BEYOND MYSTICISM

The Modern Northwest

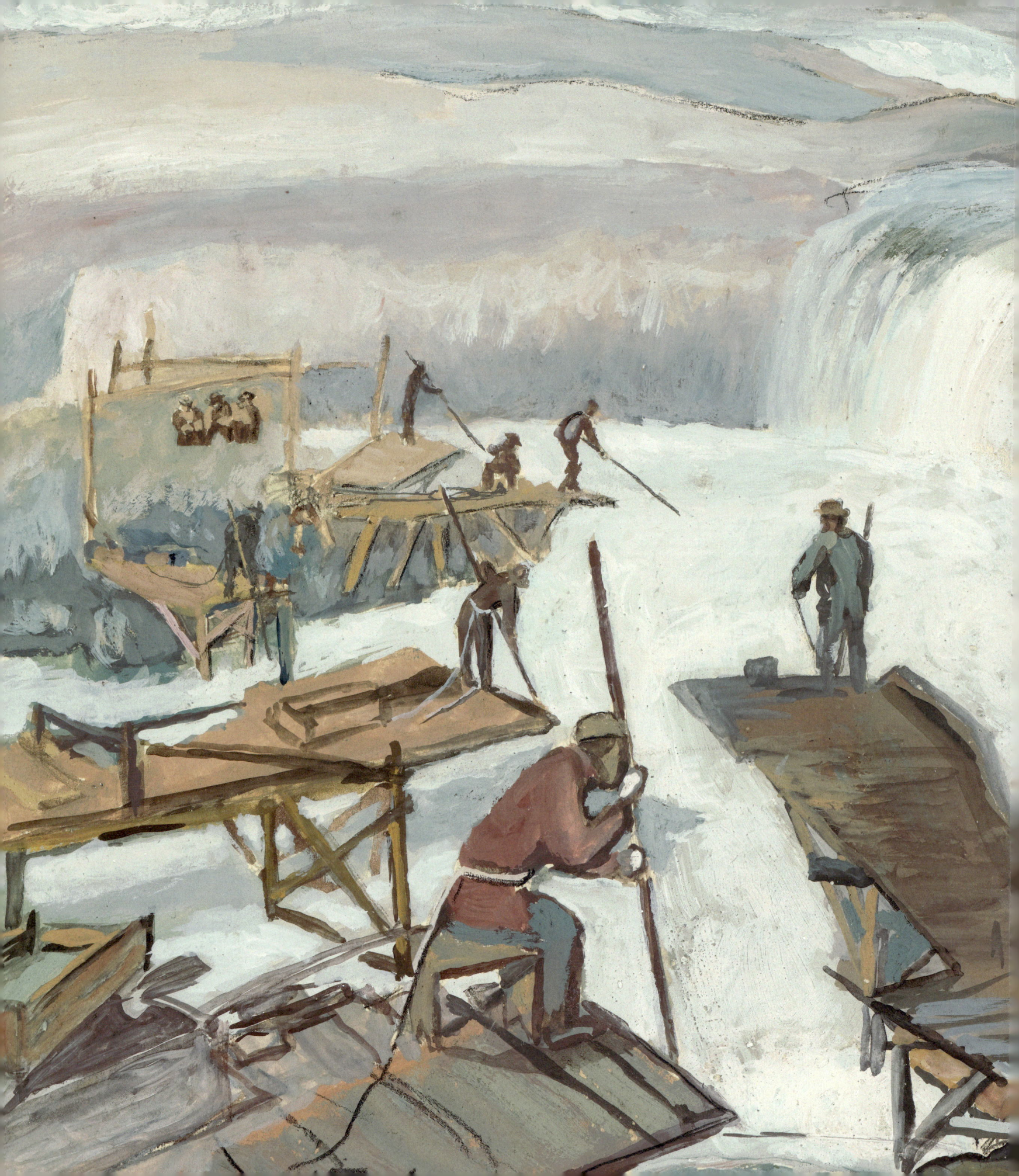

Theresa Papanikolas

BEYOND MYSTICISM

The Modern Northwest

Seattle Art Museum

University of Washington Press
Seattle

CONTENTS

FOREWORD AND ACKNOWLEDGMENTS

The Seattle Art Museum has a long history of celebrating the art of our region—in our galleries, through our exhibition program, and with our unparalleled permanent collection. *Beyond Mysticism: The Modern Northwest* adds a fresh perspective to this legacy by considering the development of Northwest Modernism in tandem with the rapid growth and urbanization of the city of Seattle, the transformation of its natural environment, and its orientation to the Pacific. Through an array of paintings, sculptures, prints, drawings, and photographs, the exhibition both demonstrates what made Modernism in the Puget Sound unique and brings to light its continuities with American Modernism more broadly. It also reveals the artistic, social, environmental, and political concerns of many of the region's most prominent artists.

A project of this magnitude requires the generosity of numerous individuals and organizations. We are grateful to the many supporters who made *Beyond Mysticism* possible. The exhibition is generously funded by substantial grants from 4Culture and ArtsFund. Major support came from the Bette and David Sprague Exhibition Endowment and the Wyeth Foundation for American Art. We also extend our gratitude to Eric Peterson and Barbara Pomeroy, and to the Twining Humber Fund for their support.

We would also like to thank the directors and staffs of the lending institutions who assisted us in bringing together such a remarkable assortment of artworks: the Art Bridges Foundation, Bentonville, Arkansas; the Art Institute of Chicago; the Dalí Museum, St. Petersburg, Florida; the Gilcrease Museum, Tulsa; the Henry Art Gallery, University of Washington, Seattle; the Menil Collection, Houston; the Museum of History and Industry (MOHAI), Seattle; the Northwest Museum of Arts and Culture, Spokane, Washington; the Philbrook Museum of Art, Tulsa; the Portland Art Museum, Oregon; the Rose Art Museum, Brandeis University, Waltham, Massachusetts; the Smithsonian American Art Museum, Washington, DC; the Tacoma Art Museum, Washington; Tsutakawa Art Legacy LLC; the Whitney Museum of American Art, New York; and the Wing Luke Museum, Seattle. In addition, we thank Bill and Holly Marklyn, Fay Hauberg Page and Nathanial Page, and an anonymous private collection for generously agreeing to part with their treasures and share them with us.

At the Seattle Art Museum, Theresa Papanikolas, Ann M. Barwick Curator of American Art, the curator of *Beyond Mysticism* and author of this exhibition catalogue, brought substantial expertise in American Modernism to the project and devoted over three years to researching the art and history of the Puget Sound. On the curatorial team, José Carlos Diaz, former Susan Brotman Deputy Director for Art, moved the project forward at the administrative level, with support from Senior Manager for Exhibitions and Publications Samantha Best, Exhibitions Coordinator Katherine Hamilton, Print and Content

Supervisor Danelle Jay, Librarian Yueh-Lin Chen, and former Emerging Arts Leader Intern Ash Gingery. Registrars for Exhibitions Jennifer Garpner and Megan Peterson, along with Director of Registration Suzan Şengöz, undertook the extensive task of coordinating loans and the movement of artworks, while Assistant Registrar for Rights and Reproductions Ian Baker and Museum Photographer Scott Leen oversaw photography of the permanent collection. Exhibition Designer Justin Scoltock brought his usual impeccable taste to designing the exhibition, while the installation crew—Drew Davis, Meredith Wadell, Anthony Elech, Andrew Malcolm, and Michael Milano—led by Chief of Installation Design and Registration Nate Peek and Lead Preparator Joshua Gosovich, brought care and finesse to installing it in the galleries. Jane Lang Davis Chief of Conservation Nicholas Dorman—along with his highly skilled team of collections care managers, Jakob Garfinkle, Vaughn Meekens, Marta Pinto-Llorca, and Barbara Robinson—treated and prepared over one hundred artworks for display, many exhibited at the Seattle Art Museum for the first time. Chief Development Officer Chris Landman and his team made sure funds were in place to support the project, and in this, we are especially grateful to Director of Institutional Giving Sarah Michael, Institutional Giving Manager Maria Gorbaty, and Director of Individual Giving Ilona Davis. We would also like to thank our colleagues in Education and Public Engagement, including Jason Porter, Erika Katayama, Ramzy Lakos,

Emily Gardner, Heaven Quiban, Anna Allegro, and Cristina Cano-Calhoun, for developing a rich portfolio of interpretive offerings, educational opportunities, and public programs; as well as our Marketing and Communications team—Mikhael Mae Williams, Kat Bryant Flaherty, Natalie Wiseman, Hailey Bortel, Devon DeGagne, Sarah Butler, Bella Brown, and Muneera Gerald—for amplifying the exhibition's content through strategic advertising and stylish collateral. This catalogue is the work of our colleagues at Marquand Books, Gina Broze, Kestrel Rundle, and designer Tom Eykemans, along with editor Kristin Swan, proofreader Janice Lee, and indexer Dave Luljak; we thank them for their careful editing, elegant design, and flawless production, with rights and reproduction support from Steve Sullivan, Smart Rights, and our copublisher, the University of Washington Press. And finally, we thank the museum's Operations, Security, and Visitor Experience teams for their careful stewardship of the exhibition throughout its run.

The Seattle Art Museum is uniquely positioned to take a deep dive into Northwest Modernism. We hope you enjoy this fascinating slice of the history of the Puget Sound region.

Scott Stulen
Illsley Ball Nordstrom Director and CEO

NORTHWEST MODERNISM

Getting Beyond Mysticism

In 1953, *Life* magazine published an article provocatively titled "The Mystic Painters of the Northwest: They Translate Reality into Symbolic and Distinctive Art."[1] Engineered by the art dealer Zoë Dusanne and based on the field research of *Life* staff editor Dorothy Sieberling, the article focused on four Seattle artists—Guy Anderson, Kenneth Callahan, Morris Graves, and Mark Tobey—crediting them with creating a uniquely Pacific Northwest form of Modernism characterized by "shimmering lines and symbolic forms" that "embody a mystical feeling towards life and the universe."[2] Their "mystical approach," the article went on to proclaim, reflected their finely honed awareness of the "overwhelming forces of nature which surround them," as well as "the influence of the Orient whose cultures have seeped into the communities that line the U.S. Pacific Coast."[3] Tobey, it specified, applied the lessons of Chinese calligraphy to a new way of looking at nature, while Callahan drew from nature's "symbolic aspect" to create "rocky slabs that [suggest] the social bonds and customs imprisoning men."[4] The text attributed Anderson's palette to the "gray, weathered tones" of the twigs and driftwood he collected on hikes through the region's forests and coastlines. Finally, it suggested that Graves "cast" nature "in the luminous lines and colors of Oriental art to suggest the shimmery mystery of their spiritual life."[5] By the time the article ran, all four artists had gone their separate ways. Nonetheless, the idea that they shared a distinctive Pacific Northwest artistic vision ignited by the region's landscape and distinguished by Orientalizing mysticism came to shape interpretations of their art and, by extension, perceptions of Northwest Modernism.

Beyond Mysticism: The Modern Northwest reconsiders the work of these artists as part of a panorama of Northwest Modernism, a distinct period of creative production, social change, and environmental transformation in the Puget Sound during the decades preceding World War II. Through a series of microhistories, this volume examines significant aspects of the region's Modernism, both in its local context and against the backdrop of national art historical movements. At its core is the idea that the Puget Sound, far from a remote, mysterious outpost in the northwest corner of the contiguous United States, was home to a progressive, inclusive, and cosmopolitan cultural scene whose spirit was shaped by the region's rapid urbanization, the beauty and tragedy of its natural environment, and its orientation neither to the East Coast nor to Europe but instead to the Pacific Rim.

Northwest Modernism unfolded in tandem with the growth and development of the Puget Sound as it—and especially Seattle—transitioned from pioneer outpost to urban metropolis with a public keen on establishing artistic and cultural institutions. Around the turn of the twentieth century, the art dealer Will Conant and the studio owner William W. Kellogg brought together a coalition of artists and arts enthusiasts for informal discussions in members' homes and modest exhibitions in rented rooms at the Seattle Public Library.[6] Their spirit of civic enrichment laid the groundwork for arts organizations in the Seattle area, and as their ranks grew and their activities became more systematic, they incorporated officially as the Seattle Fine Arts Society (SFAS). Founded in 1906, the SFAS aimed to "promote and cultivate the Fine Arts, and to that end maintain in the city of Seattle, art rooms or buildings and art instruction," as well as to "acquire works of art and exhibit paintings, sculpture, engravings, and other works of art; to provide lectures and generally to foster art in all its branches."[7] The organization's long-range goal was to establish a municipal art museum for the use and enrichment of the Seattle community, and to that end it staged an ambitious exhibition program that included an inaugural display of Japanese prints followed by a selection of works by the American artist John La Farge—the city's first solo presentation of an internationally renowned artist.[8] The society held these shows in a series of downtown Seattle office buildings and, starting in 1912, thanks to an advantageous partnership with the American Federation of Arts, regularly and consistently presented an encyclopedic range of artwork from all over the world; the SFAS also showcased the work of local artists through its prestigious and competitive Annual Exhibition of Northwest Artists.[9] In 1933, the society—by now reincorporated as the Seattle Art Institute—formally became the Seattle Art Museum, opened the doors to its permanent location in Volunteer Park, and became a nucleus for the region's artists, including those aligned with Modernism.

Additional arts organizations and artist groups further enriched cultural life in Seattle and ensured that the city was always abreast of artistic developments nationally, while small avant-garde factions introduced Modernist formal strategies and ideas into the conservative mix of local taste. Among these innovators were the Triad, comprising the printmaker Roi Partridge, the painter John Butler, and the miniaturist Clare Shepherd; the Cherry Street Art Colony, the city's first bohemian artists' community; and the circle that met regularly at the home of Margaret and Kenneth Callahan and included Graves, Tobey, and William Cumming.[10] In 1914, the piano teacher Nellie Cornish founded the Cornish School of Allied Arts (now the Cornish College of the Arts), which rapidly expanded into the largest music school west of Chicago. The Cornish School incorporated dance, drama, and the visual arts for a truly immersive and interdisciplinary arts education. It attracted a distinguished faculty that included Tobey, Graves, and the composer John Cage, as well as an inclusive and talented student body that counted the dancer Merce Cunningham among its members.[11] In 1918, the School of Painting and Design was established at the University of Washington under the direction of the painter Ambrose Patterson, and by 1930, under the leadership of the painter Walter Isaacs, it had expanded to twelve instructors and entered into partnership with the university's Henry Art Gallery. The gallery, founded in 1927, showed the Seattle entrepreneur Horace Henry's collection of nineteenth- and twentieth-century paintings, as well as the work of artists associated with the university. The Seattle Camera Club, established in 1924 by Kyo Koike with a charter membership of Japanese American photographers and national figures such as Imogen Cunningham and Ella McBride, advanced pictorial photography in Seattle, while the Northwest Printmakers, formed in 1929 by a group of local artists, promoted the cause of printmaking.[12] In 1935, the Group of Twelve, a loose alliance of progressive artists that included Callahan, Graves, Tobey, Ambrose Patterson, Viola Patterson, Kenjiro Nomura, Kamekichi Tokita, and Takuichi Fujii, had its first exhibition and published the pamphlet *Some Works of the Group of Twelve*, further raising the profile of Modernism in Seattle.[13]

The four essays in this volume explore key themes of Northwest Modernism. "The City and Industry: Modernist Regionalism in the

Puget Sound" reveals how a diverse assortment of artists active in 1930s Seattle responded to the rapid growth, both structurally and culturally, of the new city. These artists found their national counterparts in Precisionist and American Scene painters such as Charles Sheeler, Reginald Marsh, and Archibald John Motley Jr., who likewise captured the energy and built environment of the United States' metropolitan centers. In Seattle, the Japanese American artists Nomura, Tokita, and Fujii recorded the proliferation of roadways, buildings, and billboards in what is now the city's International District, while the photographer Albert Smith Sr. documented the jazz scene thriving on nearby Jackson Street. The work of painters such as Tobey, Callahan, Cumming, and Z. Vanessa Helder captured local agricultural and industrial landscapes, as well as the workers who occupied them and drove the region's economy.

"Kenneth Callahan and Morris Graves: The Northwest Landscape Through an Ecocritical Lens" zeroes in on the two artists, showing how their depictions of the Pacific Northwest landscape cautioned against the ill effects of urbanization and industrialization. In responding to the Puget Sound region's deep forests and abundant flora and fauna, Callahan and Graves expressed their concern for the natural environment and its transformation in the name of progress. Not only does their work align with that of American Modernists likewise attuned to the specificities of place, such as Georgia O'Keeffe, it also makes powerful statements about the ephemerality and fragility of ecosystems and advocates for holistic approaches to nature that make space for its equilibrium and connection to humanity—as a unifying force that has come to be described as "mystical."

"Uncanny Landscapes: The Surreal Northwest" considers whether this perceived mysticism was in fact a form of Surrealism. Many Northwest Modernists—among them Louis Bunce, Leo Kenney, Malcolm Roberts, and Margaret Tomkins—absorbed, assimilated,

and ultimately transformed Surrealist imagery and ideas. In this they looked to the work of Salvador Dalí, Yves Tanguy, and other internationally renowned artists as powerful examples of Surrealist strategies—such as exploring dreams, understanding the subconscious, experimenting with psychic automatism, and contemplating metamorphosis—through which they could move beyond landscape and the American scene to achieve intuition, introspection, and self-actualization.

The final essay, "A Pacific Perspective?: Northwest Abstract Expressionism," follows the trajectory of Northwest Modernism during and immediately following World War II, when a core group of artists—among them Tobey, Paul Horiuchi, and George Tsutakawa—developed a regional form of Abstract Expressionism allegedly inspired by the artistic and philosophical traditions of the Pacific Rim, most notably those of East Asia and Northwest Coast Native communities. While it is true that the Pacific Northwest is oriented geographically more to the Pacific than to Europe, it is also true that Northwest Abstract Expressionism originated in a critical climate where primitivism and Orientalism prevailed, and claims to influence and affinity (and acts of appropriation) were accepted at face value. Within this context, Asian American and Native artists such as Horiuchi and Tsutakawa or Julius Twohy and Joseph Hillaire—as well as their strategies for navigating modernity—were considered in the essentialist light of their communities, if not overlooked entirely. The influence of Asian and Northwest Coast Native art must be considered alongside that of regionalism, ecocriticism, urbanization, and Surrealism, within the broader context of the development of Northwest Modernism and the place and time in which it unfolded. Beyond its so-called mysticism, the story of Northwest Modernism is a story of the Puget Sound.

Notes

1. "Mystic Painters of the Northwest."

2. "Mystic Painters of the Northwest," 84. For the article's origins, see Junker, *Modernism in the Pacific Northwest*, 61.

3. "Mystic Painters of the Northwest," 84.

4. "Mystic Painters of the Northwest," 84, 87.

5. "Mystic Painters of the Northwest," 87, 88.

6. For the history of the Seattle Fine Arts Society, see Calhoun, *Seattle Heritage*, 19. See also Seattle Art Museum archives, housed in University of Washington Library Special Collections.

7. Quoted in Calhoun, *Seattle Heritage*, 19.

8. Calhoun, *Seattle Heritage*, 22.

9. The American Federation of Arts is a nonprofit body founded in 1909 to organize traveling exhibitions for museums nationally and internationally.

10. For the Triad, see Martin and Bromberg, *Shadows of a Fleeting World*, 10; for the gatherings at the Callahans' home, see Cumming, *Sketchbook*.

11. For the history of the Cornish School, see Cornish, *Miss Aunt Nellie*.

12. For the Seattle Camera Club, see Martin and Bromberg, *Shadows of a Fleeting World*; for the Northwest Printmakers, see archives housed at the Seattle Art Museum and the University of Washington.

13. *Some Works of the Group of Twelve*.

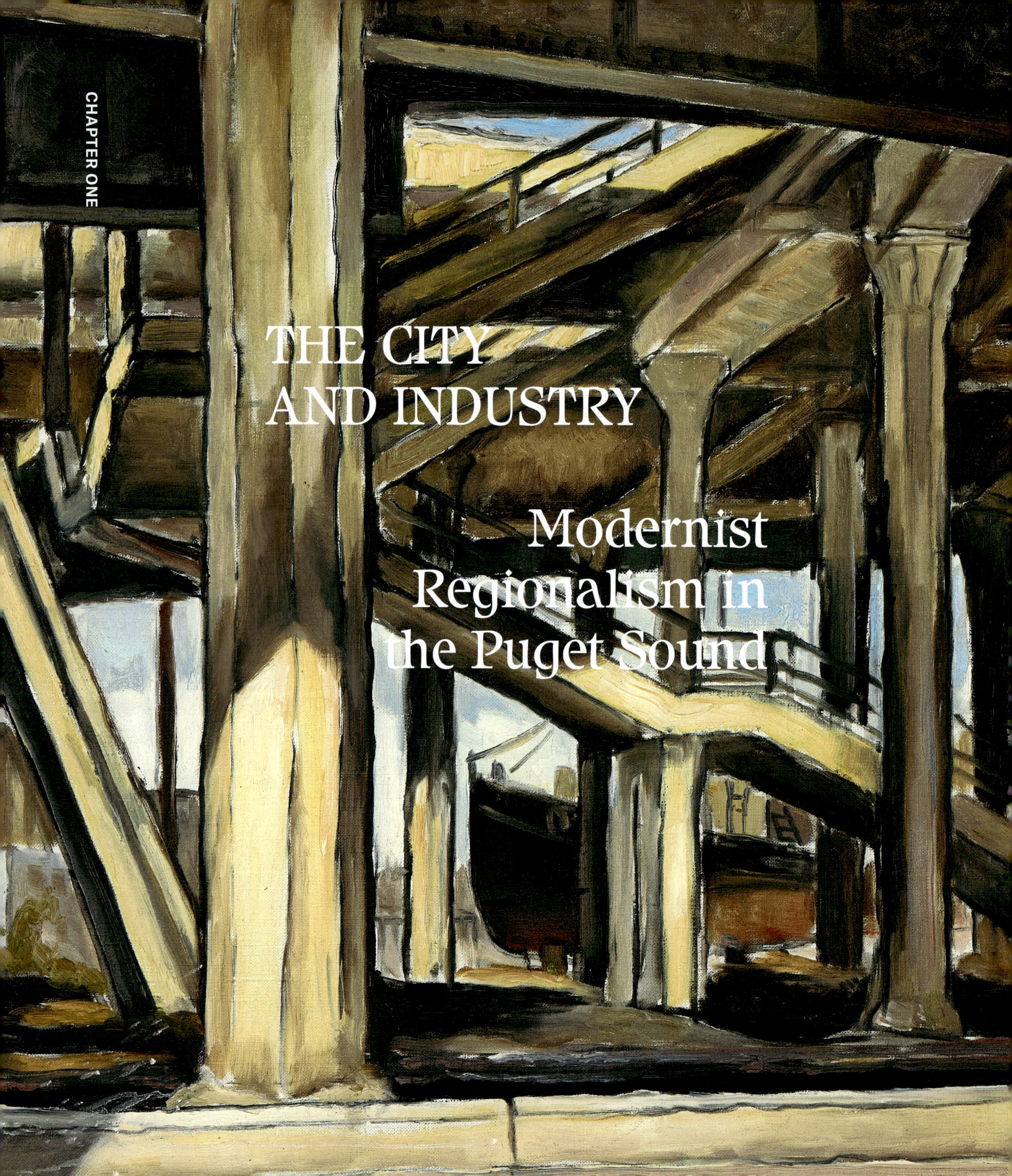

CHAPTER ONE

THE CITY
AND INDUSTRY

Modernist
Regionalism in
the Puget Sound

amekichi Tokita's *Drugstore* (1933, plate 1) and Mark Tobey's *Working Man* (1942, plate 67) reveal a side of Northwest Modernism that is decidedly not mystical. *Drugstore* is a place-portrait of Seattle prior to World War II, when small businesses crowded the city's urban core and announced their wares with a cacophony of signboards, while *Working Man* portrays an archetype of the laborers who moved through and populated these commercial corridors. Both paintings adopt the social realist approach that dominated American art during the Great Depression, when artists such as Edward Hopper, Grant Wood, Thomas Hart Benton, and Reginald Marsh captured the nation's landscapes, livelihoods, and industries in easily readable styles.[1] Tokita and Tobey likewise responded to the American scene in literal and accessible ways; what sets them apart is how deeply their work embodies the specific changes happening in the Puget Sound. The Northwest regionalism that Tokita, Tobey, and their artistic cohorts developed during the 1930s and 1940s reflects the history and growth of metropolitan Seattle—its infrastructure, its economy, and, whether directly or implicitly, its people.

Building the Northwest

The city of Seattle originated as an interloper in a complex ecosystem that had for centuries sustained Coast Salish communities, who historically moved in seasonal migrations through the waterways, mountains, and tidelands of the Puget Sound, and who valued—and continue to value—this natural environment as a nurturing force and a powerful source of knowledge.[2] While the balance they maintained with the landscape continued with the arrival of European explorers and fur traders beginning in the late eighteenth century, the Donation Land Claim Act of 1850 signaled the onset of radical change. This legislation brought waves of homesteaders from the East Coast and the Great Plains to Oregon Territory (which included present-day Washington), luring them with the promise of 320 acres of land for each white male US citizen over the age of eighteen. These colonizers brought with them a very different view of nature: What Native communities honored as a sacred resource, they exploited as raw material—land for building, trees for lumber, deep waters for commercial fishing and shipping—to be extracted, monetized, and transformed into a new Pacific Northwest economy.[3] By the time Washington became a state in 1889, a city stood on the original homeland of the Coast Salish people, with a busy waterfront (fig. 1) and a thriving business district. The population of Seattle had jumped from around 3,500 in 1880 to about 31,000 in 1889; by the Klondike Gold Rush of 1896, it stood at just under 42,000, nearly doubling, to 80,000, only two years later.[4]

Accommodating the city's rapid growth meant reengineering its tidelands, wetlands, and hills, transforming them from impassable terrain into navigable watercourses, traversable

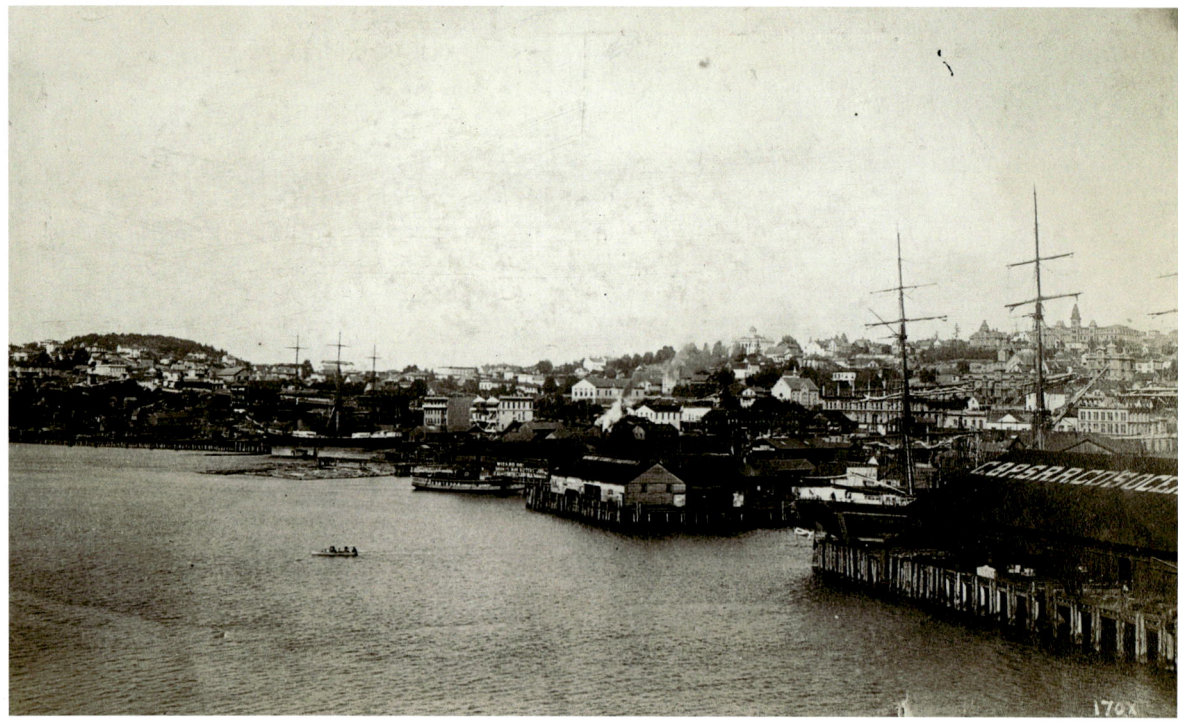

Fig. 1. Seattle waterfront view north from South Washington Street, 1887. Seattle Public Library, Seattle Historical Photograph Collection, spl_shp_5187

roads, and inhabitable property. City planners and civil engineers redesigned the region's waterways, dredging and diverting rivers and lakes into canals, culverts, and pipelines for the movement of water and watercraft; logged off its old-growth forests in support of urban development; and converted coastlines into harbors for the fisheries, canneries, sawmills, flour mills, railroads, docks, shipyards, and wharves that drove the city's economy. In 1898, the city embarked on a two-decade process of reshaping its hilly terrain, a massive series of nearly sixty projects that involved razing several steep inclines, emptying the debris into Elliott Bay (with obvious environmental repercussions), reconfiguring more than twenty streets, and moving or displacing their residents (fig. 2). In 1909, work began on a series of canals that would connect Lake Washington on the city's east side with Puget Sound to the west, an undertaking that required lowering the lake's water level, building a system of locks between Shilshole Bay and Salmon Bay, and reversing the flow of the Cedar River into the lake to provide sufficient waterflow for the locks.

Where the Cedar and White Rivers originally converged to form the Duwamish, the Army Corps of Engineers built another wide canal, opening the surrounding lowlands for development and, in the process, destroying salmon runs and the ecosystems that sustained them. Reengineering the city's waterways paved the way for a series of dams and hydroelectric plants on the Cedar and Skagit Rivers, localizing the city's utilities and making them more affordable. Between 1880 and 1930, Seattle and the land on which it stood were, whether for good or ill, more profoundly and completely transformed than any other place in the United States, a massive reordering of nature at a rapid pace to pave the way for an urban future.[5]

The restructuring of the city's landscape and the explosion of infrastructure that followed in the 1930s and 1940s can be traced through a series of paintings of the Puget Sound region, starting with Jacob Elshin's *Mill* (1934, plate 3). The Russian-born Elshin arrived in Seattle in 1923 and by the early 1930s was creating paintings for the Public Works of Art Project (PWAP) under the Works Progress

Administration (WPA) and completing commissions for the US Treasury Department's Section of Painting and Sculpture. These programs were established under President Franklin Delano Roosevelt's New Deal to support artists and make art accessible to the general population, and they sustained the livelihoods of many Northwest Modernists, including Mark Tobey, Morris Graves, Kenneth Callahan, Ambrose Patterson, and Ernest Ralph Norling.[6] With its blocky forms and earthy palette of blues and oranges, *Mill* reflects Elshin's indebtedness to the nineteenth-century French painter Paul Cézanne. Painted for the PWAP, it shows the rapid redevelopment of the Seattle waterfront following the rerouting of the Duwamish River. In the foreground is the messy tangle of docks, watercraft, and fisheries that separated land from water and disrupted

the Native communities that had long relied on the coastline for sustenance. In the middle ground is Harbor Island, then the largest artificial island in the world, created in 1909 from land dredged from the Duwamish River and removed during the regrading of Jackson and Dearborn Streets.[7] Rising from the hulking ships and diminutive wharves at the island's edges is Fisher Flouring Mills, established in 1911, the largest of the more than 160 flour mills that dotted the state of Washington and processed the grain supply for the city's growing settler population.[8] Aligned with American regionalism and topographically accurate, this painting captures the redevelopment and industry in Seattle during the early twentieth century.

In Tokita's *Bridge* (1931, plate 4), the busy waterfront is obscured by the network

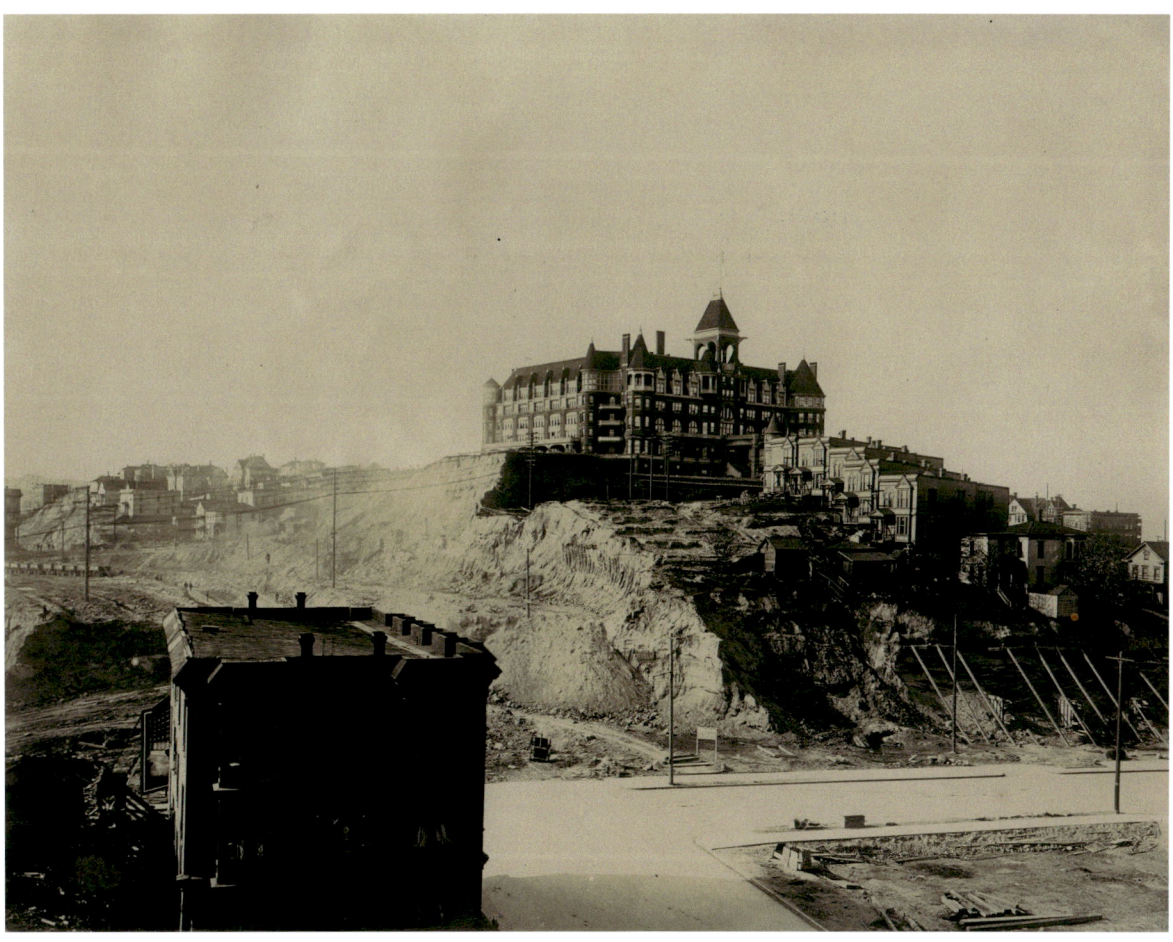

Fig. 2. View of regrade work, north from Second Avenue and Pine Street, Seattle, ca. 1906. Seattle Public Library, Seattle Regraded Photograph Collection, spl_dr_033

of trusses and bridges built for the railroads and other conveyances that transported people and goods inland from the docks to points throughout the region. These elevated thoroughfares created mayhem on the city's coastlines, which, already overbuilt, were now forced to withstand the added pressure of locomotive and vehicular traffic, as well as the flammable oil and embers they disgorged, making fire a constant and catastrophic threat.[9] In *Bridge*, Tokita pictures this urban infrastructure as an elaborate, invasive grid that sidelines the harbor and pushes it into the background. Born in Japan, he stopped in Seattle on his way to Chicago in 1919 and decided to stay, pursuing a successful career as a sign painter and co-owner of Noto Sign Company; with his business partner, Kenjiro Nomura, he practiced oil painting on the side.[10] Early training in calligraphy as a youth in Japan served Tokita well when developing the precision required to paint lettering for signs, and 1930s American Scene painting provided a model for the realist style and regionalist subject matter in his paintings. He once stated that his artistic aims were "found in Cézanne and . . . developed through the methods used by Sesshū," a master of Japanese ink painting.[11] *Bridge* affirms these two paradigms of the European and Asian traditions: the planes of the structure's massive supports demonstrate Tokita's understanding of Cézanne's form, while the intricate web of their configuration shows his grasp of Sesshū's line.

Z. Vanessa Helder's series of twenty-two paintings documenting the construction of Grand Coulee Dam captures the industrialization of waterways beyond Seattle that impacted the Puget Sound region. On the Columbia River, about eighty-five miles northwest of Spokane, Grand Coulee Dam is by far the largest and most ambitious of the many public works projects initiated under the New Deal. It was built between 1933 and 1942 to generate the hydroelectric power required to produce aluminum for western Washington's airplane industry and to harness irrigation for

eastern Washington's agriculture. Today, it continues to supply electricity and water in the Northwest and remains the largest power station—and the largest concrete structure— ever built in the United States.

Helder, who rose to national attention for her participation in the 1943 exhibition *American Realists and Magic Realists* at the Museum of Modern Art in New York, specialized in watercolors redolent of the Precisionism of Charles Sheeler and ideal for capturing the dam's intrusion into the stark landscape of the Columbia Plateau, as in *Coulee Dam, Looking West* (1939–41, plate 11).[12] Helder had moved to Spokane from Seattle in 1939 to teach at the new WPA-funded Spokane Art Center and, immediately fascinated with the dam's construction, gained access to the site—the only woman to do so. Under the constant supervision of an escort, she explored the complex's power plants, irrigation pumps, ditches, spillways, and reservoirs, but she was not permitted to draw on the premises. Instead, she made field sketches of the dam from a nearby vista house and the community of Electric City, capturing it from the elevated vantage point offered by these locations. She also depicted the neighborhoods reserved for workers (for example, plates 15, 22), as well as natural landmarks such as Kettle Falls (plate 19), an important Native fishing site until it was flooded by Lake Roosevelt upon the completion of the dam. In these works, Grand Coulee Dam and its elaborate infrastructure descend upon the vast Columbia River, alter its flow, invade the surrounding landscape, and disrupt the livelihoods of the people who lived there. Like their urban counterparts, Helder's paintings of the dam and its environs reveal not only the massive scale of industry but also its impact on the human and natural environment.

Labor and Community in the Northwest

The city views and streetscapes that proliferate in the work of Seattle artists from the 1930s and 1940s reflect the character and composition of the neighborhoods at the city's core. Nomura's *Street* (ca. 1932, plate 35) is a view of Yesler Way, a busy artery within walking distance of his sign-painting business and one of the many Seattle spaces that found their way into his paintings. Noto Sign Company was at the epicenter of Nihonmachi, the city's large Nikkei community, made up of emigrants from Japan and their US-born descendants. Nihonmachi thrived from the 1890s, when Japanese immigrants began to arrive in Seattle to fill the labor void left by the Chinese Exclusion Act of 1882, until the forced incarceration of West Coast Japanese Americans during World War II. Nomura had come to the United States with his parents in 1907 at the age of eleven and moved to Seattle when he was sixteen, working first for a shopkeeper and then as an apprentice sign painter before eventually opening Noto Sign Company and bringing on Tokita as co-proprietor. He studied painting with Fokko Tadama, a local painter of Dutch Indonesian descent who taught many Japanese American students, and exhibited regularly in the Seattle Fine Arts Society's annual Exhibition of Northwest Artists. When the Seattle Art Museum opened its doors in 1933, his was the first solo show.[13]

In *Street*, deep perspectival space emphasizes Yesler's steep slope and the multistory buildings lining it, as well as the tracks for the streetcars that carried workers from downtown Seattle to suburbs to the east. These tracks expose the racial segregation that led to the formation of Nihonmachi: Streetcar suburbs were historically restricted by covenant to white homeowners, excluding the city's Nikkei residents, who were prohibited from owning property regardless due to being denied US citizenship under federal law.[14] Indeed, even as Seattle promoted itself as the gateway to Asia, anti-Asian racism and exclusionism still prevailed, and Nihonmachi—captured in *Street* and numerous other works by local Nikkei artists— was the only place where the city's Japanese American residents could build businesses, livelihoods, and community.[15]

Racial covenants similarly impacted the city's Black community, segregating it within the Yesler-Jackson area in downtown Seattle and, later, the Central District to the east.[16] Yesler-Jackson was on the dividing line between the immigrant and working-class neighborhoods on the city's south end and the upper- and middle-class neighborhoods to the north, and its Black residents, most of them migrants from the American South, brought jazz to Seattle.[17] By the 1920s, the speakeasies and clubs of Yesler-Jackson had become the heart of the city's music scene as they sidestepped Prohibition—in place in Washington since 1916—thanks to a corrupt city government paid to look the other way. Night spots such as the Blue Note, the 908 Club, the Green Dot, and the Black & Tan staged a whirlwind of performers, including legends such as Ernestine Anderson, Cab Calloway, Louis Armstrong, Billie Holiday, Dizzy Gillespie, Count Basie, Quincy Jones (who graduated from Seattle's Garfield High School) and his childhood friend Ray Charles (who lived in Seattle as a teenager in the 1940s), and a multitude of local favorites such as Palmer Johnson, Floyd Standifer, Woody Woodhouse, and Vernon Brown. Beginning in the early 1940s, Albert Smith Sr., Seattle's premier Black photographer, took candid photographs of the Jackson Street jazz scene and sold them to clubgoers through his business, Al Smith: On the Spot. His shots of Armstrong (1944, plate 41), Calloway (ca. 1947, plate 44), Basie, Fats Waller, Jimmie Lunceford, Katherine Dunham, Lionel Hampton (1946, plate 43), Duke Ellington, Tommy Dorsey, Harry James, and many others reveal a world of performers and patrons that finds its national counterpart in the jazz paintings of Archibald John Motley Jr. (plate 52), who, like Smith, captured the thriving nightlife in America's historically Black neighborhoods.[18]

South of Nihonmachi and Yesler-Jackson were the unregulated shantytowns, encampments, and transient residential districts that housed and supported Seattle's substantial working class. By 1930, the city numbered more than 300,000 residents and was the nucleus of a vast labor network generated by the recruitment and exploitation of Indigenous and immigrant populations, including the local Duwamish tribe, removed from its traditional homelands and displaced to the city's south end; Native communities from throughout the Pacific Northwest; and Asian, European, and American laborers.[19] Almost exclusively single and male, this labor force cycled in and out of the city according to the production schedules of its manufacturing and extraction industries.

These workers, along with the largely Nikkei and Black Seattleites who owned the businesses and single-occupancy hotels that supported them, inhabited the neighborhoods along Yesler Way that, in 1939, were targeted for Yesler Terrace, a new development of low-income family housing. Built with Seattle Housing Authority funds, Yesler Terrace was the first of several initiatives intended to eradicate urban blight; instead, it destroyed a community by restricting property ownership through racial covenants and, in the case of Asian Americans, underscored alien land laws that kept them from living anywhere else in the city. Yesler Terrace, though touted as racially diverse, was initially available almost exclusively to white married couples, which meant that the neighborhood's original residents—mostly single men, noncitizens, or both—were forced to relocate to the handful of neighborhoods in the Central District and North Capitol Hill that had relatively few residential restrictions.[20]

Fay Chong's *Yesler Housing Project* (ca. 1942, plate 34) depicts the newly constructed Yesler Terrace and its impact on the neighborhood. Chong grew up in Seattle and studied painting and printmaking at Broadway High School, as well as calligraphy during visits to China, where he was born.[21] Encouraged by Tobey and Graves, he applied his knowledge of calligraphy to watercolor views of urban Seattle. In this work, a neat row of structures, accessible only by a narrow road, rests,

practically hidden, atop a steep bluff that dominates the composition. Sapling trees, scrub, new growth, and an assortment of utility poles suggest the recent demolition of the dwellings and businesses that previously stood on the site, while Yesler Terrace represents the new development that replaced them.

Tobey captured the energy and psychology of Seattle's crowded urban core in his paintings and drawings of Pike Place Market. One of the nation's oldest continuously operated farmers markets, Pike Place Market was established in 1907 as a venue where farmers could offset inflation through direct sales and as a gathering spot where local consumers could shop economically for food and other items. In *E Pluribus Unum* (1942, plate 65), the continuous lines of the artist's white writing trace a throng of shoppers in a labyrinth of market stalls offering meat, fish, produce, baked goods, cheese, and other sundries. *Rummage* (1941, plate 66) shows the market's sprawling Rummage Hall and the multitudes that gathered there regularly to barter used goods amid the rationing and scarcity of resources during World War II. "So many things are offered for sale," Tobey wrote. "Plants to be replanted; ropes of all kinds; antiques; Norwegian pancakes made by an old sea captain . . . It has been for me a refuge, an oasis, a most human growth, the heart and soul of Seattle."[22] *Time Off* (1941, plate 68), a scene of working men on break, shows the market as a haven for the city's laborers, who, as Tobey put it, "gathered in groups like islands in the constant stream of people [away from] their furnished rooms and rundown hotels."[23]

Tobey was not alone in portraying Seattle's working class. Labor and laborers proliferate in art produced in the Puget Sound region during the Depression, rounding out the many scenes of the infrastructure and mechanisms of production with portraits of the anonymous multitudes that powered them. Ernest Norling's *The Timber Bucker* (ca. 1934, plate 69) pays tribute to the lumberjacks of western Washington's logging industry. Dominating the composition are the remains of an enormous old-growth evergreen being "bucked" into manageable lengths by a ripsaw-wielding logger. Aided by this devastating implement, he overpowers the ancient tree, subjecting it to human will and the inevitable march of progress. An active participant in New Deal art programs, Norling was one of fifty Washington participants in the PWAP, for which *The Timber Bucker* was painted, and he made sketches documenting the reforestation, roadwork, and erosion control undertaken by the Civilian Conservation Corps. A celebration of Washington's lumber industry and the people who made it happen, *The Timber Bucker* is related to Norling's murals for the Bremerton Post Office, which he did on commission for the United States Treasury Department's Section of Painting and Sculpture as part of its program to embellish public buildings with scenes of regional economies in action.

The Treasury Department murals were meant to celebrate American industry and exploits during one of the nation's bleakest hours, yet they overlooked—or ignored—the actual toil and danger of labor. Artworks created on the margins of government channels during the Depression, however, expose many of the challenges faced by the Puget Sound's working class. Kenneth Callahan's *The Accident* (1939, plate 73), for example, presents a disquieting scene of two men stranded in a remote landscape following a field catastrophe. It reflects the hazards—falling timber, malfunctioning machinery, inclement weather, precarious terrain—of agricultural and industrial labor in the Pacific Northwest. Callahan had traveled to Mexico in 1938 to learn from and work with the muralists José Clemente Orozco, Rufino Tamayo, and, to a lesser extent, Diego Rivera, and he internalized not only the literal details of their paintings, prints, and murals but also their sympathy for and elevation of the working class. He brought this understanding to bear on depictions, for both public commissions and private consumption, of the lives and livelihoods of the lumberjacks, shipwrights,

fishermen, and dockworkers who made up western Washington's workforce.[24]

Inspired by Callahan, William Cumming applied the broad forms and clear delineation of Mexican mural painting to his figural works. Highly skilled as a draftsman, Cumming specialized in capturing the human body in motion, and his work-life vignettes are dynamic renditions of the physical effort, daily drudgery, and economic challenges of labor in Depression-era Seattle.[25] *Worker Lifting a Rock* (1940, plate 75) captures the toil of clearing the rough terrain around the Puget Sound to make room for the infrastructure of industry. A broad-shouldered rock picker braces himself as he prepares to move a massive boulder, while a second, larger rock awaits the grueling cycle of excavation. *Worker Resting* (1941, plate 76) reflects the sheer exhaustion of hard labor as a wage earner, pausing on his lunch break, reclines under the weight of his tired muscles. *Planting the Flare* (ca. 1945, plate 77) shows a lumberjack readying to install an acetylene torch on a job site. Inscribed on the wall behind him is the slogan "21 united can win," echoing the era's familiar appeals for solidarity and, perhaps, pointing to the upsurge in left-wing union activity in Seattle during the 1930s as a result of worker unrest and higher-than-average unemployment.[26] A union sympathizer and a member of the Communist Party from 1945 until 1957, Cumming was acutely aware of the hardship faced by his workplace comrades. In paintings such as *Abandoned Factory* (1939, plate 78) and *Skidroad Group* (ca. 1940, plate 79), he exposed privation and job loss during the Depression, when manufacturing plants shut down and their employees were forced to linger penniless on the street corners and sidewalks of Seattle.

The explosive development of the Puget Sound region, the settlement and migration of its people, and the physical and economic impact of its industries find their way into the work of the region's artists during the 1930s and 1940s. Scenes of Seattle's congested waterfronts; its buildings, streets, and neighborhoods; its commerce and manufacturing; and its indefatigable working class show the city's transformation from balanced ecosystem to teeming municipality over generations of settlers, and they signal the hardship, segregation, and displacement of its most marginalized residents. While these works align with 1930s American Scene painting, they tell a story that is specific to Seattle and the Puget Sound, a cautionary tale of the consequences of replacing an abundant, life-sustaining landscape with a barren infrastructure in conflict with it.

Notes

I would like to thank Pam McClusky for her helpful feedback on an earlier version of this essay.

1. For American art between World Wars I and II, see Barter, *America After the Fall*; Park and Markowitz, *Democratic Vistas*; Rudnick et al., *Art for the Millions*; Saab, *For the Millions*; Wagner, *1934*; and, for the Pacific Northwest, Bullock et al., *New Deal Art in the Northwest*.

2. For the impact of urban growth on the ecosystems and Native communities of the Puget Sound, see Klingle, *Emerald City*, especially chapters 1 and 2.

3. Klingle, *Emerald City*, chapter 1.

4. Klingle, *Emerald City*, 54.

5. For Seattle's physical transformation in the late nineteenth and early twentieth centuries, see Klingle, *Emerald City*; Morgan, *Skid Road*; and Klingle, "Reclaiming Nature."

6. For support for artists under the New Deal, see Bullock, *New Deal Art in the Northwest*; Park and Markowitz, *Democratic Vistas*; Rudnick et al., *Art for the Millions*; and Wagner, *1934*.

7. Wilma, "Harbor Island."

8. For Fisher Flouring Mills, see Long, "Fisher Flouring Mills"; and Reed, "Flour Milling in Washington."

9. Klingle, *Emerald City*, 60.

10. For Tokita's biography and art, see Johns, *Signs of Home*.

11. *Some Works of the Group of Twelve*, n.p.

12. For Helder's activities at Grand Coulee Dam, see Martin, *Austere Beauty*, 28–29.

13. For Nomura's biography and art, see Johns, *Kenjiro Nomura, American Modernist*.

14. For the segregation of Seattle and the formation of Nihonmachi, see Asaka, *Seattle from the Margins*, especially chapter four.

15. Barbara Johns has researched Seattle's Nihonmachi in the work of its Japanese American artists. See especially Johns, "Knowing Your Place."

16. Taylor, *Forging of a Black Community*.

17. For the Jackson Street jazz scene, see de Barros, *Jackson Street After Hours*; and Faltys-Burr, "Jazz on Jackson Street."

18. For Al Smith, see Blecha, "Al Smith"; and Lawson, *Seattle on the Spot*.

19. For Seattle's labor force, see Asaka, *Seattle from the Margins*, chapter 5.

20. Asaka, *Seattle from the Margins*, chapter 5.

21. Tsutakawa, "A Canvas Diary," 77.

22. Tobey, *World of a Market*, n.p.

23. Tobey, *World of a Market*, n.p.

24. Callahan wrote about his interest in Mexican art in a review of a 1936 exhibition at the Seattle Art Museum. See K. Callahan, "Seattle Art Museum," 16 February 1936. For his travels in Mexico, see M. B. Callahan, *Margaret Callahan*, 18–25. For the influence of Mexican Modernism in the United States, see Haskell, *Vida Americana*.

25. For Cumming's life and art, see Cumming, *Sketchbook*.

26. Gregory, "Seattle Labor History Highlights."

PLATES

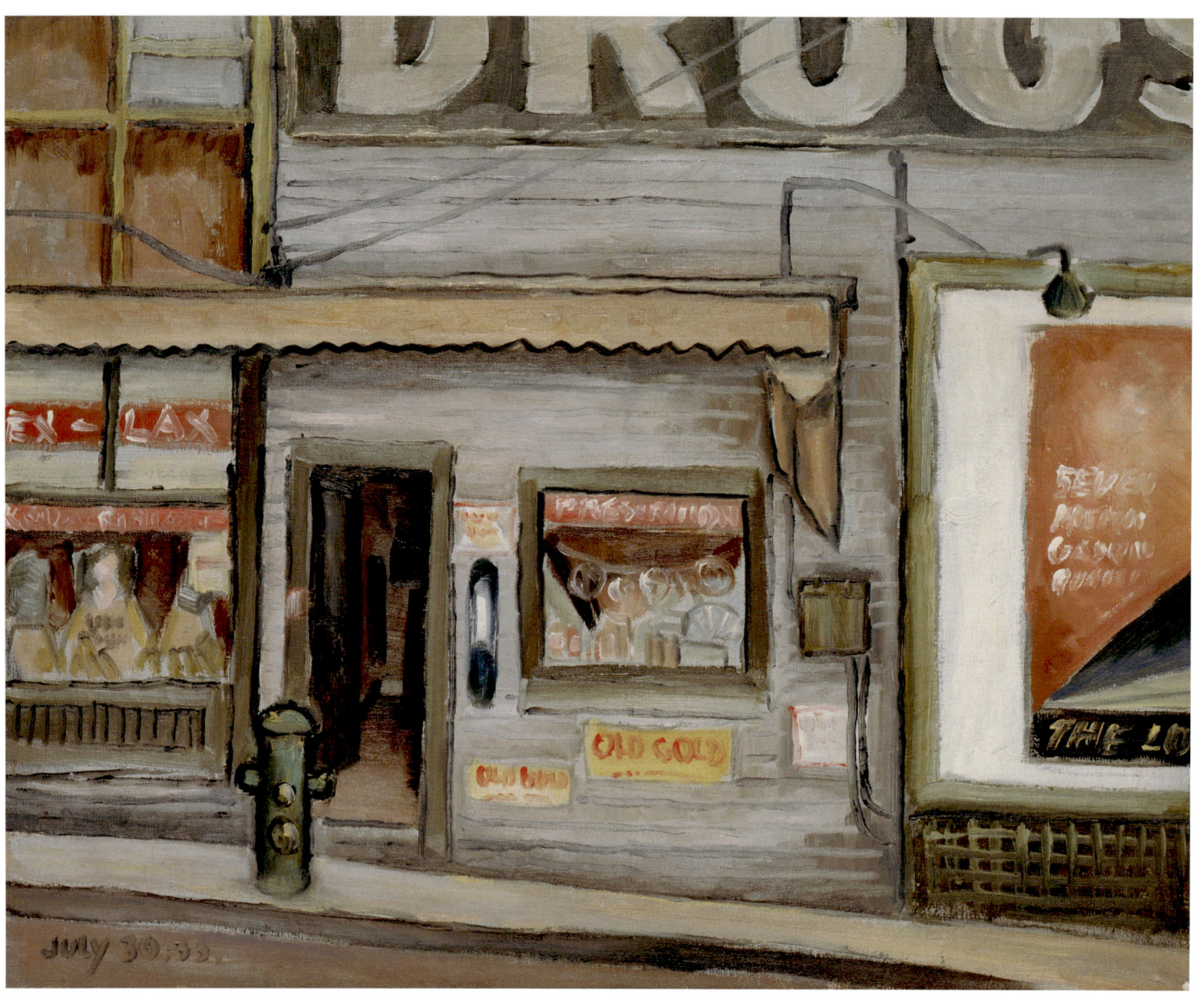

1 Kamekichi Tokita, *Drugstore*, 1933, oil on canvas

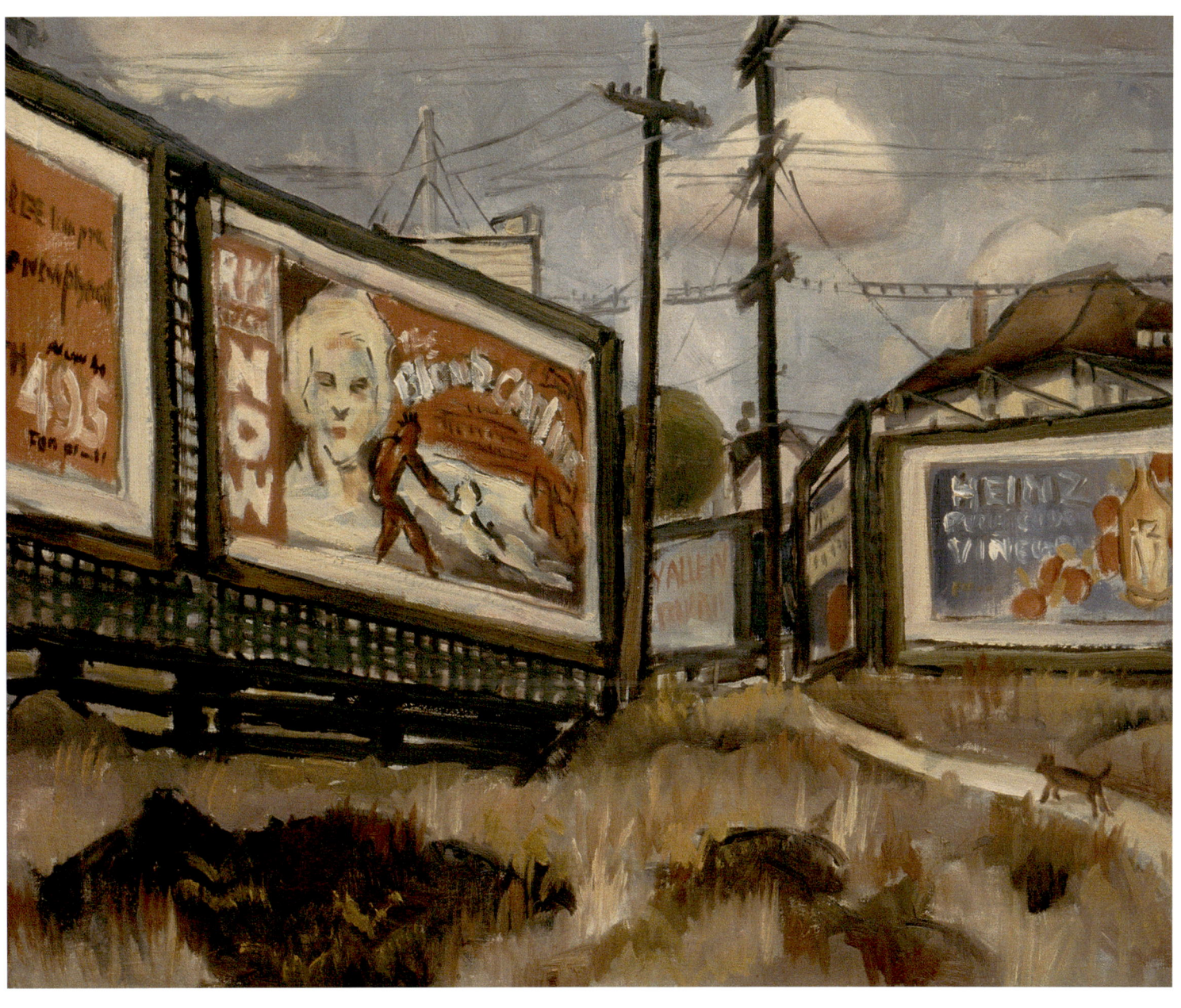

2   Kamekichi Tokita, *Billboard*, 1932, oil on canvas

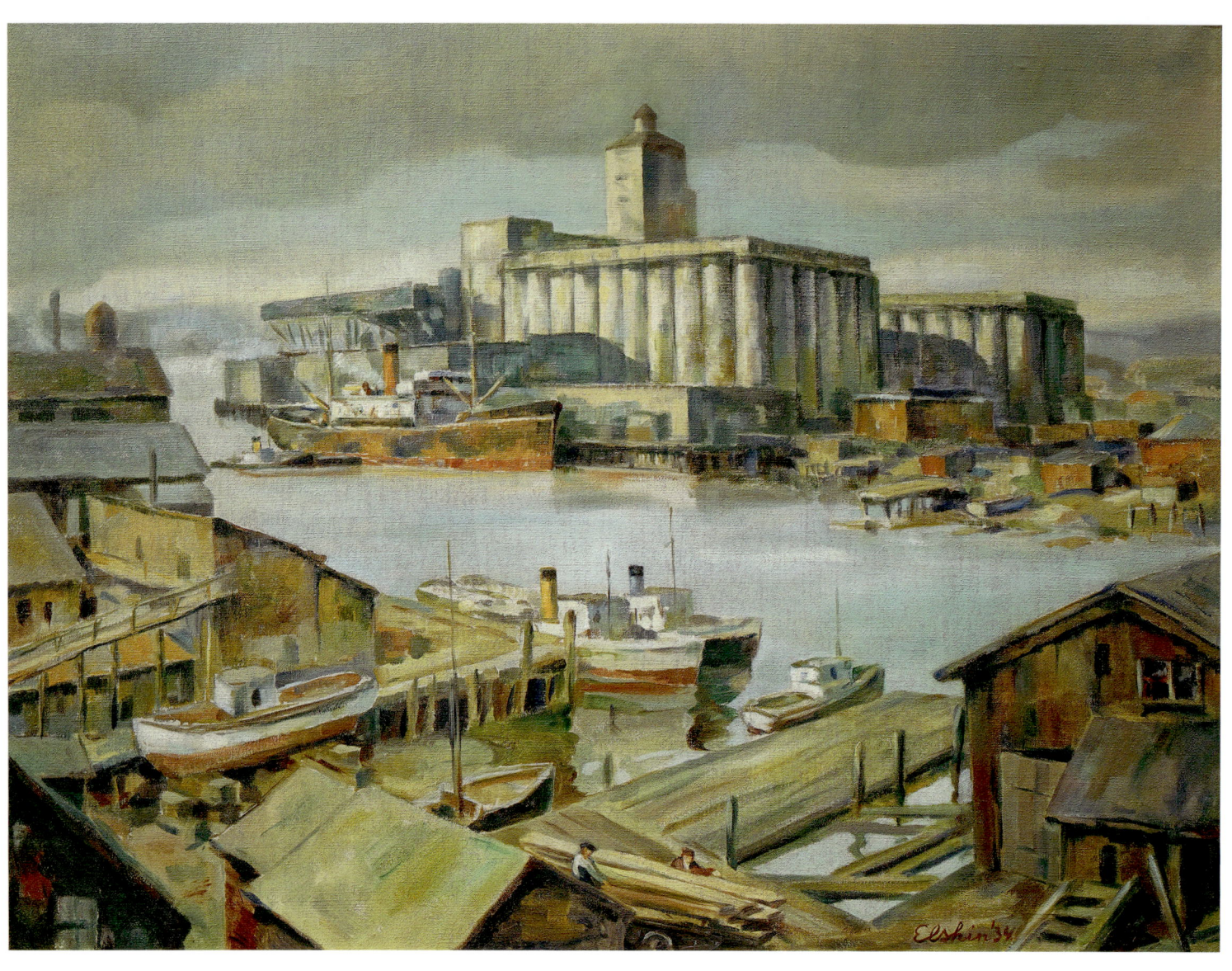

3 Jacob Elshin, *Mill*, 1934, oil on canvas

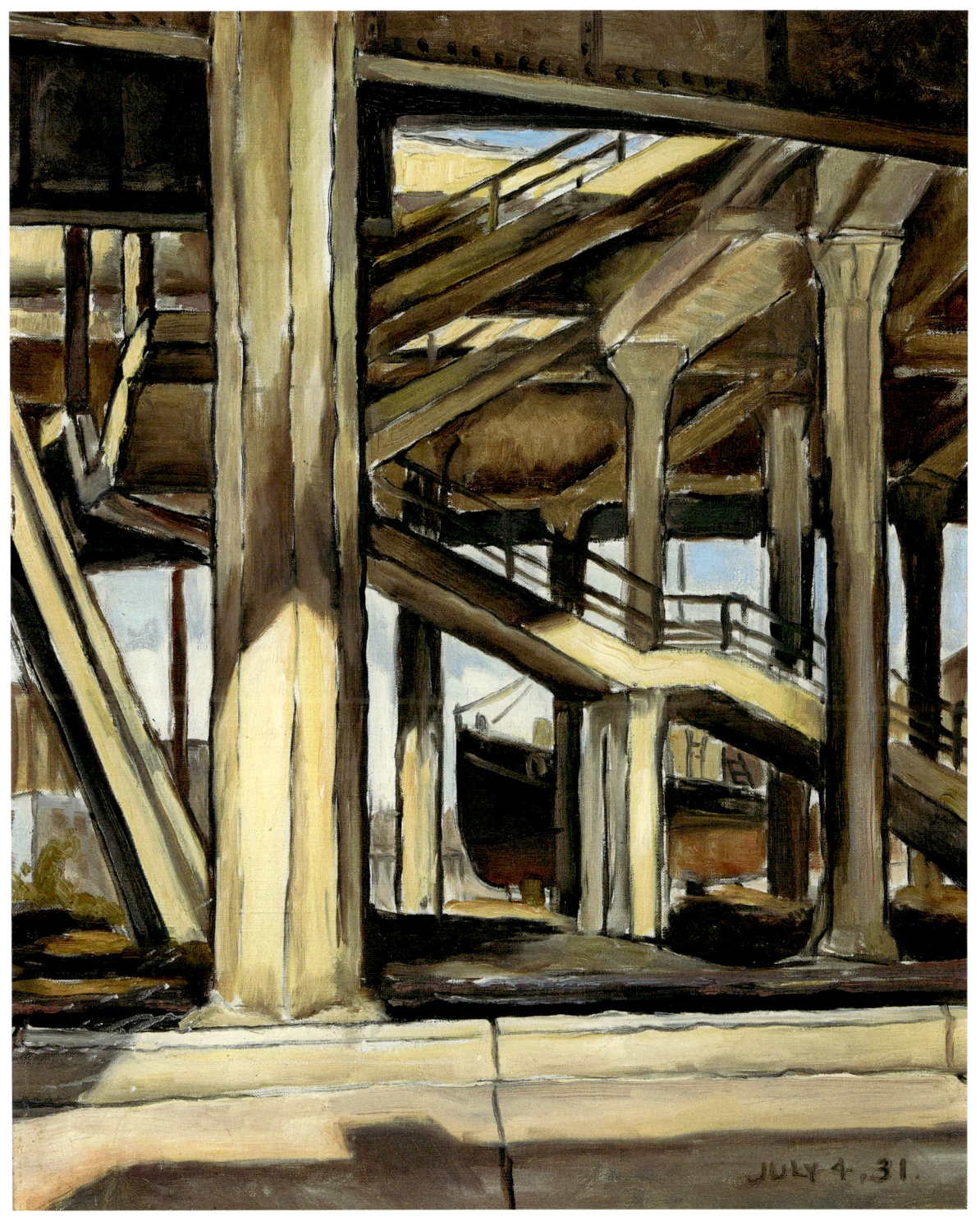

4 Kamekichi Tokita, *Bridge*, 1931, oil on canvas

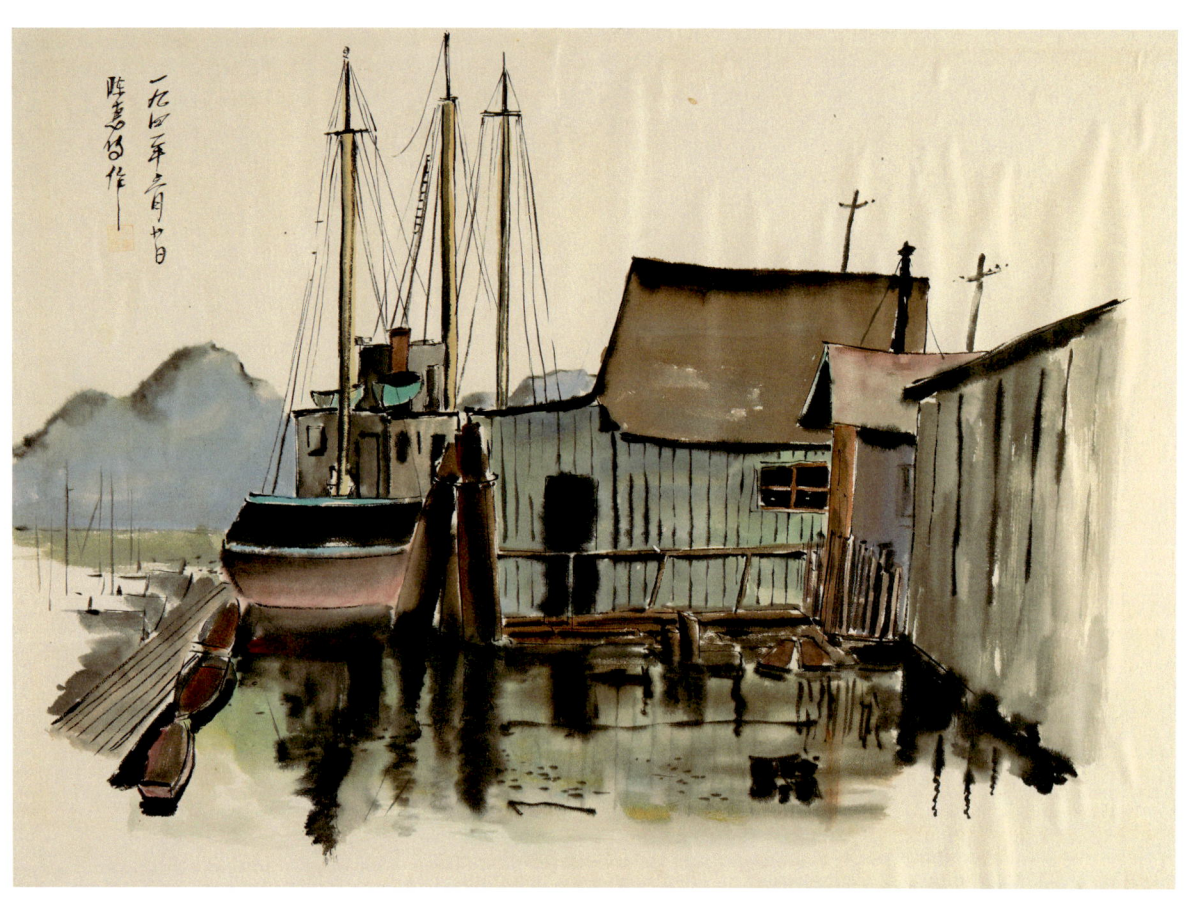

5 Fay Chong, *Lake Union Mooring*, ca. 1942, watercolor

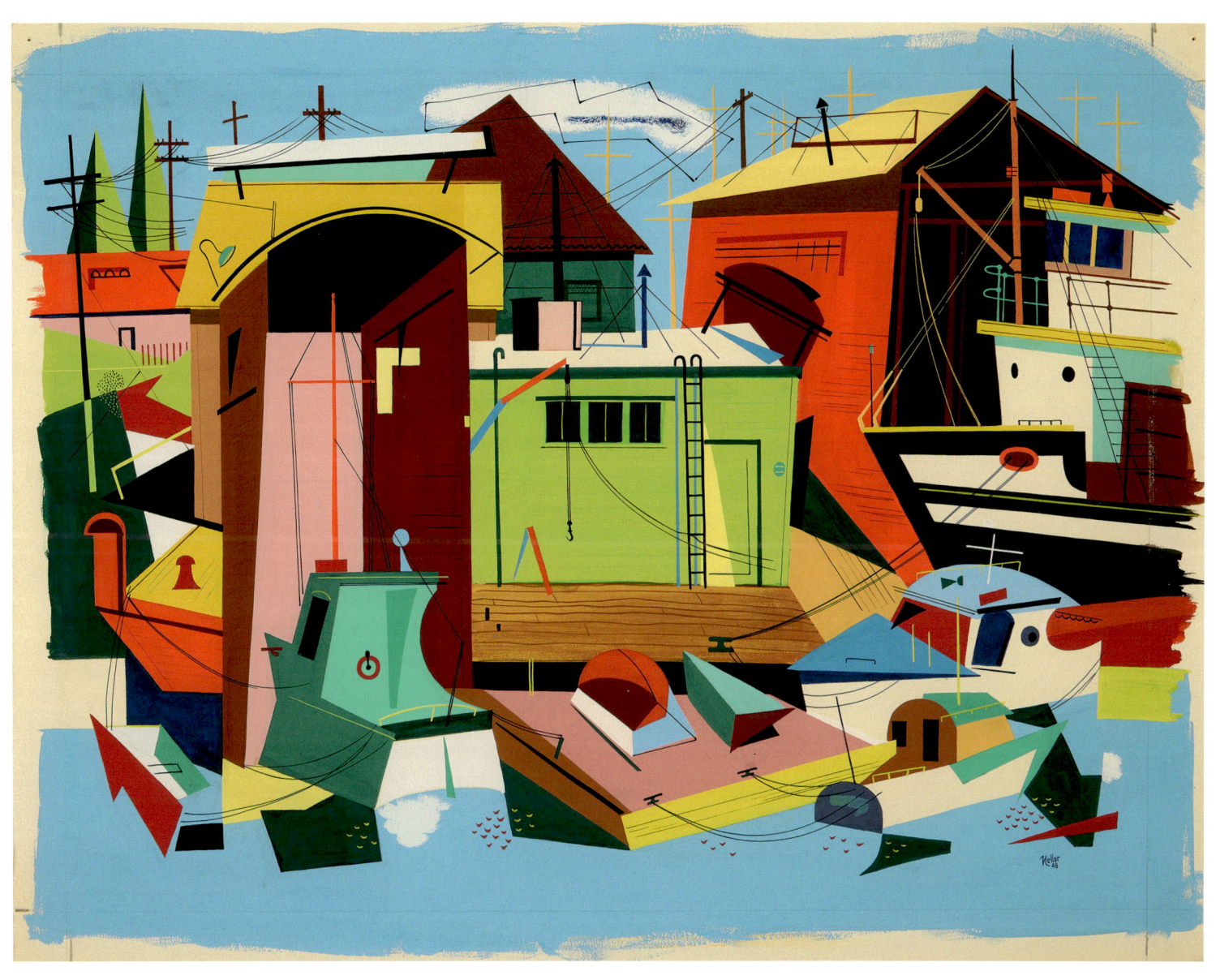

6 William L. Nellor, *Merry Pranks*, 1949, tempera on paperboard

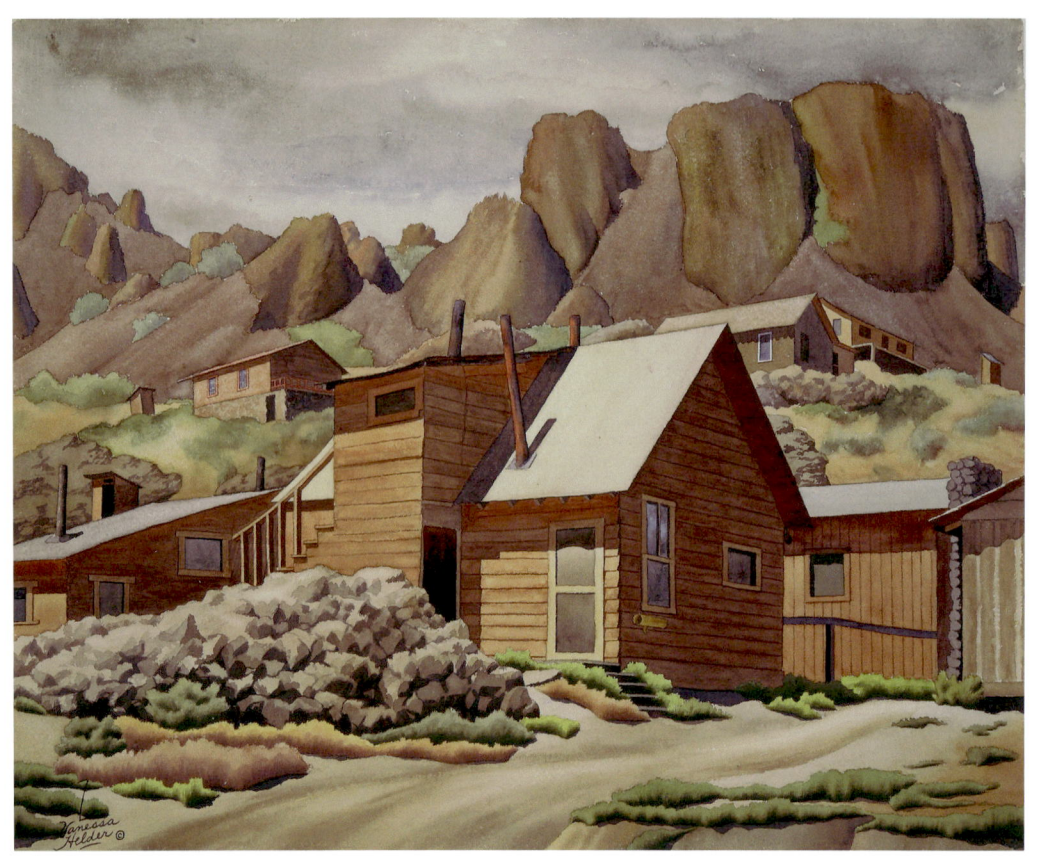

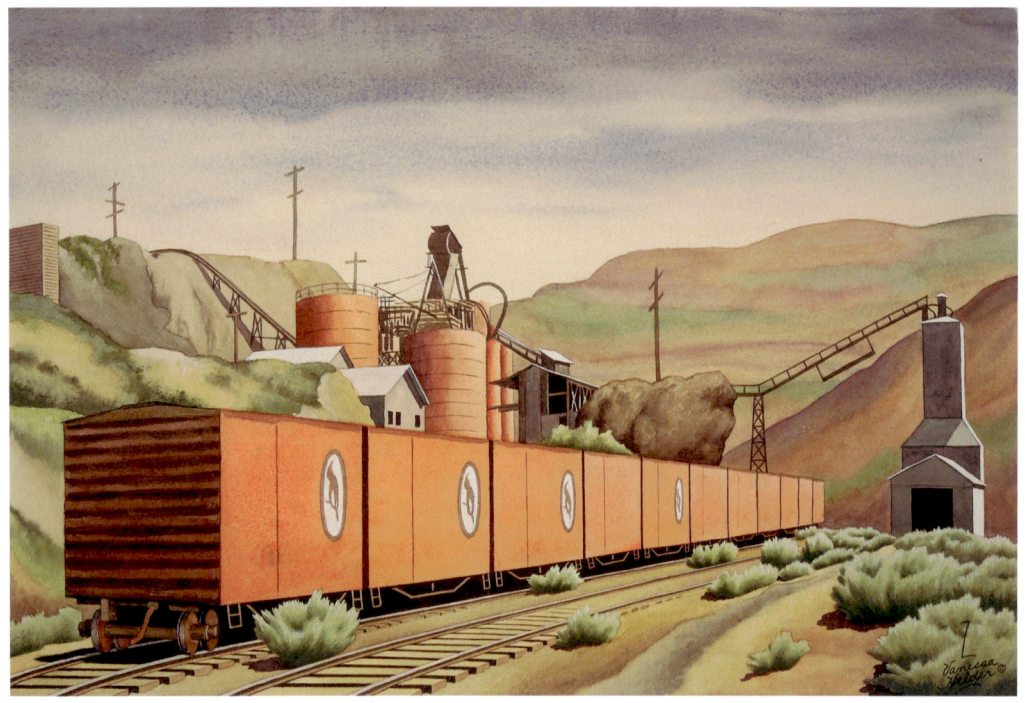

7 Z. Vanessa Helder, *B Street—Residence District*, 1939–41, watercolor

8 Z. Vanessa Helder, *Cement Silos*, 1939–41, watercolor

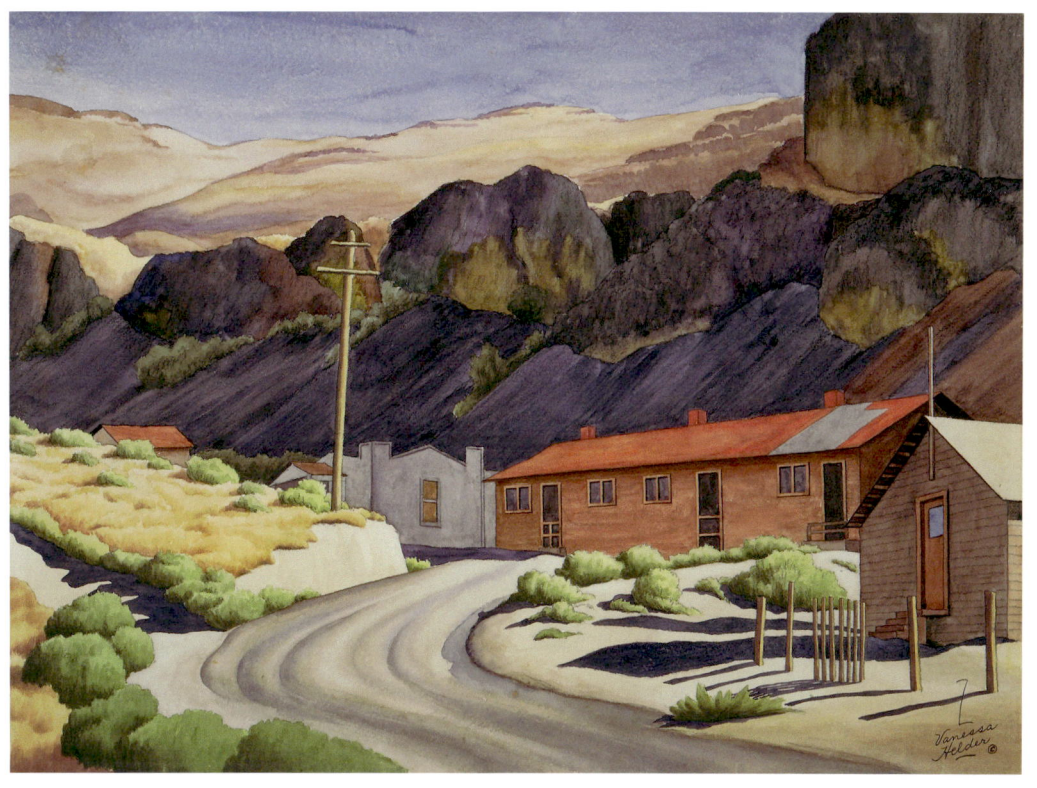

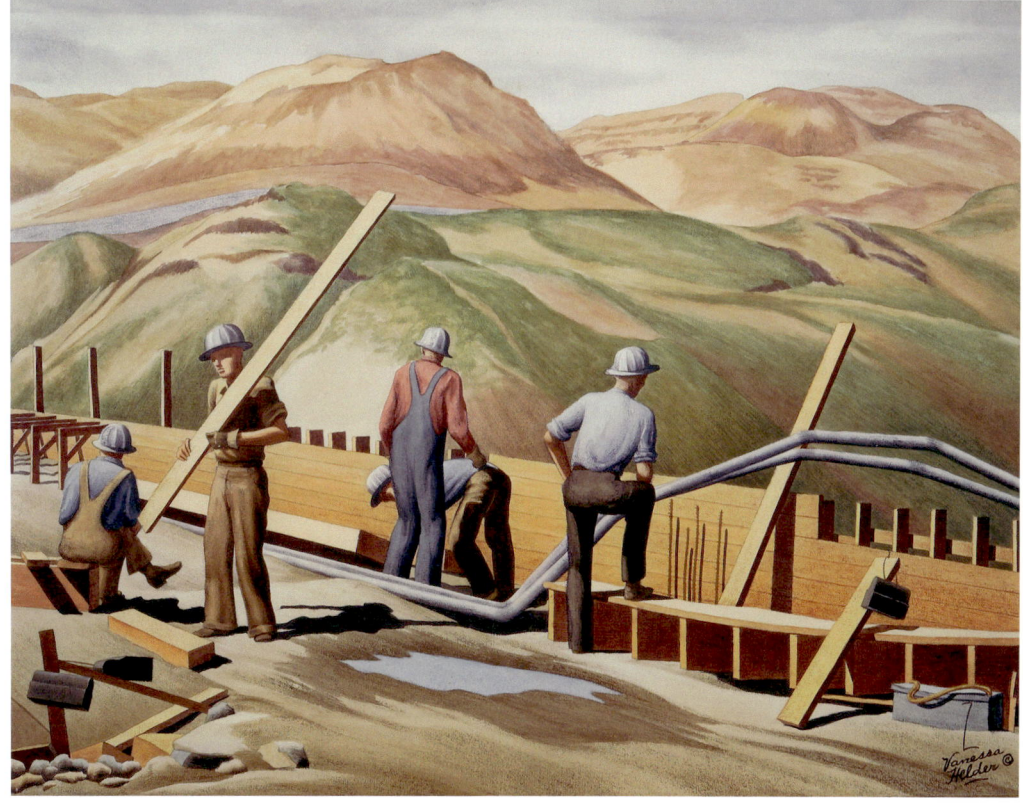

9 Z. Vanessa Helder, *Cliff Drive*, 1939–41, watercolor

10 Z. Vanessa Helder, *Construction Crew*, 1939–41, watercolor

31

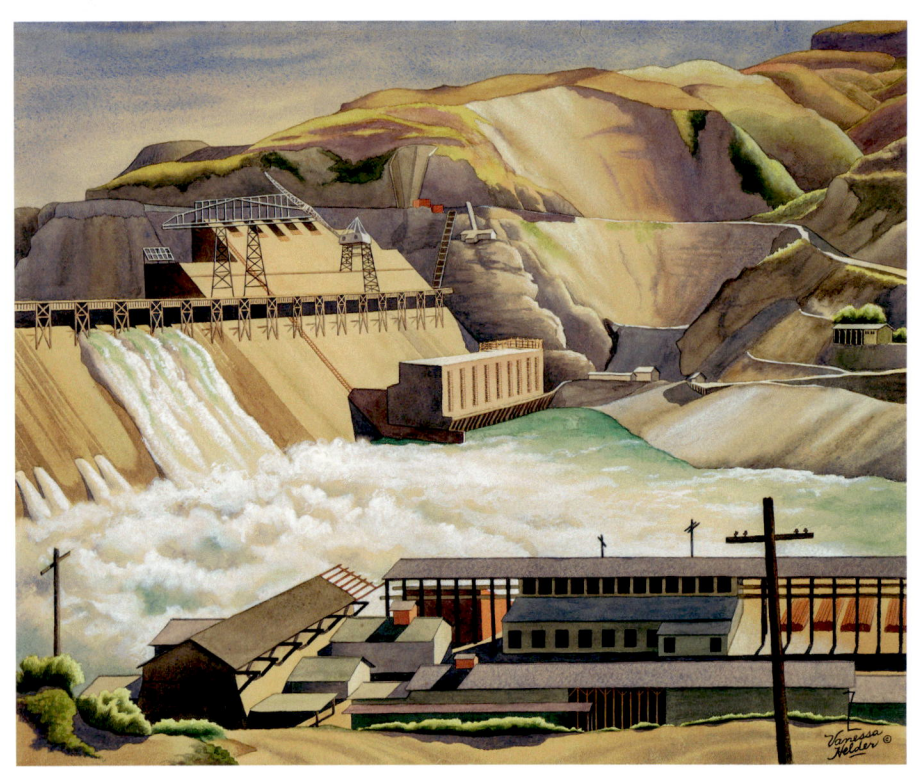

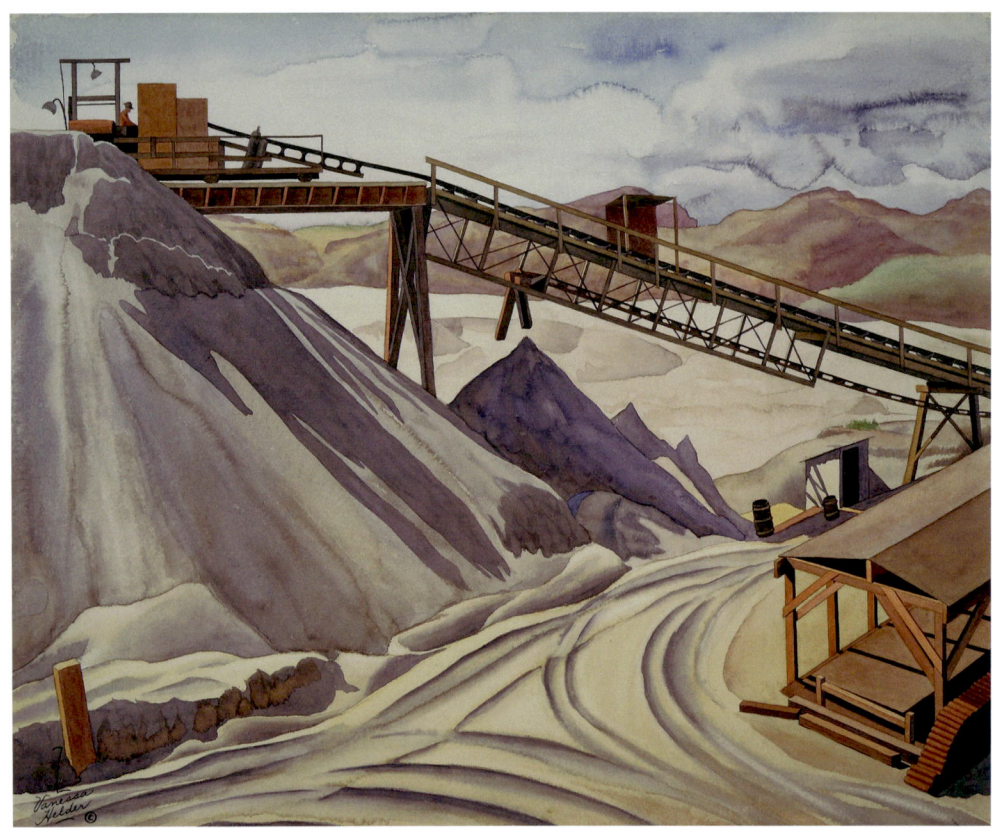

11 Z. Vanessa Helder, *Coulee Dam, Looking West*, 1939–41, watercolor

12 Z. Vanessa Helder, *Conveyor Belt*, 1939–41, watercolor

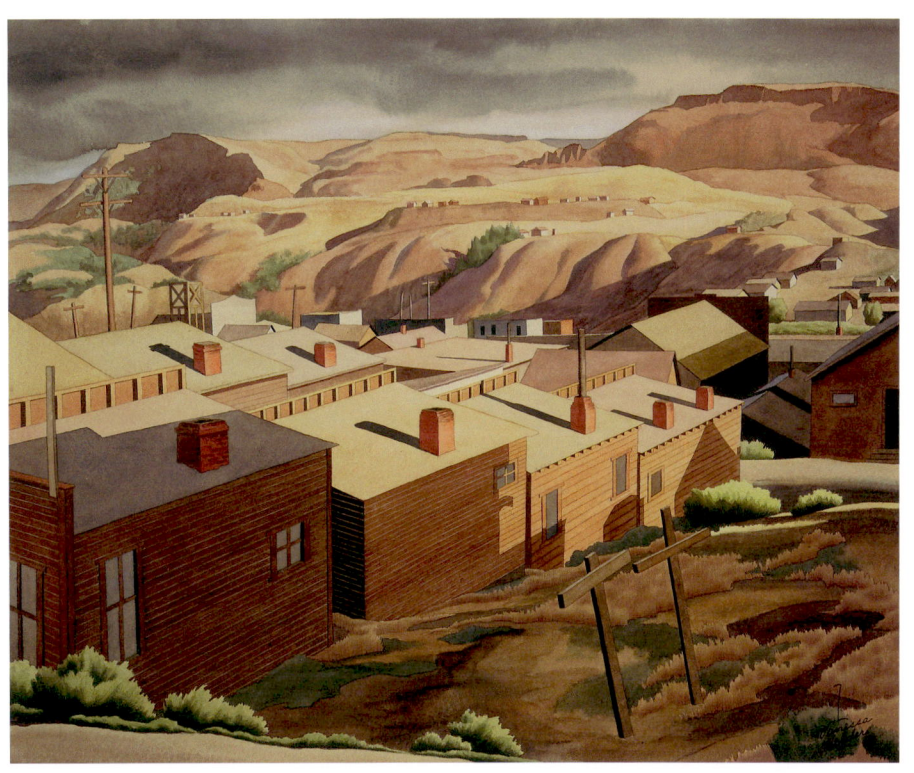

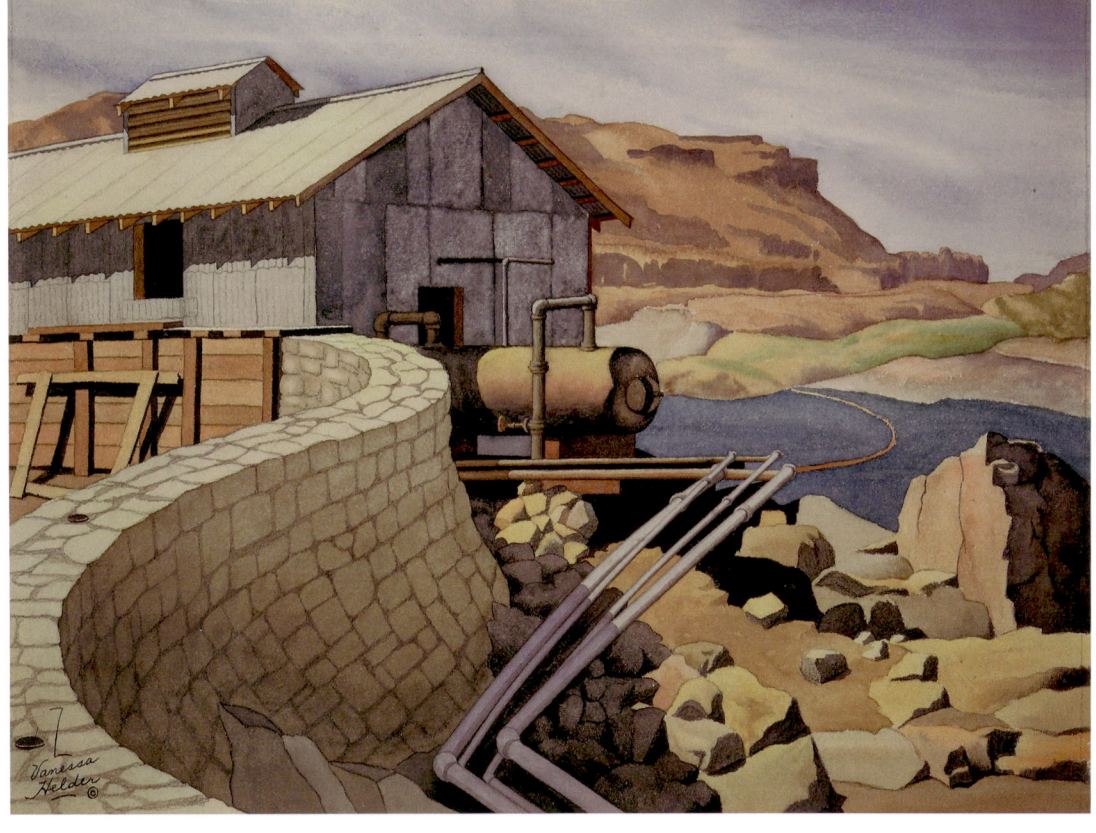

13 Z. Vanessa Helder, *Grand Coulee*, 1939–41, watercolor

14 Z. Vanessa Helder, *East Grout Shed*, 1939–41, watercolor

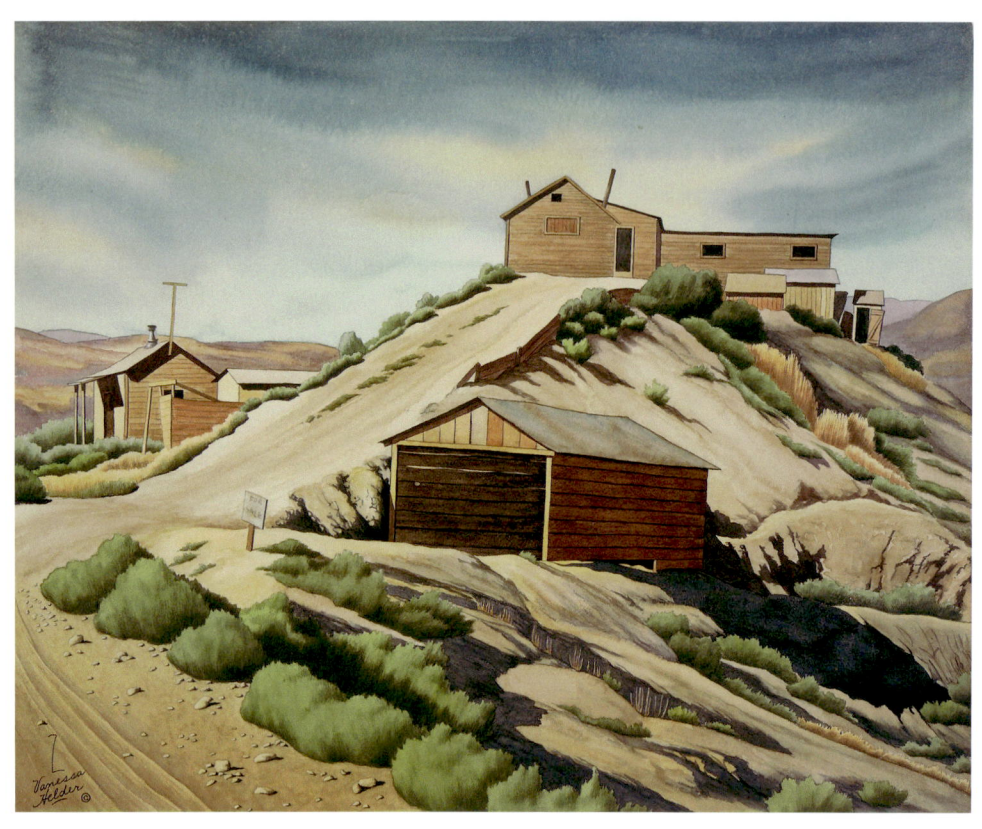

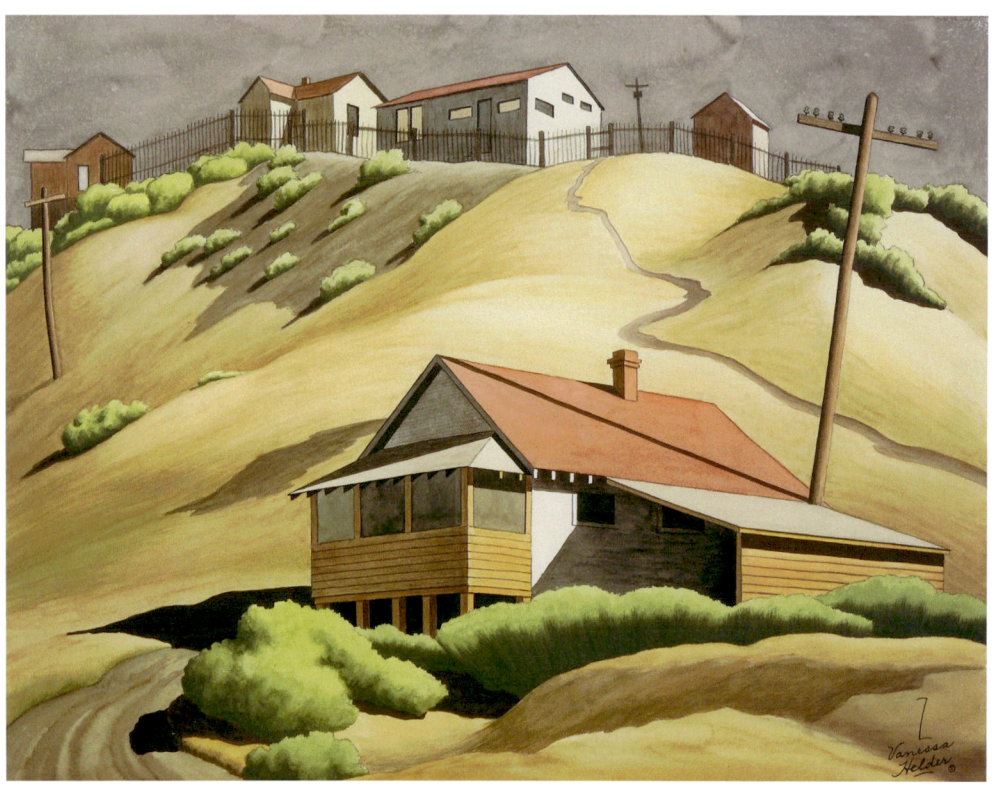

15 Z. Vanessa Helder, *Hilltop House*, 1939–41, watercolor

16 Z. Vanessa Helder, *Grand Coulee Heights*, 1939–41, watercolor

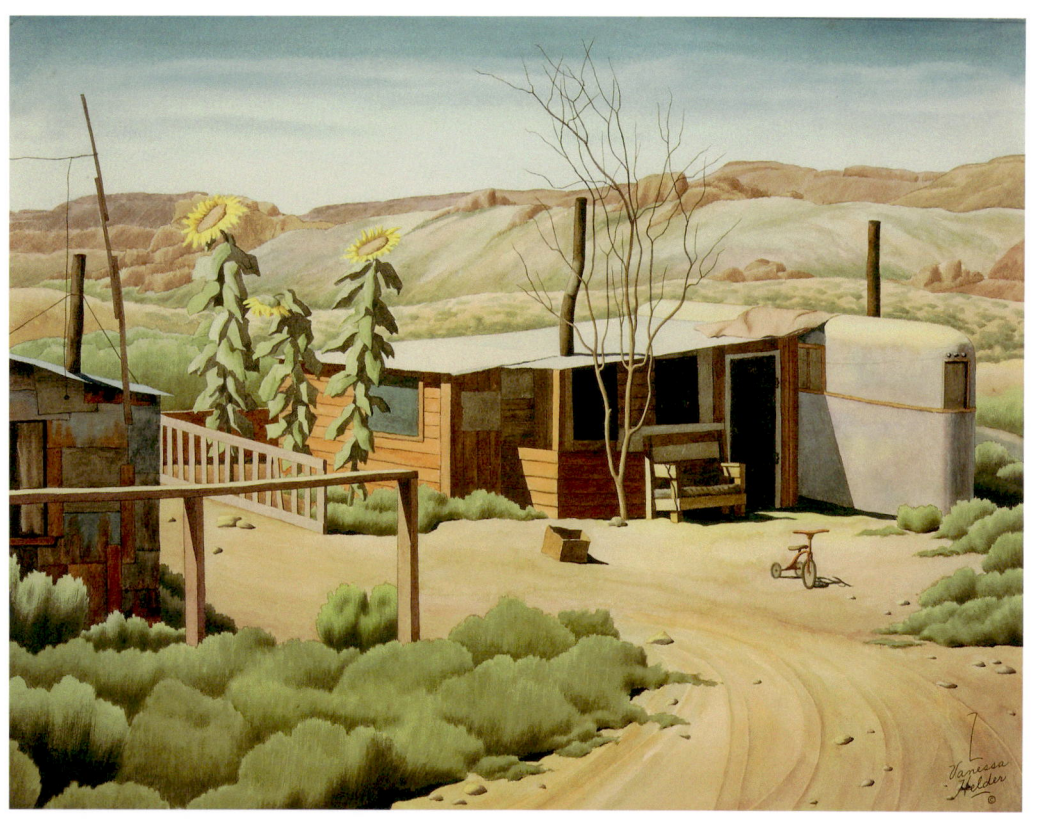

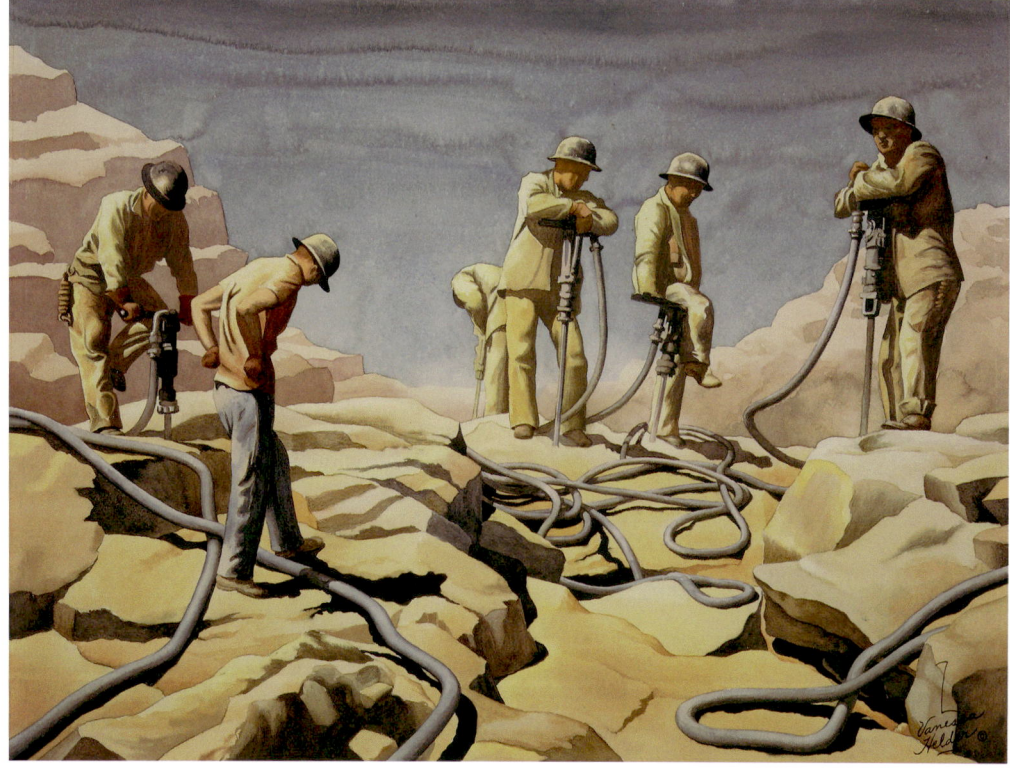

17 Z. Vanessa Helder, *Hooverville, Coulee Dam*, 1939–41, watercolor

18 Z. Vanessa Helder, *Jackhammer Crew*, 1939–41, watercolor

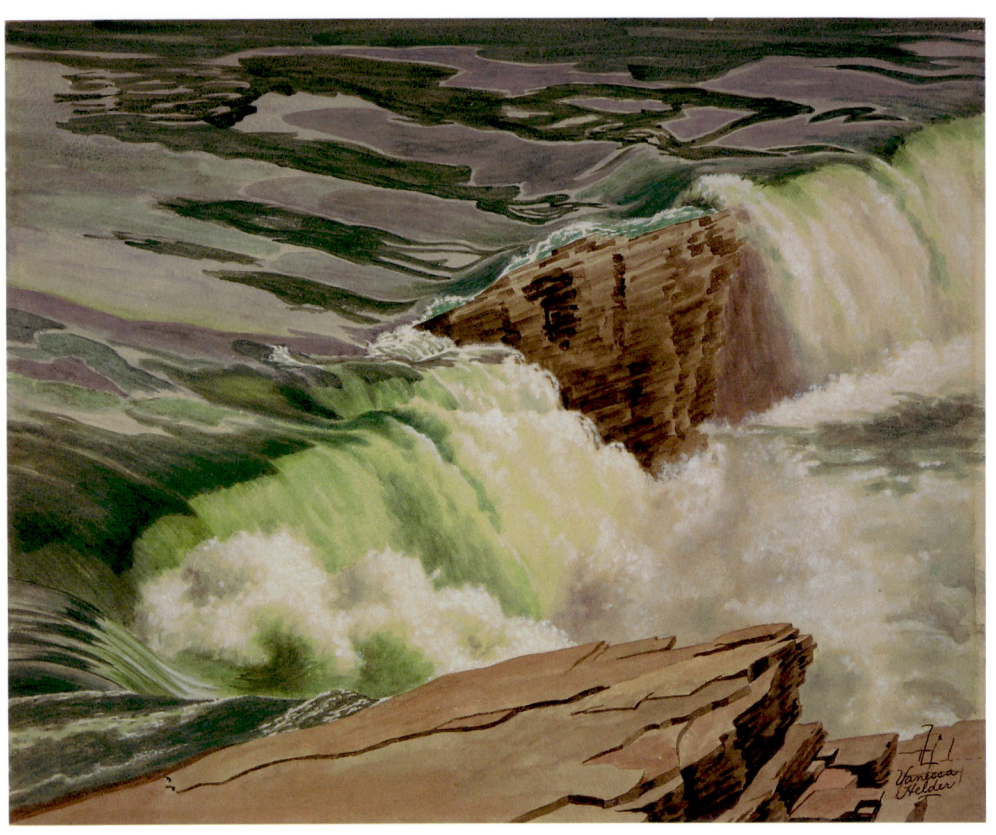

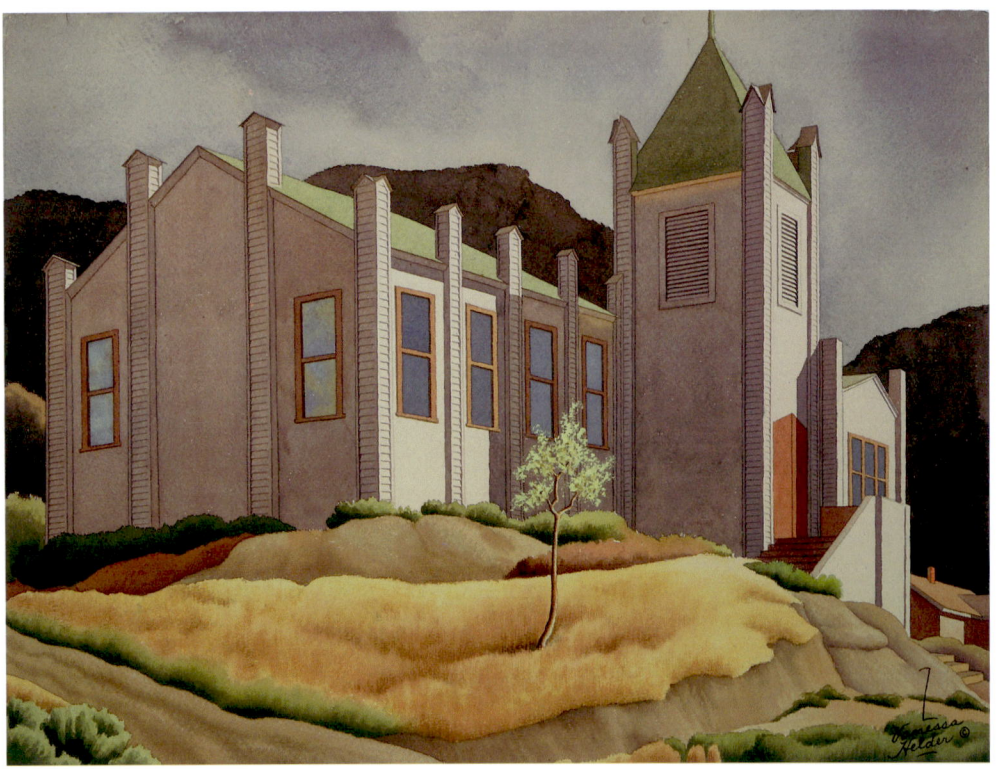

19 Z. Vanessa Helder, *Kettle Falls*, 1939–41, watercolor

20 Z. Vanessa Helder, *Methodist Church in Coulee Heights*, 1939–41, watercolor

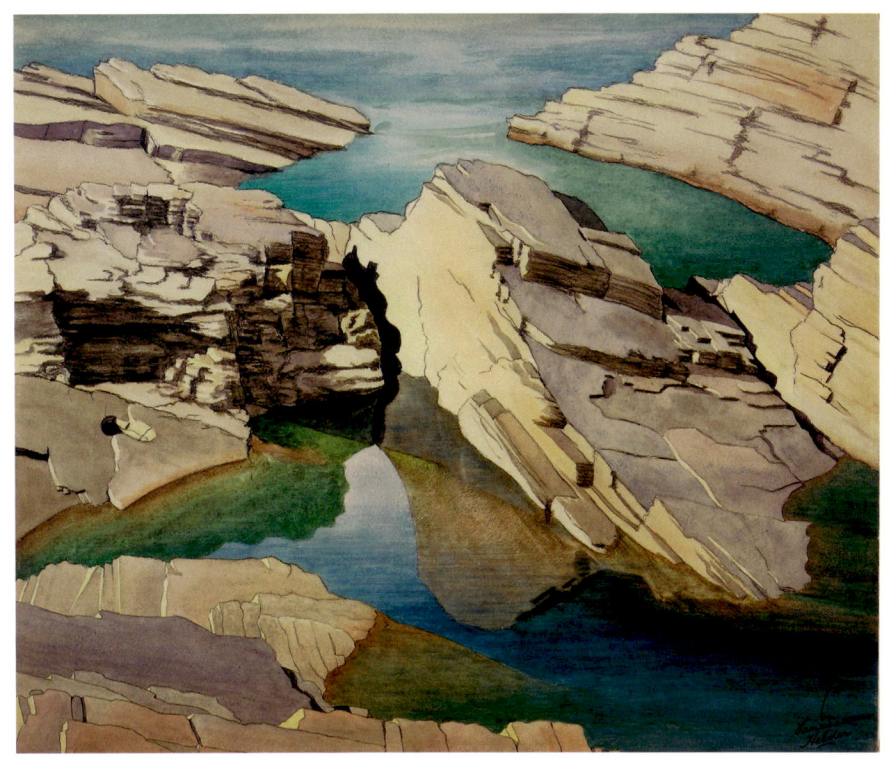

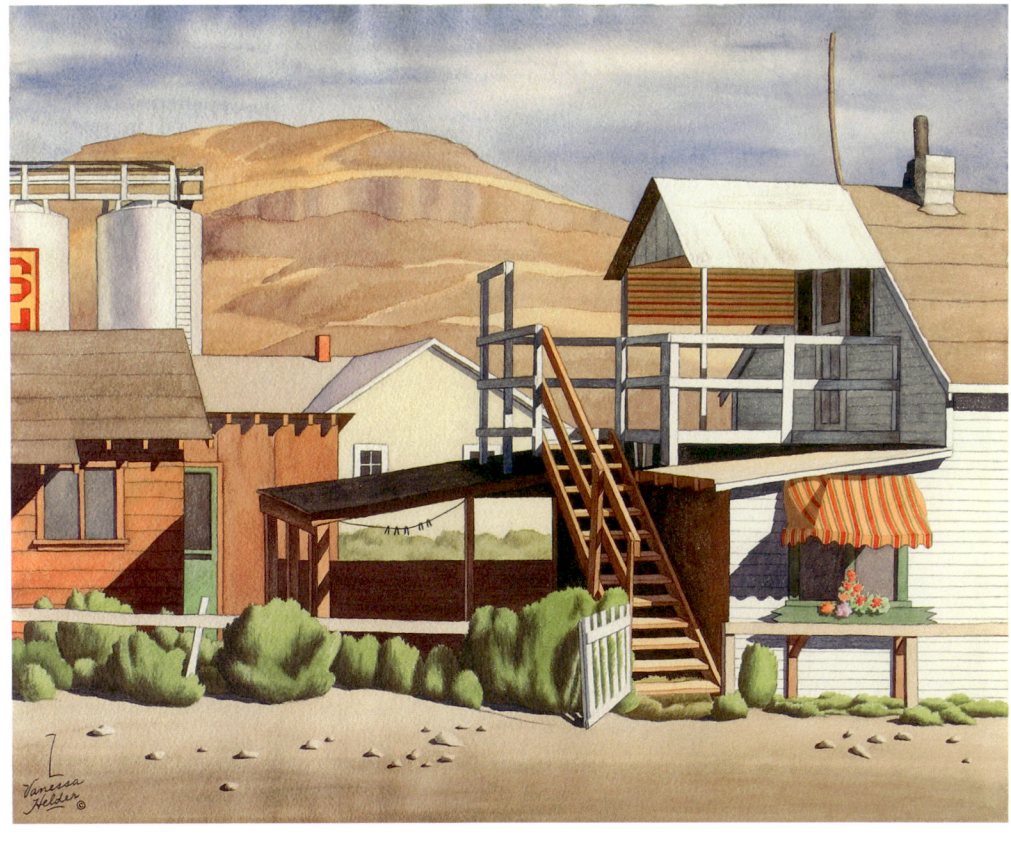

21 Z. Vanessa Helder, *Pool Below Kettle Falls*, 1939–41, watercolor

22 Z. Vanessa Helder, *Neighbors*, 1939–41, watercolor

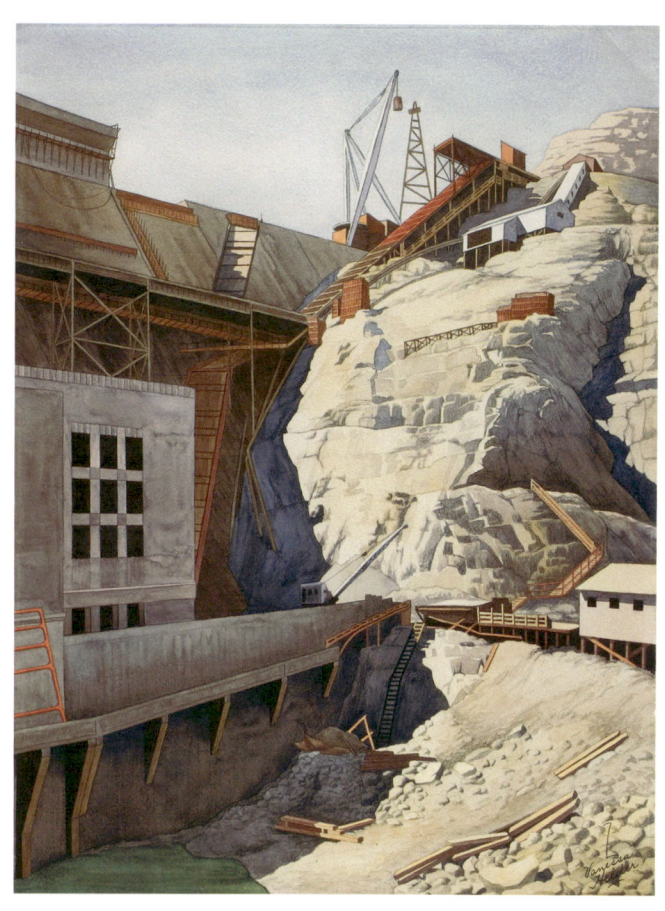

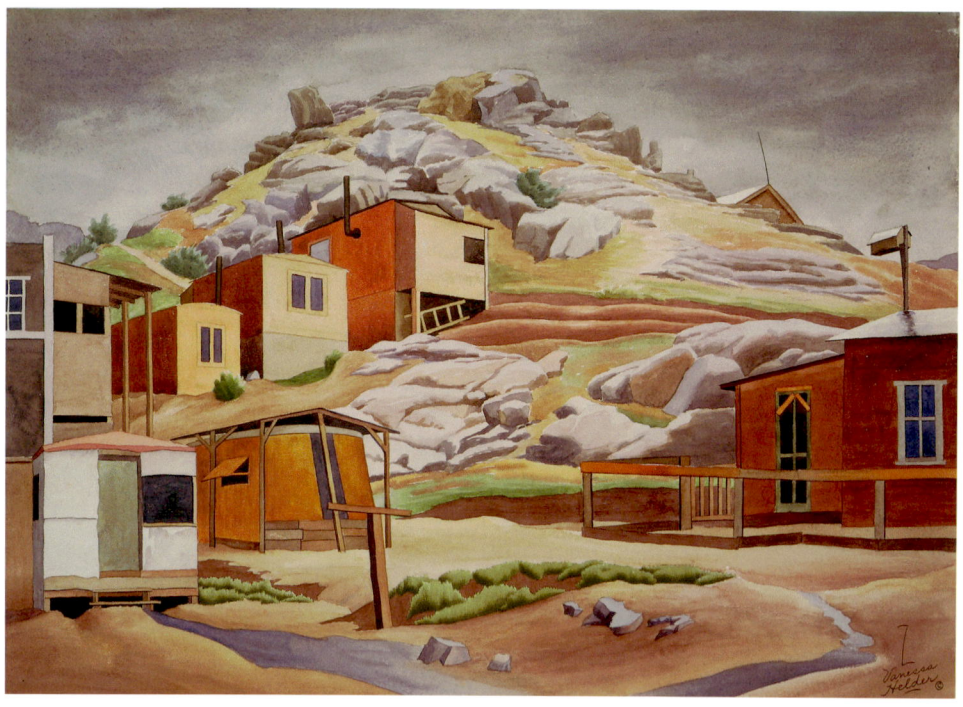

23 Z. Vanessa Helder, *Rocks and Concrete*, 1939–41, watercolor

24 Z. Vanessa Helder, *Rainy Afternoon*, 1939–41, watercolor

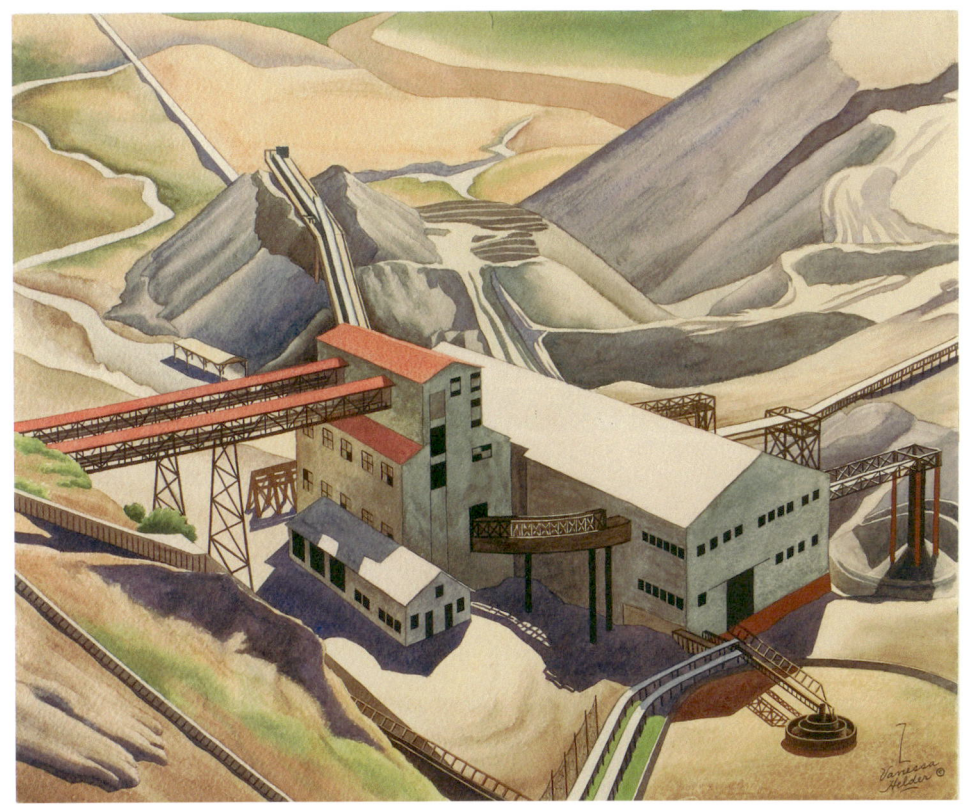

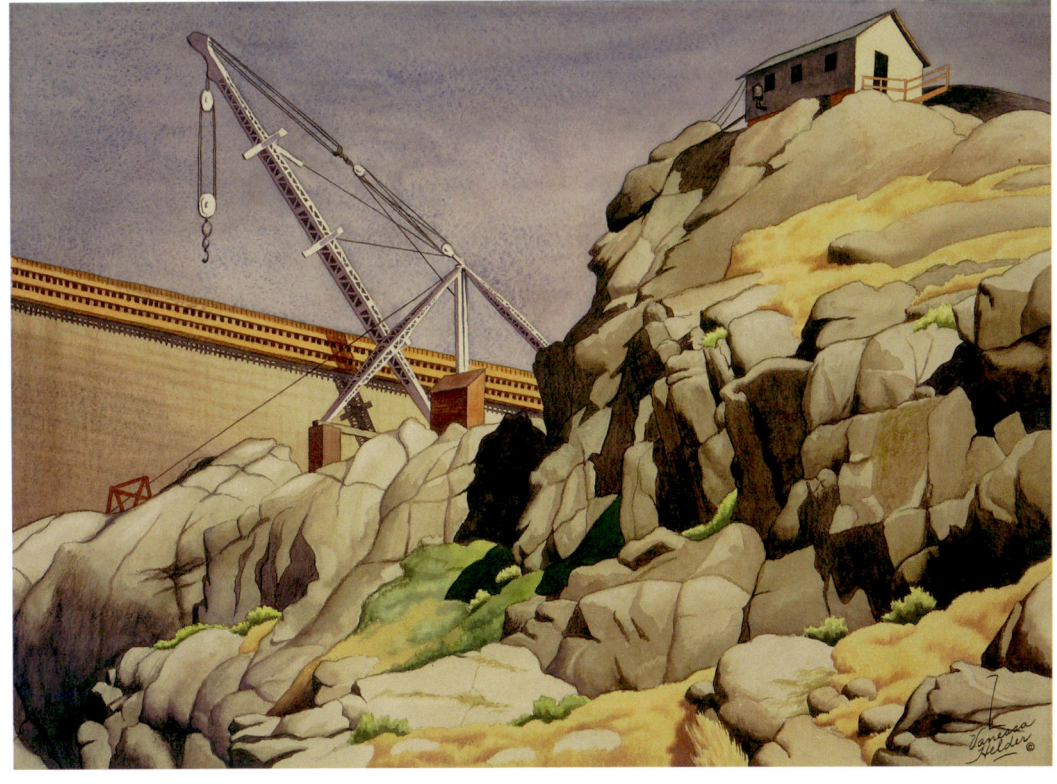

25 Z. Vanessa Helder, *Sand and Gravel Works*, 1939–41, watercolor

26 Z. Vanessa Helder, *Stiff-Legged Crane*, 1939–41, watercolor

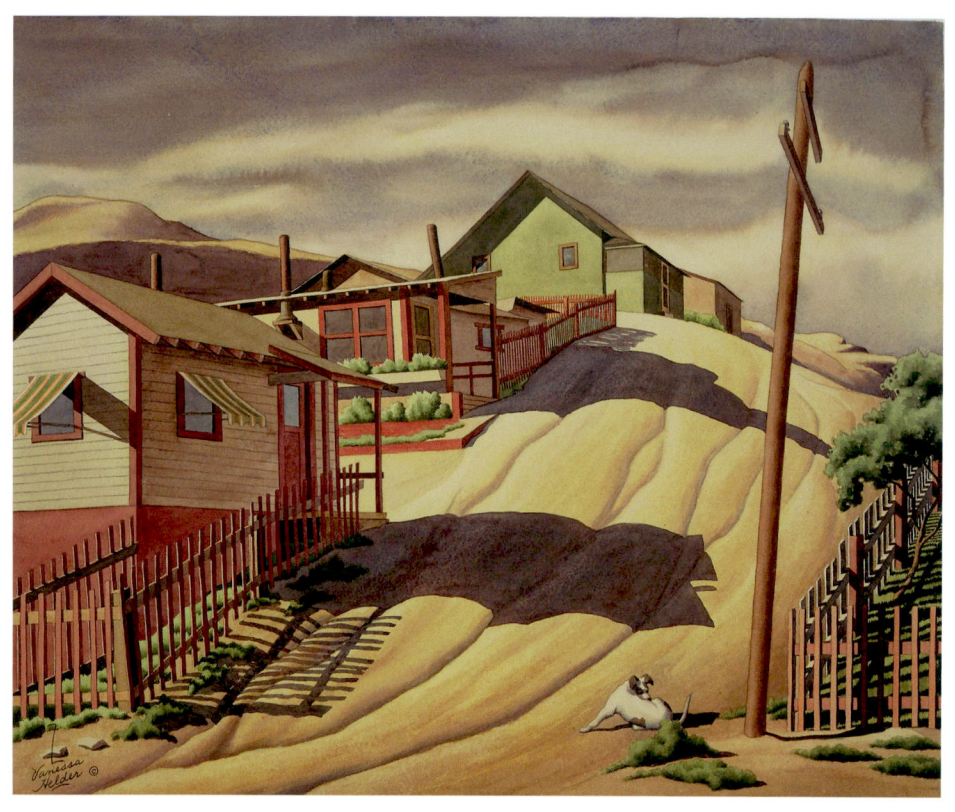

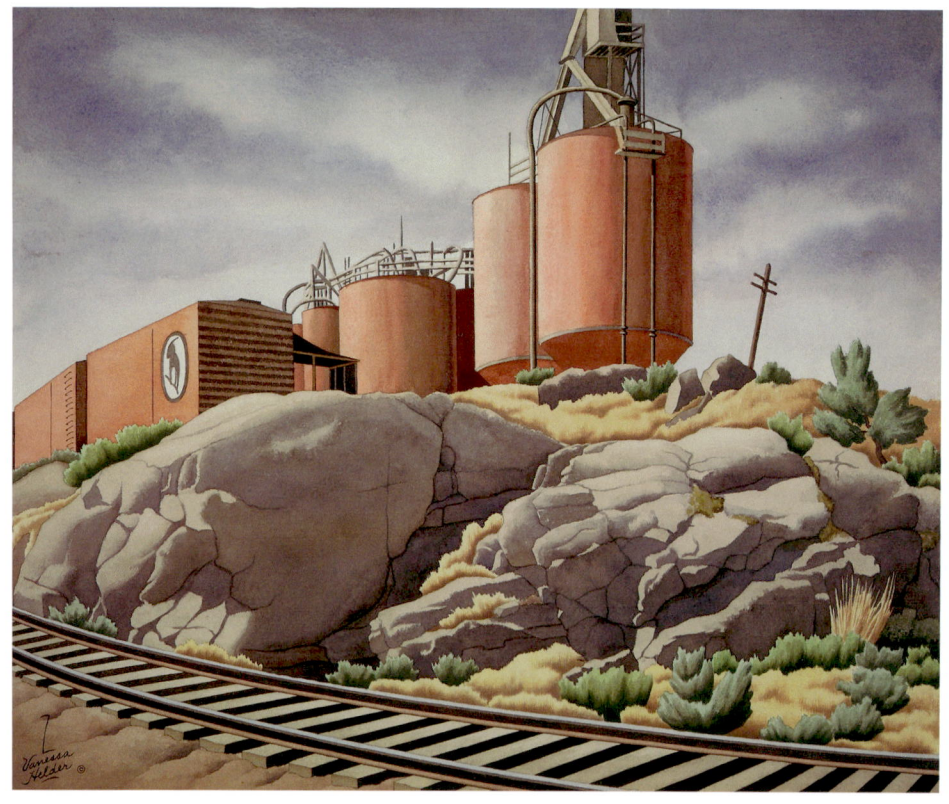

27 Z. Vanessa Helder, *Sunday Morning in Grand Coulee*, 1939–41, watercolor

28 Z. Vanessa Helder, *Tanks and Track*, 1939–41, watercolor

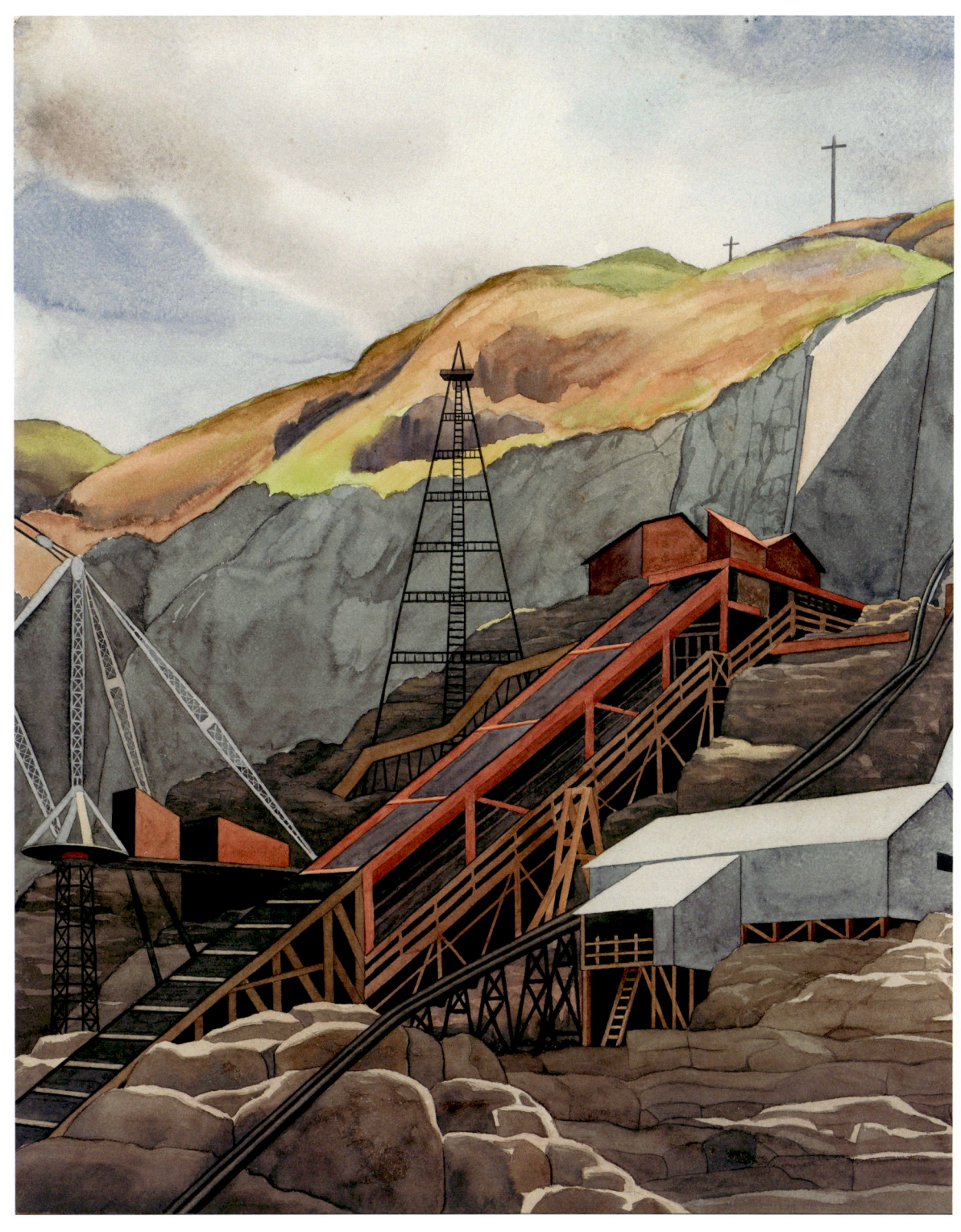

29 Z. Vanessa Helder, *Coulee Dam Construction: Skip Way and Grout Shed*, 1939, watercolor

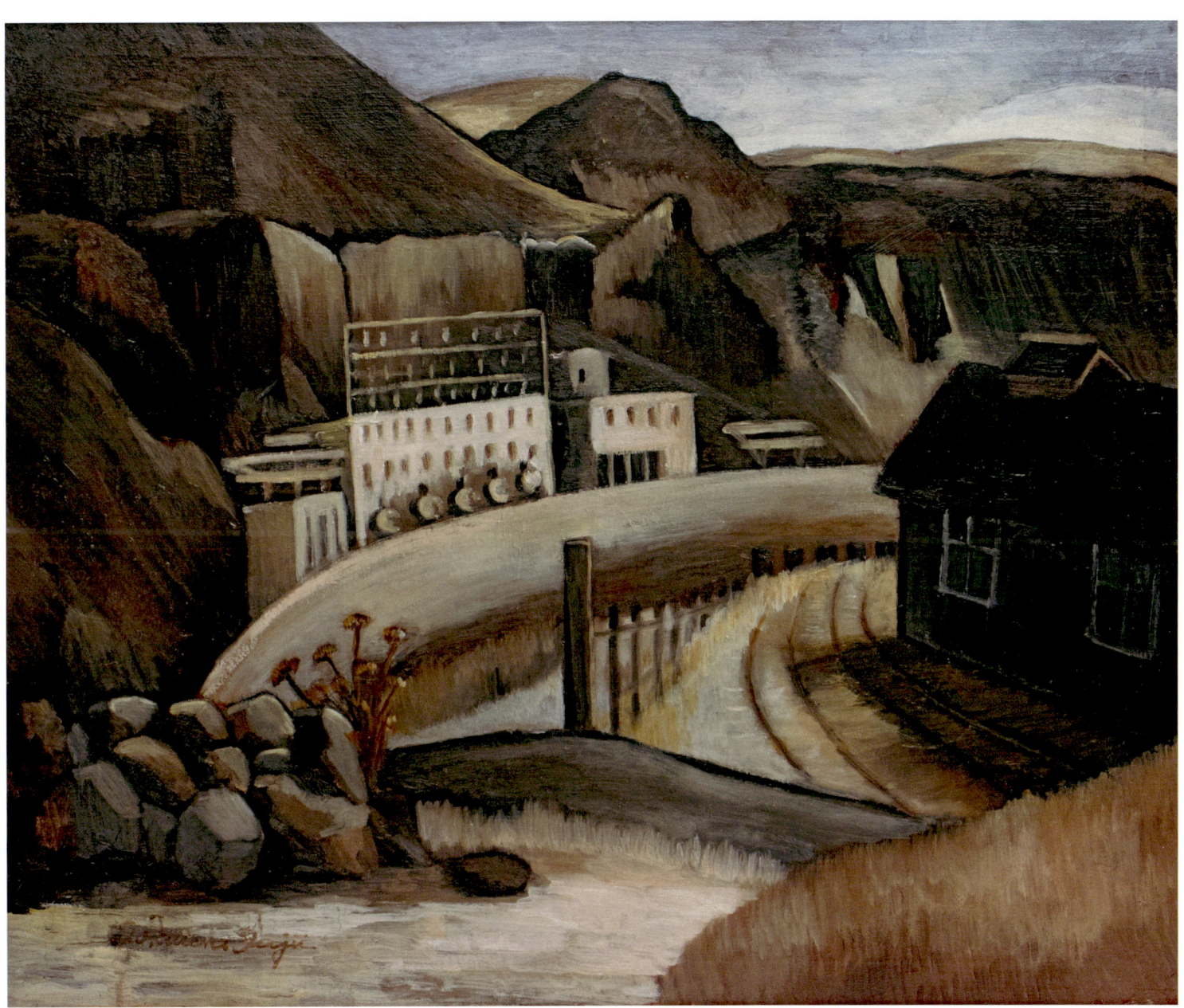

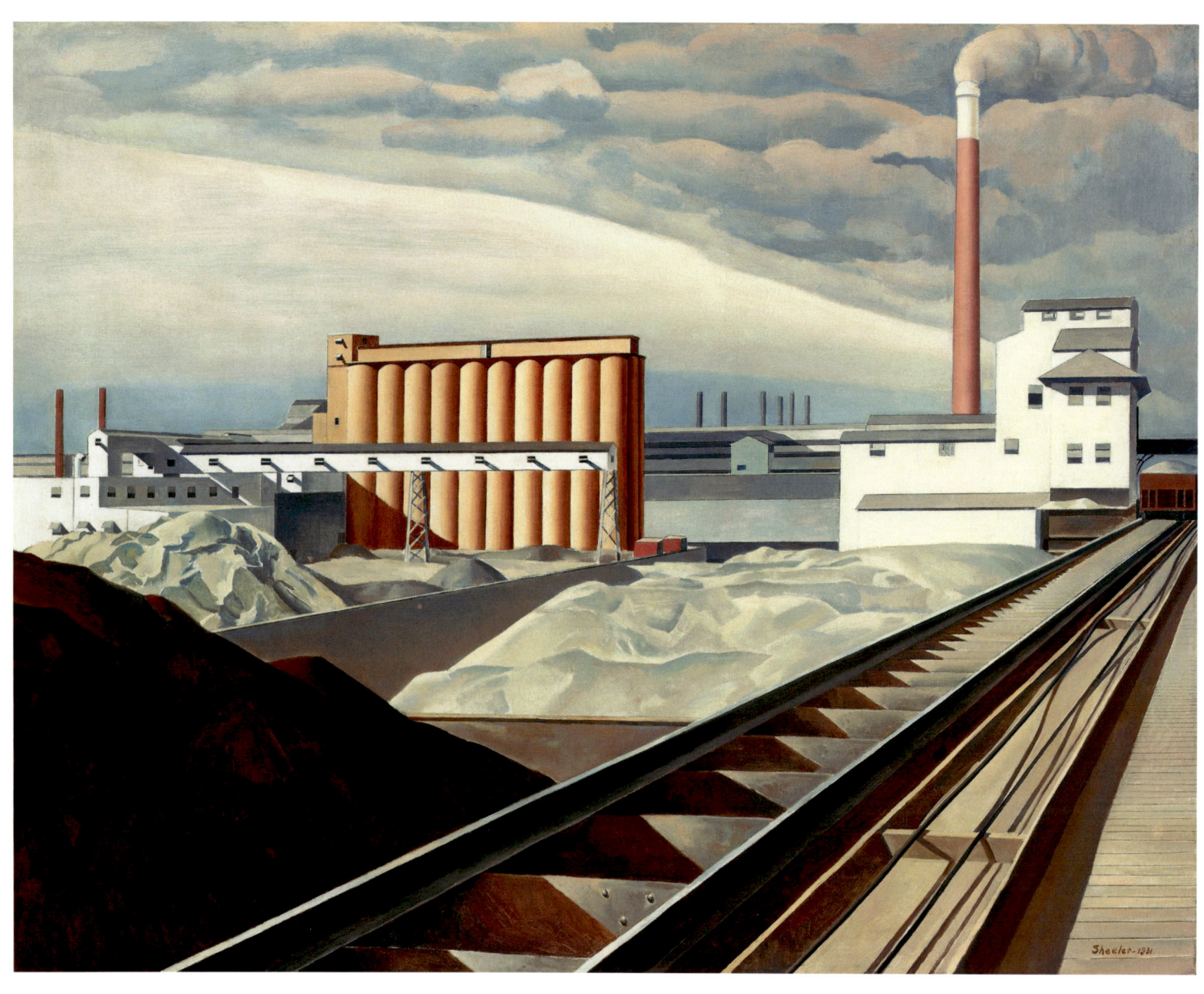

31 Charles Sheeler, *Classic Landscape*, 1931, oil on canvas

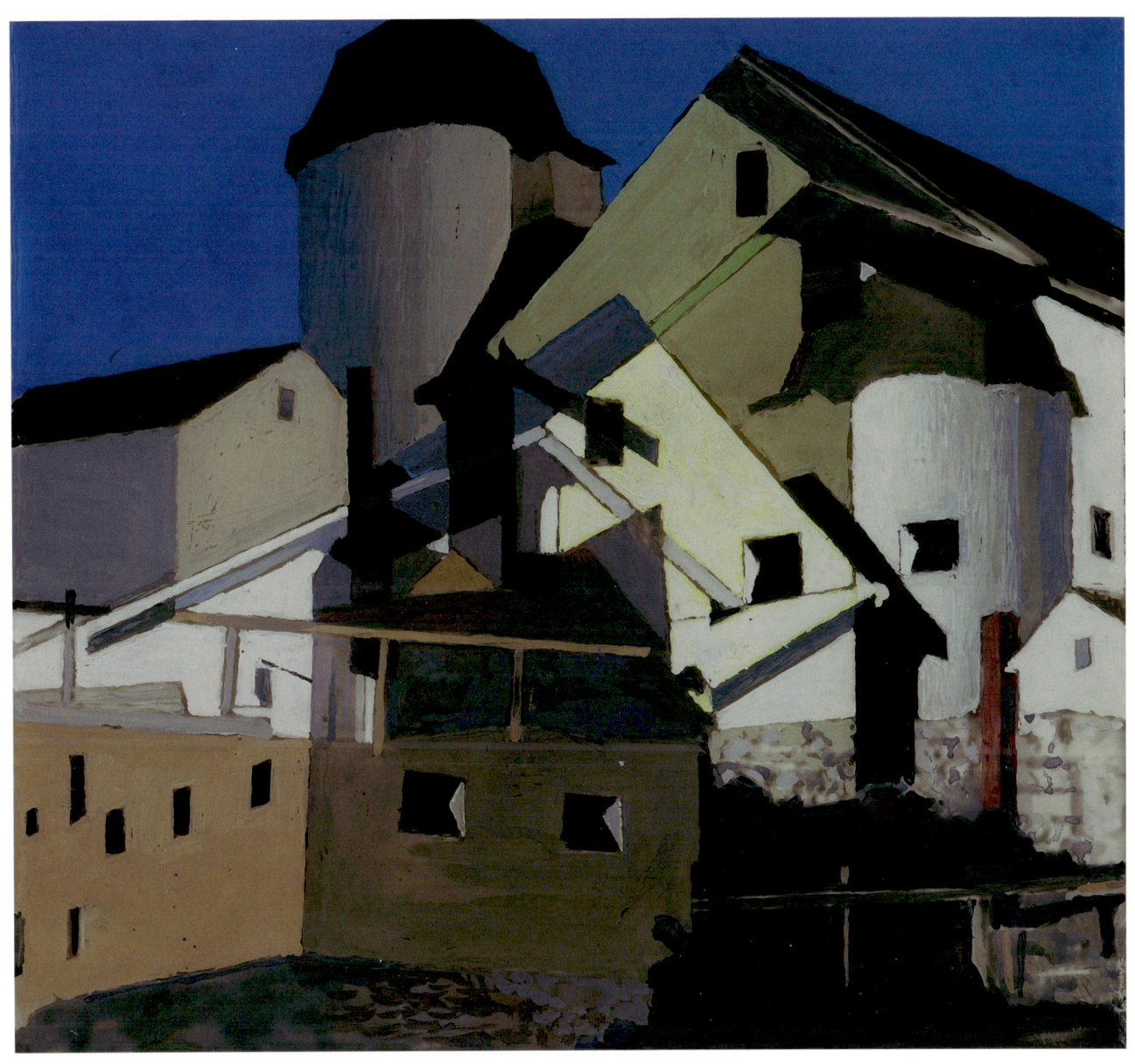

32 Charles Sheeler, *Composition Around White*, 1957, tempera on plexiglass 45

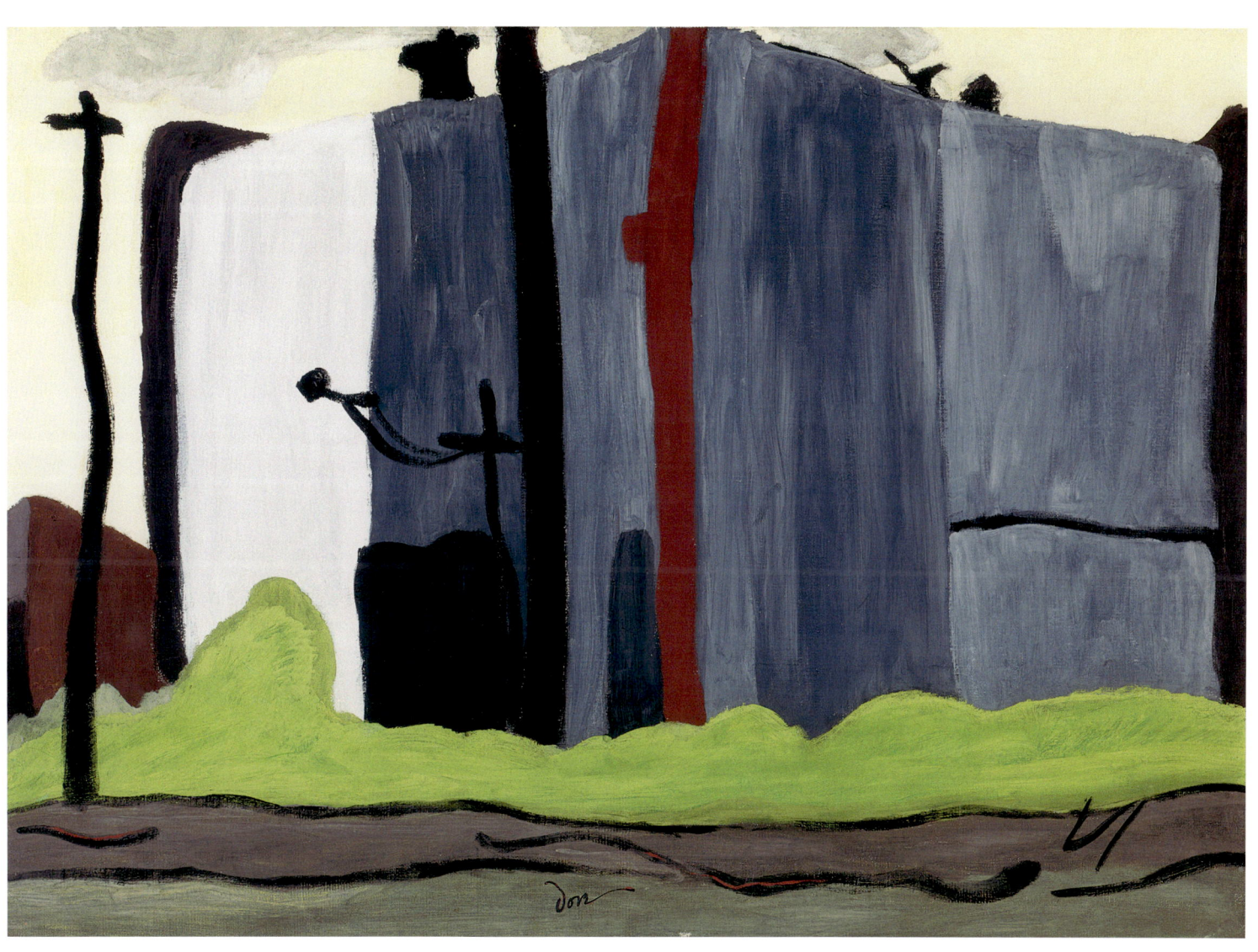

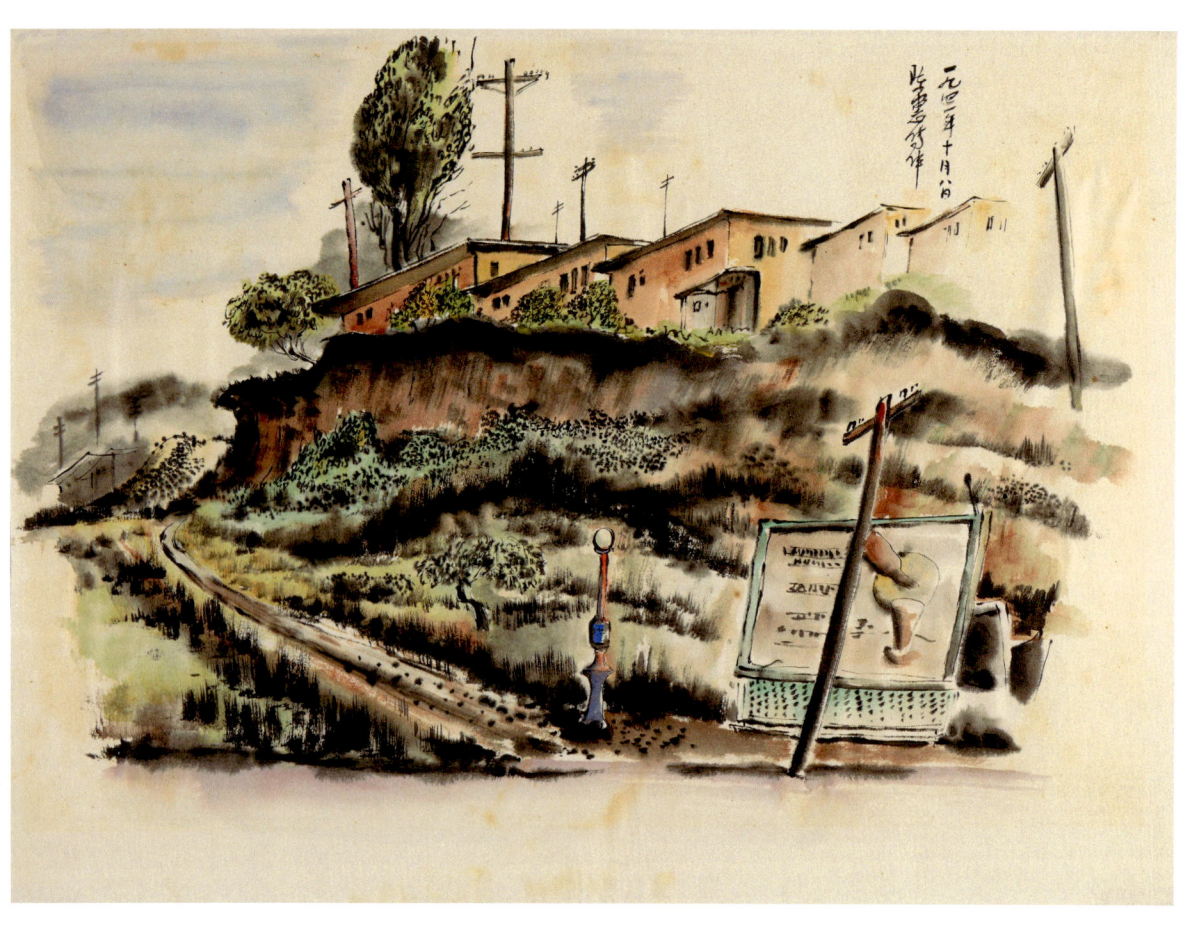

34 Fay Chong, *Yesler Housing Project*, ca. 1942, watercolor

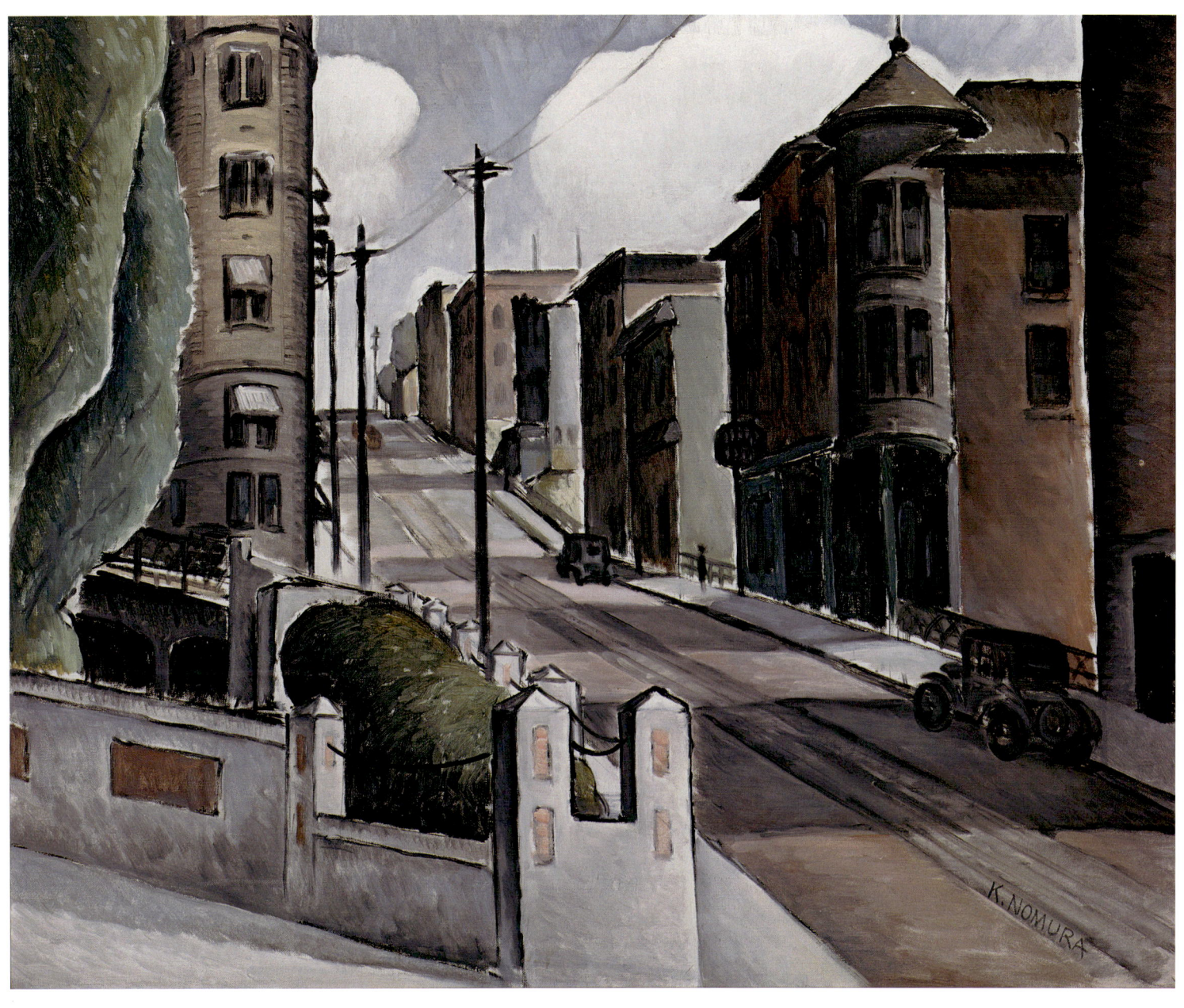

35 Kenjiro Nomura, *Street*, ca. 1932, oil on canvas

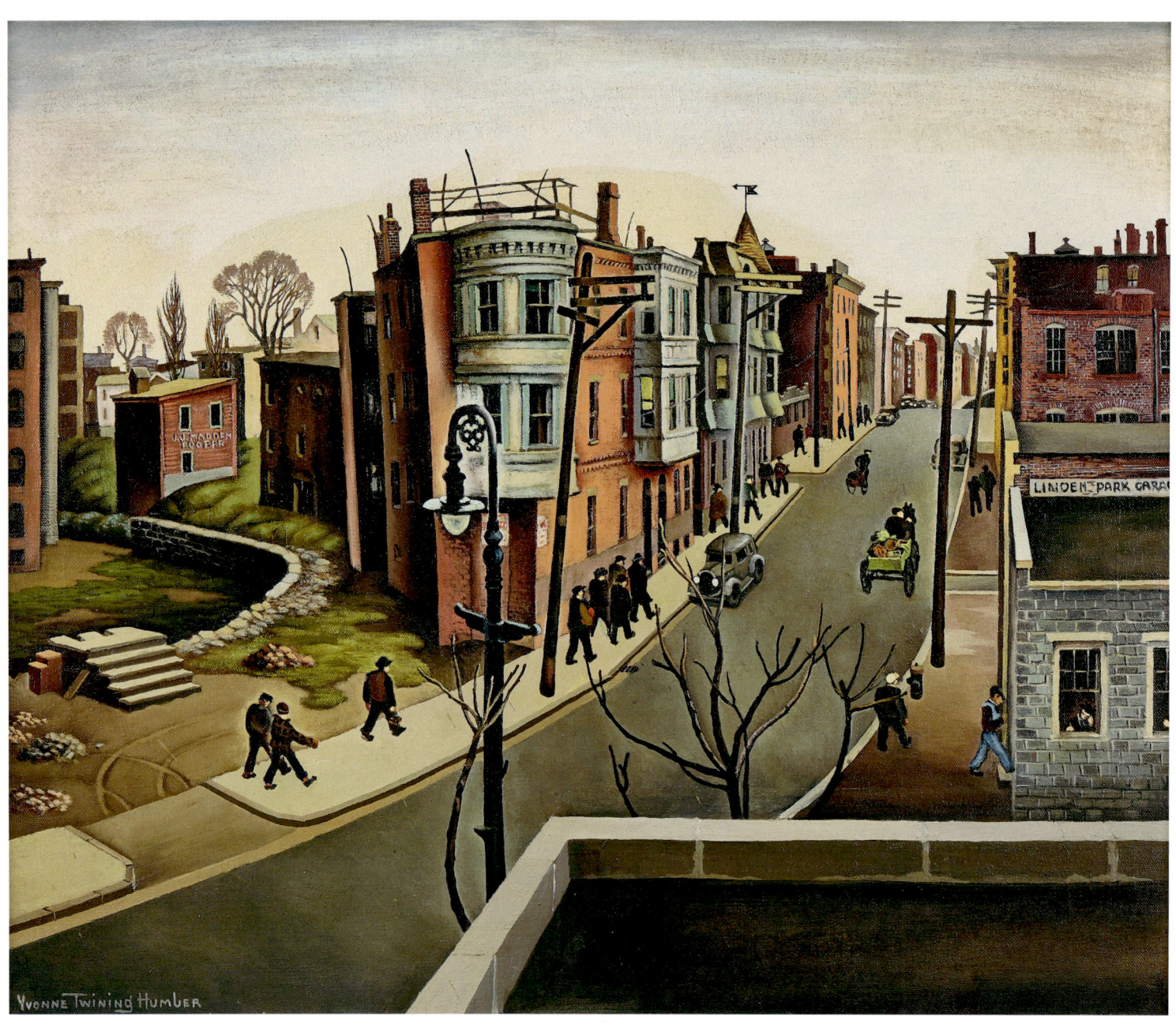

36 Yvonne Twining Humber, *Suburban Street*, 1940, oil on canvas

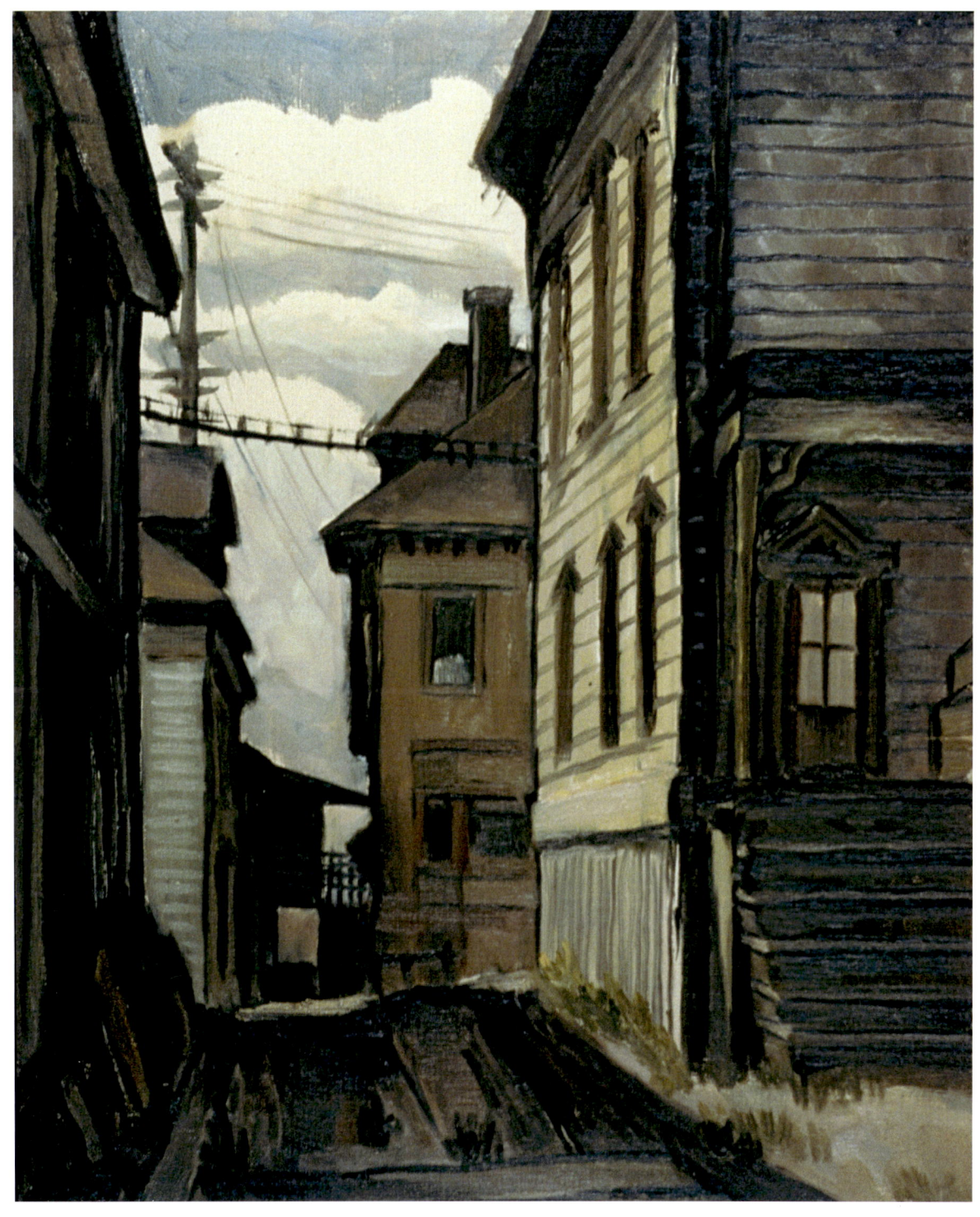

37 Kamekichi Tokita, *Alley*, ca. 1929, oil on canvas

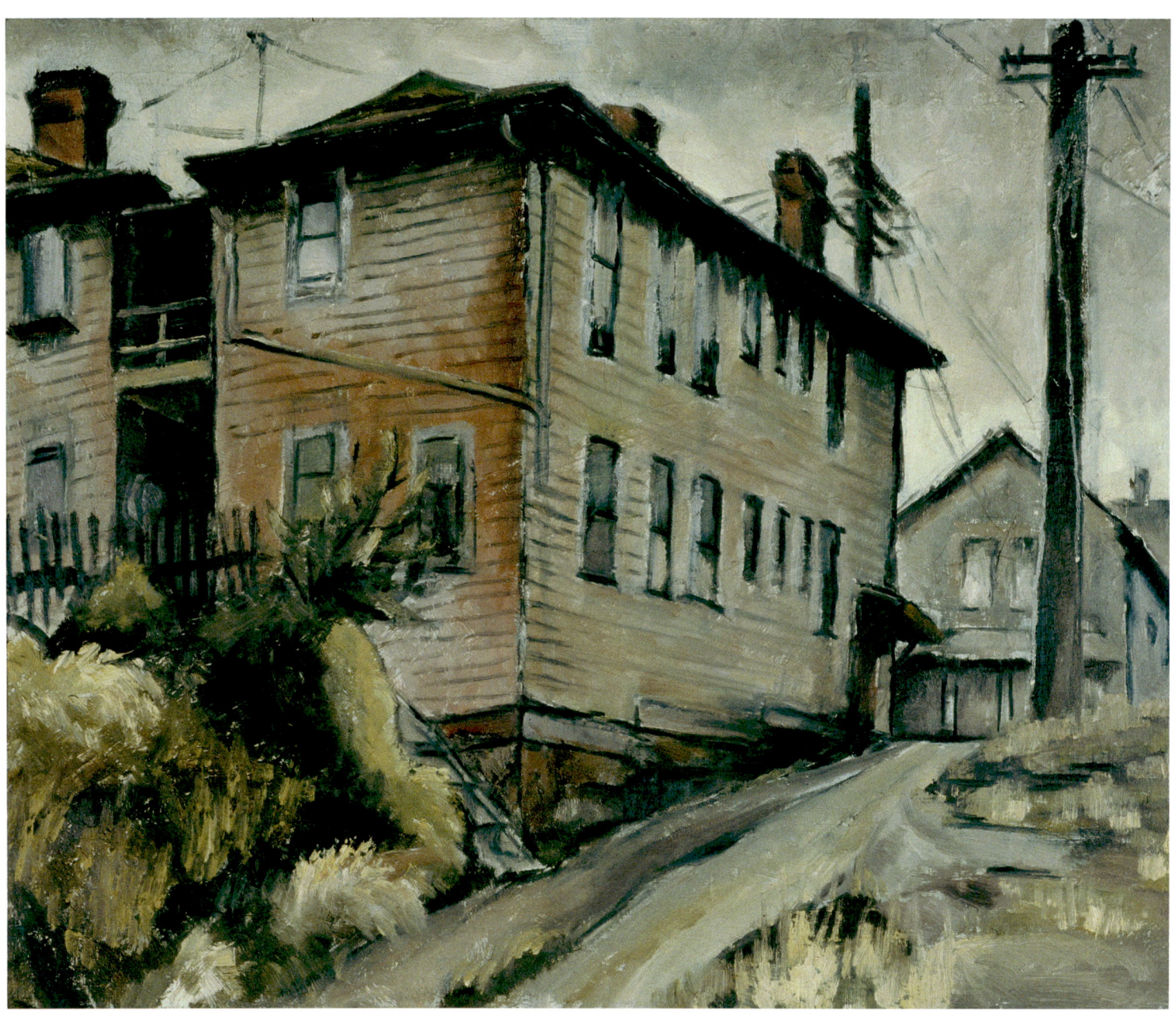

38 Kamekichi Tokita, *House*, ca. 1930, oil on canvas

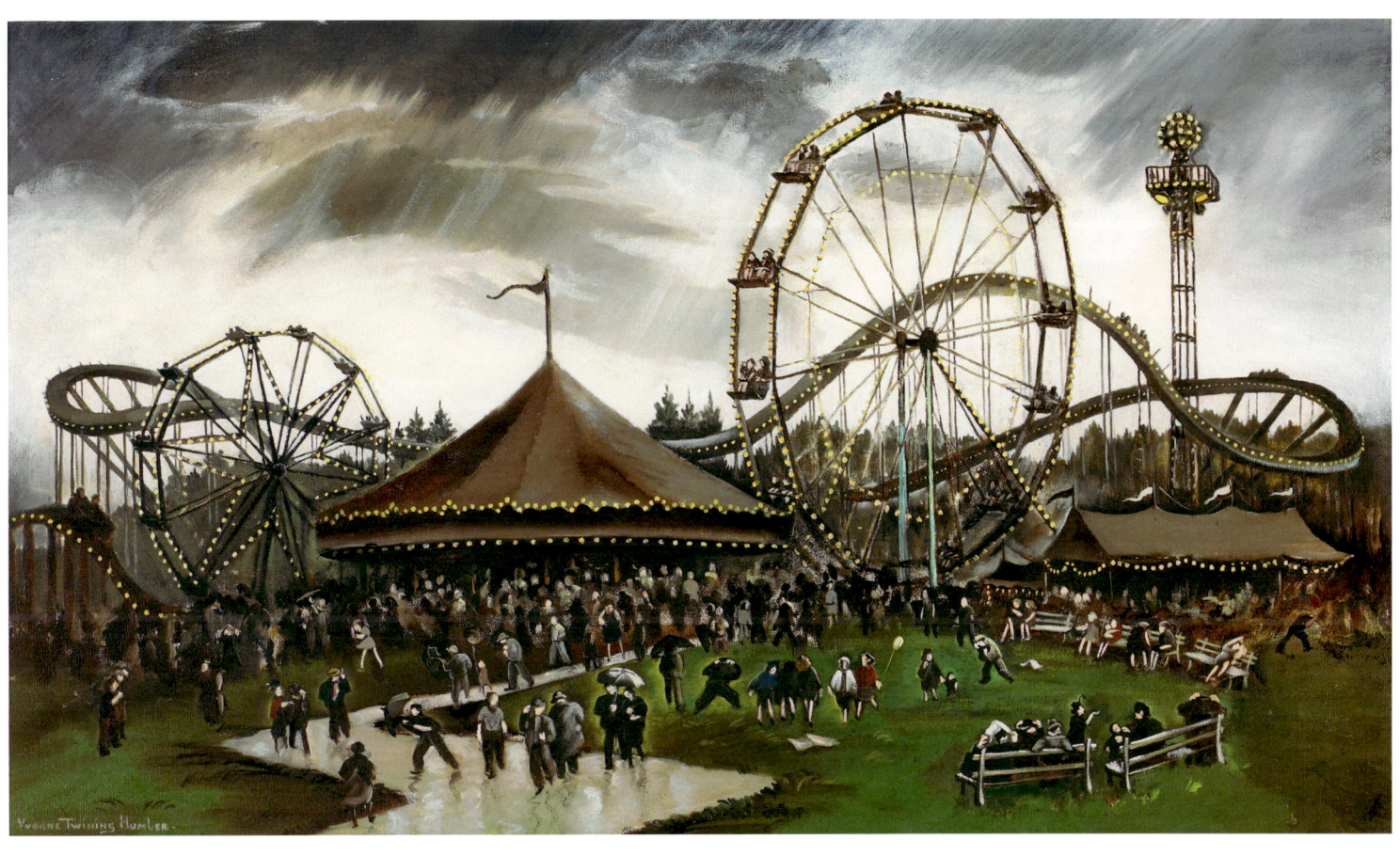

39 Yvonne Twining Humber, *Spoiled Carnival*, 1946, oil on canvas

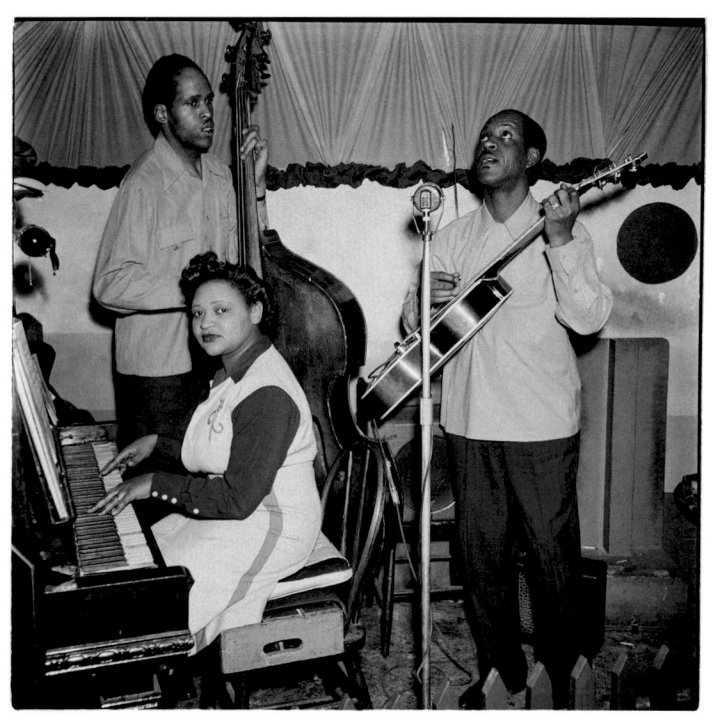

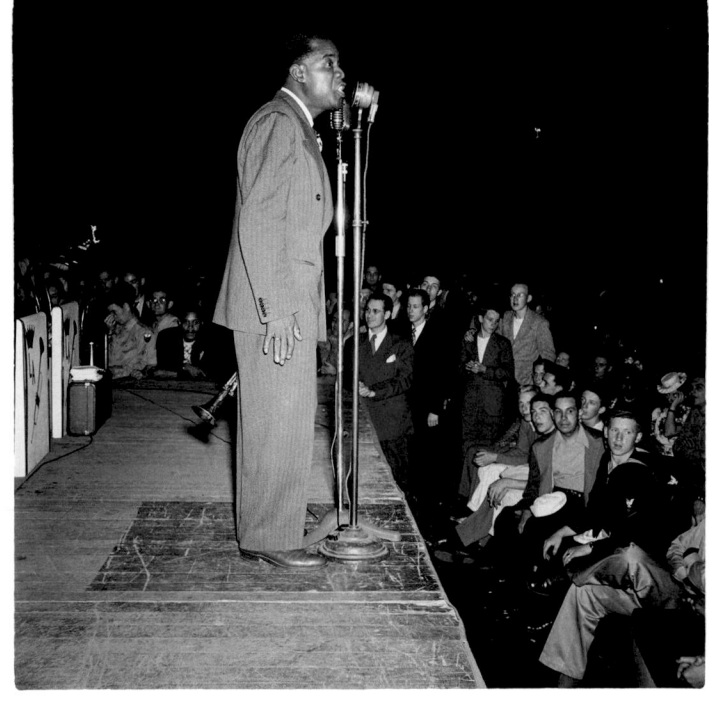

40 Albert Smith Sr., *Jazz Trio on Stage at the Basin Street Club, Seattle, March 24, 1945*, 1945, digital scan of a black-and-white acetate negative

41 Albert Smith Sr., *Louis Armstrong Onstage at the Civic Auditorium, Seattle, July 17, 1944*, 1944, digital scan of a black-and-white acetate negative

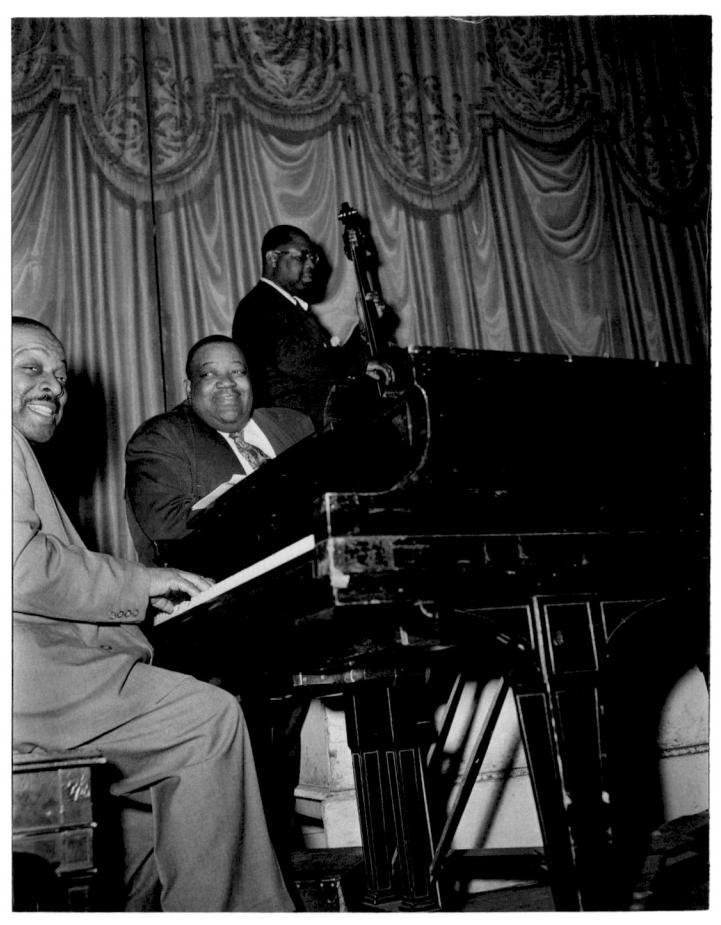

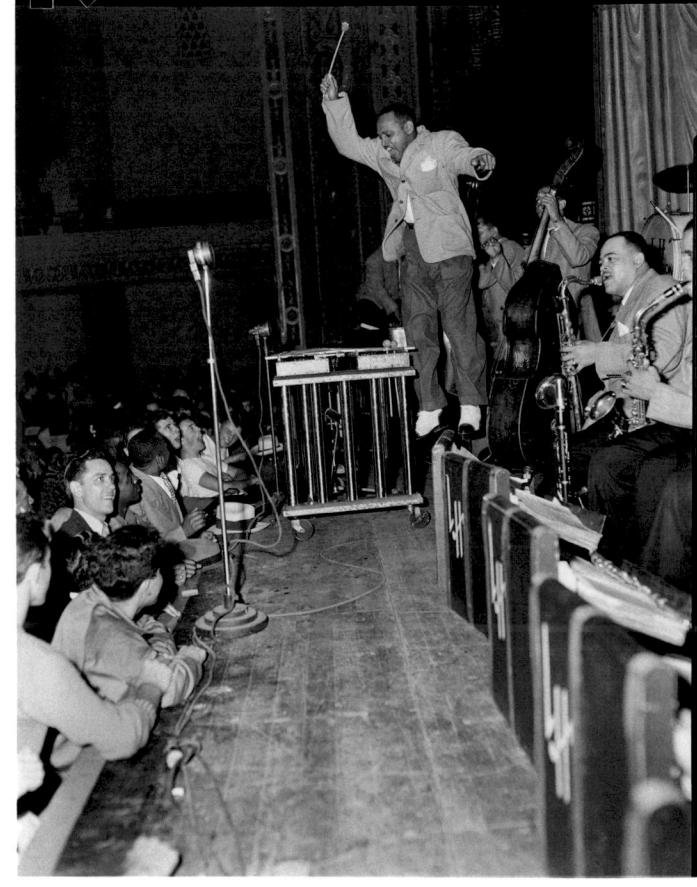

42 Albert Smith Sr., *Count Basie at the Piano, Seattle, November 27, 1946*, 1946, digital scan of a black-and-white acetate negative

43 Albert Smith Sr., *Lionel Hampton and His Orchestra Playing at Civic Auditorium, Seattle, August 7, 1946*, 1946, digital scan of a black-and-white acetate negative

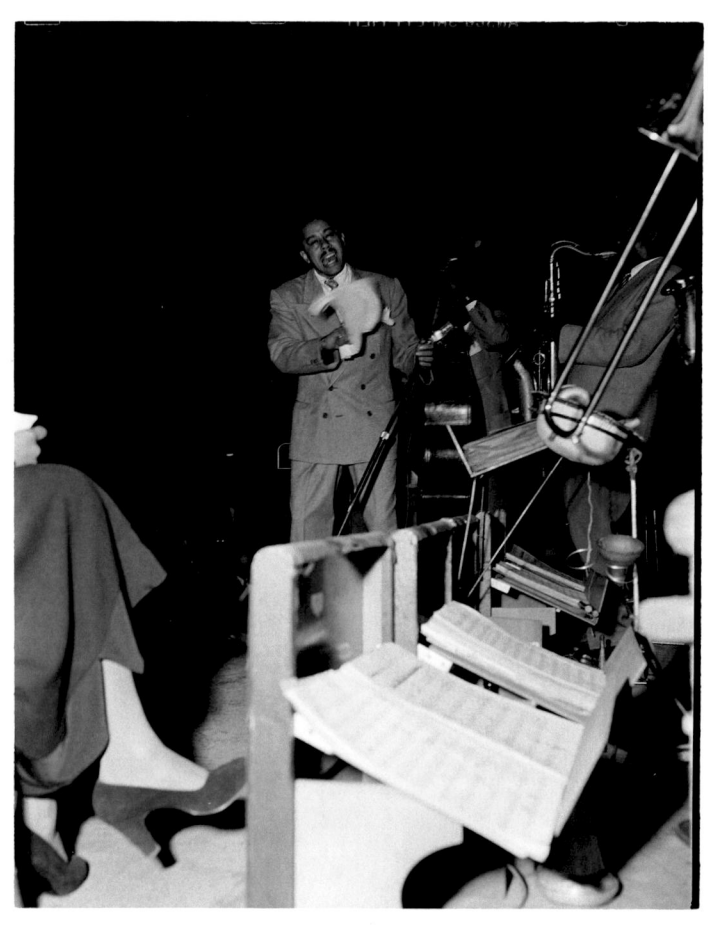

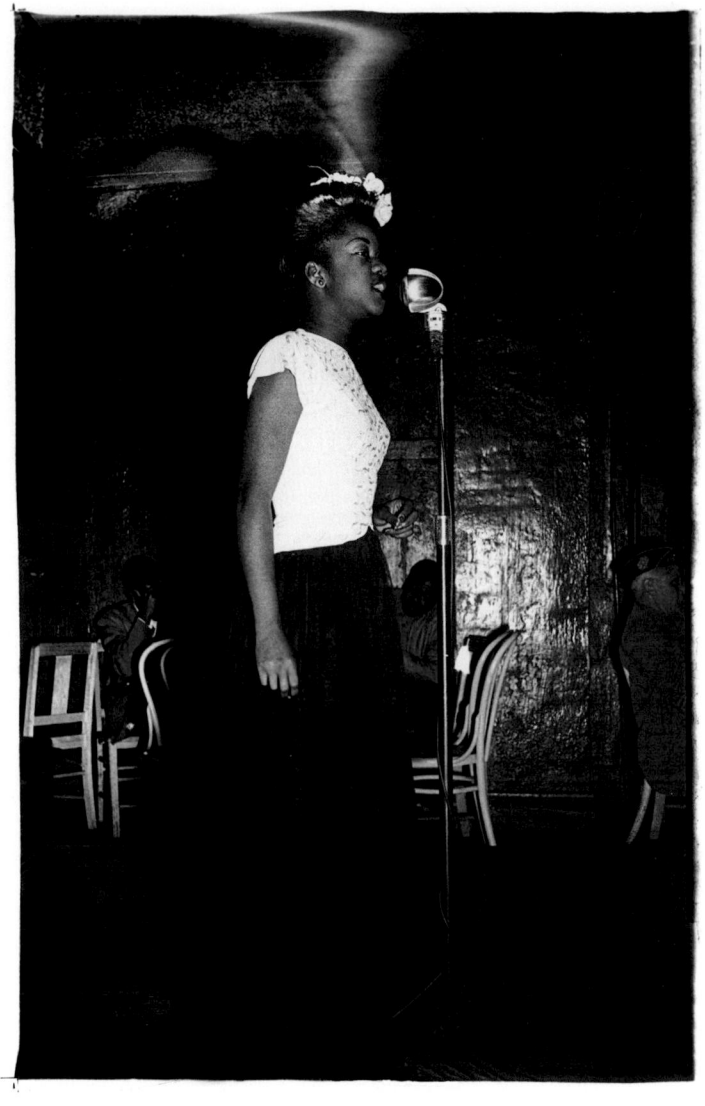

44 Albert Smith Sr., *Cab Calloway Singing on Stage at the Civic Auditorium, Seattle, circa 1947*, ca. 1947, digital scan of a black-and-white acetate negative

45 Albert Smith Sr., *Ernestine Anderson Singing at the Black & Tan, Seattle, circa 1947*, ca. 1947, digital scan of a black-and-white acetate negative

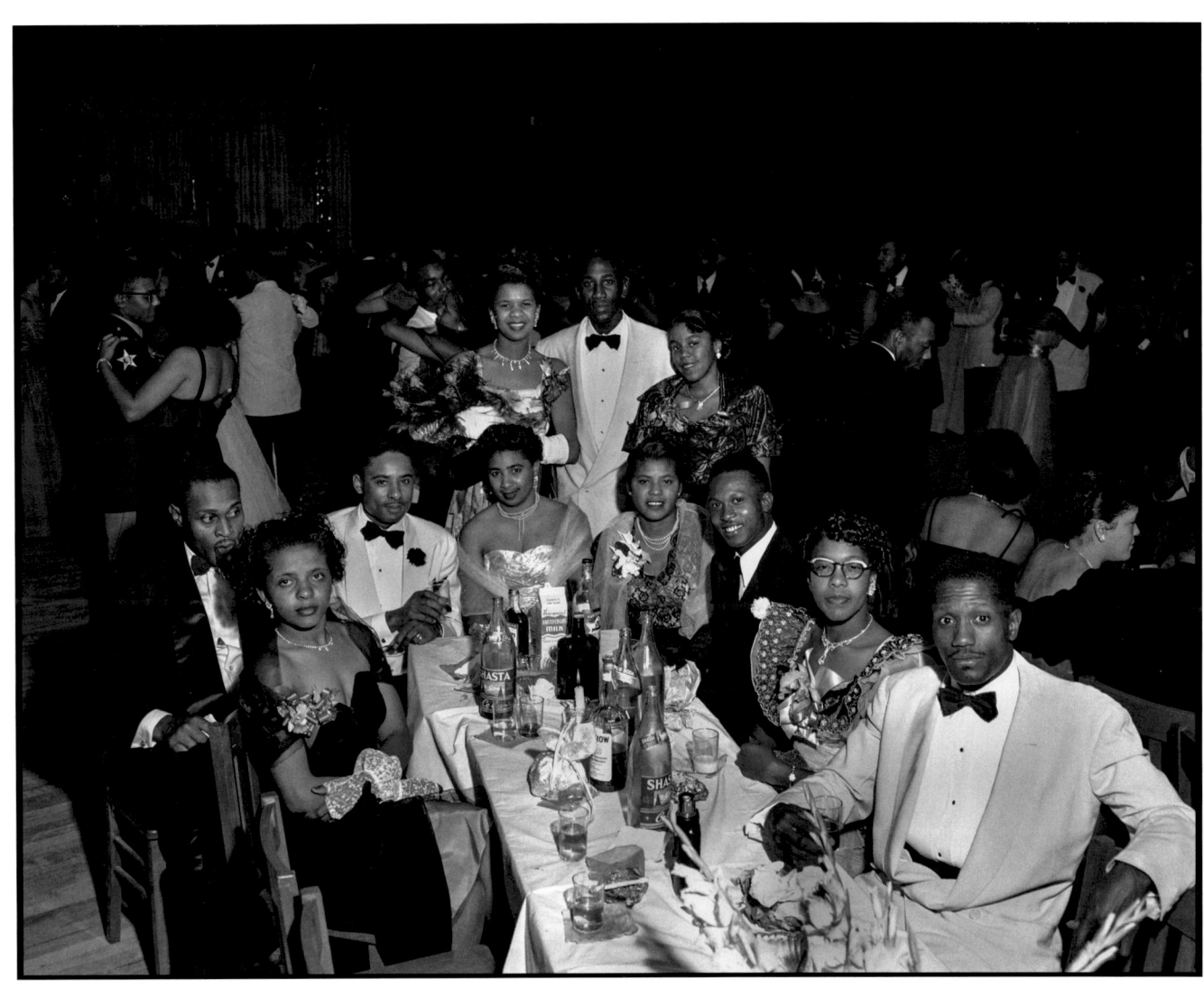

46 Albert Smith Sr., *Group Around Table at the Black & Tan, Seattle, circa 1947*, ca. 1947, digital scan of a black-and-white acetate negative

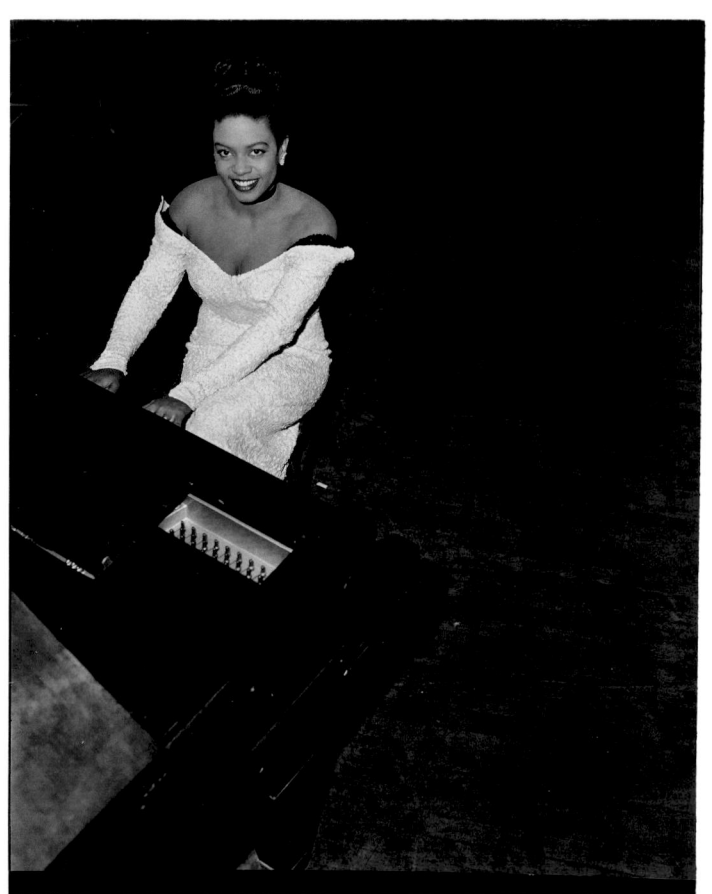

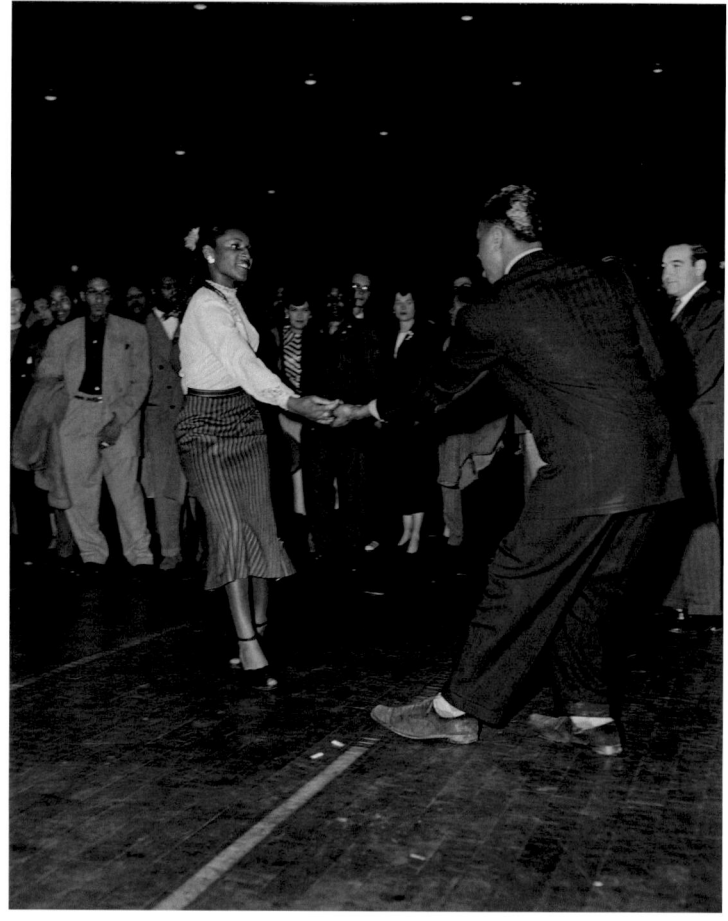

47 Albert Smith Sr., *Hazel Scott at the Piano at the Civic Auditorium, Seattle, October 11, 1947*, 1947, digital scan of a black-and-white acetate negative

48 Albert Smith Sr., *Jitterbug Dancers at Cab Calloway Performance, Seattle, circa 1947*, ca. 1947, digital scan of a black-and-white acetate negative

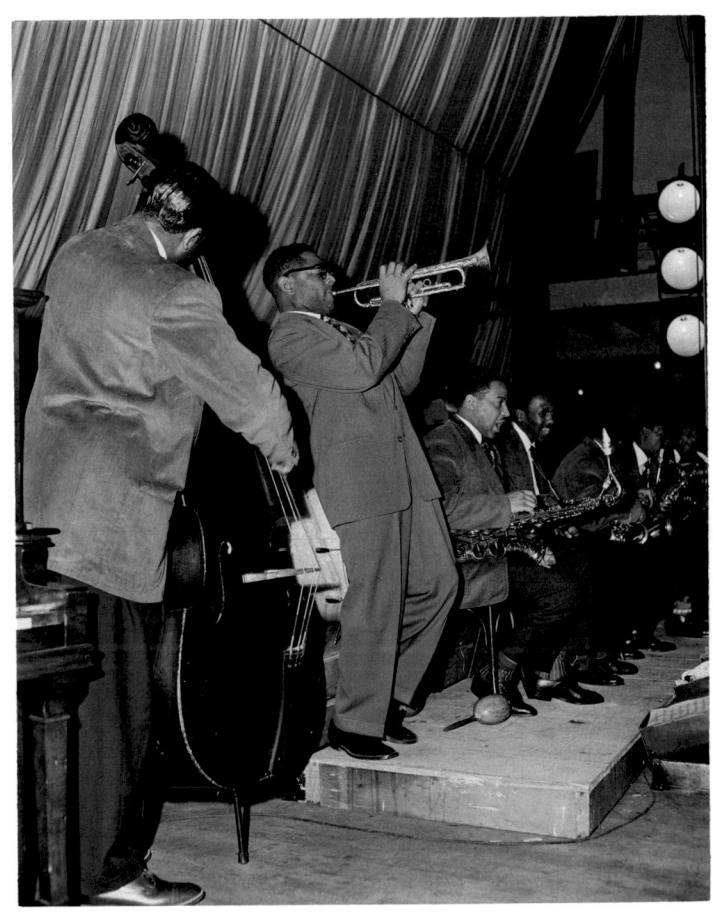

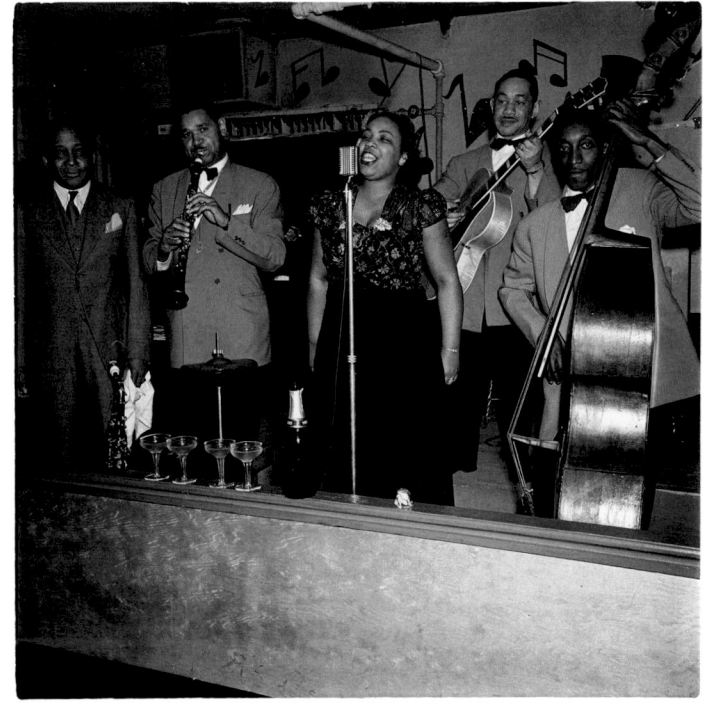

49 Albert Smith Sr., *Dizzy Gillespie and His Orchestra Performing at the Senator Ballroom, Seattle, February 19, 1949*, 1949, digital scan of a black-and-white acetate negative

50 Albert Smith Sr., *Singer and Jazz Band at the Black & Tan, Seattle, circa 1947*, ca. 1947, digital scan of a black-and-white acetate negative

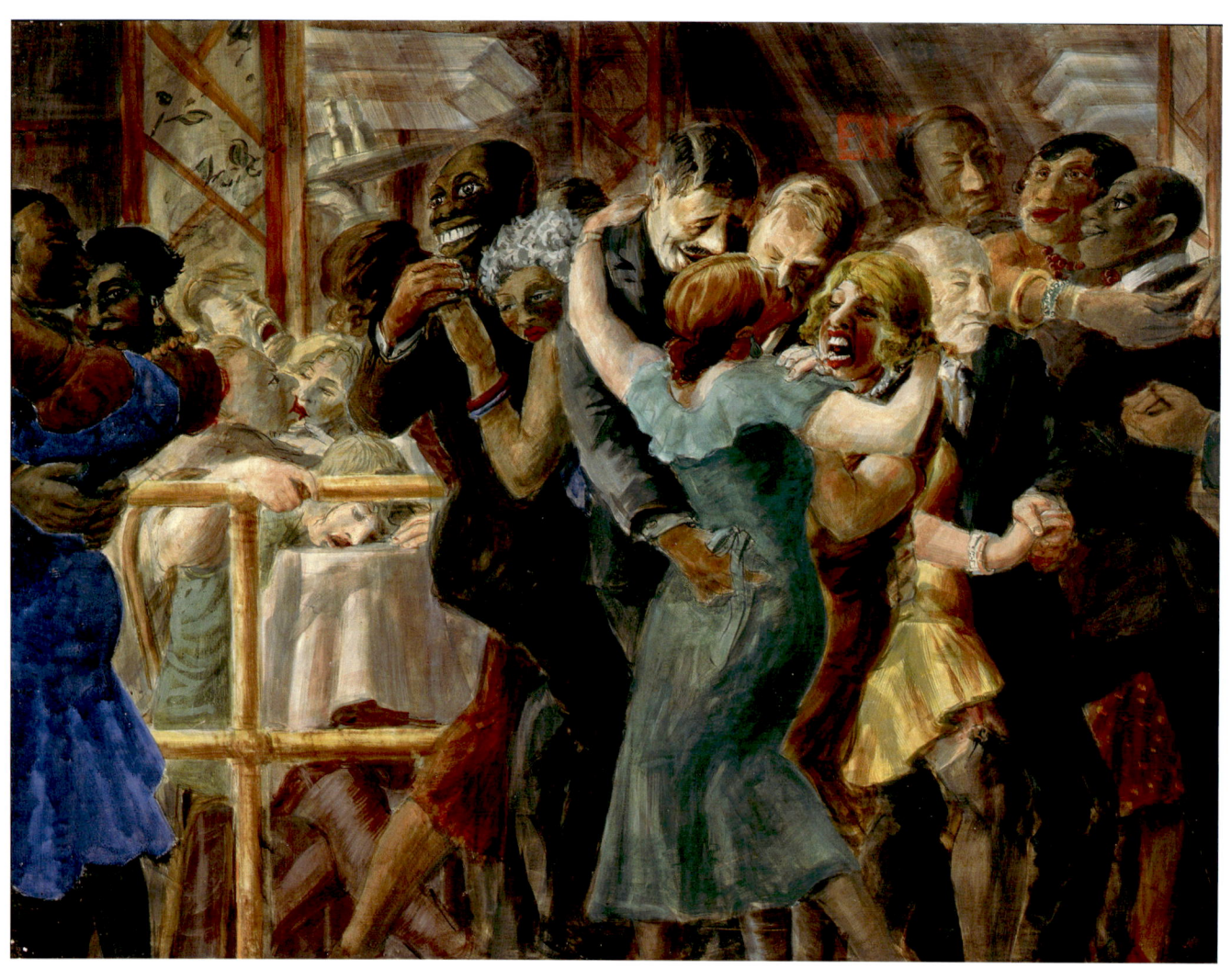

51 Reginald Marsh, *Tuesday Night at the Savoy Ballroom*, 1930, tempera on composition board

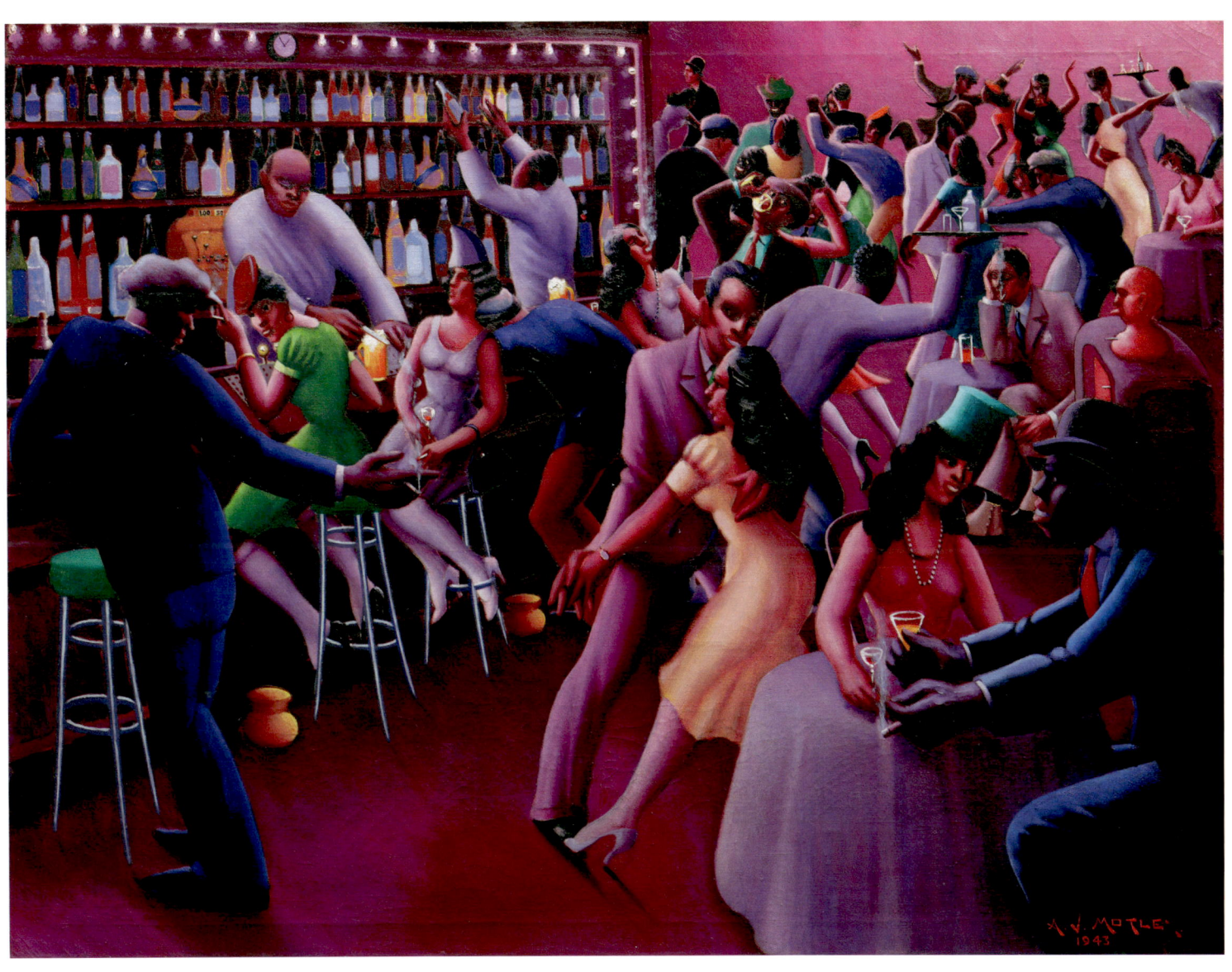

52 Archibald John Motley Jr., *Nightlife*, 1943, oil on canvas

53-64 Mark Tobey, *12 Market Scenes, Being Sketches of Seattle Public Market Between 1939 and 1941*, 1939–41, ink and watercolor on paper

62

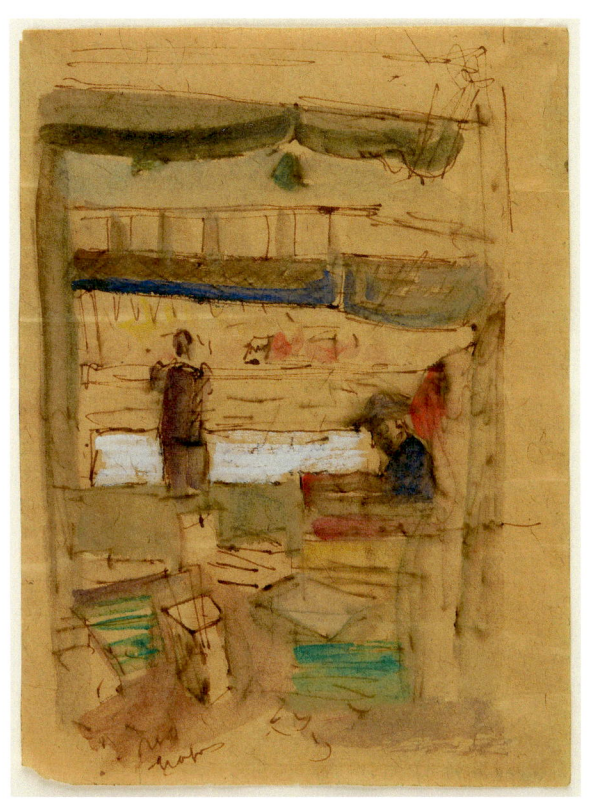
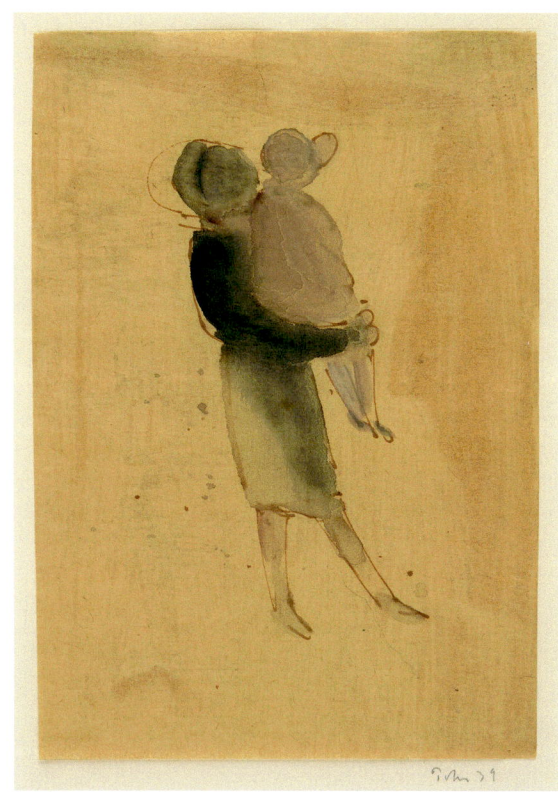
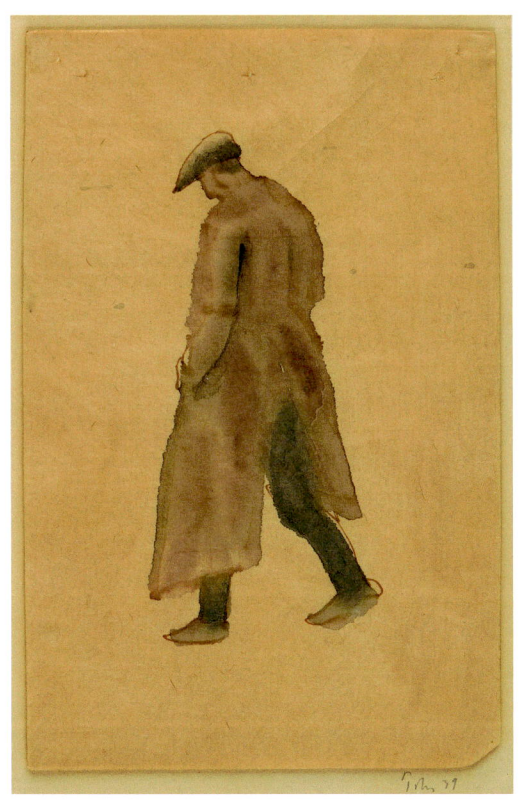
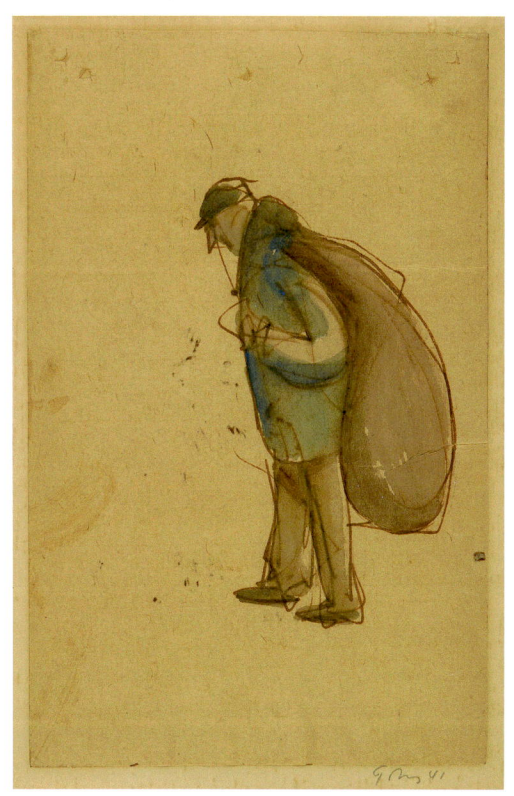

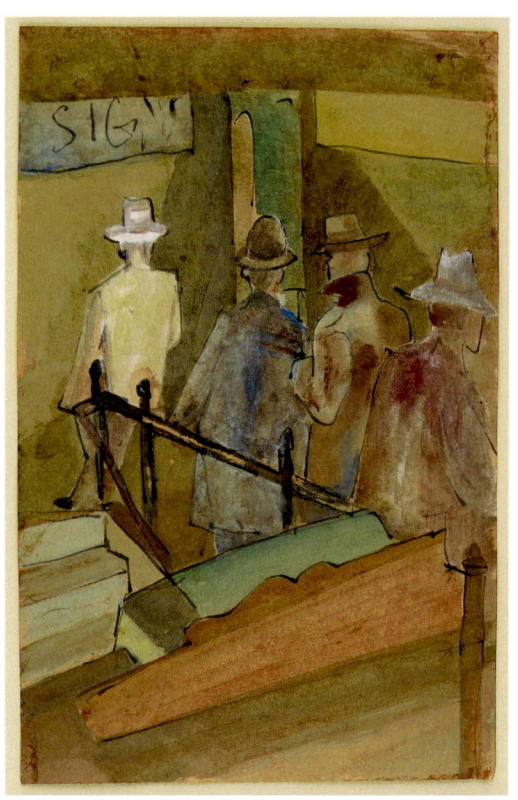
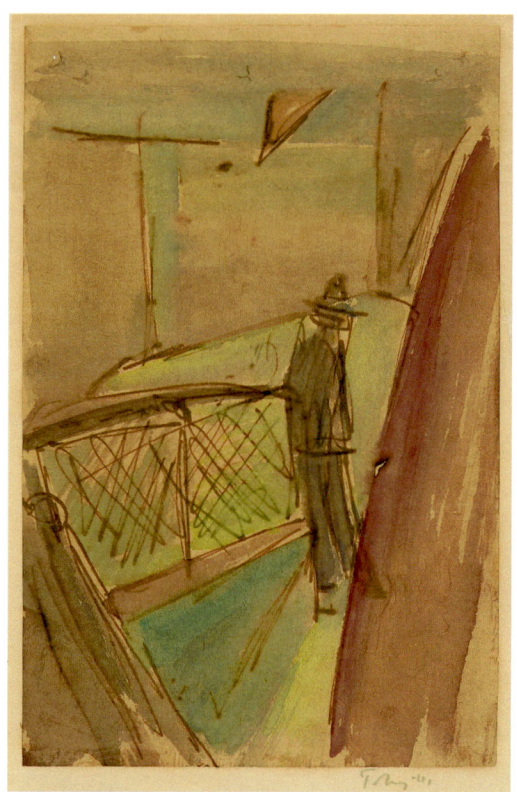
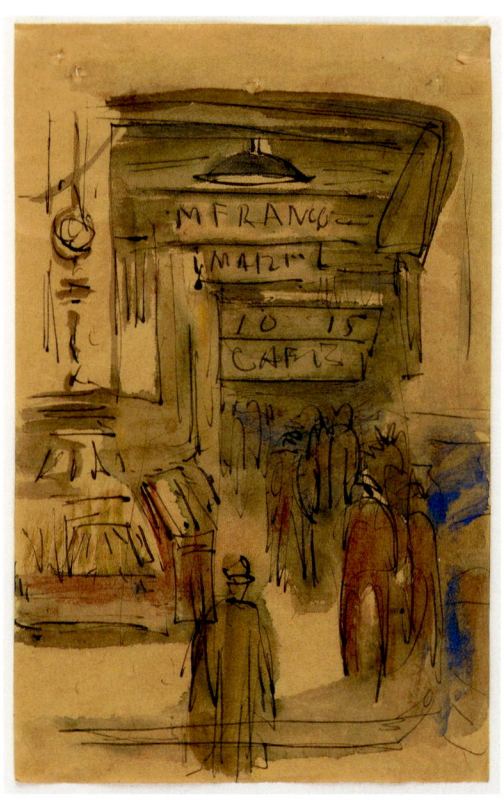
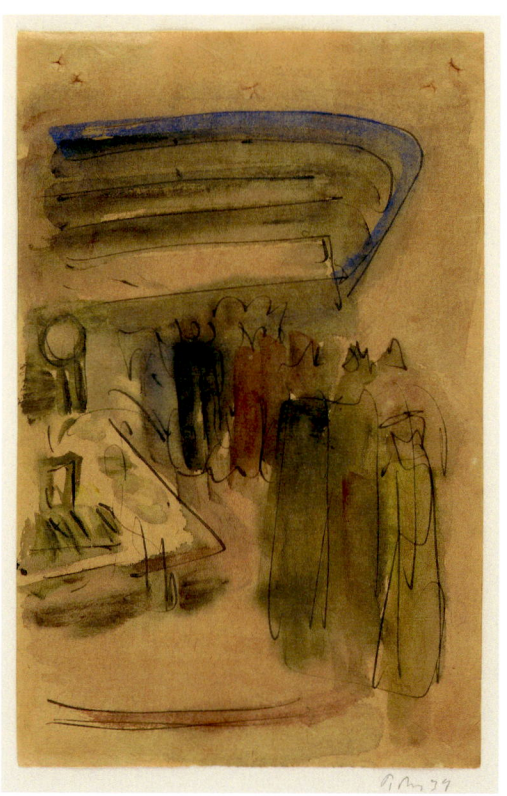

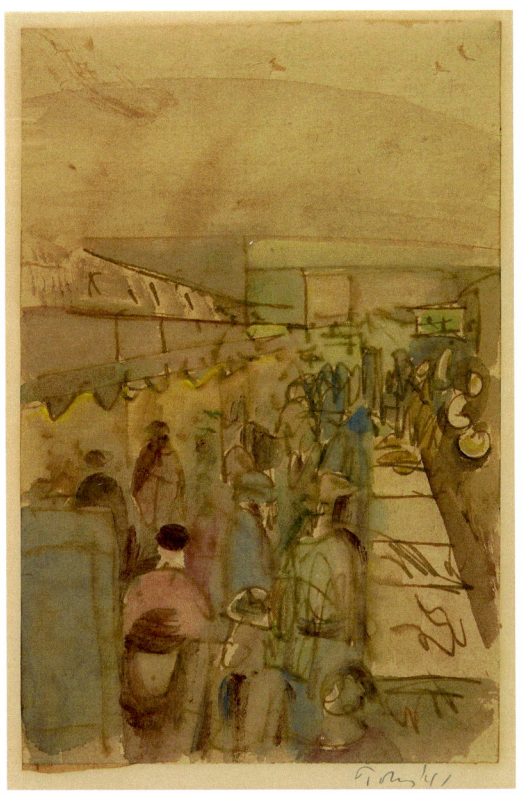

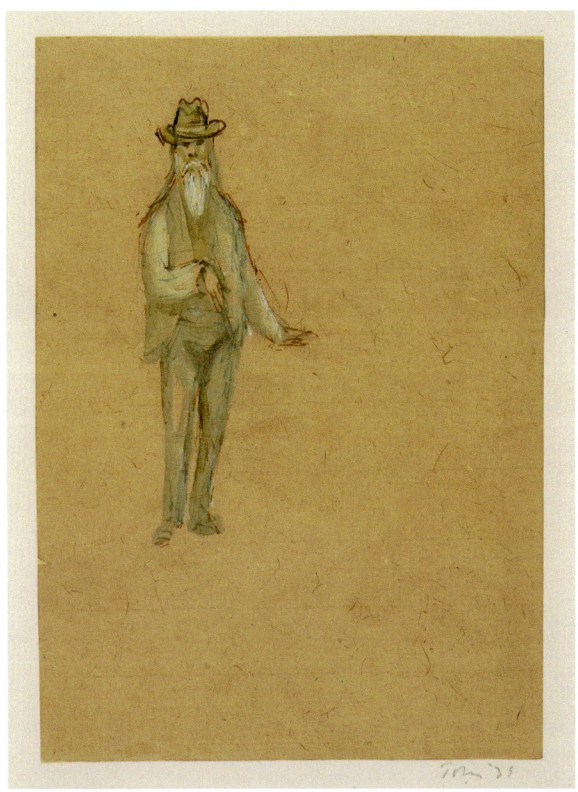

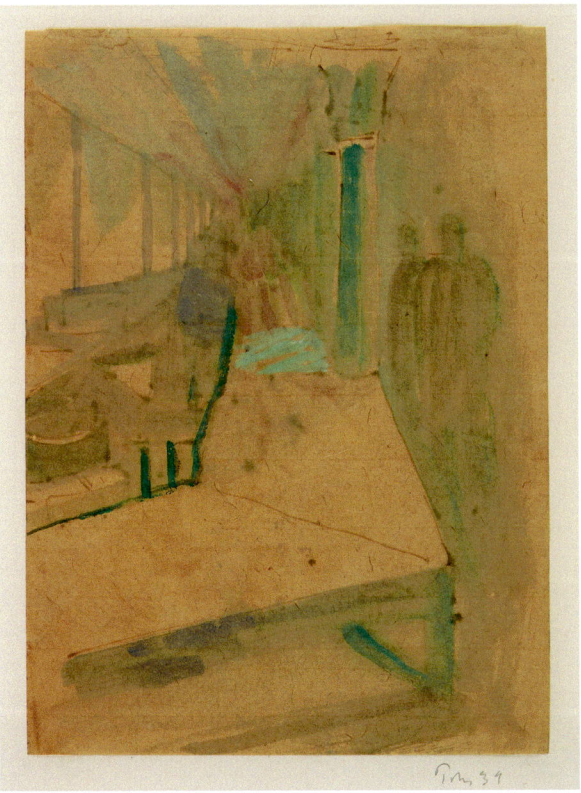

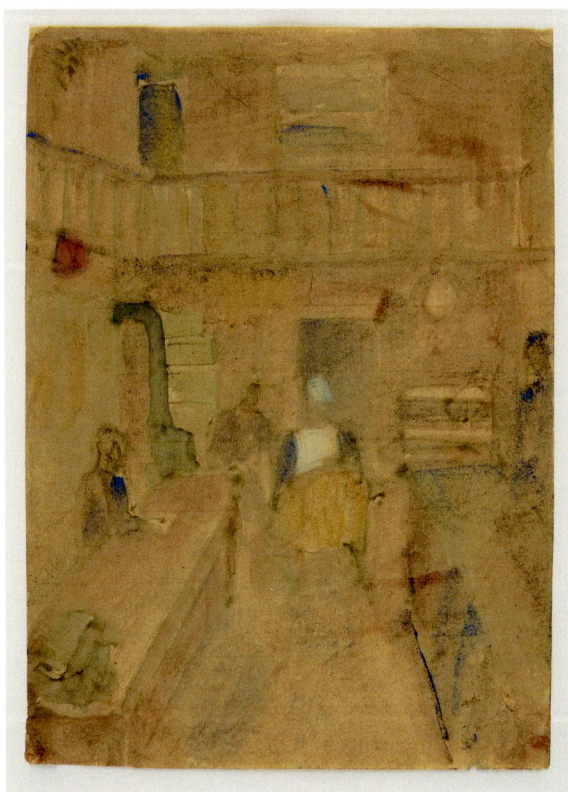

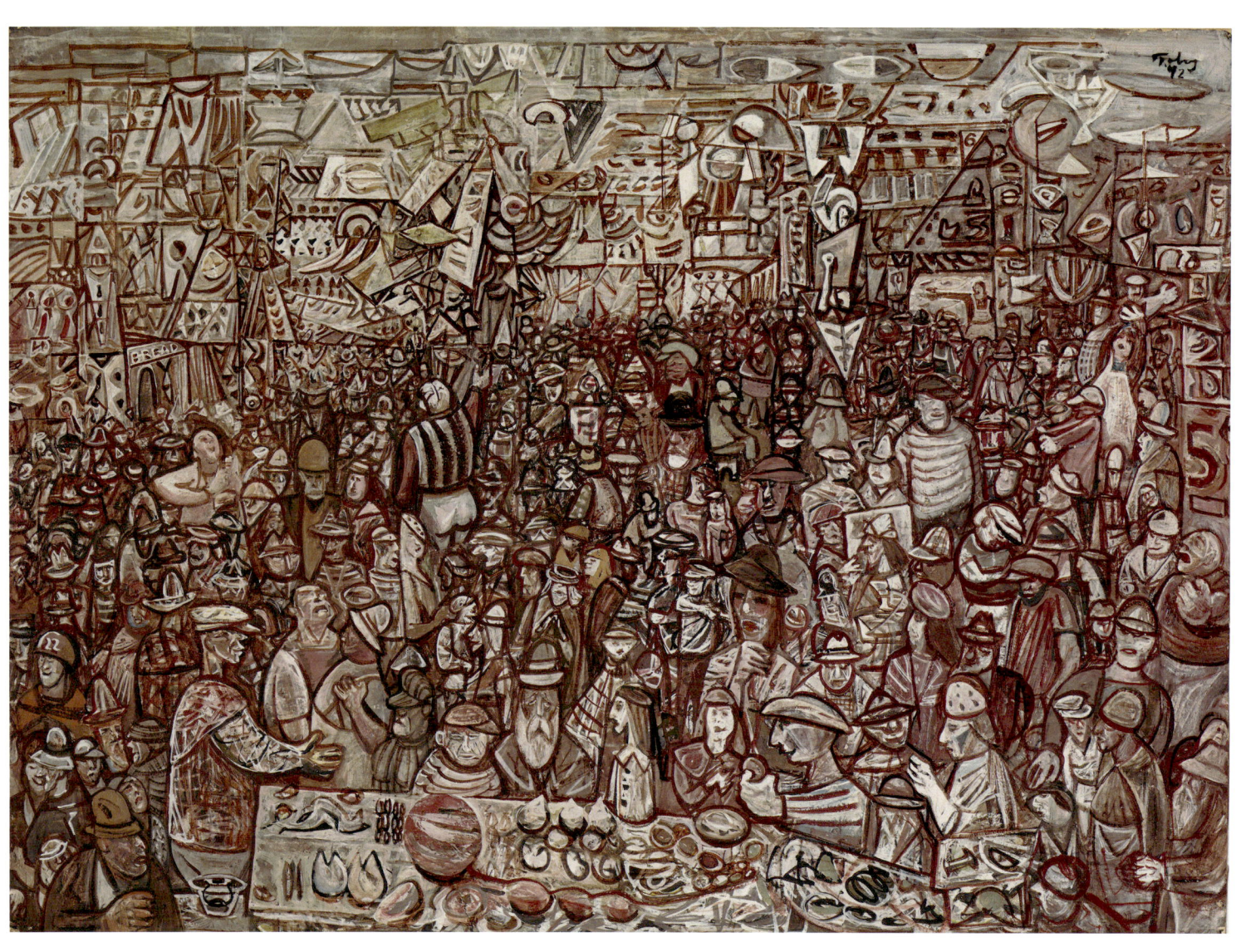

65 Mark Tobey, *E Pluribus Unum*, 1942, watercolor on paper mounted on paperboard

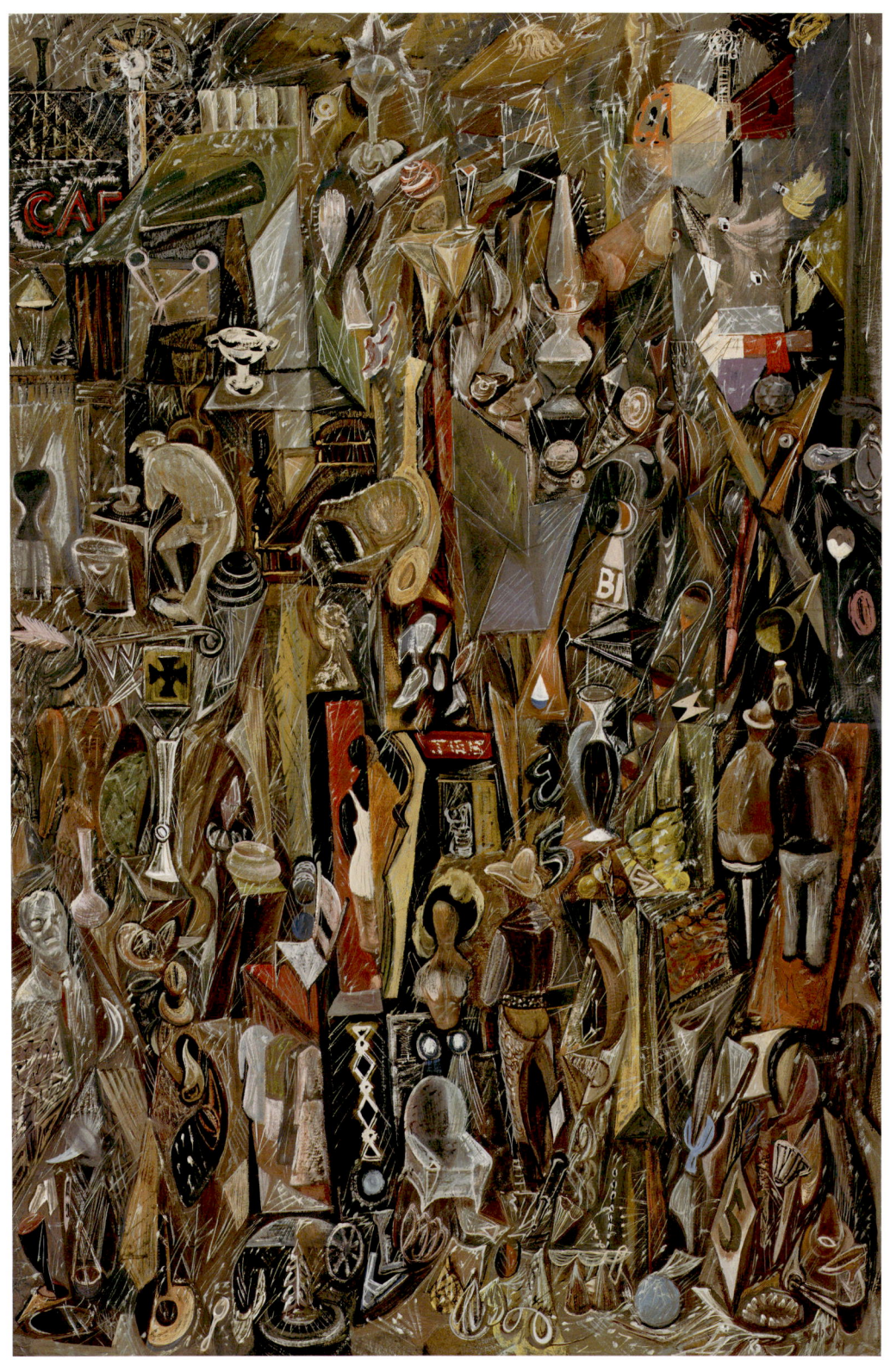

66 Mark Tobey, *Rummage*, 1941, watercolor on paperboard

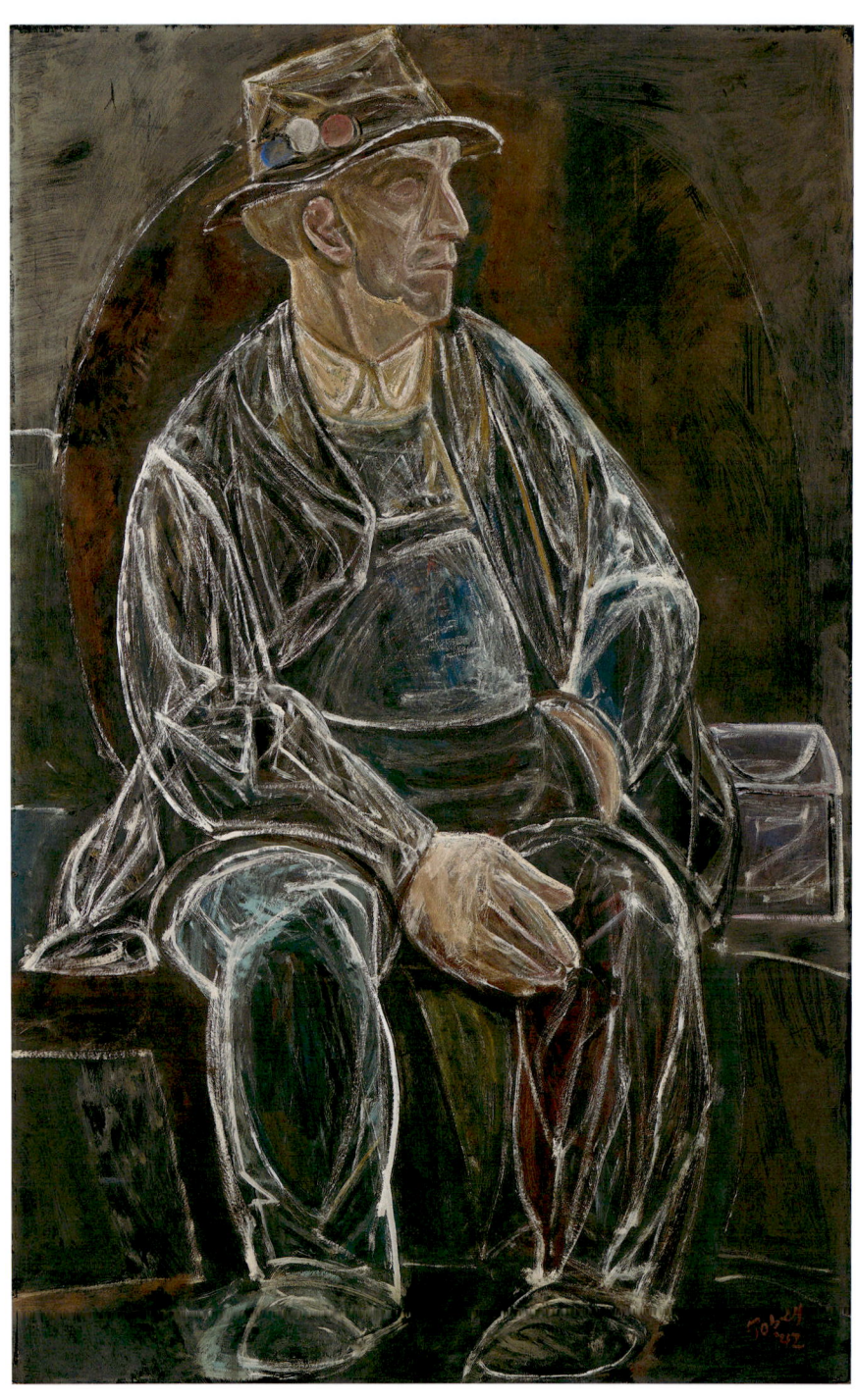

67 Mark Tobey, *Working Man*, 1942, gouache on board

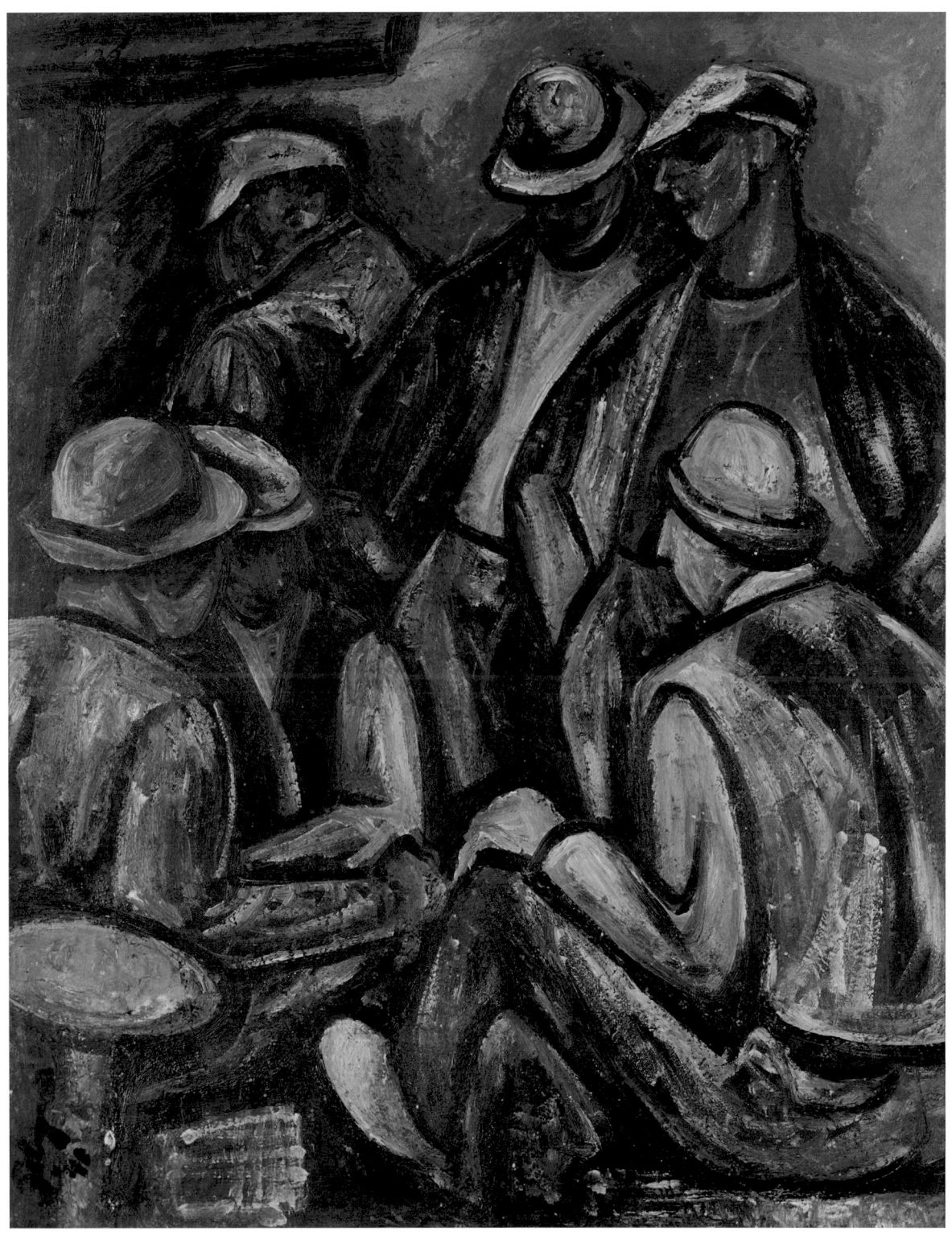

68 Mark Tobey, *Time Off*, 1941, oil on board

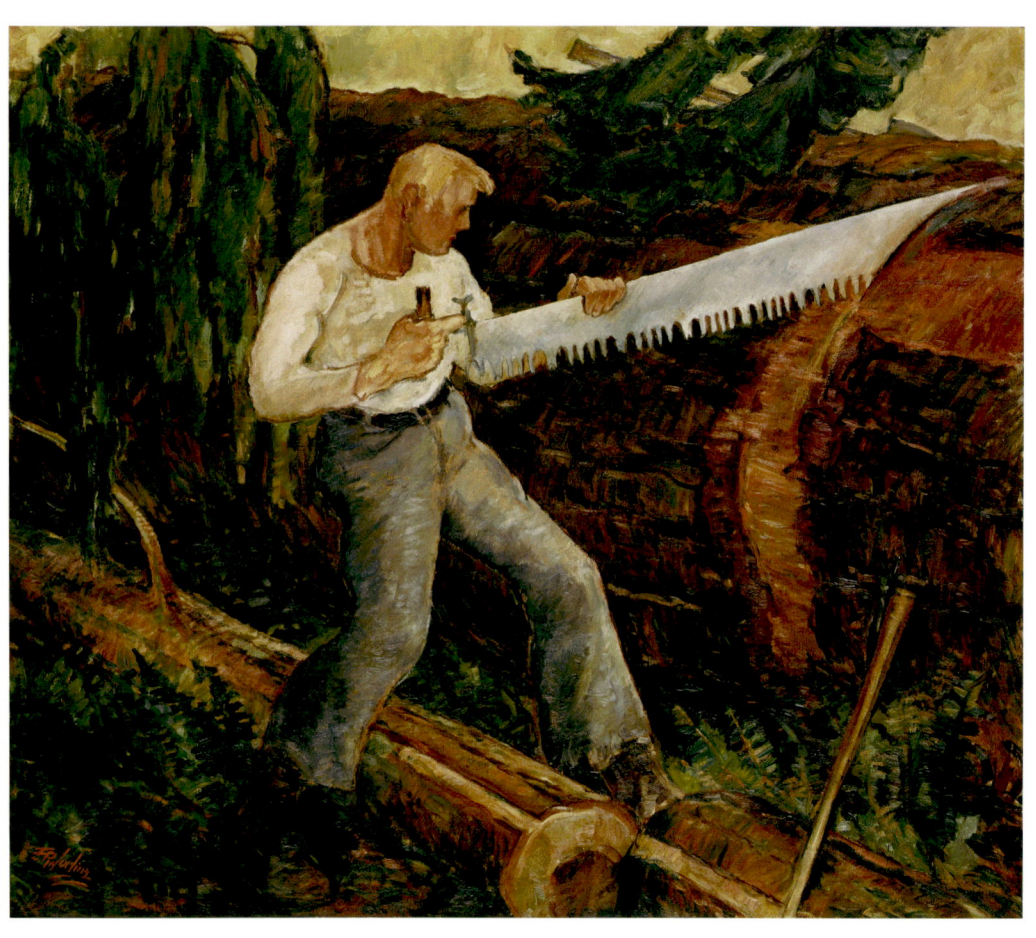

69 Ernest Ralph Norling, *The Timber Bucker*, ca. 1934, oil on canvas

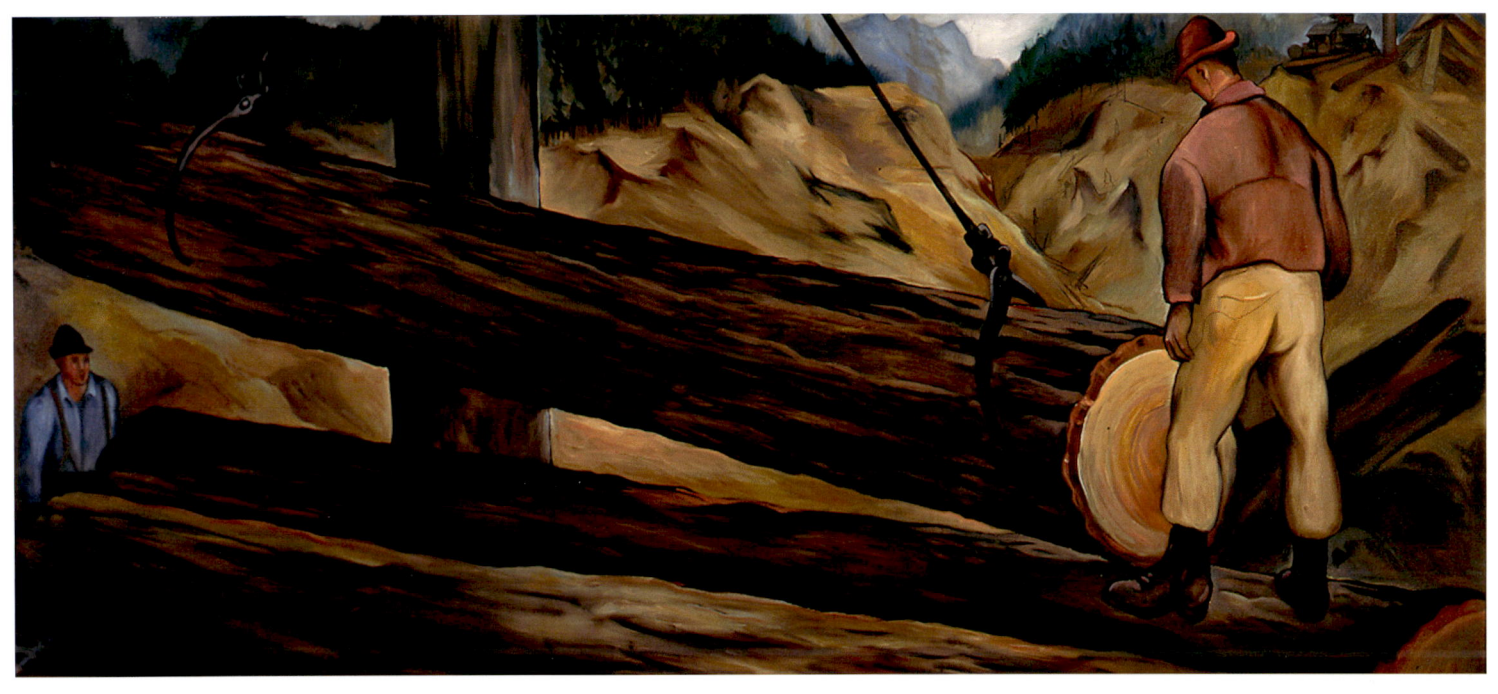

70 Kenneth Callahan, *Weyerhaeuser Company Mill B Mural Panel (Loggers with Chokers)*, 1944, oil on canvas

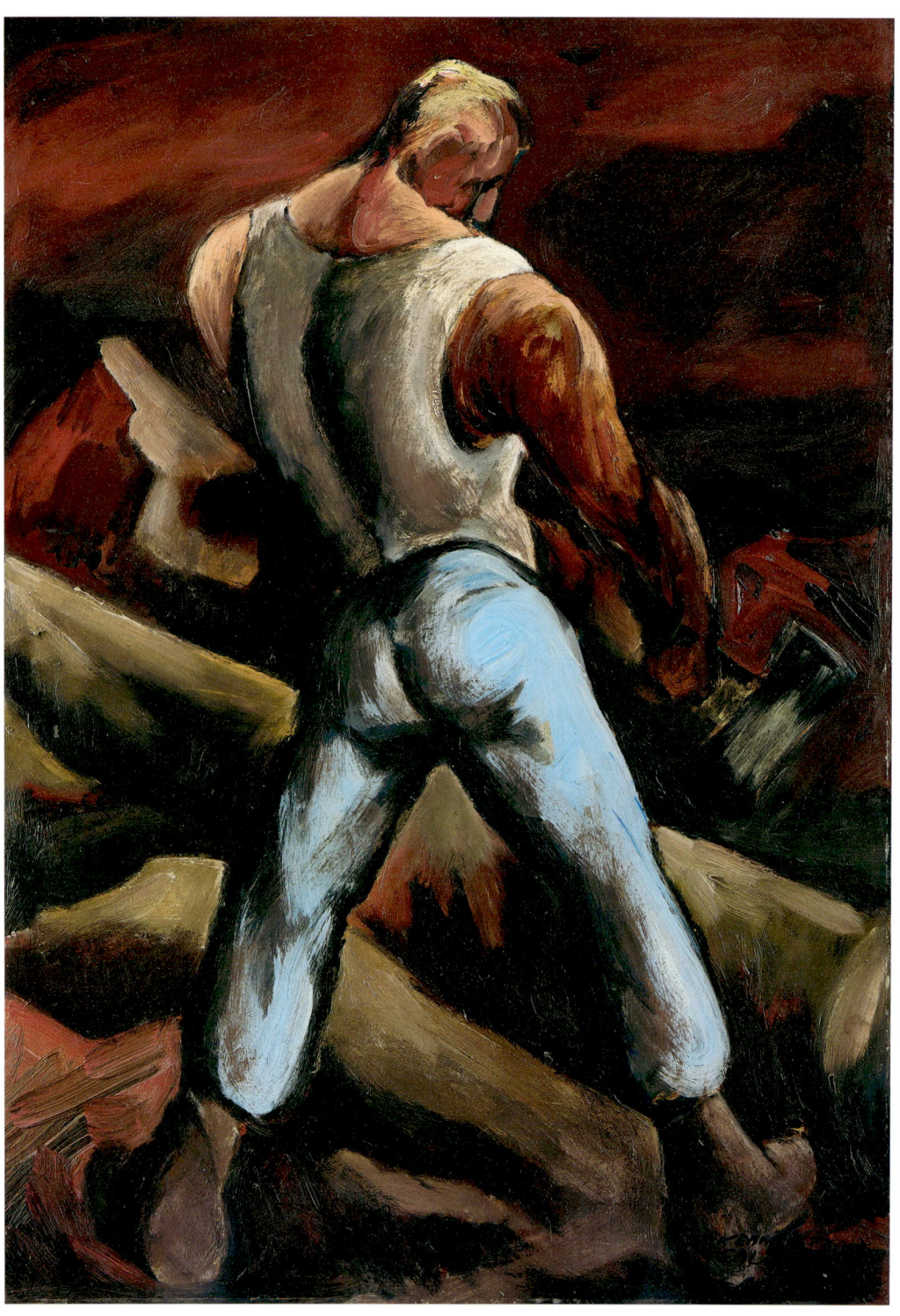

71 Kenneth Callahan, *Feller*, 1934, oil on board

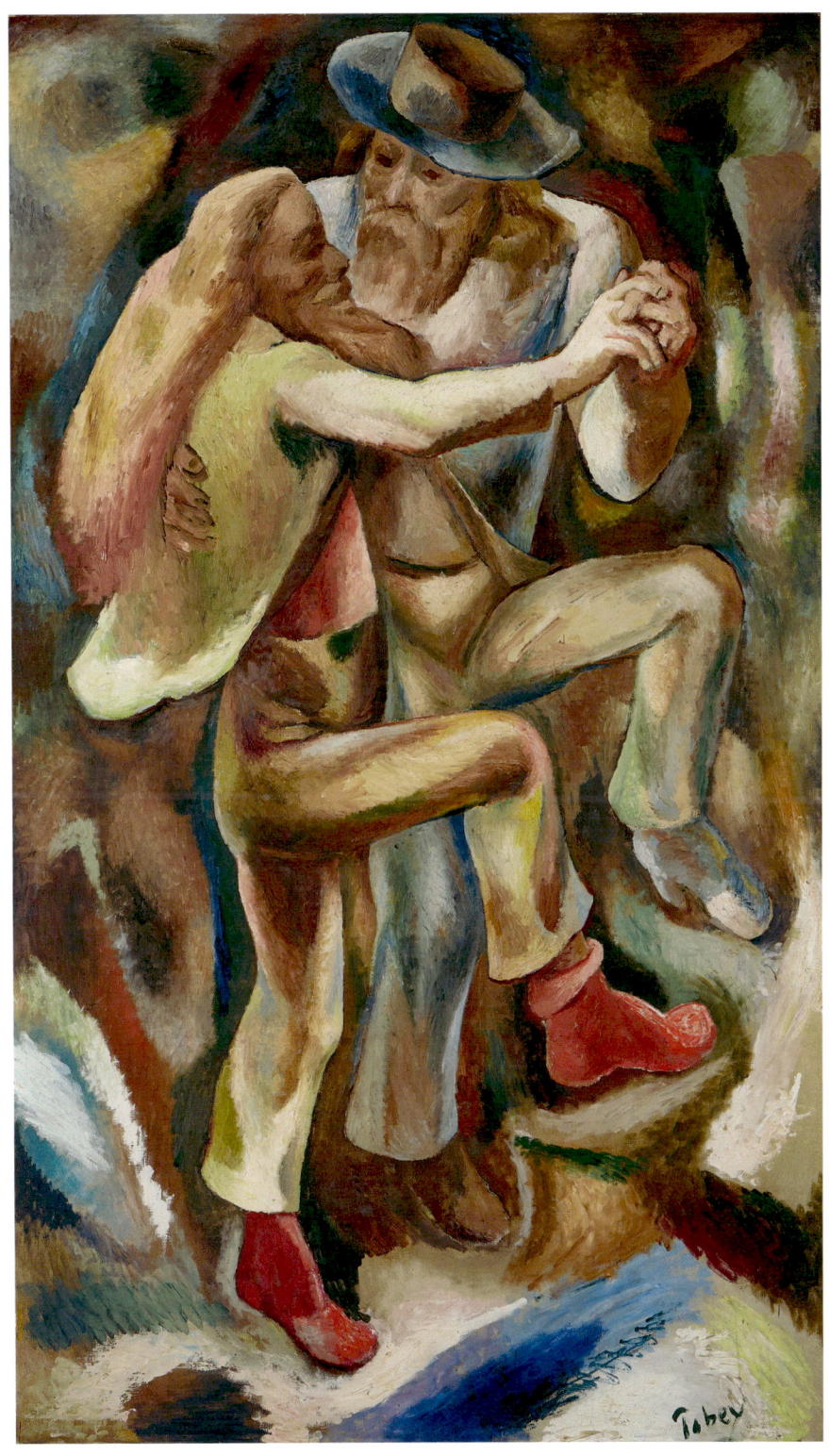

Mark Tobey, *Dancing Miners*, ca. 1922–27, oil on canvas

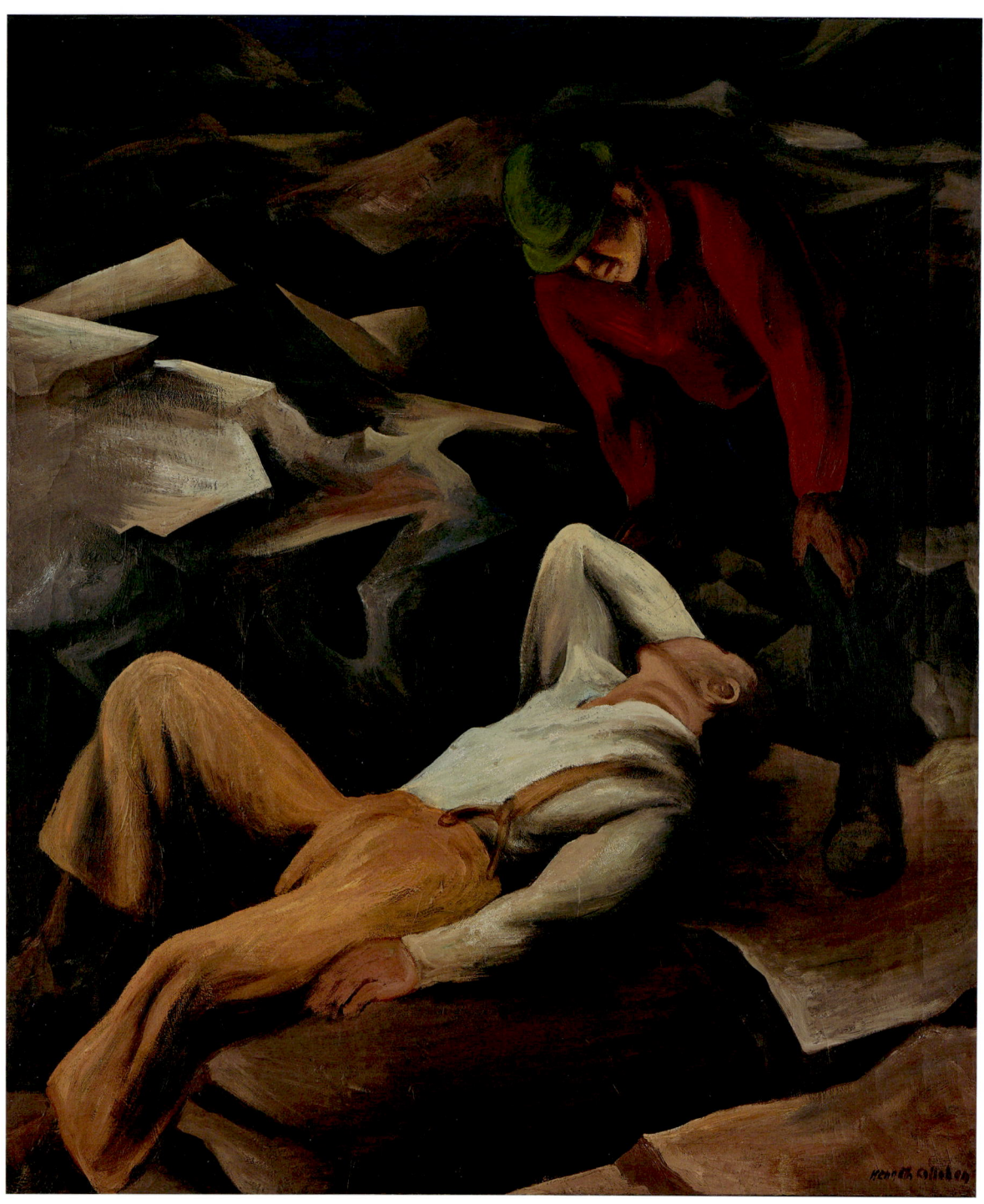

73 Kenneth Callahan, *The Accident*, 1939, tempera on canvas

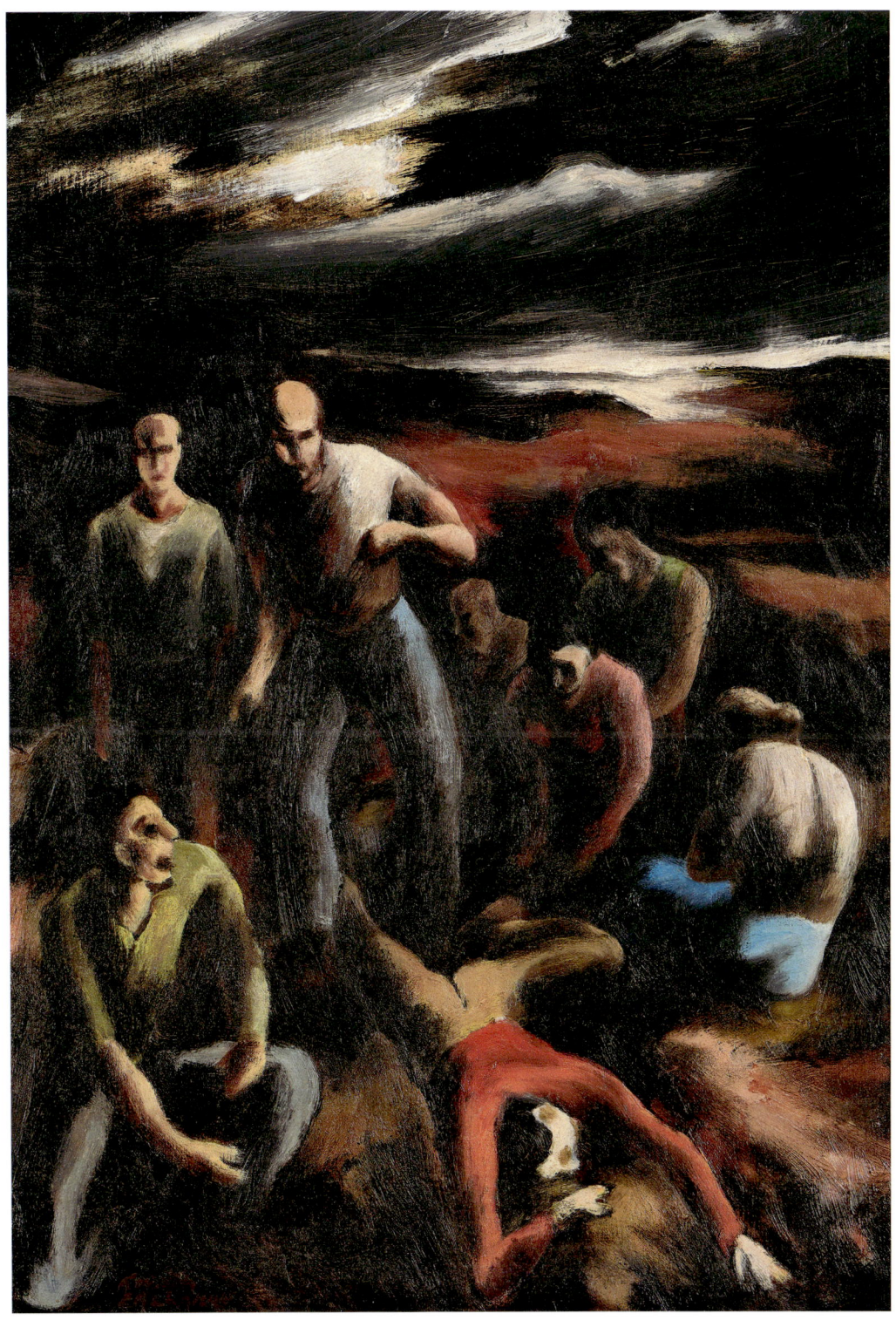

Kenneth Callahan, *The Storm*, 1938, oil on wood

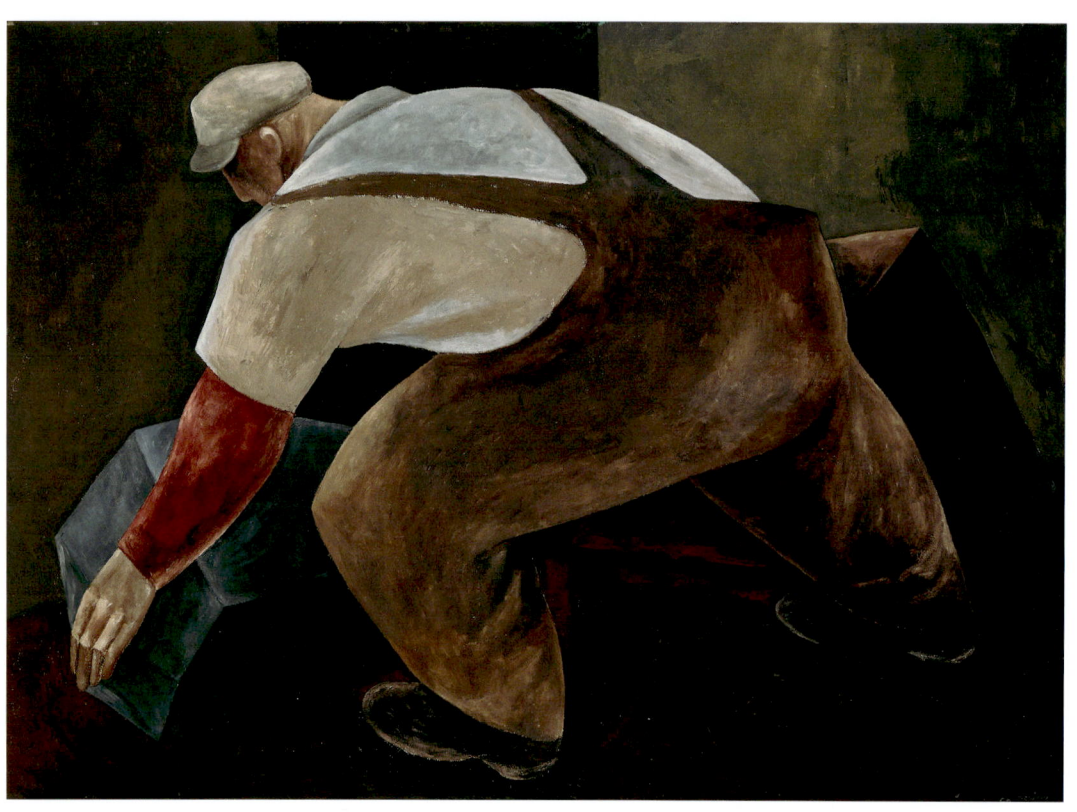

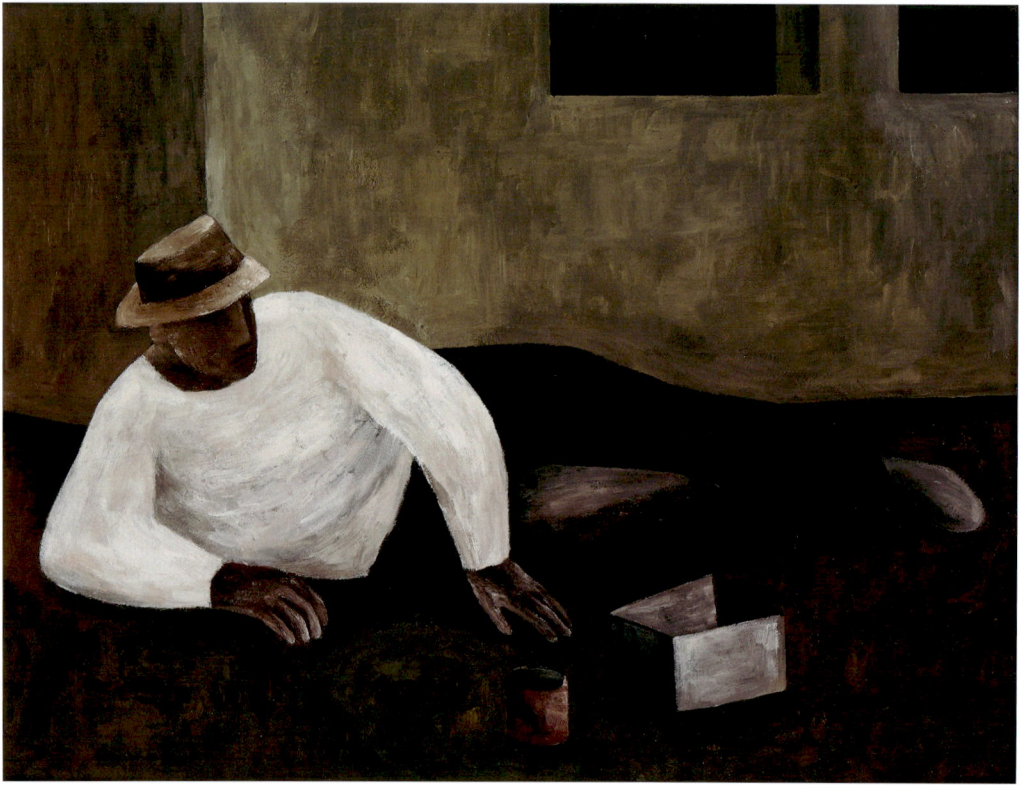

75 William Cumming, *Worker Lifting a Rock*, 1940, tempera on board

76 William Cumming, *Worker Resting*, 1941, tempera on board

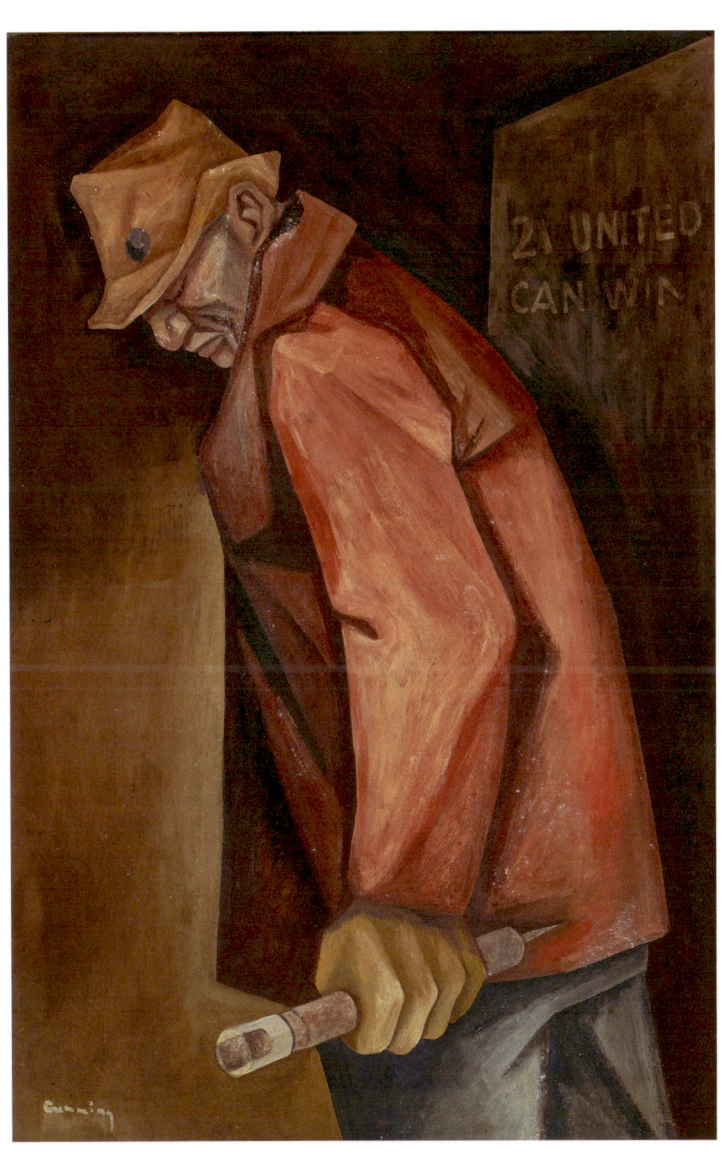

77 William Cumming, *Planting the Flare*, ca. 1945, gouache on board

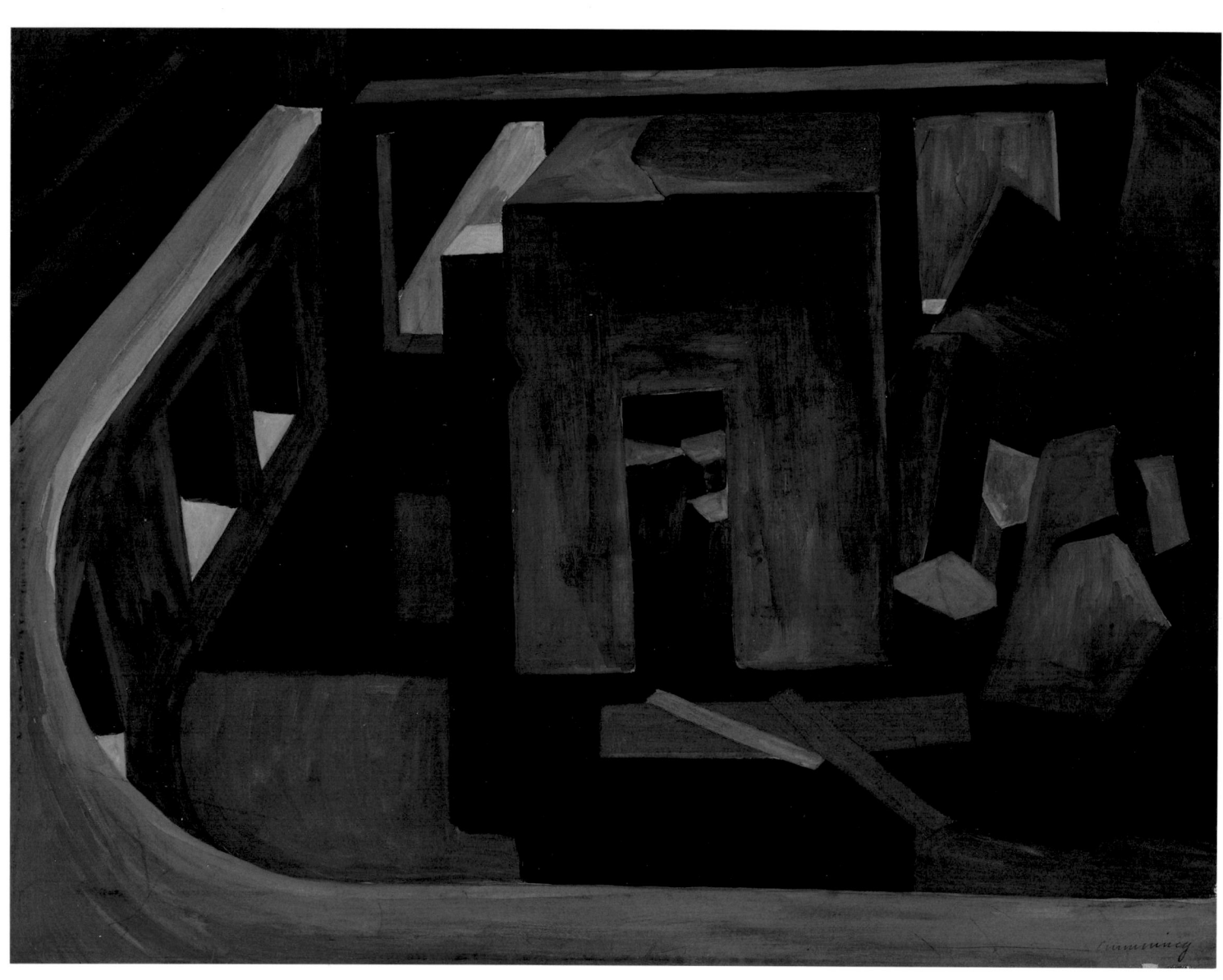

78 William Cumming, *Abandoned Factory*, 1939, tempera on board

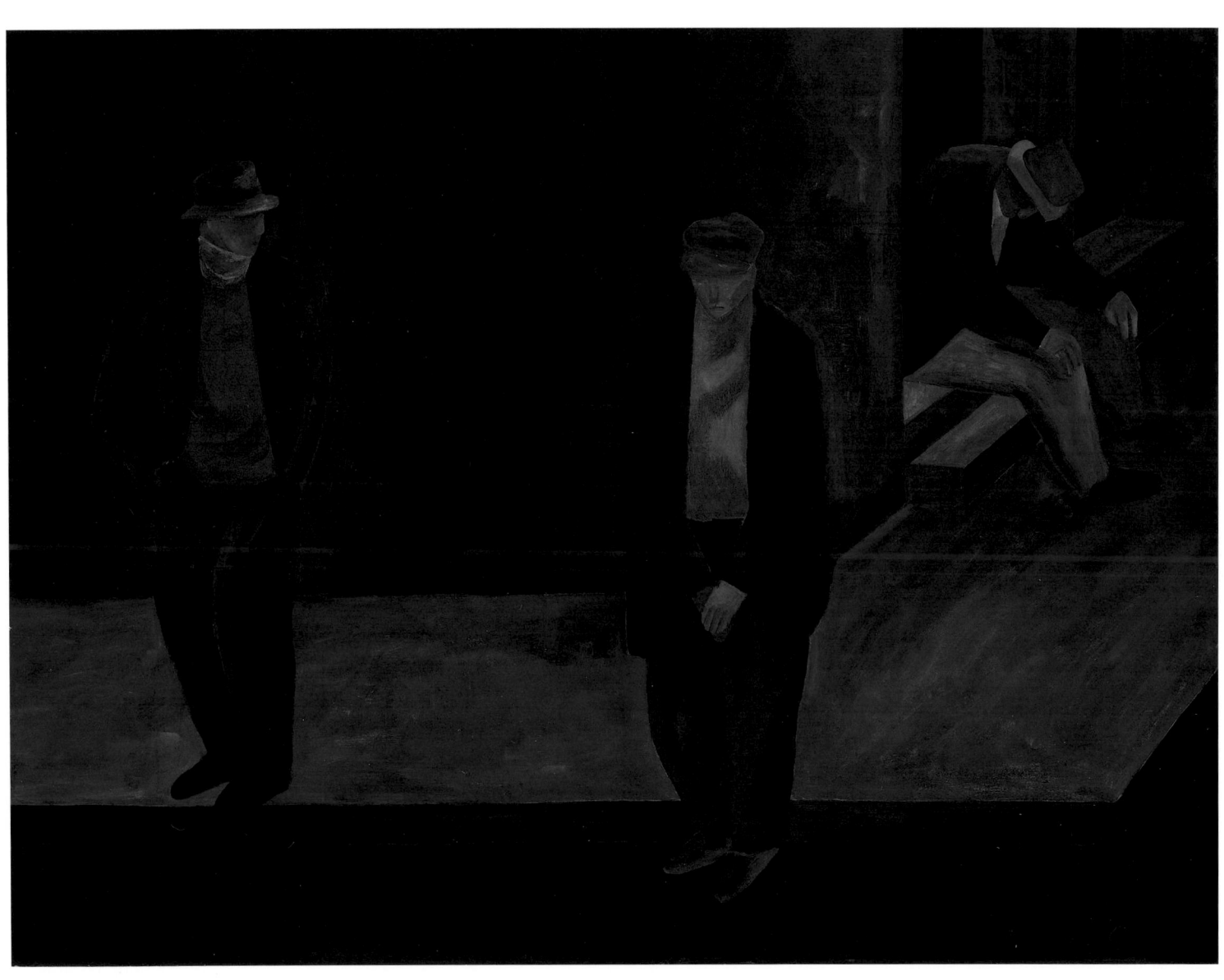

79 William Cumming, *Skidroad Group*, ca. 1940, tempera on board

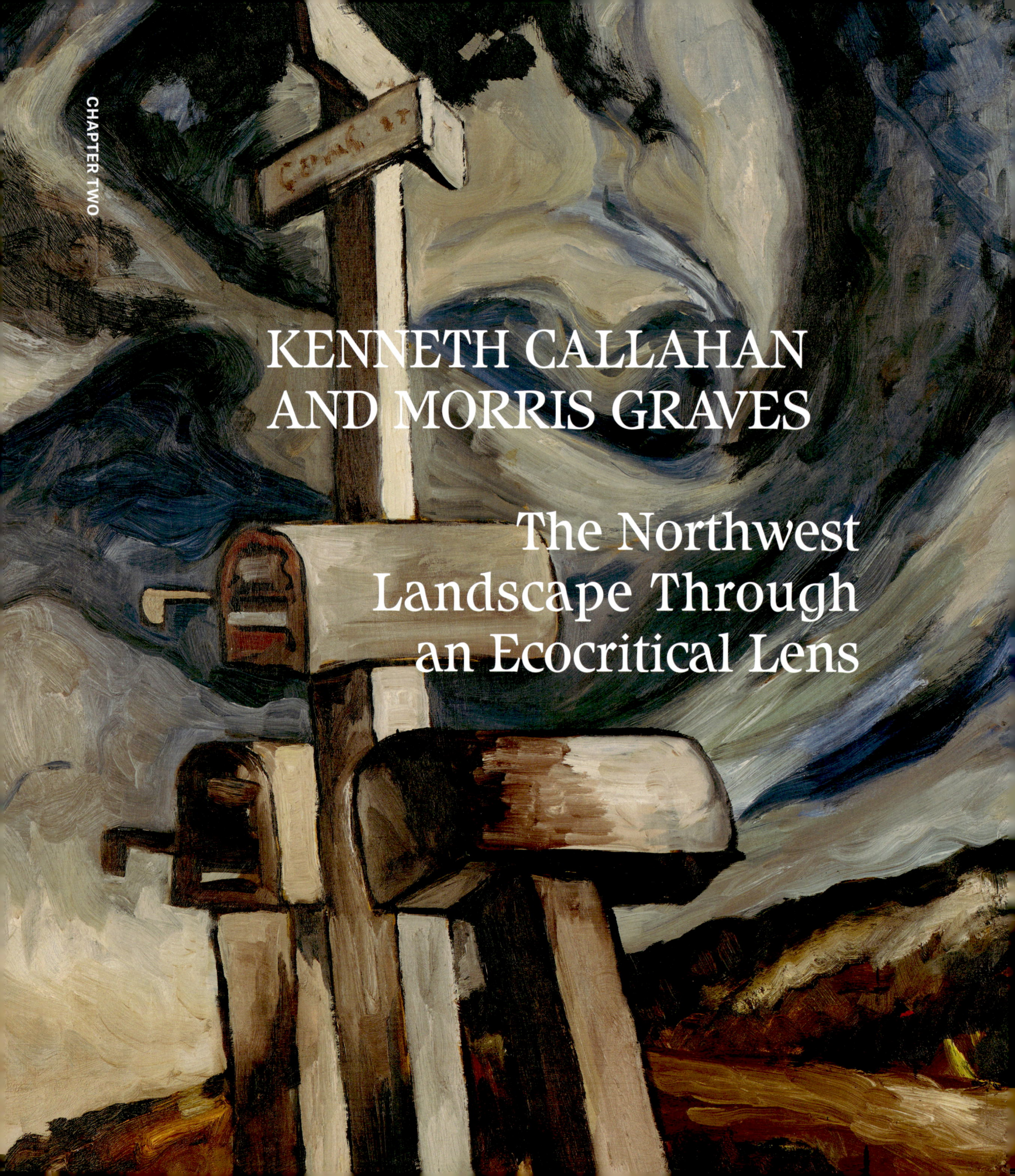

CHAPTER TWO

KENNETH CALLAHAN AND MORRIS GRAVES

The Northwest Landscape Through an Ecocritical Lens

In 1984, Jaune Quick-to-See Smith (Citizen of the Confederated Salish and Kootenai Nation) embarked on a series of paintings about climate disaster. Inspired by words attributed to Chief Seattle's 1855 address to the US government at the signing of the Treaty of Point Elliott, Smith's *Chief Seattle* series is, like the Duwamish and Suquamish leader's address, a chilling indictment of heedless disregard for the earth.[1] Each painting in the series takes on an urgent environmental issue, from acid rain and the weakening ozone layer to polluted air and contaminated water, and Smith's massive triptych *The Spotted Owl (C.S. 1854)* (fig. 3) relates specifically to the Pacific Northwest. The artist grew up in western Washington and maintained close ties in the region throughout her life, and she was

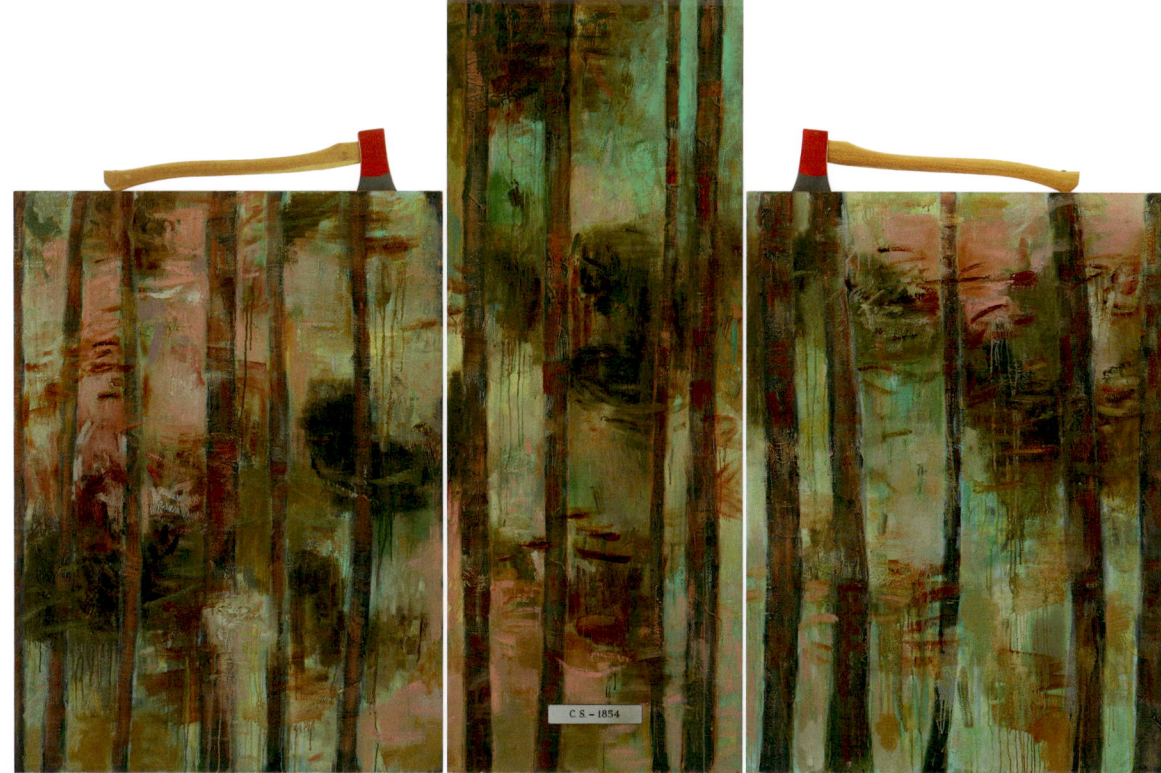

Fig. 3. Jaune Quick-to-See Smith (Native American, Citizen of the Confederated Salish and Kootenai Nation, 1940–2025), *The Spotted Owl (C.S. 1854)*, 1989, mixed media on canvas, axes, 80 × 116 in. (triptych). Private collection, courtesy of Garth Greenan Gallery

C.S. – 1854

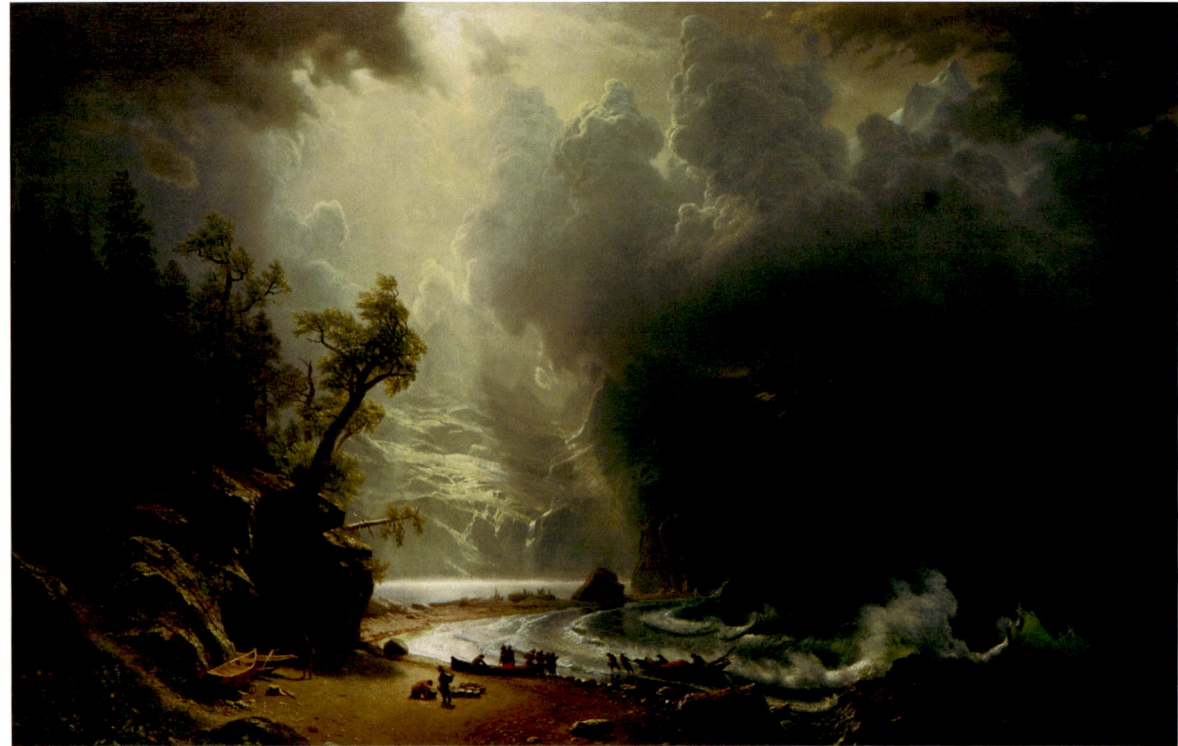

Fig. 4. Albert Bierstadt (American, 1830–1902), *Puget Sound on the Pacific Coast*, 1870, oil on canvas, 52½ × 82 in. Seattle Art Museum, Gift of the Friends of American Art at the Seattle Art Museum, with additional funds from General Acquisition Fund, 2000.70

outspoken about the impact of the logging industry on the Northwest's fragile ecosystems. She recalled working in a roadside diner on Snoqualmie Pass, watching trucks full of timber rumbling up and down the mountain, and described witnessing the devastation of clear-cutting as she flew over the Cascade Range.[2] In *The Spotted Owl*, Smith's woodsy palette, a pair of axes, and the conspicuous absence of the eponymous owl evoke the obliteration of the Northwest's ancient forests and the threat logging poses to native species like the northern spotted owl. Cutting down forests diverts rainwater, depletes watersheds, disrupts the migration of nutrient-rich salmon, and destroys natural habitats. For Smith, big lumber may benefit the Northwest's economy, but it wreaks havoc on the region's natural environment.[3]

Anticipating Smith's ecocriticism by roughly half a century are Kenneth Callahan's and Morris Graves's mountain views. These works recast the sublime drama of American landscape painting in Pacific Northwest terms, but they also, like Smith's *Spotted Owl*, allude to the harmful impact of clear-cutting. In Callahan's *Evening Mist in Mountains* (ca. 1940, plate 80), rugged peaks meet blustery skies, resilient terrain sustains dark forests, and the jagged remains of felled trees fan out across a swath of wasted land. Graves similarly included barren snags and razed earth in his early painting *Logged Mountains* (ca. 1935–43, plate 81).

These melancholy vistas evoke the singular look and feel of the Pacific Northwest's most remote wooded areas, where both Callahan and Graves traveled and, at times, lived in order to paint and connect with nature, and where they also witnessed industry's ruinous effects in action. With their decimated vegetation and scorched terrain, these two artists' paintings have much to say about nature and its exploitation for industrial purposes. For them, as for Smith, the impact of resource extraction on the beauty and ecological complexity of the Pacific Northwest was a vexation, and their work underscored

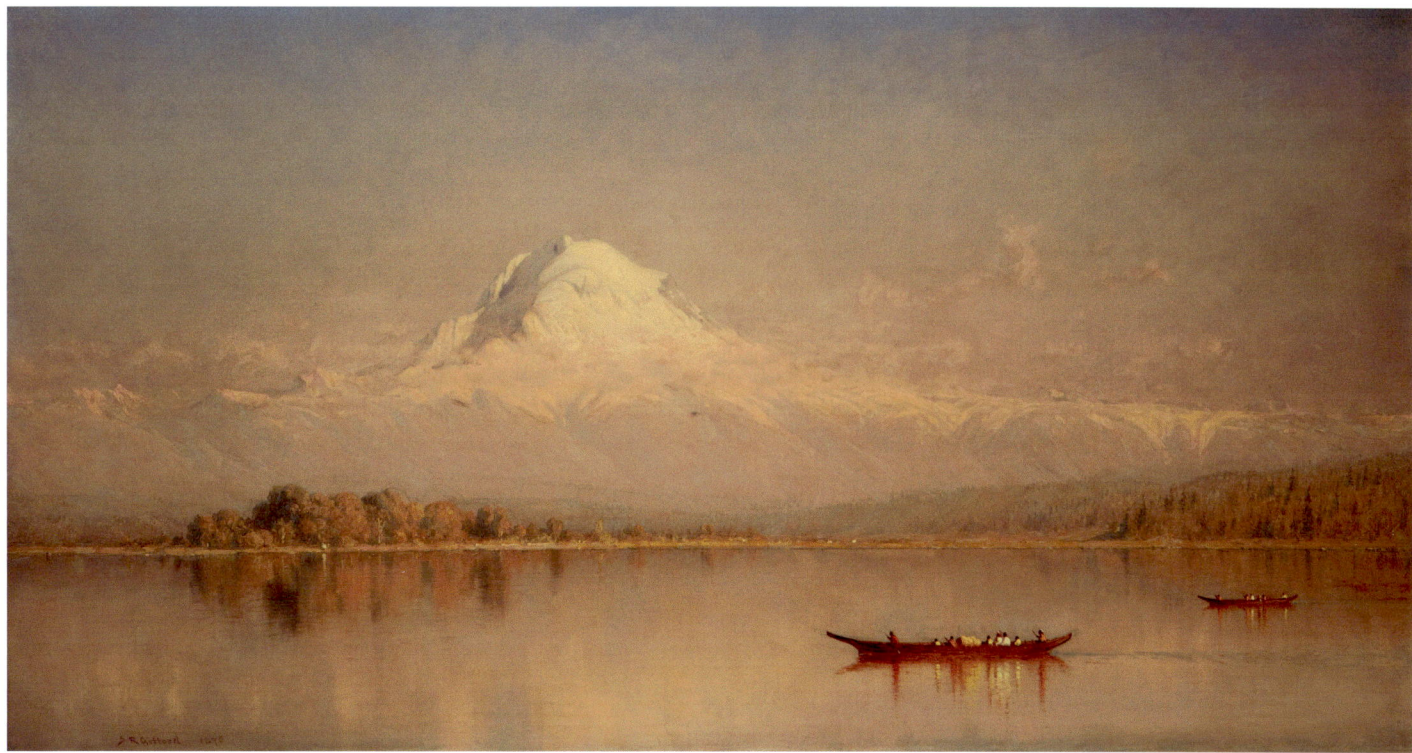

this threat to the landscape, extrapolated its consequences, and offered a road map for redemption.

Landscape painting has had a long and storied history in the work of American artists trained in the Western tradition, where nature is meant to be beheld, possessed, partitioned, and explored—in contrast to Indigenous worldviews that prioritize living with, honoring, and experiencing the land. In the nineteenth century, Hudson River School artists such as Albert Bierstadt (fig. 4) and Sanford Robinson Gifford (fig. 5) routinely traveled to remote locales and created panoramic views, establishing the nation's natural landmarks and offering frameworks for experiencing them. These artists perpetuated the myth of the American wilderness as something vacant, unpopulated, and there for the taking, and its inhabitants—if they were pictured at all—were depicted as characters in this narrative, engaged in traditional practices and unadulterated by contact with non-Natives.[4] In the twentieth century, artists such as Georgia

O'Keeffe (plates 87, 88) advanced the American landscape tradition in Modernist renderings of singular places—for O'Keeffe, this meant New Mexico, upstate New York, and even Hawai'i. Like the work of her Hudson River School forerunners, O'Keeffe's topographies are beautiful yet empty.

In the natural world of Northwest Modernism, however, living creatures—human and animal—are ever present, whether literally or implicitly, and artists advocated for a reverential approach to nature that was, intentionally or not, more aligned with Native worldviews. While Callahan and Graves emphasized the costs that extractive industries imposed on the land, many artists in the region represented nature as a life-sustaining force. Kenjiro Nomura, for example, focused on the farms and pastures that dotted rural areas on the outskirts of Seattle, which he painted and sketched on weekend excursions with his business partner and fellow artist Kamekichi Tokita. Generations of Nikkei truck farmers, who brought their own produce to market rather than relying on distributors, grew the bulk of the region's produce supply on this land, and Nomura captured its abundance in the cultivated fields, bountiful vegetation, and overall serenity of paintings such as *Red Barns* (1933, plate 84).[5] Julius Twohy (Ute) similarly pictured the human and natural worlds in harmony. A collaborator with Callahan on murals for Washington Marine Hospital, Twohy was one of the relatively few Native artists to benefit from art programs under the New Deal, for which he created prints and murals merging abstract form with pan-Indian imagery (plates 161–66). In his painting *Celilo Falls* (1945, plate 85), however, he departed from this stylized approach to show Native fishing activity at an important site on the Columbia River just east of the Cascades. There, members of local tribes exercised their treaty-protected right to catch salmon using traditional methods, stationing themselves on platforms constructed over the rushing river and using the centuries-old dip-netting technique to snare the migrating fish.

Callahan shared Nomura's and Twohy's appreciation of the nurturing landscape and understood the natural world as a reflection of the totality of the human experience, where art was the embodiment of "a holistic vision of cosmic unity" and the expression of a deep connection to the cycles of life.[6] "I think there's a basic rhythm, a basic current," he suggested, "obvious in the movements of waves in the sand patterns and mountains and animals and the flowing of blood."[7] In *Mail Boxes* (1935, plate 86), eddies of cosmic energy animate three letterboxes and the sky and landscape that surround them, signaling human presence in harmony with nature. Yet, even as Callahan, Nomura, and Twohy advanced their holistic approaches to the Northwest landscape, the landscape itself was undergoing physical and geopolitical changes. By the mid-twentieth century, Nikkei farmers had been forced to sacrifice their fertile land and endure mass incarceration during World War II; Celilo Falls had been flooded by the construction of the Dalles

Dam in 1957; and the equilibrium in nature that Callahan had observed had been irrevocably upended by the Northwest logging industry (fig. 6).

Disenchantment in the Wilderness: Callahan's Mountain Landscapes

According to Callahan's wife, the journalist Margaret Bundy Callahan, "nature was one of the primary sources for Kenneth's paintings . . . as necessary to [his] physical and mental well-being as food and drink."[8] To meet this need, he routinely retreated into the remote wilderness. During World War II, he spent three summers stationed on fire lookouts high in the Cascades, where, with little else to do but contemplate the vast forest, he sketched and painted the surrounding landscape and reflected on humanity's connection to nature, "the inter-relation of man, rock and elements; the creation and the disintegration, repeated over and over: man into rock, rock into man, both controlled by sun and elements."[9] Even before this wartime service, Callahan had been making regular excursions into Washington's backcountry. In 1938, he and Margaret rented a cabin at Robe Ranch on the Stillaguamish River, near Granite Falls in the North Cascades, spending all their free time there and eventually, in 1945, purchasing 160 nearby acres with fellow artist Guy Anderson.

By then, Callahan had witnessed the visible violation of Washington's forests when, in the mid-1930s, he visited a logging camp near Pysht on the Olympic Peninsula and observed timber felling in action. With the crew, he traveled along rough mountain roads and narrow, winding railways far back into the densest part of the forest. There, he saw lumberjacks cutting down giant old-growth evergreens and rigging spar trees to direct felled tree trunks down the mountain to waiting transports.[10] Margaret Callahan, who had accompanied her husband, also noted the depletion of these ancient forests and, in her memoirs, foretold its devastating legacy:

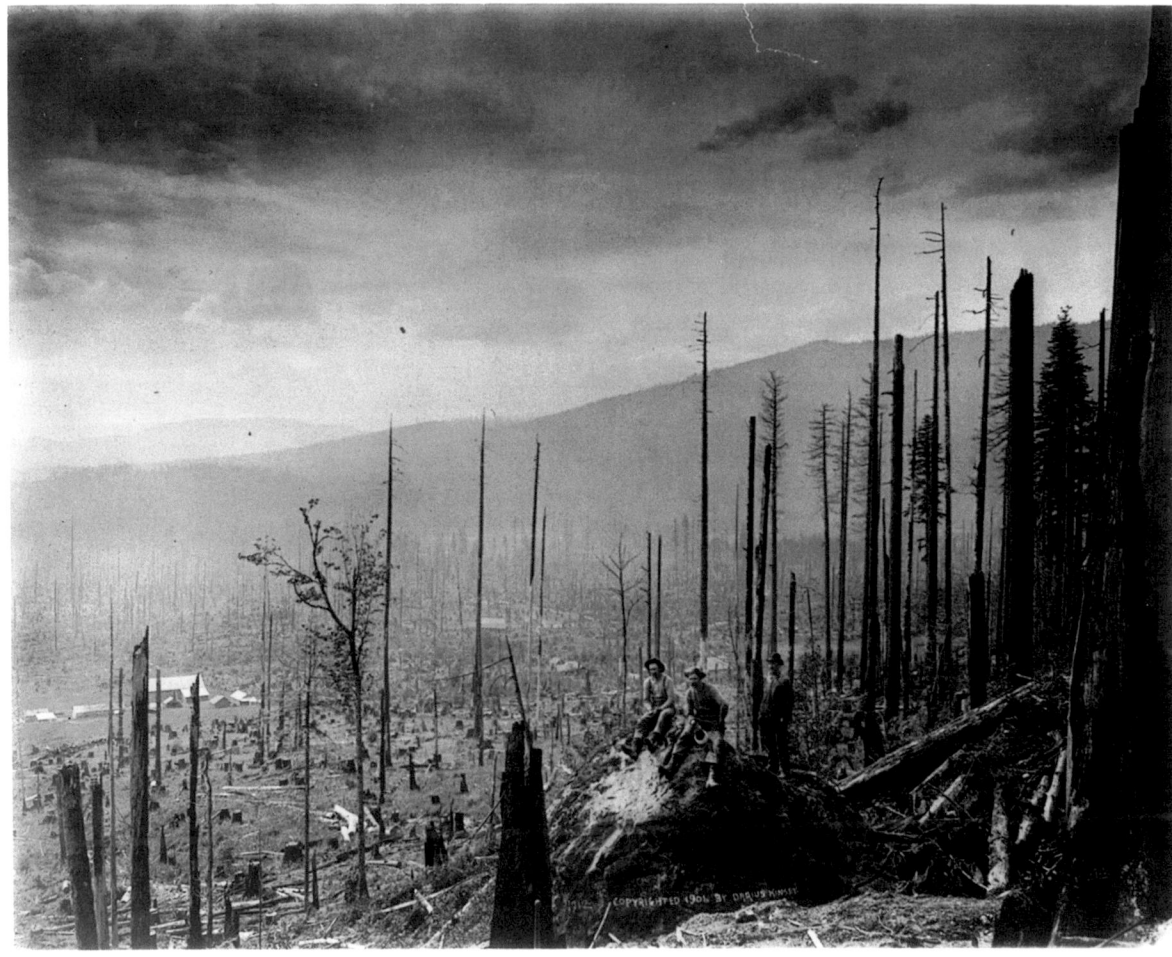

Fig. 6. Darius Kinsey (American, 1869–1945), *Three Men in Devastated Forest, Logging in the Cascade Mountains, near Seattle, Washington,* ca. 1906. Library of Congress Prints and Photographs Division, Washington, DC

And in five years or maybe ten, according to the crew, you won't find this kind of logging going on in the backwoods because there won't be any forests like these left. Not for another fifty years, when the second growth matures, will there be anything called woods here at all. By that time maybe they'll know enough not to mow down the forests like hayfields. Maybe selective logging will be the rule.[11]

Following this experience, Callahan painted *Logging Rail Road Construction* (1937, plate 89), a complex scene of the human and environmental cost of logging. A large group of men engage not in sawing timber but in building one of the railroads used to transport lumber workers into the forests and sawed-off logs out of them. Tracklayers and graders level railbeds, haul ties, position tracks, and pound spikes, while the surrounding landscape, barren and brown, bears the visible scars of depletion. More than a record of the strain of hard labor, this painting warns of environmental disaster to come. Narrow-gauge railroads made it possible to expand the lumber industry inland from coastal regions to Washington's most remote wooded areas, where its impact, by the mid-1930s, was obvious and profound. Even as the railroad workers in Callahan's painting carve their lethal path into the forest's farthest reaches, it appears that the forest itself has already suffered the devastating impact they herald.

By the time Callahan painted *Logging Rail Road Construction*, big lumber had been a presence in the Washington wilderness for decades. It originated in the 1840s, when forests in the Cascade Range and Olympic Mountains, deemed unsuitable for farming, were targeted instead to supply timber for the building boom that followed the 1848 California Gold Rush and the rapid development of western Washington a few decades later. The industry's growth accelerated with the completion of the transcontinental railroad in 1883, which made it possible to ship lumber to distant points at reasonable rates, paving the way for mammoth Midwestern operations such as Weyerhaeuser Timber Company to relocate to the Pacific Northwest after Great Lakes timber supplies were depleted. By 1900, lumber—and its subsidiaries, pulp and paper—dominated the Puget Sound economy, and, from then until World War II, vast ancient forests and their ecosystems were annihilated. Efforts at reforestation on the part of the US Forest Service only exacerbated the devastation by replacing slow-growing native trees with fast-growing, easily regenerated Douglas firs. Forest biomes were transformed into tree factories with minimal life-sustaining capacities.[12] Callahan's painting of a mountain railroad in progress and future wasted landscape maps the development, growth, and devastating impact of the lumber industry; far from the exuberant natural equilibrium of *Mail Boxes*, it shows the natural environment fighting for its life.

Logging Rail Road Construction is related to Callahan's mural cycles documenting the logging industrial complex, beginning with the massive, noncommissioned *Logging the Northwest* (1935, no longer extant) and culminating in eighteen murals for the staff cafeteria at Weyerhaeuser's Company Mill "B" in Everett, Washington, its largest and most productive sawmill. Designed to bolster company morale by celebrating its workers, the series pictured each step in the process of transforming forests into lumber, under the benevolent gaze of the folk hero and lumberjack alter ego Paul Bunyan.[13] The panel *Loggers with*

Chokers (1944, plate 70) shows two loggers using a chain mechanism, known as a choker, to manipulate the remains of an immense tree onto a transport and out of the forest, while *Weyerhaeuser Mill* (1944, plate 90) offers a commanding view of the mill complex humming with production as it processes the cut timber. Neat rows of flatbed trailers laden with fresh planks indicate the plant's profitability, even as subtle references—smokestacks spewing noxious plumes of black ash, the brown and depleted earth on which the complex sits—signal its impact on the environment. In the distance is the blue expanse of the Snohomish River and the green carpet of the forests beyond, reminders of the natural world sacrificed to big business.

Consequences: Graves's Menagerie

Graves, like Callahan, also withdrew into the wilderness, first escaping periodically to a rented cabin on the Callahans' acreage near Robe Ranch and eventually, in 1940, building a home and studio of his own on an isolated promontory in Skagit County known as the Rock. There, in extreme solitude, he spent long nights walking the property, listening to the calls and movements of animals and marveling at their resonance in the quietude of nature. "You could hear the cattle, or a dog barking," he wrote, "from a great distance. The sound carried clearly, intensely. Living alone in that forest . . . you spent a lot of time outside, just listening and hearing what happened in the night—the forest creatures."[14] In Graves's series *In the Night*, he conjured visual equivalents for these unseen yet audible nocturnal beings and the deep connection he felt with them (plate 94). Like Callahan, he believed that humans should live *"searchingly close to nature"* so that "from the mist to the mountain—even from the molecule to the cosmos—[it would be possible to] dream deeply down into the kelp beds *and not let one fleck of the significance of beauty* pass unappraised and unquestioned and unanswered."[15]

Graves shared Callahan's environmentalism and holistic view of nature, but his focus was on small-scale flora and fauna, whose biomes and habitats he painted even as he witnessed their encroachment by industrialization and urban development. From the Rock, he could hear the construction and expansion of the naval air station on Whidbey Island, headquarters to the squadrons of aircraft that patrolled the Puget Sound during World War II. Farther afield, he knew that forests and wetlands were continuing their transformation from ecosystems to ecotechnological systems harnessed and shaped for economic ends.[16] As forests collapsed under the weight of the logging industry and watersheds fell victim to dredging, rerouting, and damming, native species were being deprived of the territories necessary for their survival. Salmon were cut off from the instinctual migratory routes that brought strict order to their anadromous life cycles, and without the presence and residue of these fish along rivers and waterways, plant life and species up and down the food chain were deprived of nitrogen and other essential nutrients.[17]

Echoing this cascade of ecological events, Graves's birds and other animals became imperiled, as in the confined and anxious *Bird Sensing the Essential Insanities* (1944, plate 108); his landscapes turned discordant, as in the crushed and beleaguered *Spring with Machine Age Noise No. 3* (1957, plate 96); and his state of mind became increasingly agitated. In the late 1940s, he left the Rock and settled at Careläden, a wooded estate to the south near Edmonds, Washington. His time there, however, was brief. With massive Boeing and Weyerhaeuser plants just to the north in Everett, there was no escaping the area's urban sprawl and the disappearance of its ecosystems. "I hate the crushing 'progress' that is killing this Far West country," he wrote to his New York art dealer, Marian Willard. "The roads that have been smashed through a woods in a day—a single day!—with bulldozers . . . and the houses (flashy shacks) that are being built in

a day along these roads . . . breaks my heart—HELL is here and now in all its Dante terror."[18] By this time, his works had evolved beyond critique of the logging industry to signal the environmental apocalypse of polluted water, depleted natural resources, contaminated land, and endangered species.

Recasting the work of Callahan and Graves in environmental terms adds nuance to the deforestation pictured in Callahan's *Evening Mist in Mountains* and Graves's *Logged Mountains*. While the towering peaks, misty skies, and forests blanketing the middle ground of Callahan's painting evoke the spirit of the Pacific Northwest's mountains, the untidy remains of hewn trees in the foreground foretell stark changes within the ecosystems they sustain. In Graves's painting, the mountain landscape is reduced to a handful of weathered snags and a thick layer of oozing mud left behind by the leveling of living trees, unstable and unable to sustain life. These foreboding views signal the aftermath of industry in the Pacific Northwest: logged-off woodlands, soil erosion, watershed depletion, diminished biodiversity, and habitat destruction.

Their ecocriticism joins paintings by American artists nationally who were similarly responding to the conflict between industry and nature prior to World War II. The Modernist painter Marsden Hartley, for example, celebrated the Northeastern woods and waterways of his native state as the self-styled "painter from Maine."[19] Like Callahan, however, he also captured the impact of logging. Maine has a long history of logging that dates back to the seventeenth century, when trees were sourced on Monhegan Island to replenish dwindling lumber supplies across the Atlantic in England. The industry continued to thrive well into the twentieth century, and Hartley, who was outspoken against industrial practices in Maine, referenced it in paintings such as *Log Jam, Penobscot Bay* (1940–41, plate 101), which shows lumber gridlocked on its drive down the Penobscot River to sawmills on Penobscot Bay.[20] Massive, impermeable, and full of detritus—cast-off bottles, a barrel, an old shoe—this jumble of timber is a reflection of the environmental fallout of log driving, which disrupted waterflow, littered riverbeds with sediment and debris, and deprived aquatic life of nutrients and oxygen.

Alexandre Hogue's views of Midwestern farms similarly signal the impact of industrial agriculture on land and livelihoods during the Dust Bowl. *Erosion No. 2—Mother Earth Laid Bare* (1936, plate 102) is an indictment of the practice of deep plowing, a method that left farms particularly vulnerable when the Great Plains were hit with a period of extreme drought during the 1930s. Plowing deep into the earth destroyed the surface of loam that preserved moisture-retaining grasses, resulting in soil dehydration and, eventually, copious amounts of blowing dust. In Hogue's painting, a bleak expanse of this parched and wind-swept earth stretches out before a deserted farm. Looming ominously in the foreground is a plow whose blade is perfect for breaching hardpan but detrimental to topsoil, metaphorically and rather heavy-handedly personified as a supine female nude. In *Crucified Land* (1939, plate 103), Hogue takes on overcultivation, the practice of excessive farming without seasons of respite until the soil loses its capacity to hold nutrients and water. A mammoth yield, eroded at the edges by wasteful runoff, lines up in furrows of cracked red earth that extend to the horizon, while a scarecrow, perched askew in the middle ground like an off-kilter crucifixion, bears witness to the sacrifice of nature's equilibrium by human intervention.[21]

Callahan's and Graves's scenes resonate with the environmentalism and specific sense of place in the paintings of Hartley and Hogue, and the two Northwest painters' ecocriticism remained subtly present in their work as they continued to elaborate their holistic beliefs in the animating forces in nature. Callahan's views of logged mountains eventually gave way to scenes of treacherous, otherworldly terrain, from whose chasms and caverns teem throngs of humans and animals engaged in desperate struggle (for example, plate 104). Whether visions of the future or warnings in the present, these hellscapes picture humanity and nature intertwined in a hopeless cycle, "man, rock and the elements: the creating and disintegration, over and over."[22] Graves continued to expand his menagerie with avian creatures and animals in "an evolving language of symbols with which to remark upon the qualities of our mysterious capacities which direct us toward ultimate reality . . . [and] rest from the phenomena of the external world—to pronounce it—and to make notations of its essence with which to verify the inner eye."[23] It was here that Graves found hope—hope for himself, and hope for the earth. In *Each Time You Carry Me This Way* (1953, plate 109), a drawing whose title comes from an ancient Hindu myth where Vishnu saved the earth from rising seas, an owl plucks a minnow out of a dark stream, sustaining ecological balance with the reassurance that disaster can bring renewal. For both artists, nature condemns but also forgives, depending on how it is treated.

The deep appreciation Callahan and Graves had for the Pacific Northwest landscape was tempered by their profound awareness that it was rapidly changing with advances in industry, technology, and development. They expressed this in scenes of flora and fauna that allude to the presence of the Northwest's extractive industries, and from there, they argued for the universal connectedness of all the earth's inhabitants, whether human or animal, sentient or inanimate. Their ecocriticism relates to the theories of early twentieth-century environmentalists such as the naturalist John Muir and the conservationist Aldo Leopold, both of whom were thought leaders in the development of the modern conservation movement. Muir, in particular, was highly influential on naturalist artists such as Ansel Adams. Callahan's and Graves's holistic approach to the natural world avoids the racial hierarchies implicit in Muir's and Leopold's writings, however. The two artists' observations about the universalism in nature seem closer to the radical ecology embedded in anarchist communitarianism. Its idea of mutualism between human beings, nature, and culture was highly relevant for a host of Modernist artists.[24] Notably, the French geologist and anarchist Élisée Reclus, in his 1881 treatise *The History of a Mountain*, saw regenerative potential in responsible logging practices in the Pacific Northwest and other American forests:

> When the means of access are easy . . . then the forests run great risk of being attacked by wood-cutters. If they cultivate intelligently, if they carefully regulate their cutting in such a manner as always to leave harvests of wood standing for the following years, and to develop in the forest ground the greatest possible power of production, man has but to congratulate himself upon the new riches he obtains. But when he hews down and destroys the whole forest at one blow, as if seized with a fit of frenzy, is not one tempted to curse?[25]

Reclus's vision of proactive and conscientious reforestation and its long-term benefits to ecosystems is rich with suggestion for Callahan and Graves, and the relevance of his work to theirs merits further study. In balancing their anxiety about nature's ephemerality with an inclusive message advocating for its equilibrium and connection to humanity, they sought to offer a solution to the ecological fallout of unchecked industrialization in the Pacific Northwest.

Notes

I would like to thank Pam McClusky for her helpful feedback on an earlier version of this essay.

1. The 1855 Treaty of Point Elliott was a land-use treaty that guaranteed hunting and fishing rights, as well as reservations, to all tribes represented by the Native leaders who signed it: the Duwamish, Suquamish, Snoqualmie, Snohomish, Lummi, Upper and Lower Skagit, Swinomish, and others. In return, the Duwamish tribe ceded over 54,000 acres of their homeland to Washington Territory. Despite the surrender of tribal lands, government officials and non-Native settlers almost immediately violated the terms of the treaty, sparking the "Indian War," a series of Native rebellions from 1855 to 1858.

2. Jaune Quick-to-See Smith, email to the author, 17 August 2023.

3. Young salmon migrate to the ocean from the fresh water in which they are hatched, then return to their birthplace to spawn before promptly dying. Their carcasses provide nitrogen and other nutrients to the soil and help sustain plant and animal life throughout the region. Development and engineering in the Puget Sound landscape compromised and altered the salmon runs, disrupting the life cycles of salmon and the world around them. For the life cycle and migratory patterns of salmon, see Klingle, *Emerald City*, "Prologue," 1–11.

4. For the nationalist impulse in American landscape painting, see Truettner, "Ideology and Image"; and Miller, *Empire of the Eye*.

5. Takami, "Japanese Farming."

6. Kenneth Callahan, quoted in Kingsbury, "Four Artists in the Northwest Tradition," 41.

7. K. Callahan and Kendall, "Oral History Interview."

8. M. B. Callahan, *Margaret Callahan*, 2.

9. K. Callahan, quoted in Conkelton, "Pantheon of Dreams," 65. Conkelton also discusses Callahan's wartime fire-prevention service.

10. See M. B. Callahan, *Margaret Callahan*, chapter 7, for the couple's visit to Pysht.

11. M. B. Callahan, 43.

12. Chiang with Reese, "Seeing the Forest for the Trees."

13. Burns, *Weyerhaeuser Murals*. The point at which Callahan went from recording the logging industry in commissioned murals to critiquing it is a topic for future research—especially with regards to the tragic story of *Logging the Northwest*. He undertook this massive mural cycle on his own initiative and without a commission in his basement studio at the Seattle Art Museum, where he was employed as assistant director and curator. The museum acquired the paintings in 1934 and exhibited them the following year, but then deaccessioned them in 1956, after Callahan removed them from the premises following the termination of his employment. In 1963, the murals perished in a fire at the artist's Granite Falls studio.

14. Morris Graves, quoted in Rubin, *Drawings of Morris Graves*, 62.

15. Morris Graves to Marian Willard, February 12, 1952, in Kass, *Morris Graves*, 59. The emphasis is Graves's.

16. Klingle analyzes this transformation in *Emerald City*.

17. "Prologue," in Klingle, *Emerald City*, 1–11.

18. Morris Graves to Marian Willard, February 12, 1952, quoted in Kass, *Morris Graves*, 59.

19. For Hartley and Maine, see Griffey, "Ambivalent Prodigal."

20. Karasoulas, "Marsden Hartley's Maine."

21. For Hogue's Dust Bowl scenes, see White, "Alexandre Hogue's Passion."

22. K. Callahan, quoted in Orton, "Kenneth Callahan," 22.

23. Graves, quoted in Kass, *Morris Graves*, 32.

24. For the anarchist basis of radical ecology, see Leighten and Antliff, "Kandinsky and Radical Ecology." See also Merchant, "Anarchist Social Ecology," 148–52.

25. Reclus, *History of a Mountain*.

PLATES

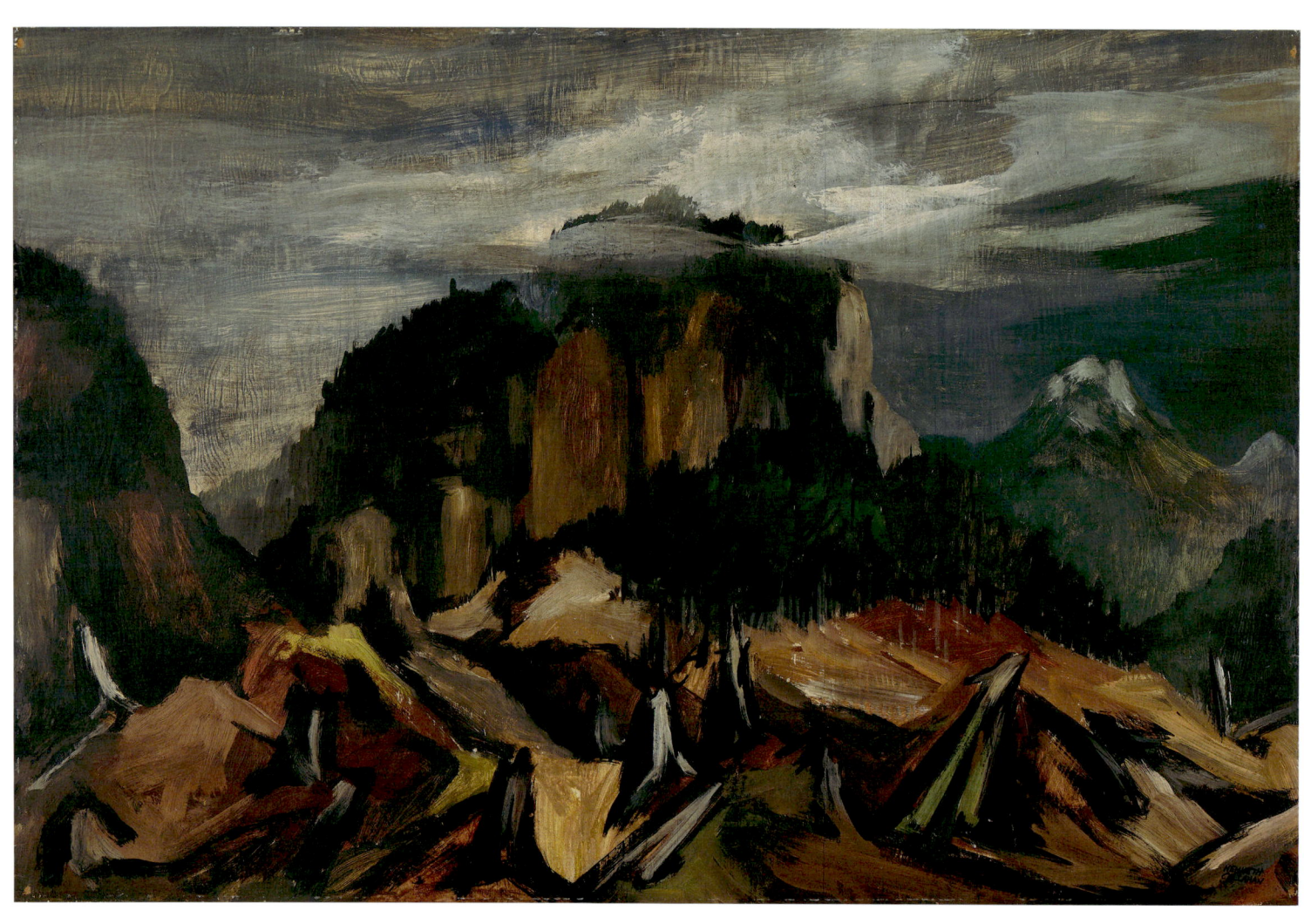

80 Kenneth Callahan, *Evening Mist in Mountains*, ca. 1940, tempera on board

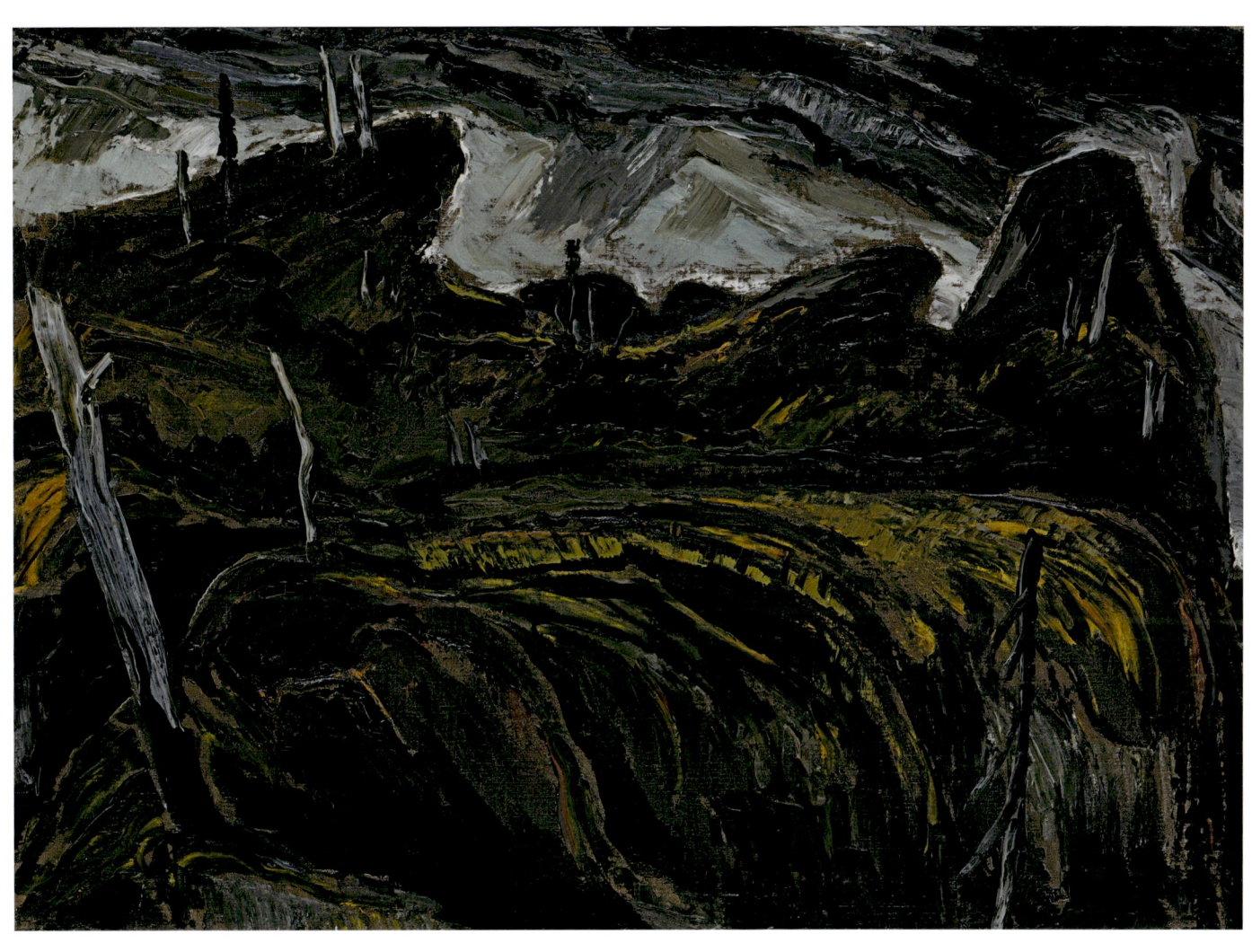

81　Morris Graves, *Logged Mountains*, ca. 1935–43, oil on canvas

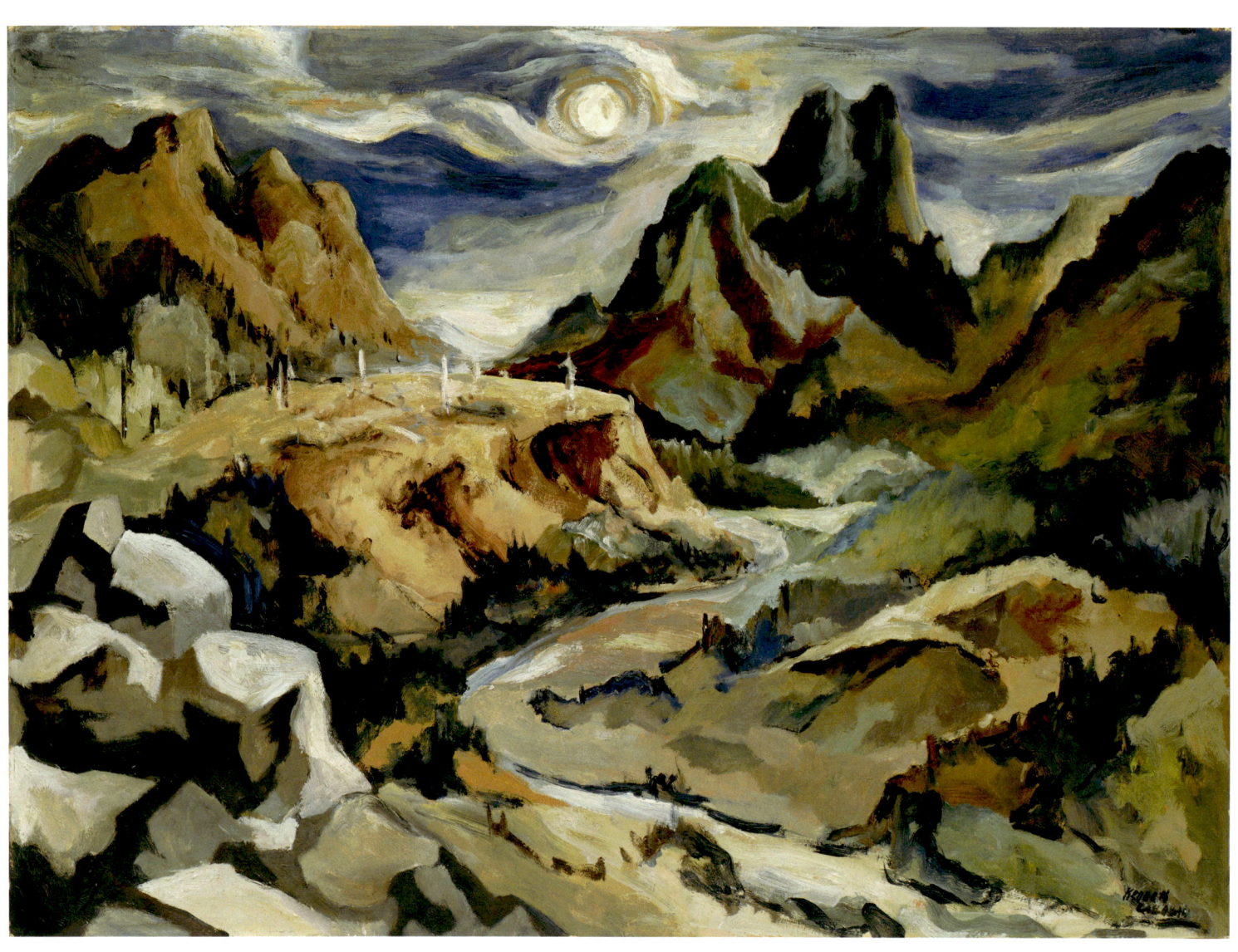

82 Kenneth Callahan, *Northwest Landscape,* 1934, oil on board

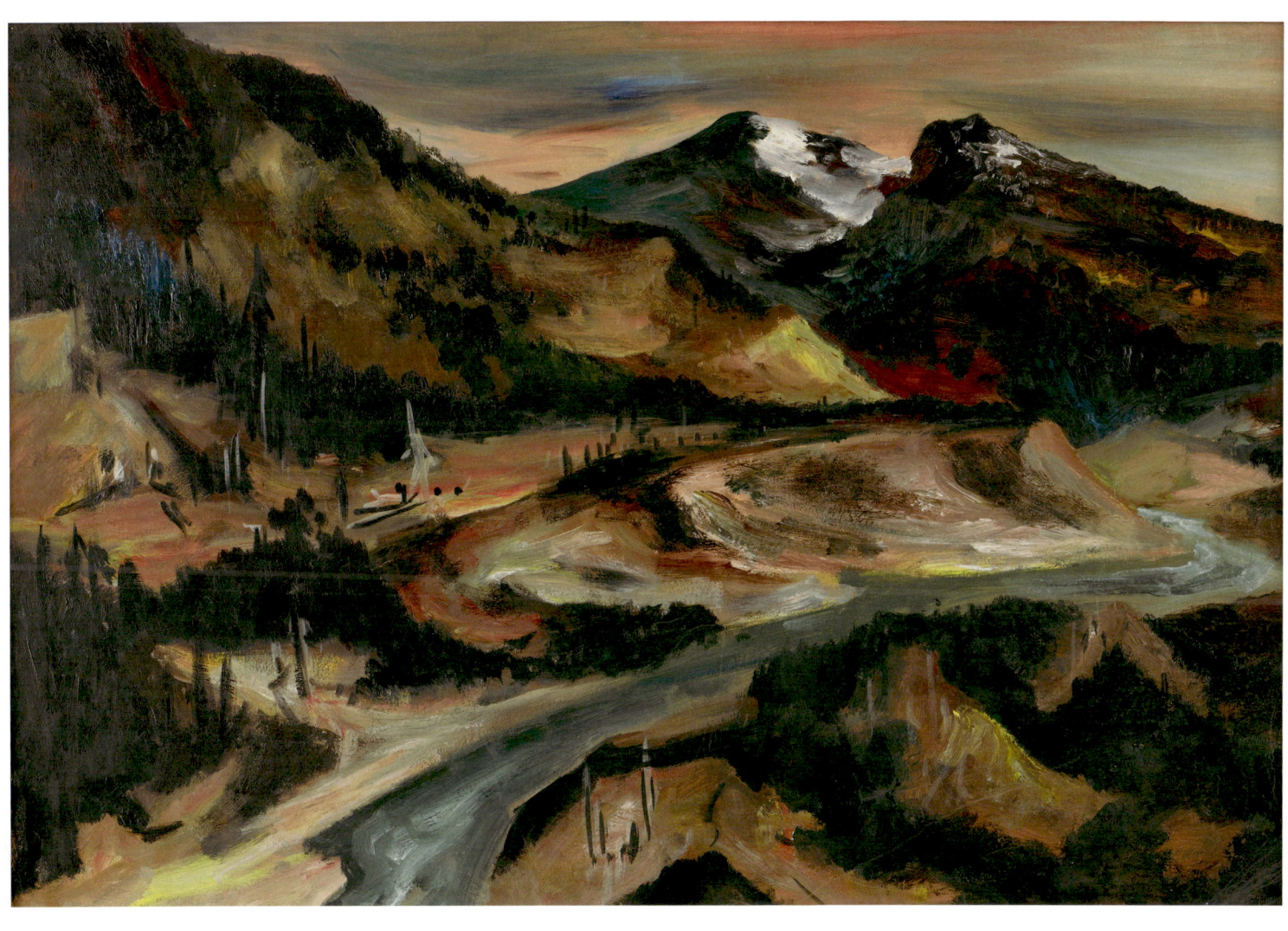

83 Kenneth Callahan, *Mountain Landscape*, ca. 1938, oil on board

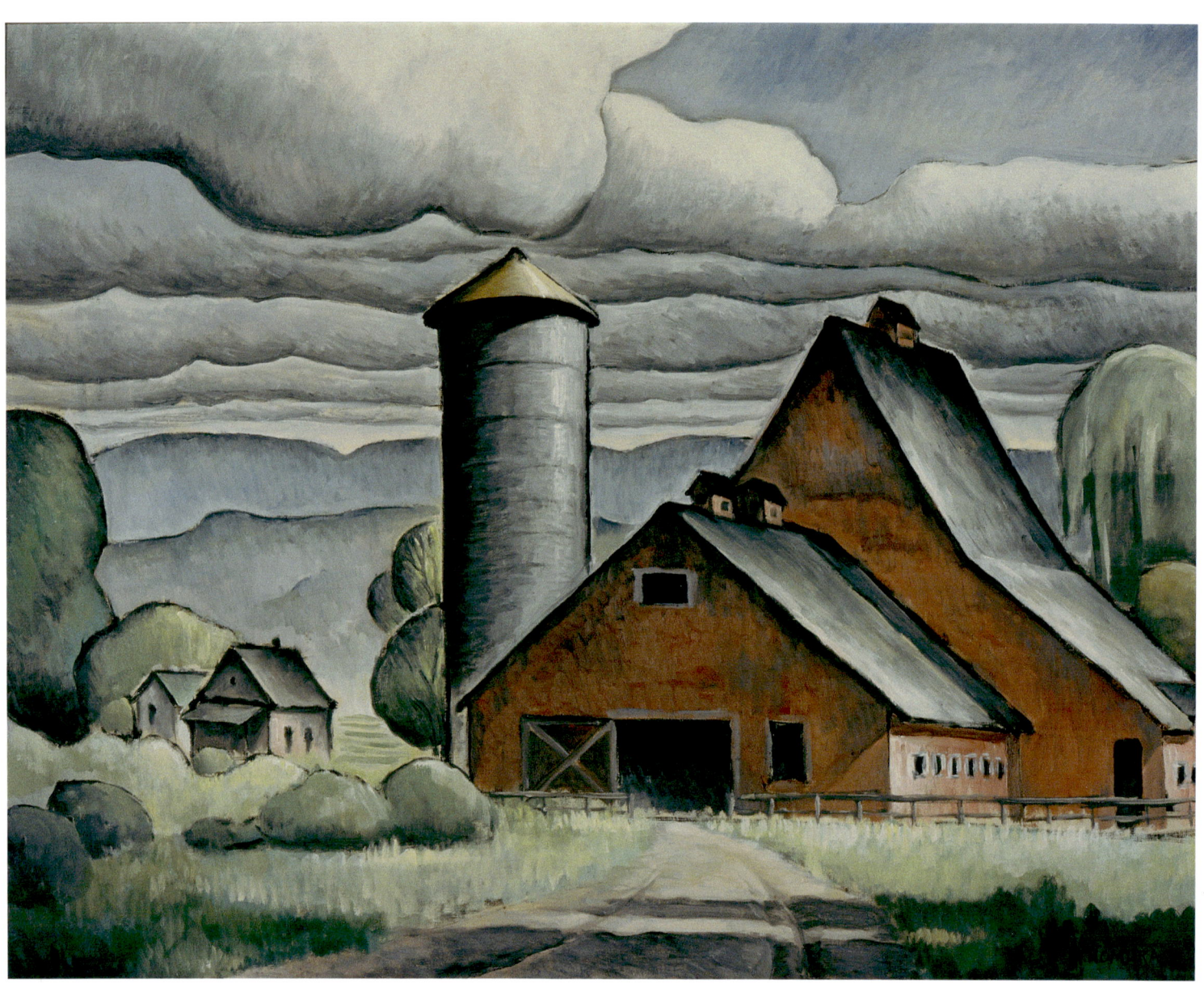

84 Kenjiro Nomura, *Red Barns*, 1933, oil on canvas

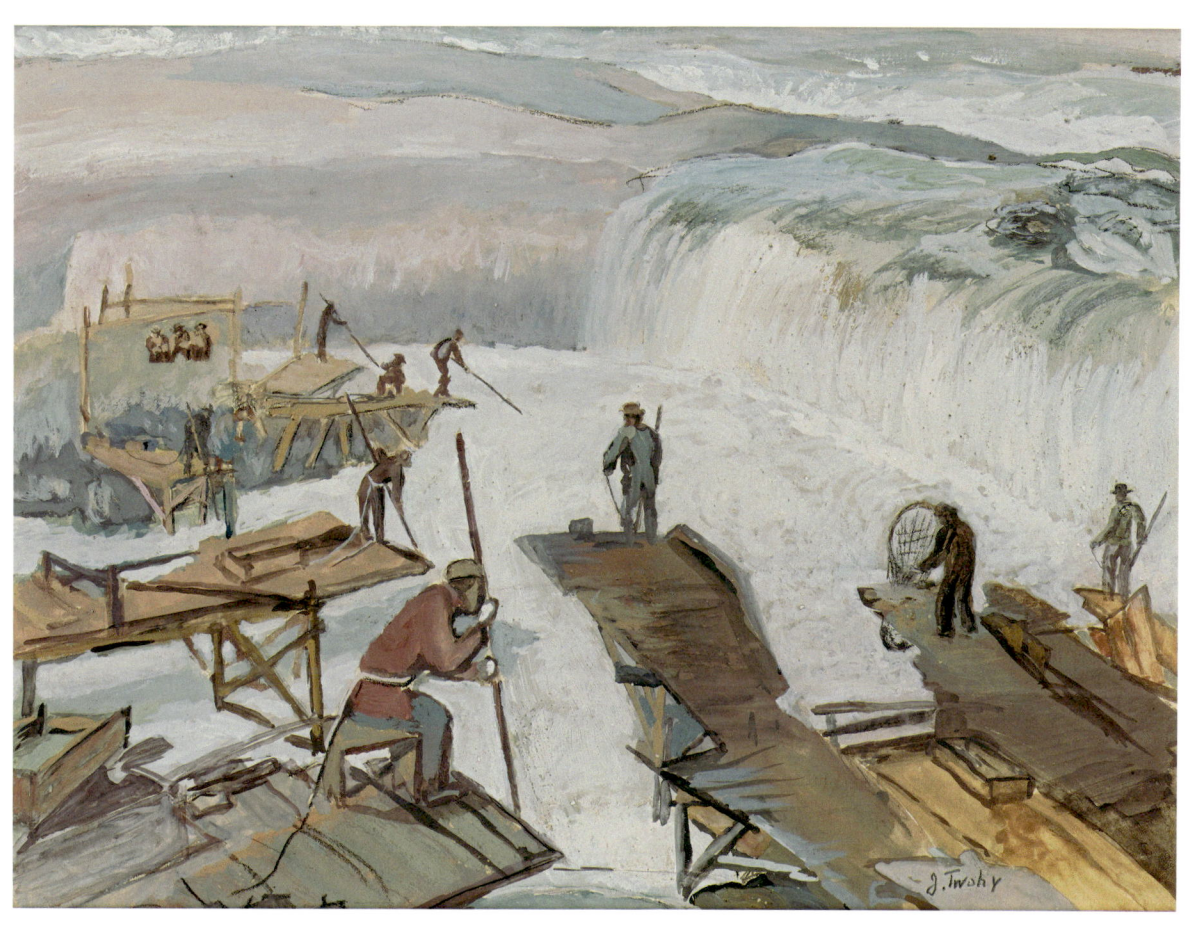

85 Julius Twohy, *Celilo Falls*, 1945, tempera on paper

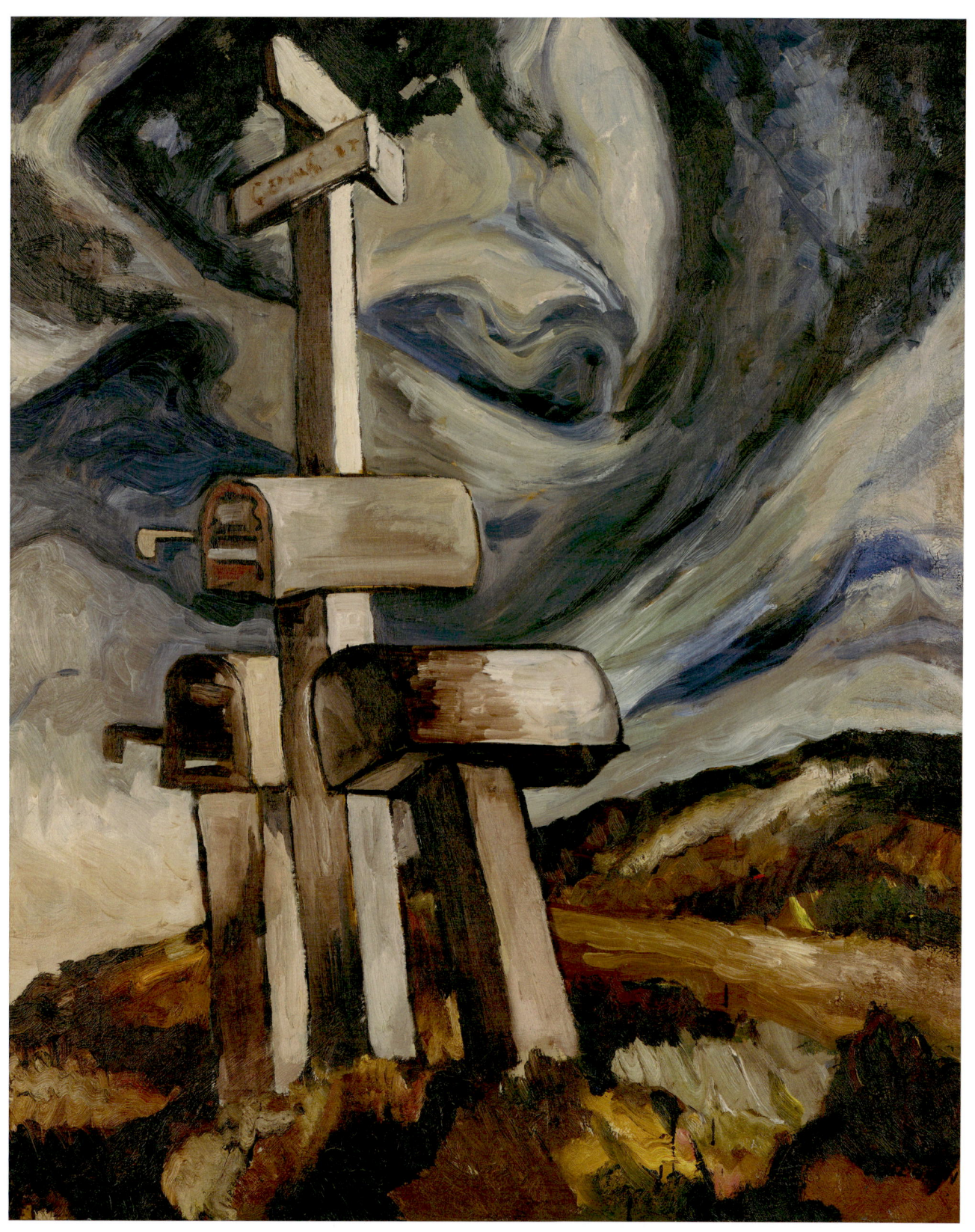

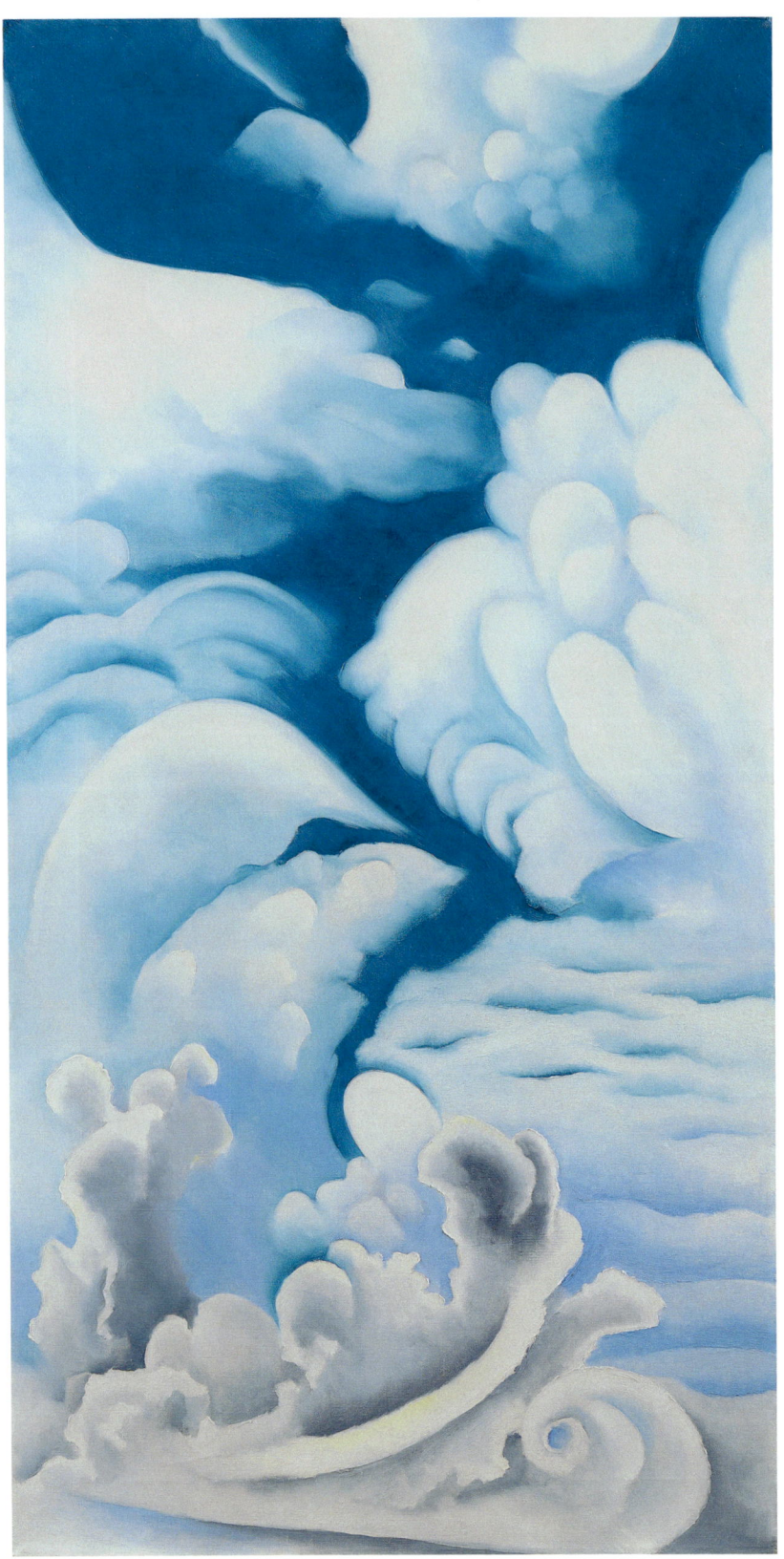

87 Georgia O'Keeffe, *A Celebration*, 1924, oil on canvas

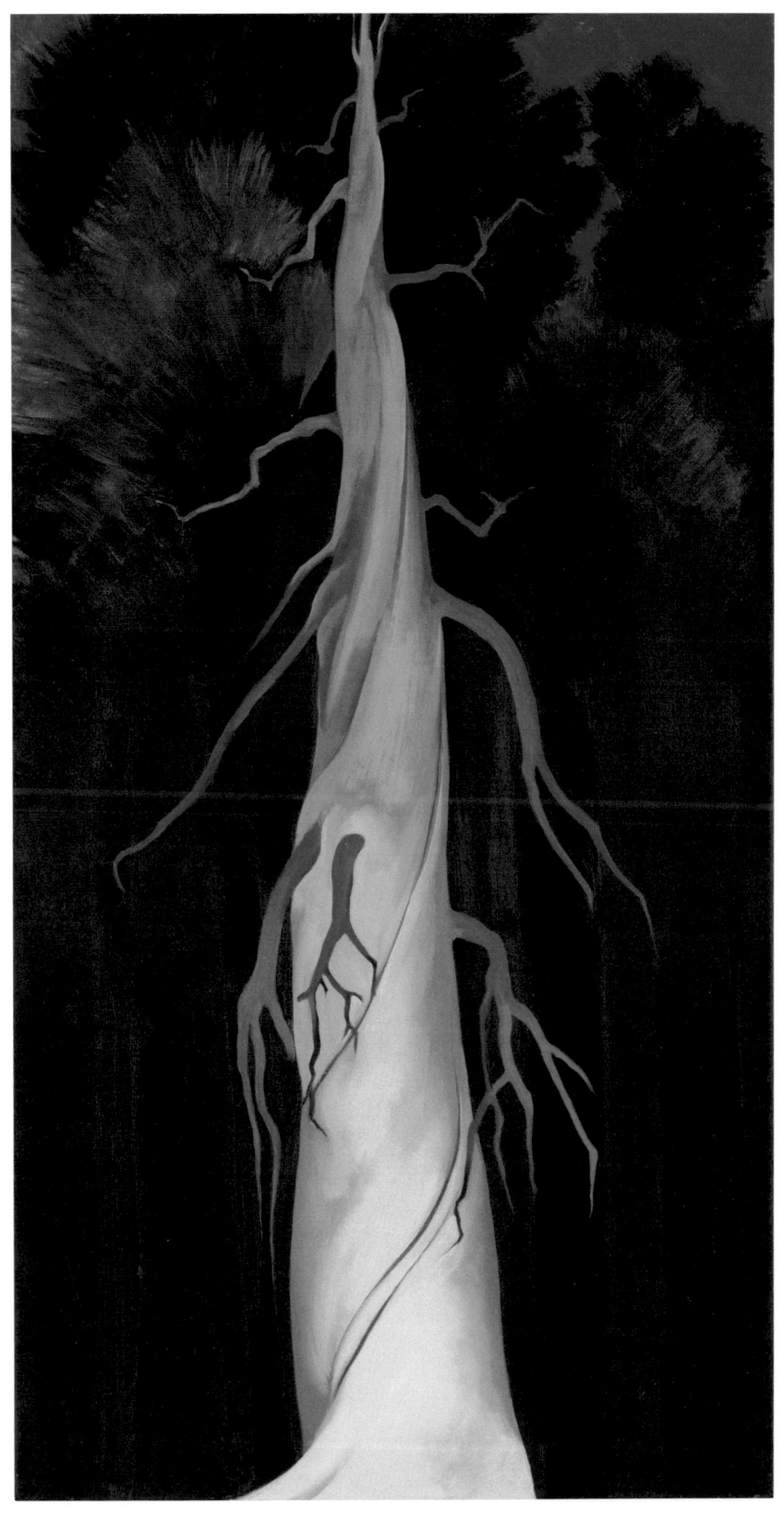

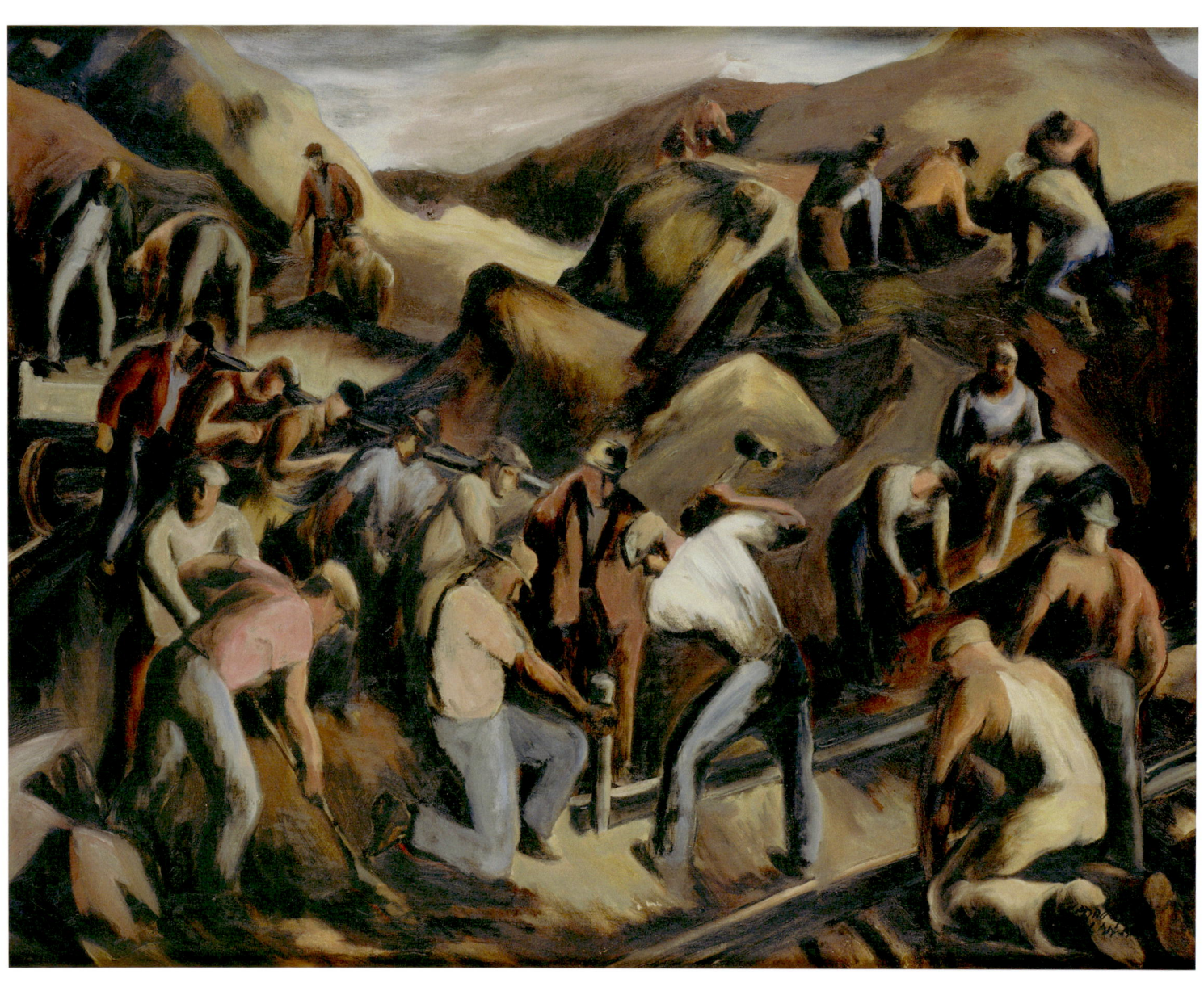

89 Kenneth Callahan, *Logging Rail Road Construction*, 1937, oil on canvas

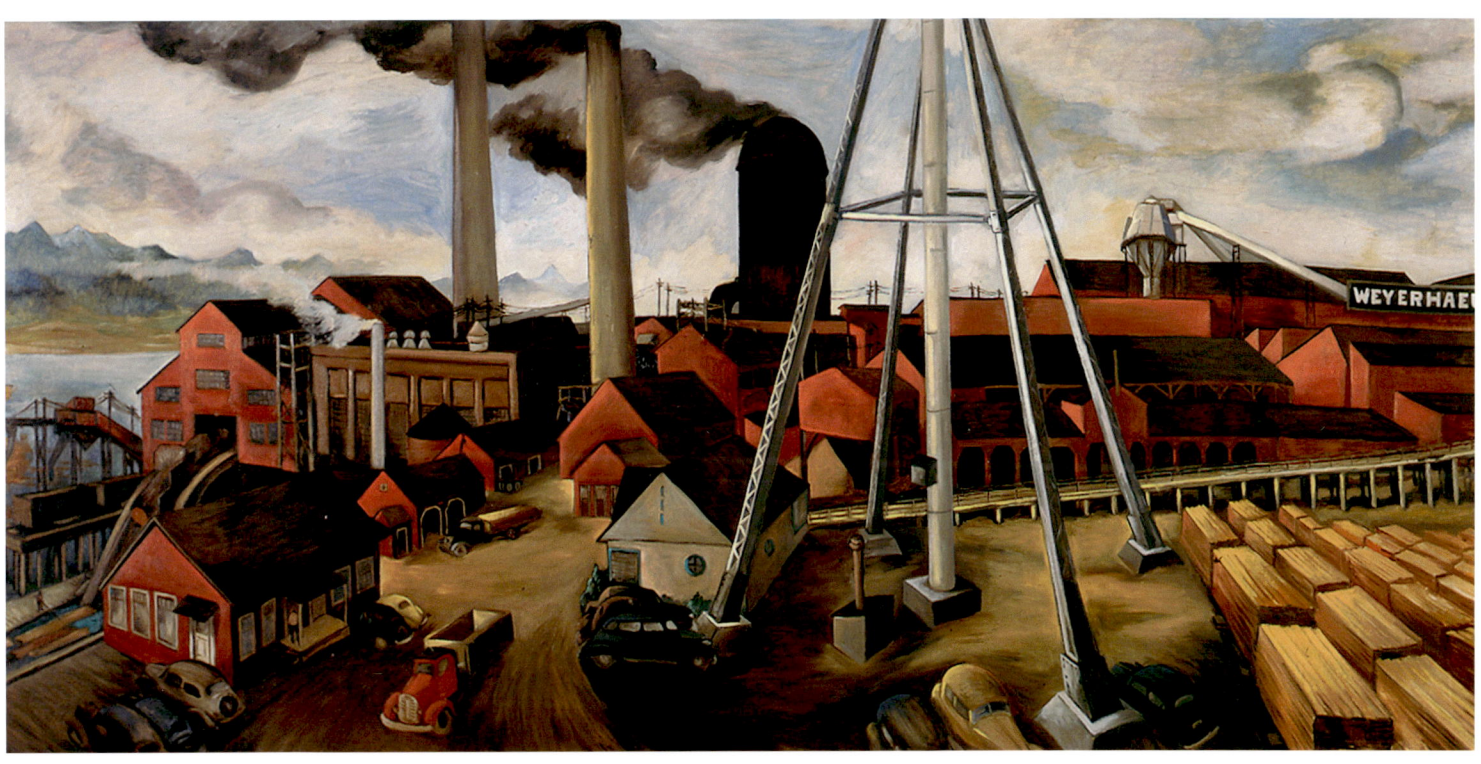

90 Kenneth Callahan, *Weyerhaeuser Company Mill B Mural Panel (Weyerhaeuser Mill)*, 1944, oil on canvas

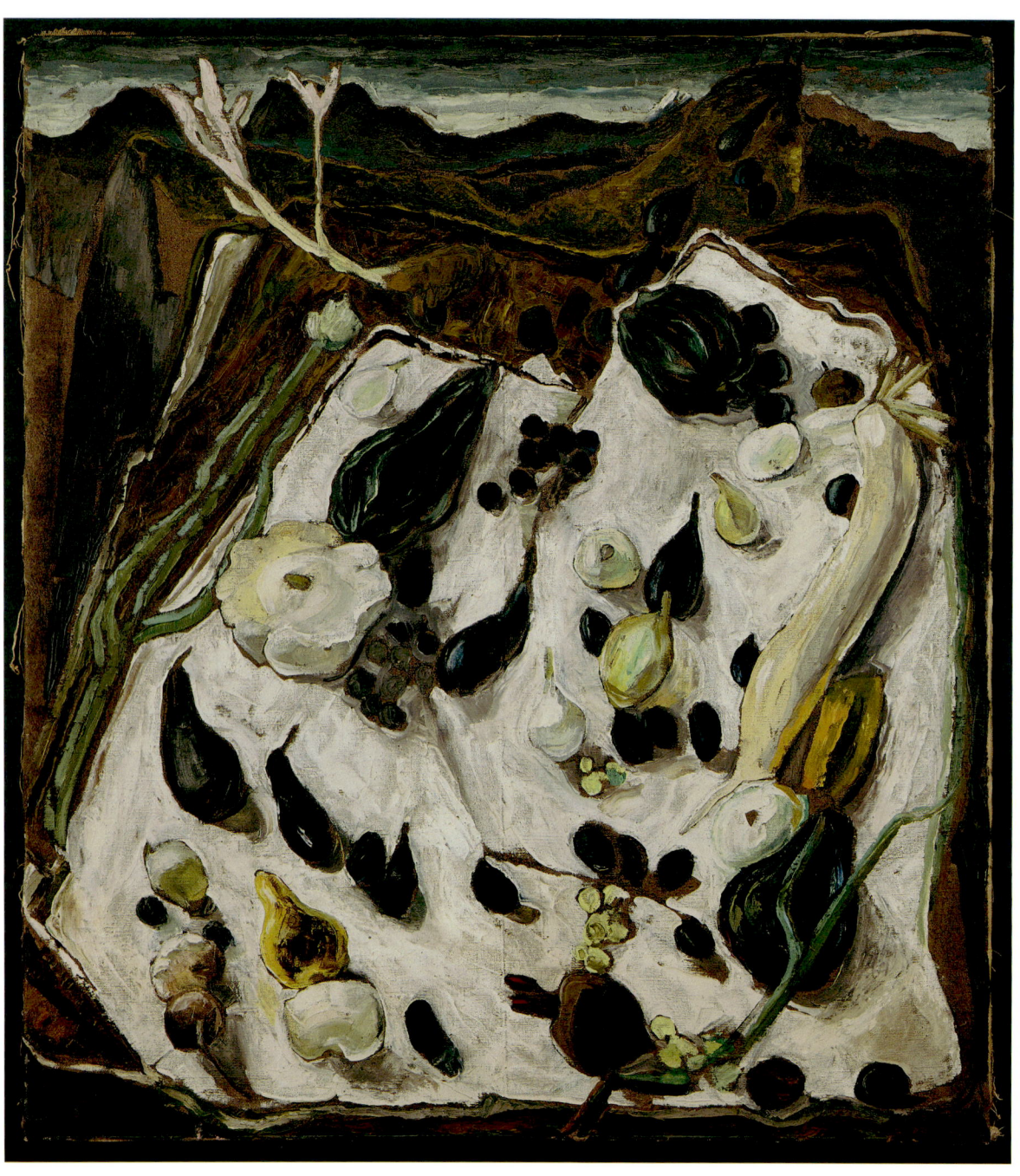

91 Morris Graves, *Summer Still Life*, ca. 1935, oil on burlap

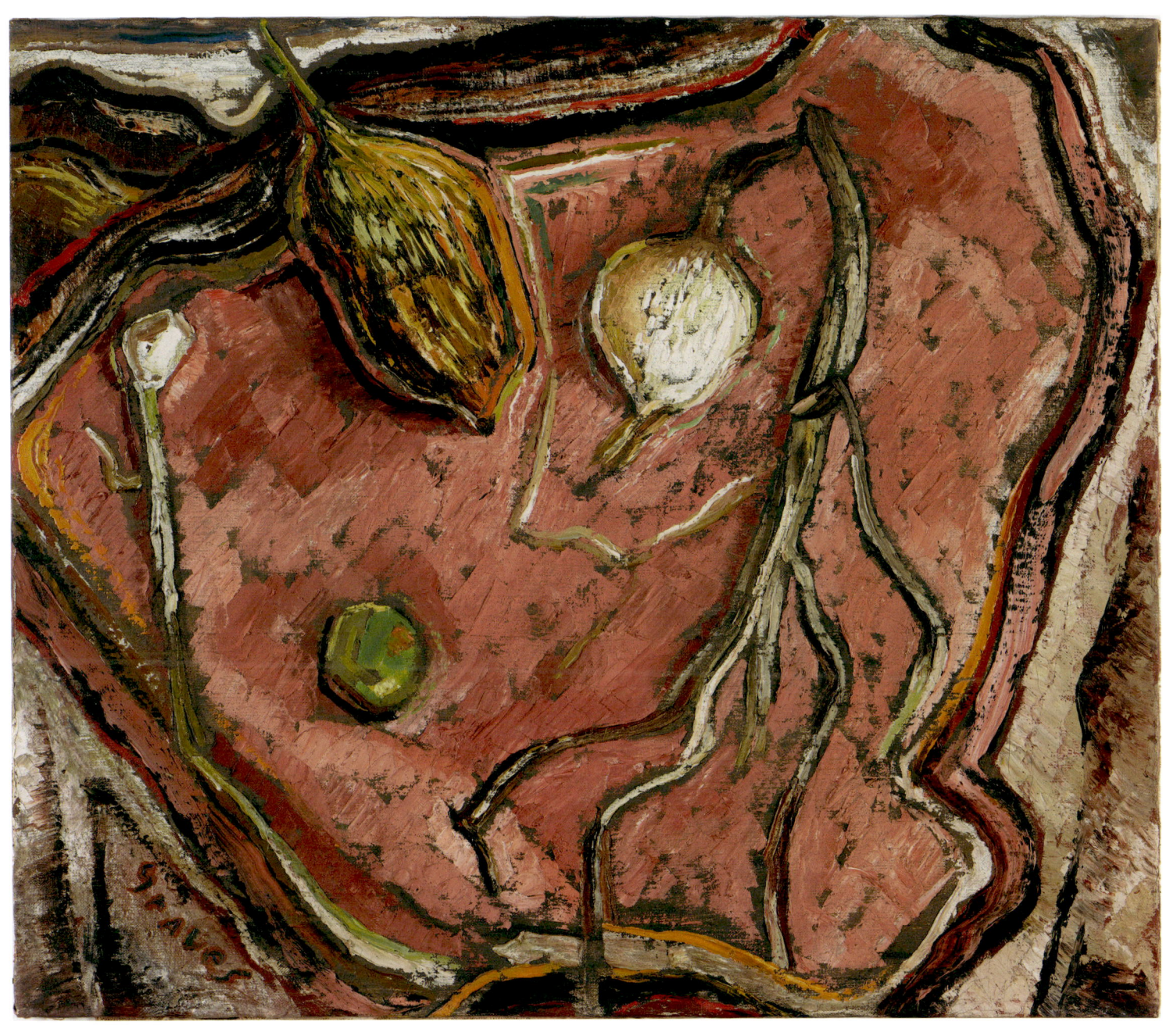

92 Morris Graves, *Still Life with Onions*, ca. 1937, oil on canvas

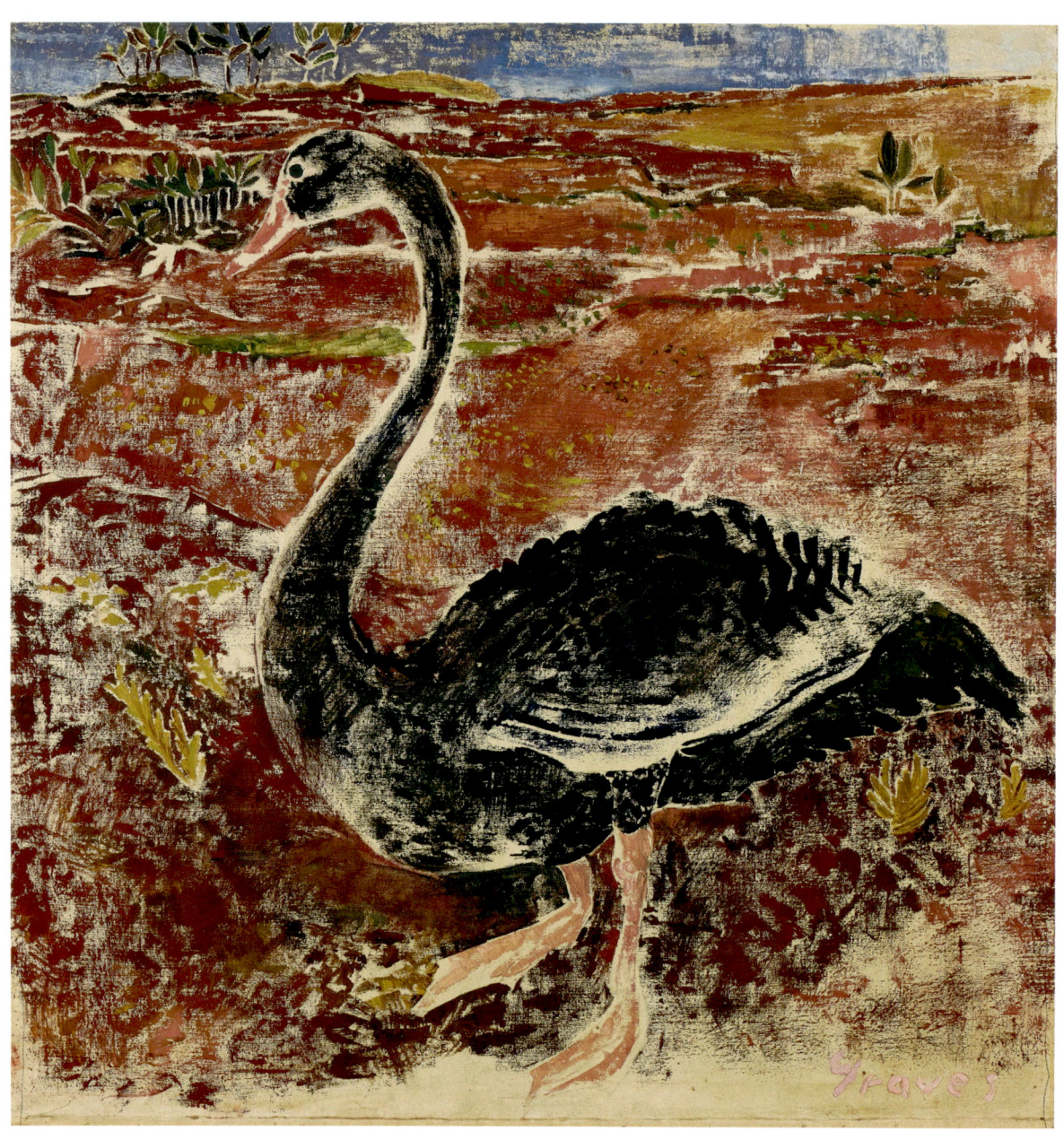

93 Morris Graves, *Moor Swan*, 1933, oil on canvas

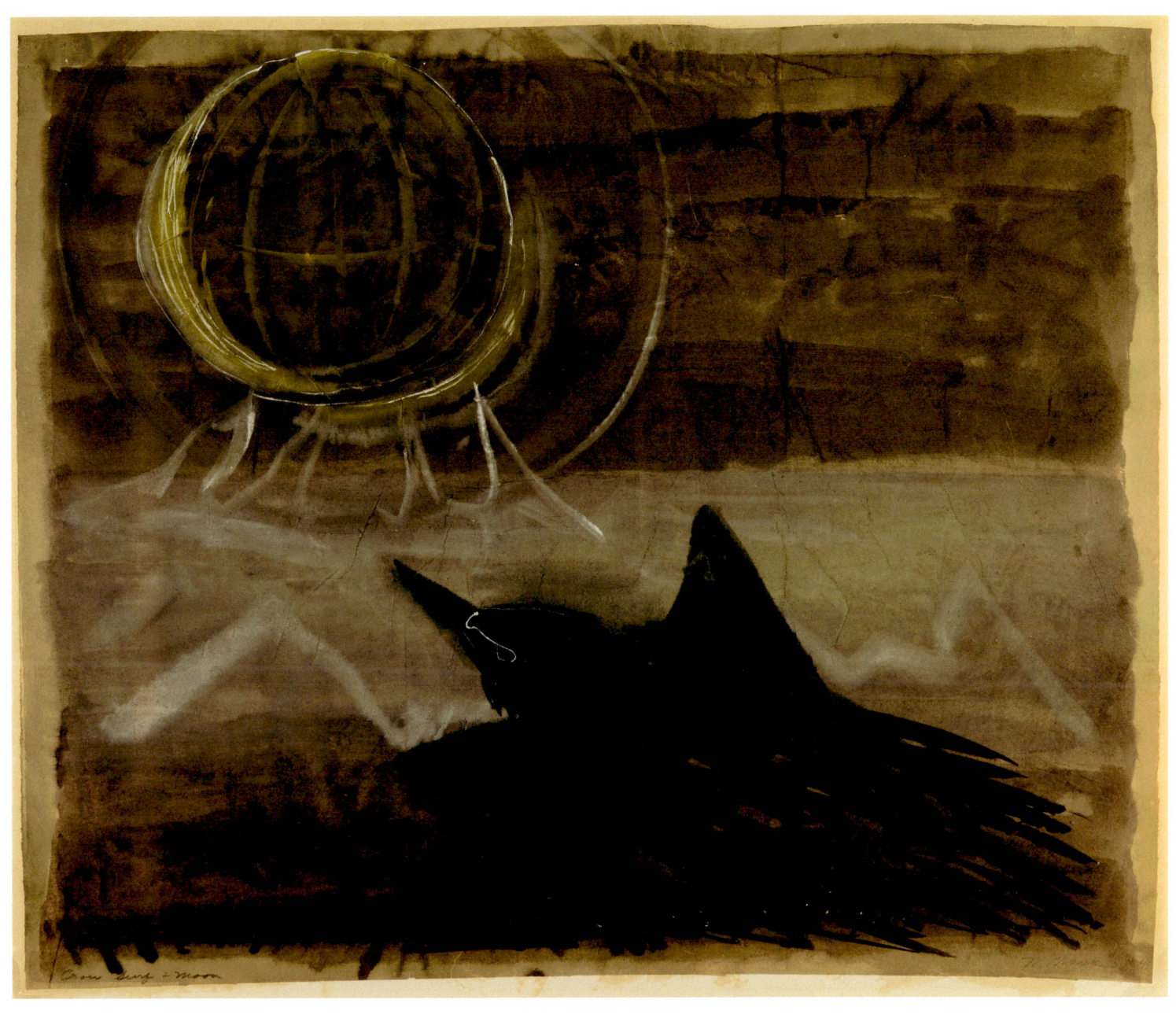

94 Morris Graves, *Crow, Surf and Moon*, 1943, ink and watercolor on Japanese paper, later mounted on rag board

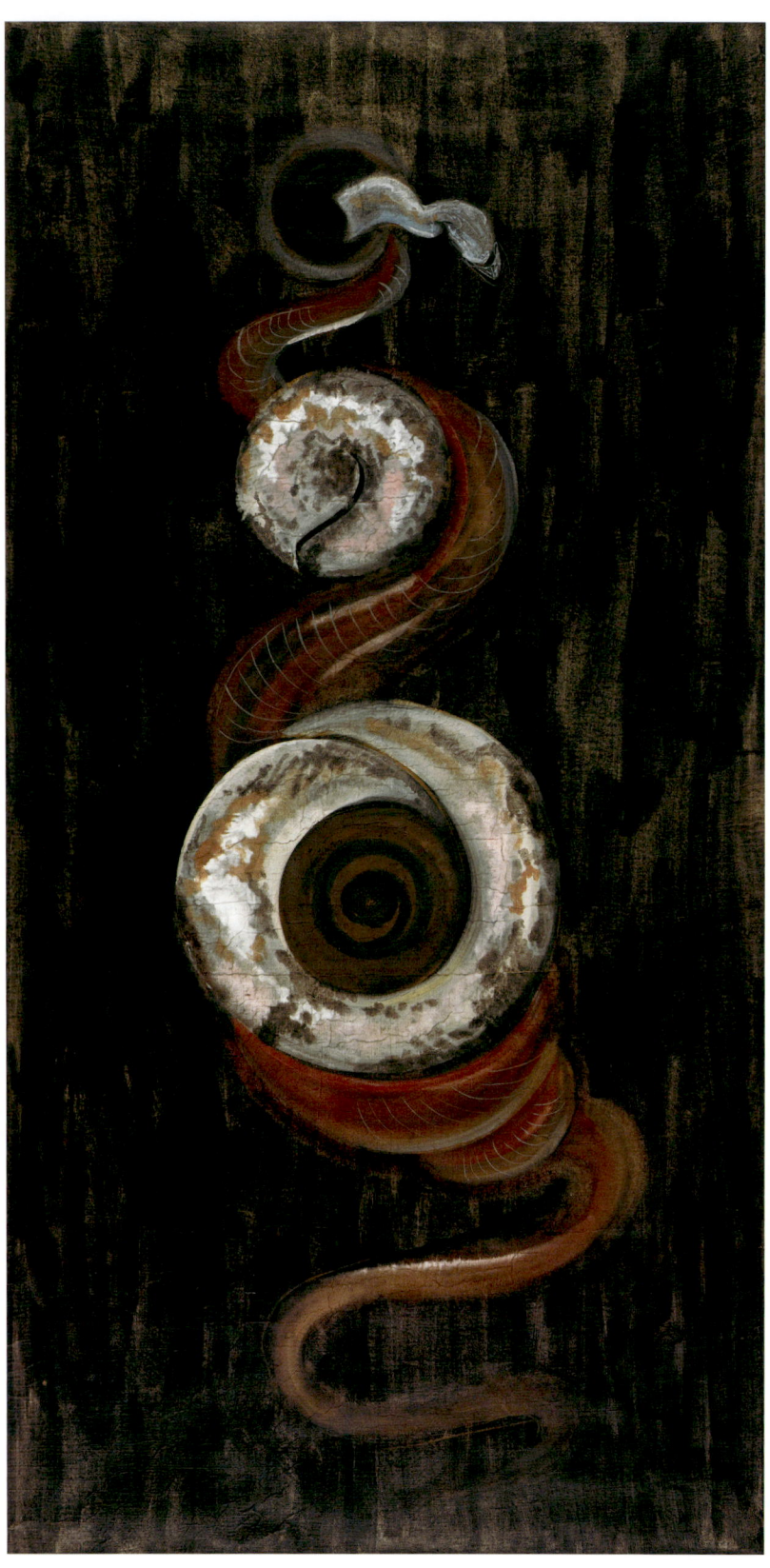

95 Morris Graves, *Night Sky No. 2*, 1944, ink and watercolor on toned Japanese paper

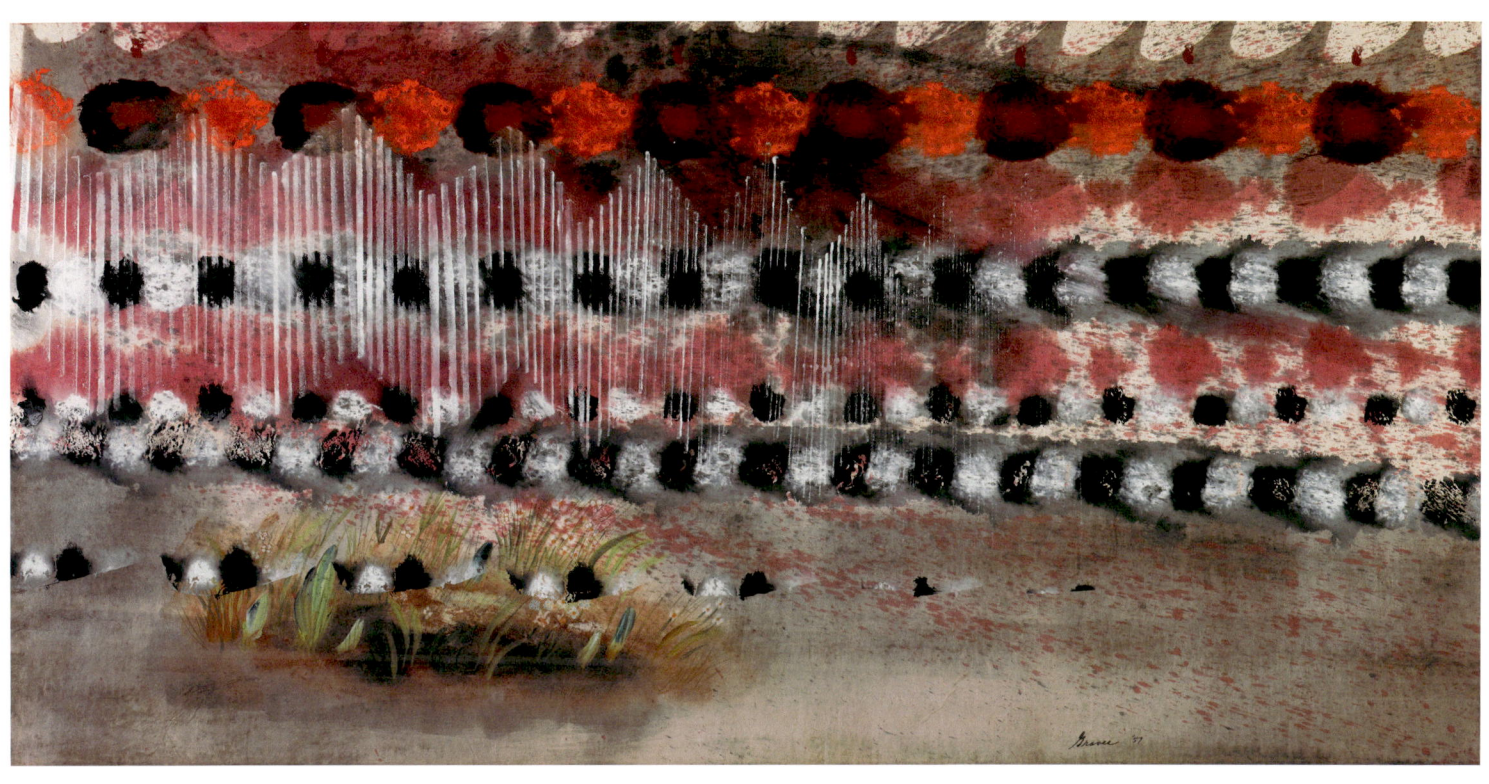

96 Morris Graves, *Spring with Machine Age Noise No. 3*, 1957, ink and watercolor on paper

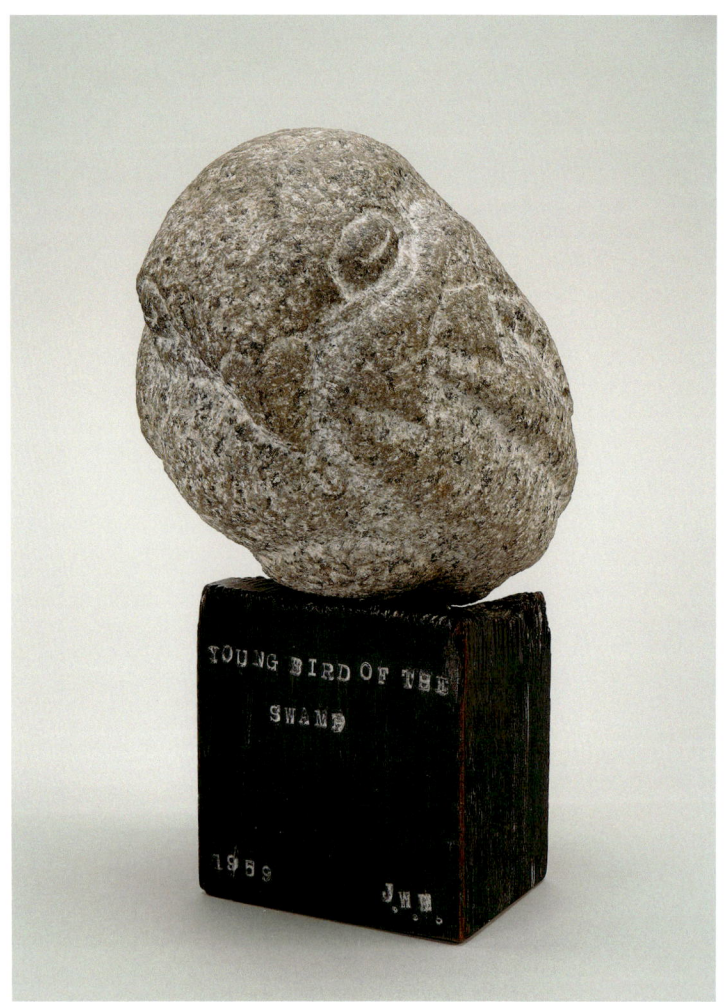

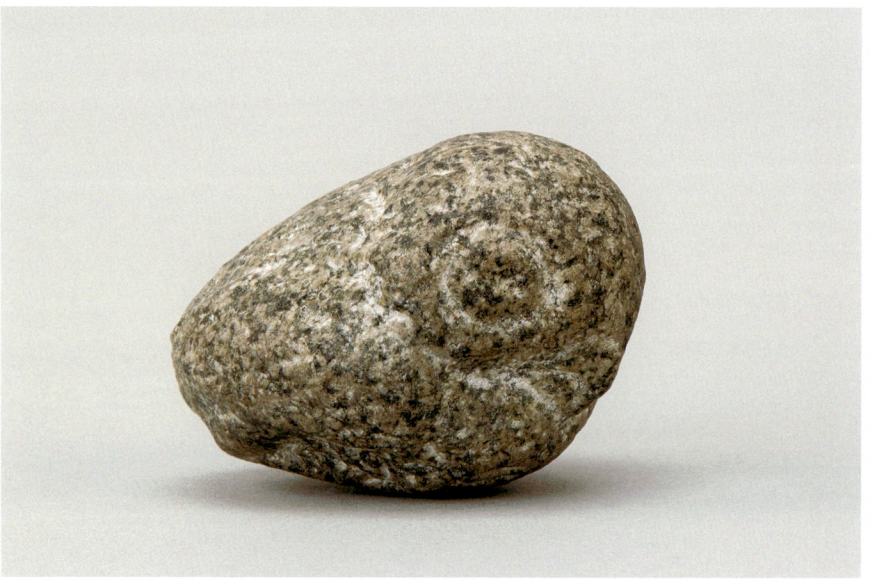

97 James Washington Jr., *Young Bird of the Swamp*, 1959, granite on wood mount

98 James Washington Jr., *Bird*, 1961, stone

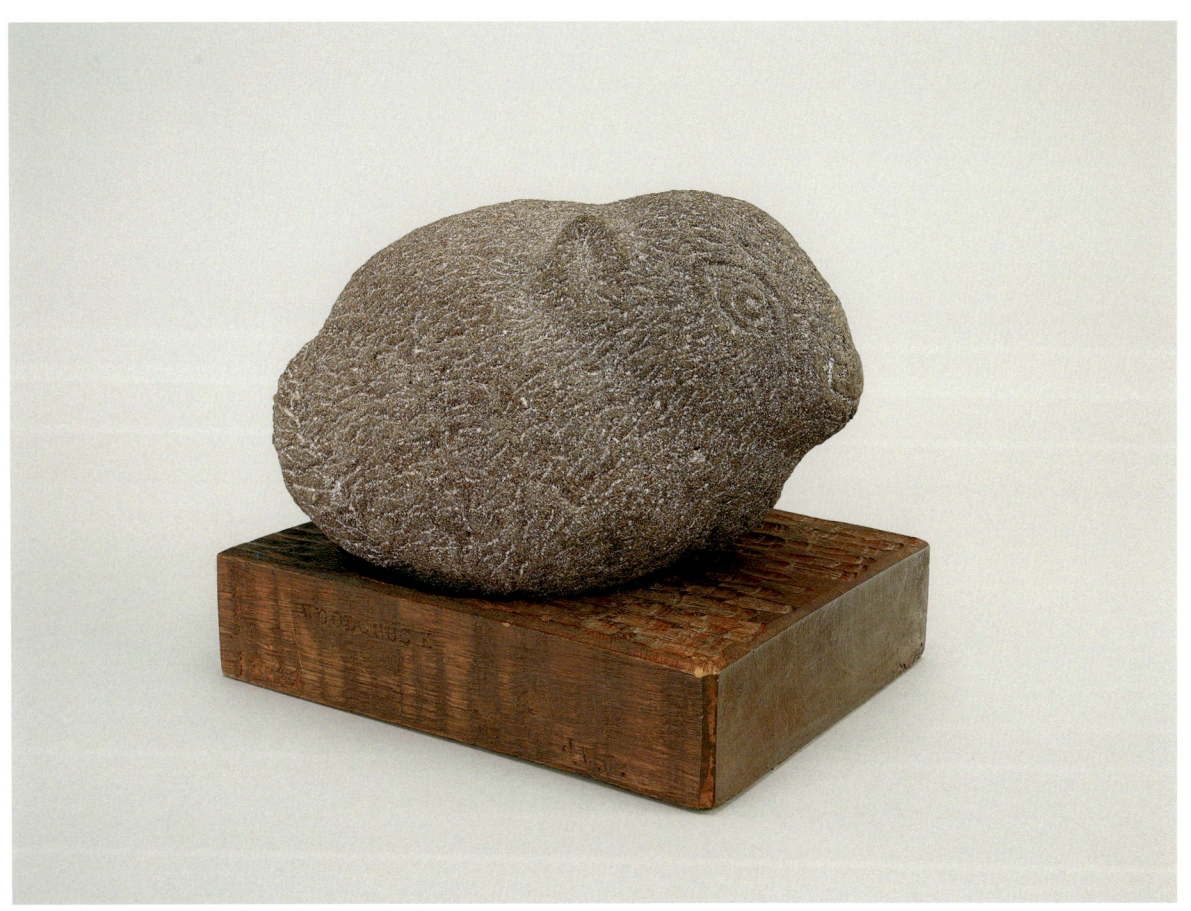

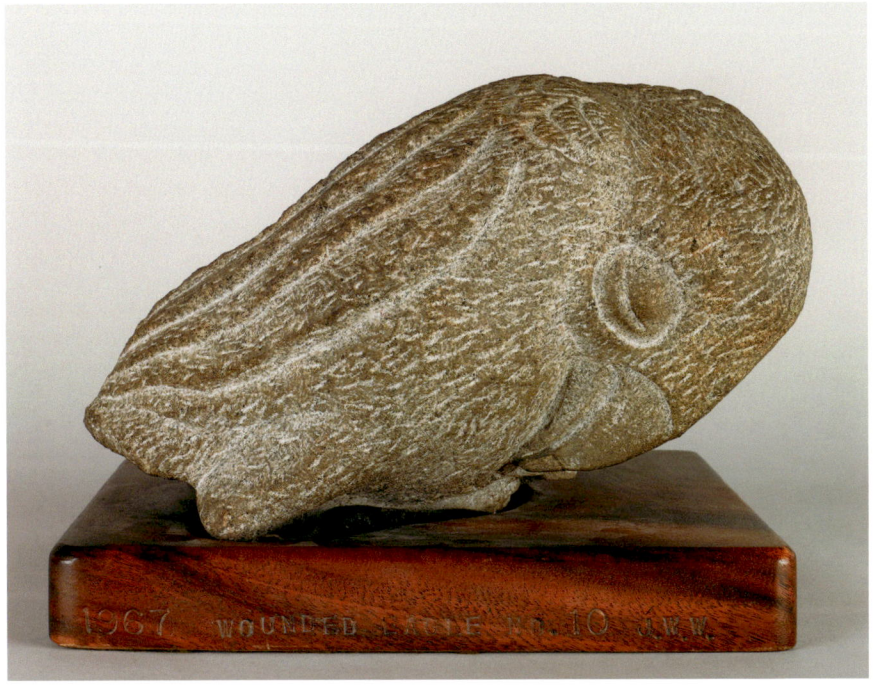

99 James Washington Jr., *The Woodchuck,*
1962, granite on wood mount

100 James Washington Jr., *Wounded Eagle
No. 10*, 1963, granite on wood mount

111

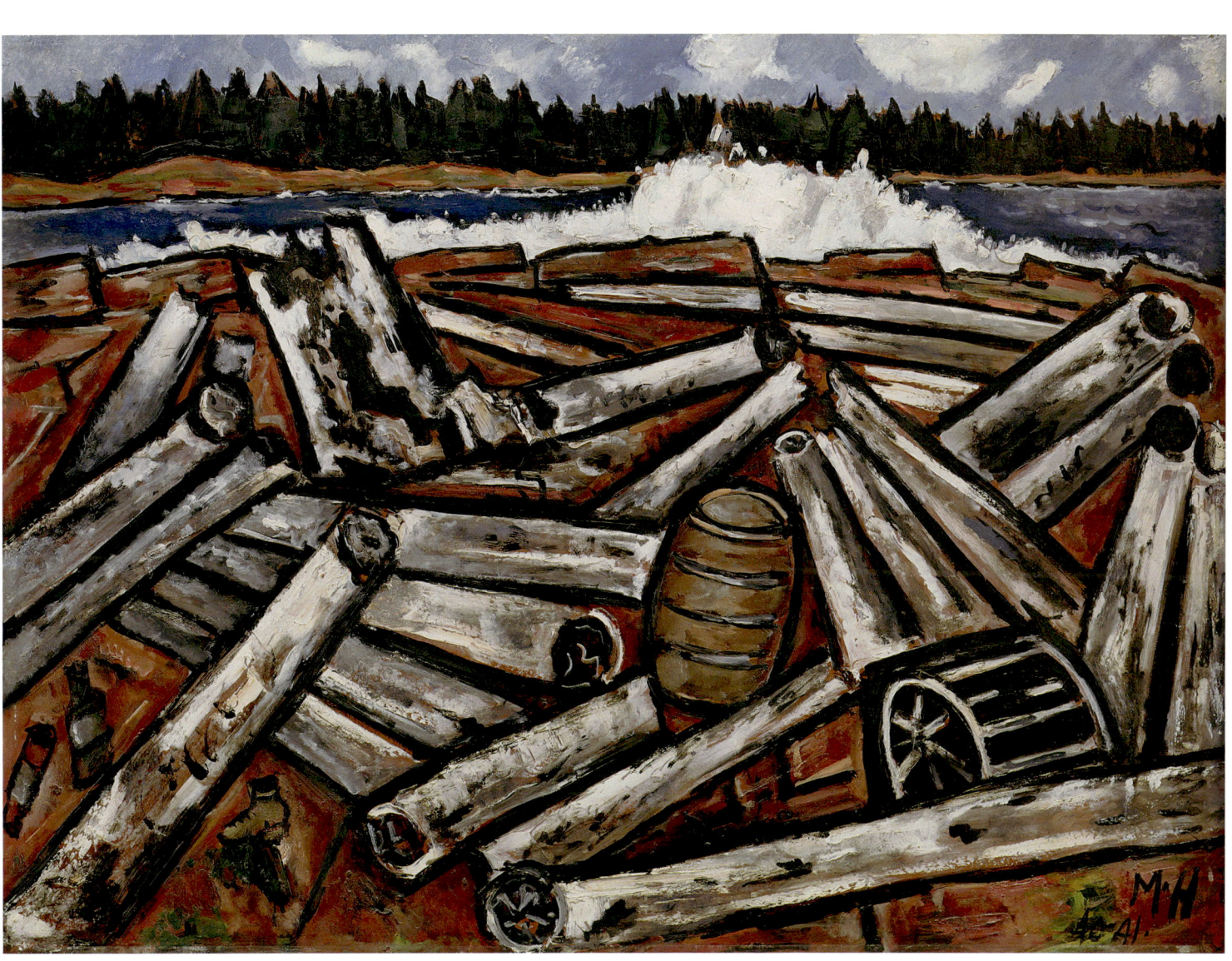

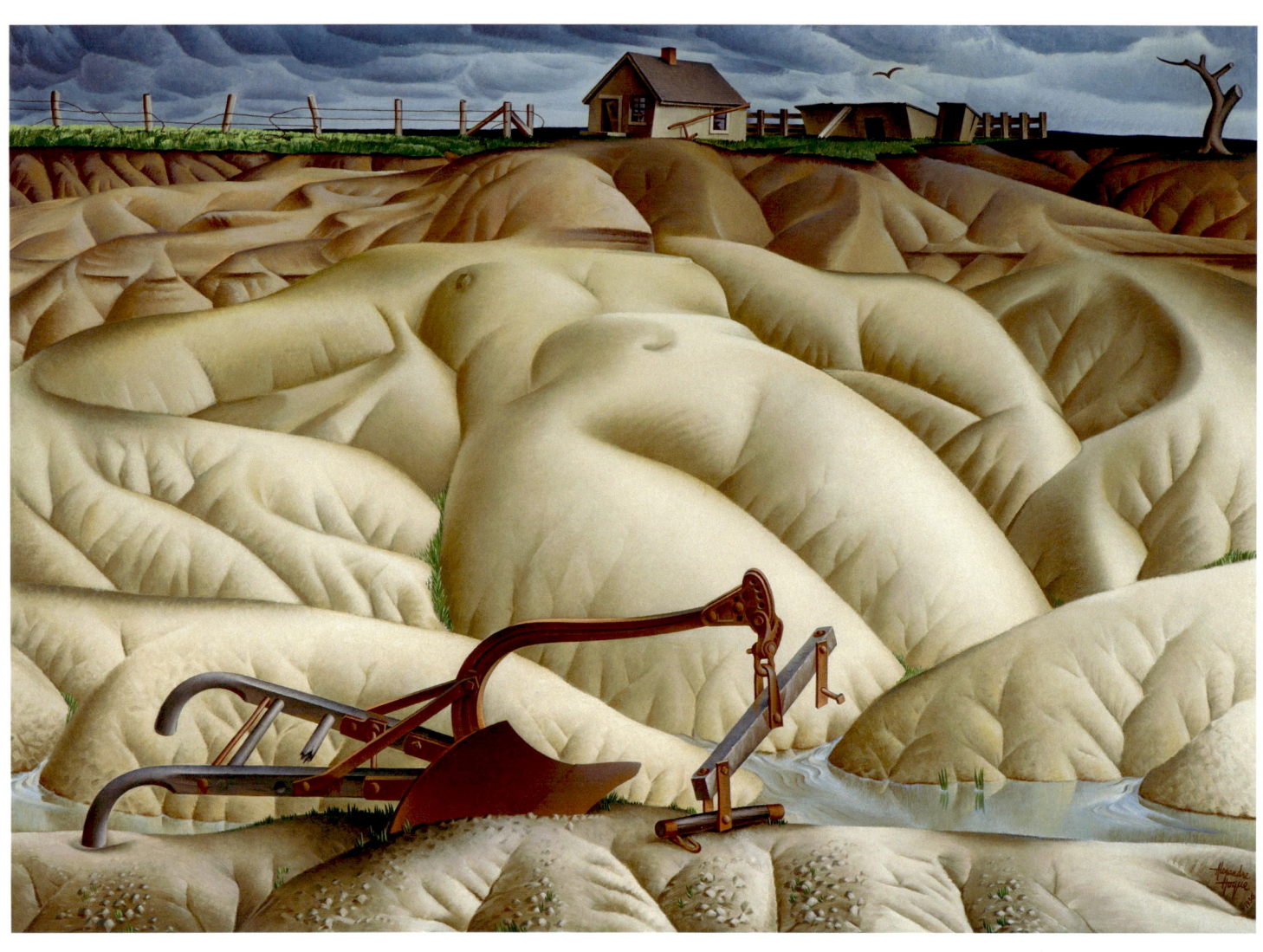

102 Alexandre Hogue, *Erosion No. 2—Mother Earth Laid Bare*, 1936, oil on canvas

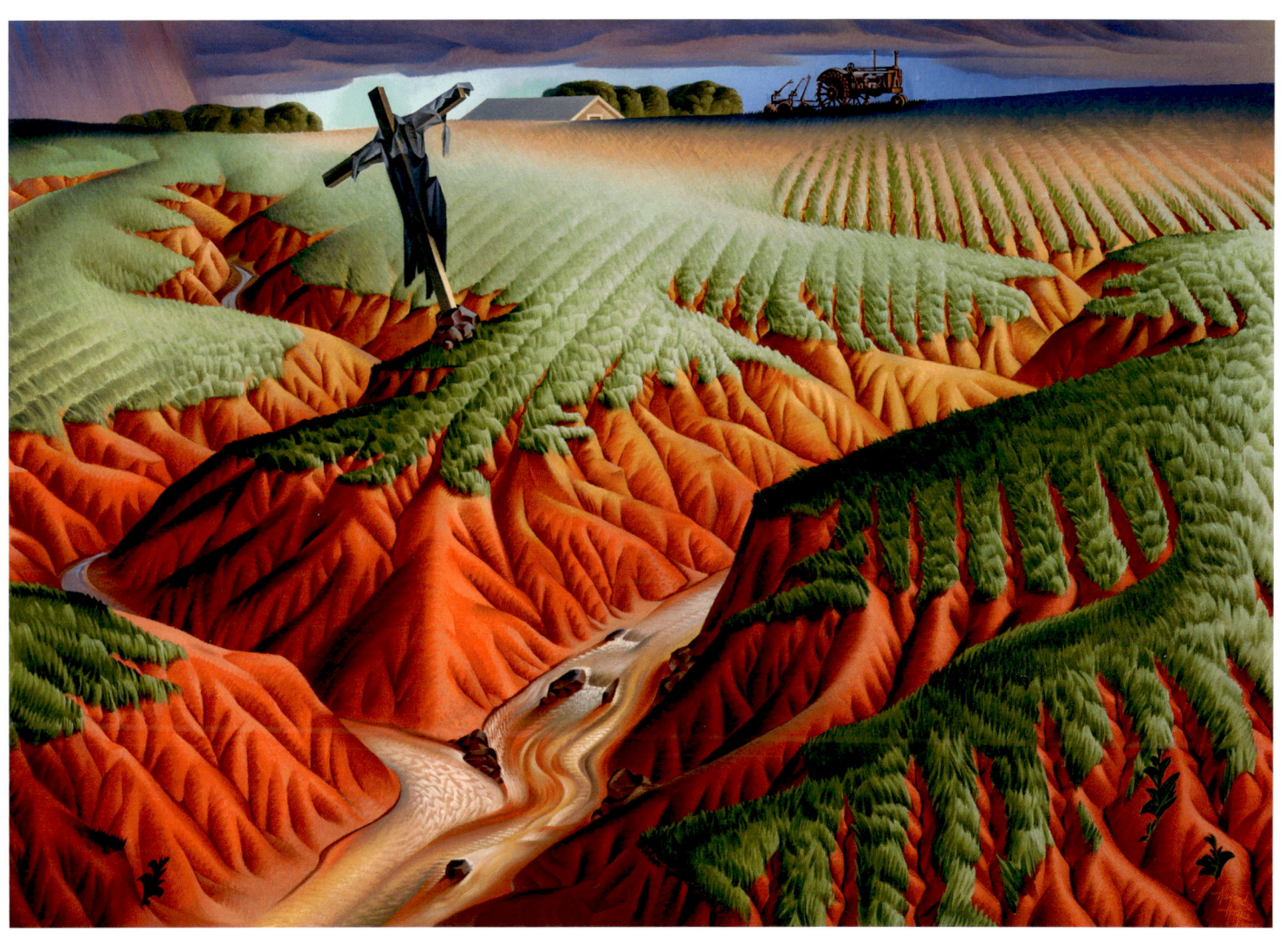

103　Alexandre Hogue, *Crucified Land*, 1939, oil on canvas

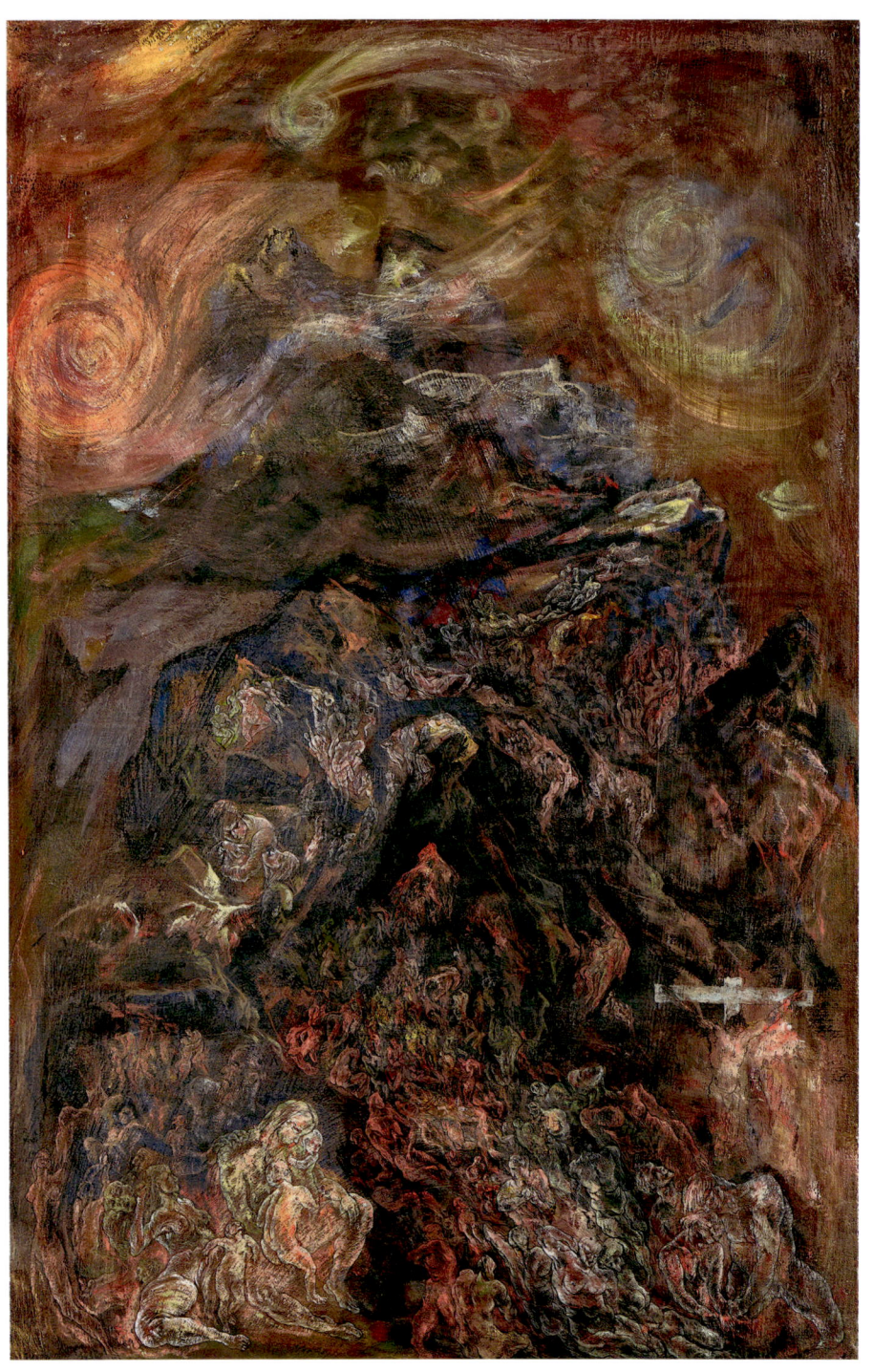

104 Kenneth Callahan, *The Mountain*, 1945–46, tempera on board

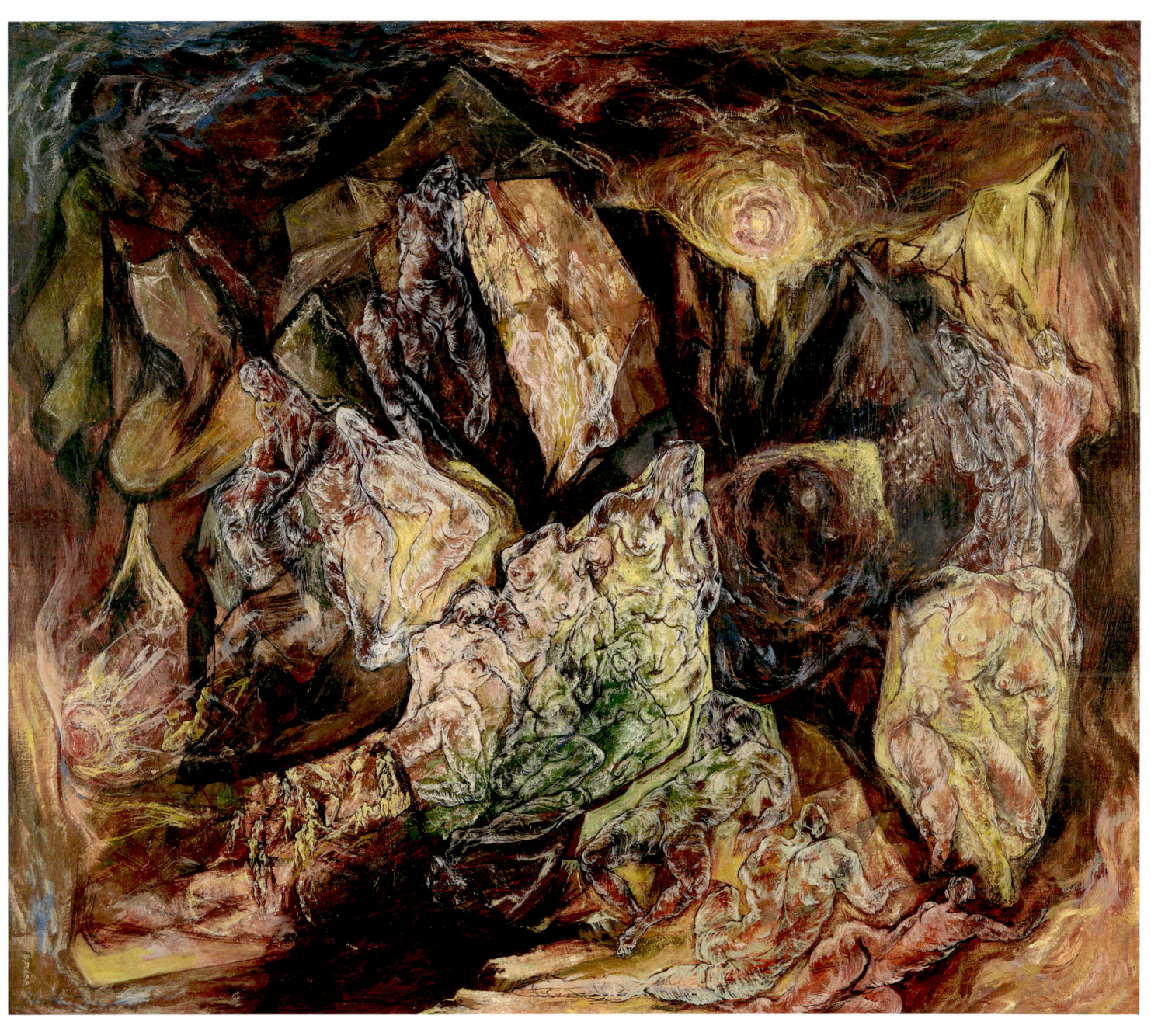

105 Kenneth Callahan, *Rocks and People*, ca. 1945–46, tempera on wood panel   117

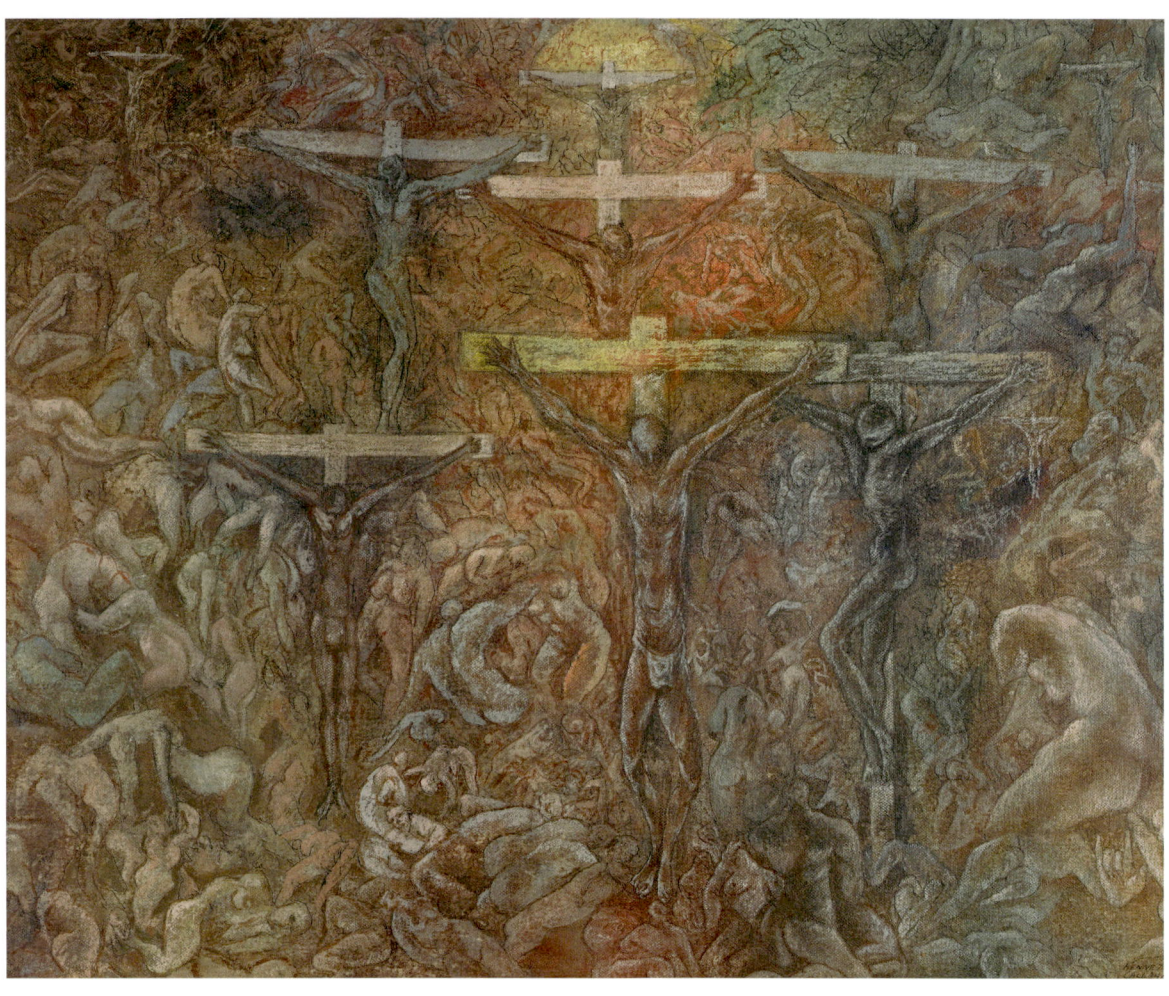

106 Kenneth Callahan, *First Seed into Last Harvest*, 1943, tempera on canvas

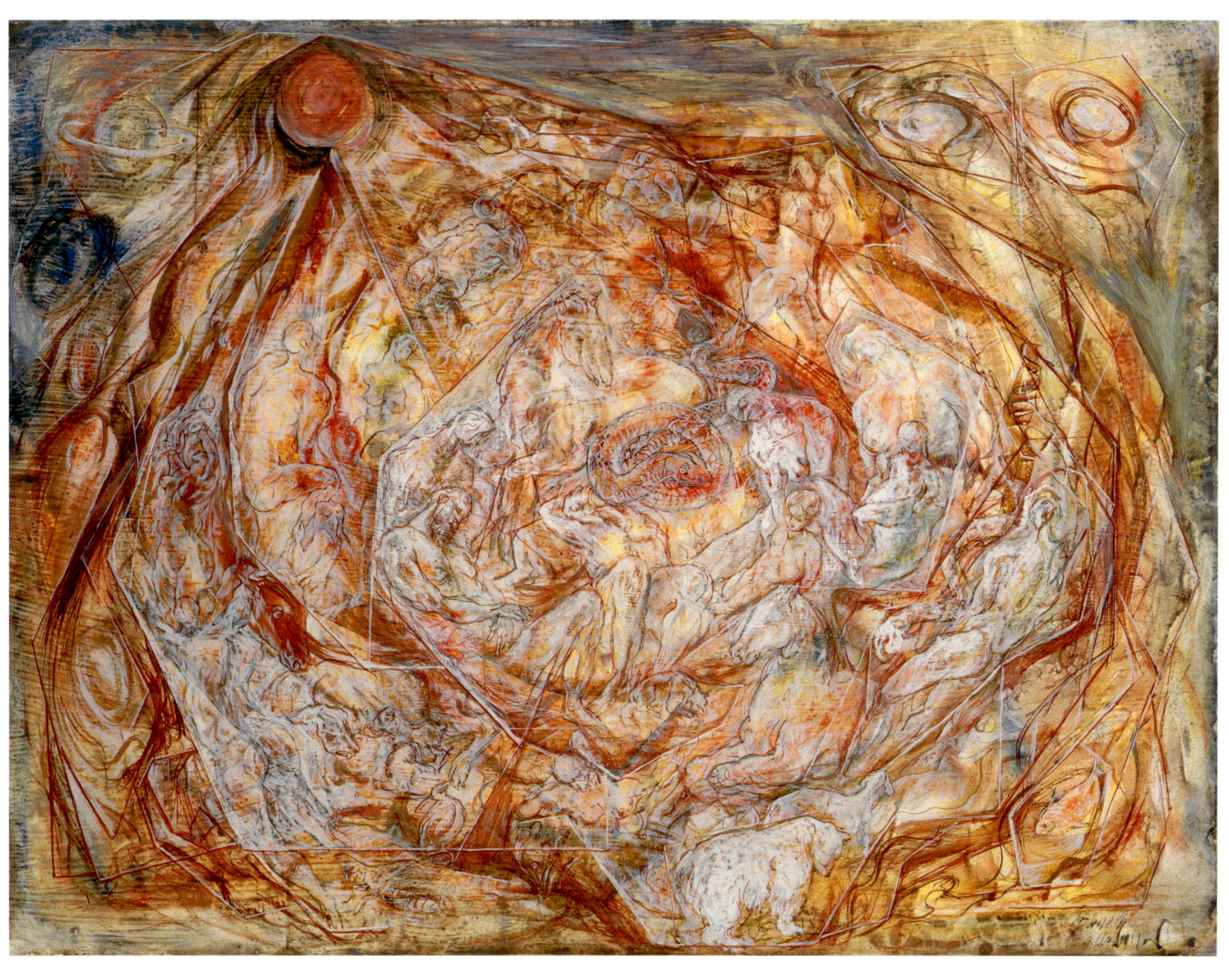

107 Kenneth Callahan, *The Seventh Day (The Seed Was in Itself)*, 1952–53, tempera on paperboard

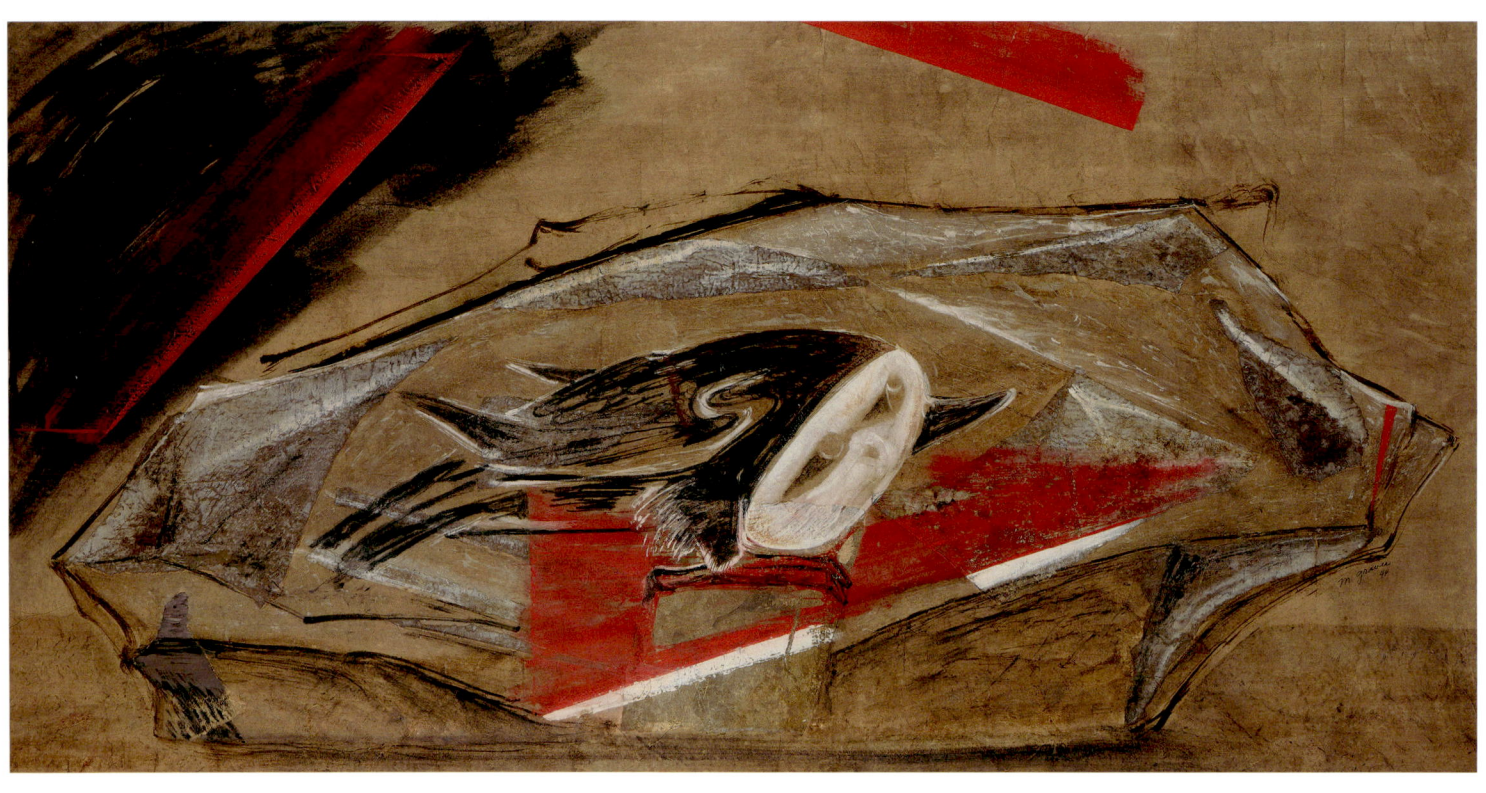

108 Morris Graves, *Bird Sensing the Essential Insanities*, 1944, tempera on paper
mounted on composition board

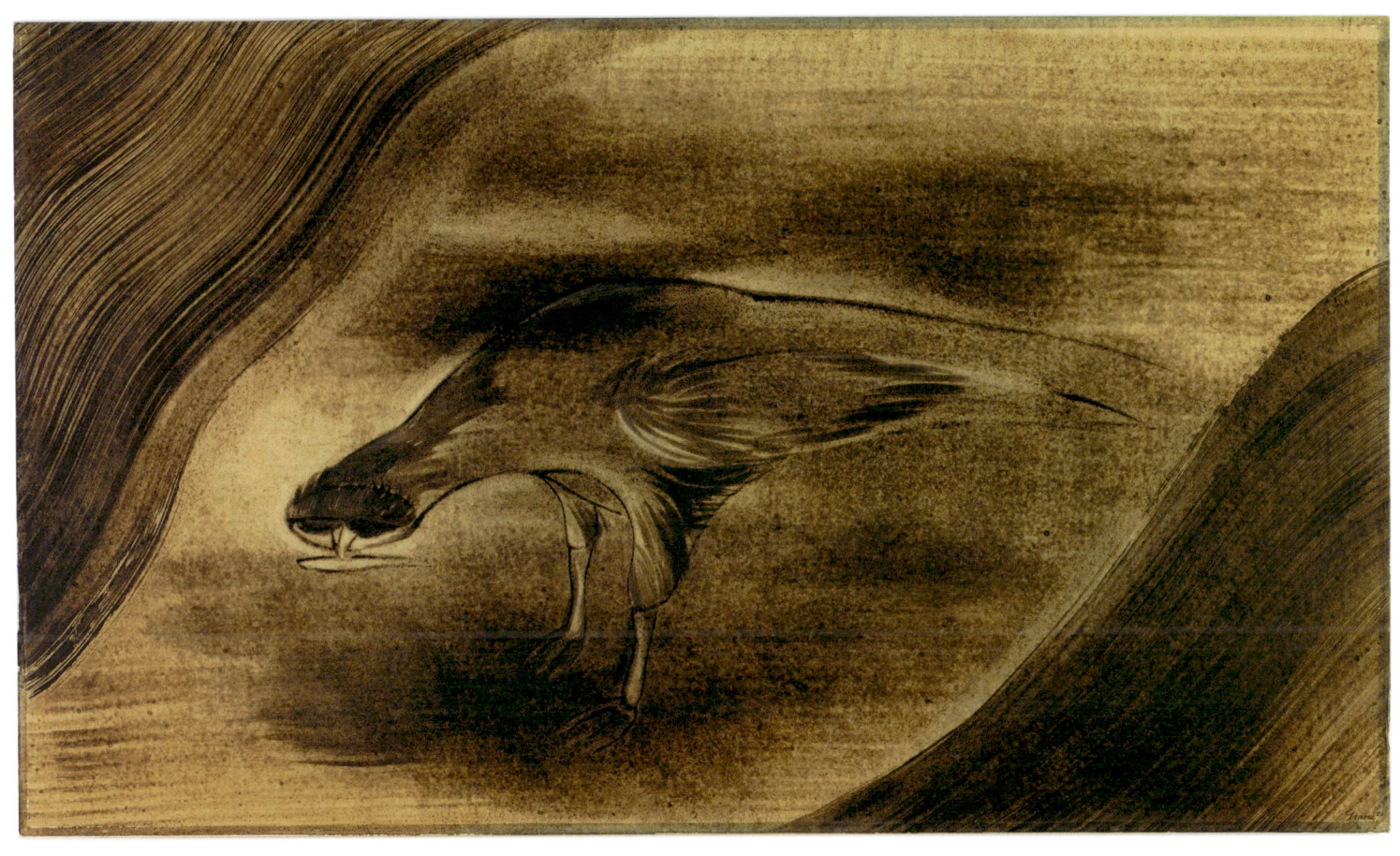

109 Morris Graves, *Each Time You Carry Me This Way*, 1953, ink and charcoal on paper mounted on heavyweight paper and fiber board

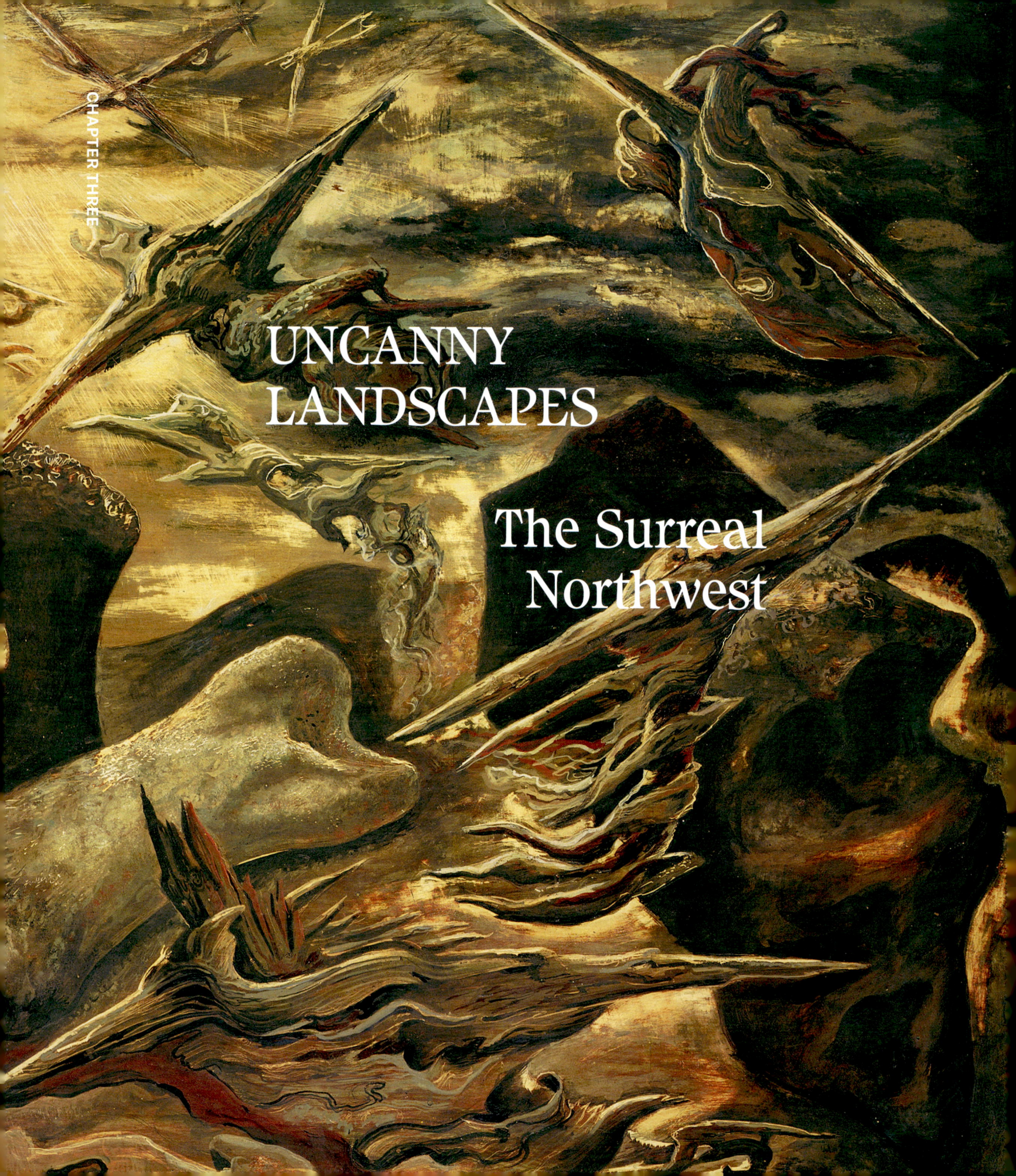

CHAPTER THREE

UNCANNY LANDSCAPES

The Surreal Northwest

Malcolm Roberts's *Drift No. 2* (1936, plate 117) introduces enigma into the Pacific Northwest landscape. All the usual elements are there: clouds, shoreline, even the driftwood remains of a felled tree, identifiable by its cleanly sliced trunk. Yet, alongside these recognizable markers of place, the hull of an improbable masted vessel—a pink claw-footed bathtub impaled by a weather vane—has run aground against the tree trunk in a parody of maritime disaster, while a second ruined vessel, a cracked pitcher, rests incongruously on the beach nearby. "Surrealism has raised its serene and crisply delightful head in [Roberts's] paintings," wrote fellow artist Kenneth Callahan.[1] Indeed, Roberts's illusionistic yet confounding Northwest scene is closer to the contemporaneous dreamscapes of Salvador Dalí than to the social realism and ecocriticism that then characterized much of the region's Modernist artworks. Recognized in his time as the "Seattle Surrealist," Roberts brought his training at the Art Institute of Chicago and his interest in the European Surrealists Dalí and, especially, Giorgio de Chirico to bear on unsettling scenes that, like *Drift No. 2*, staged unexpected objects in familiar Northwest settings.[2] The adaptation of Surrealism offered Roberts, as well as other Puget Sound artists, a novel mode of perceiving the local landscape and a way of transcending social realism in favor of intuition, introspection, and self-actualization.

Surrealism's Origins

Surrealism's journey to the Pacific Northwest followed a complex trajectory that originates in Paris in the aftermath of World War I. There, a group of artists and poets, led by André Breton and including Louis Aragon, Robert Desnos, Paul Éluard, Benjamin Péret, and Philippe Soupault, gathered in search of alternatives to the rationalism that they deemed responsible for the horror and devastation of mechanized warfare. Inspired by psychoanalysis—and the theories of Sigmund Freud, in particular—they embraced a wholesale exploration of the subconscious as an unrestricted and individualized font of creativity, inspiration, and existence. They met regularly to explore, experiment with, and expand upon the possibilities of this pure psychic automatism, looking to dreams and states of semi-wakefulness for examples of unpremeditated imagery and ideas, relinquishing narrative control through automatic writing, cultivating the hilarity and spontaneity of gameplay, and welcoming the irrational as the poetic antithesis to logic. In 1924, Surrealism made its public debut with the *Manifesto of Surrealism*, authored by Breton, who offered the following definition:

> SURREALISM, *n*. Psychic automatism in its pure state, by which one proposes to express—verbally, by means of the written word, or in any other manner—the actual functioning of thought. Dictated by thought, in the absence of any control exercised

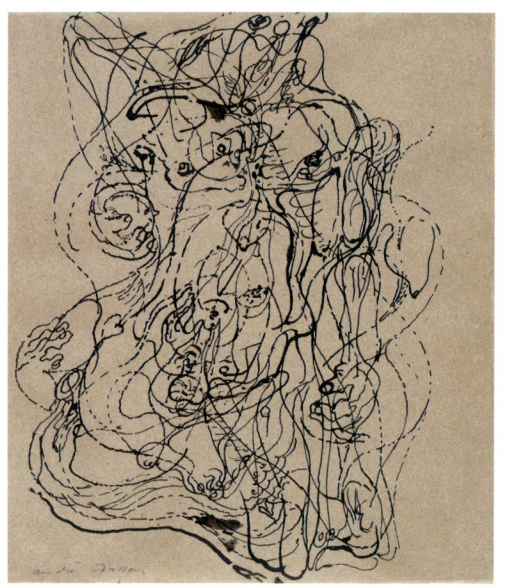

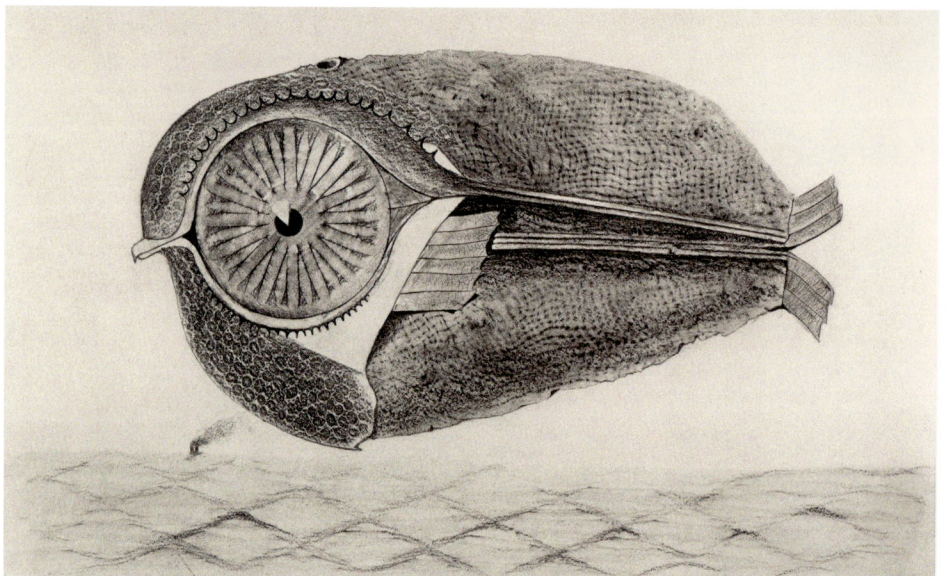

by reason, exempt from any aesthetic or moral concern.[3]

While initially focused on literature, Surrealism abounded with possibilities for the visual arts, and many artists advanced their work through various forms of psychic automatism. André Masson, for example, adapted automatic writing to the practice of drawing, releasing his mind from premeditated thought and allowing his pen to meander spontaneously over paper until intuition took over and fragments of images emerged (fig. 7). Max Ernst sourced imagery through improvised actions, making rubbings from textured surfaces—wood grain, leaves, and other objects (fig. 8)—and reading shapes into the patterns left behind, a practice he called "frottage," or pressing paper or canvas to wet pigment and using the resulting marks as the basis for formal configurations, a process known as "decalcomania." Drawings of cadavres exquises (exquisite corpses) were unmediated collaborations between several Surrealists, each adding to a shared composition without knowing what the others had contributed (fig. 9). The resulting juxtapositions of bizarre forms and disparate styles were intentionally unsettling and part of a

larger project to free the mind both to cultivate and to accept novel, often contradictory, and always uncanny associations. From there, Surrealism became performative, spilling over into daily life to encompass anything beyond the margins of rationalism: chance encounters, unexpected configurations, metamorphosis, growth, and transformation. Many Surrealists enacted these surprising associations through the practice of collage, while others—such as Dalí, Yves Tanguy (plate 114), and, before them, de Chirico (plate 112)—configured disparate objects and figures in illogical, painterly realms. In 1929, Breton issued a second *Manifesto of Surrealism*, reiterating the importance of psychic automatism, which by then had been joined by a form of Surrealist art that was veristic, unsettling, and based on the uneasy reconciliation of opposites.[4]

Surrealism eventually spread internationally, taking hold in Brussels, Copenhagen, Prague, London, and Tenerife, as well as North and South America. While Breton welcomed these transnational migrations as evidence of a cohesive global Surrealism, in reality the movement shifted to align with each of its geographic centers, becoming a rhizomatic network of unique Surrealisms varyingly connected to the original group.[5] In the United

Fig. 7. André Masson (French, 1896–1987), *Automatic Drawing*, 1924, ink on paper, 9¼ × 8⅛ in. Museum of Modern Art, New York, Given anonymously, 873.1978

Fig. 8. Max Ernst (German, 1891–1976), *The Fugitive* (*L'Évadé*) from *Natural History* (*Histoire Naturelle*), ca. 1925, published 1926, one from a portfolio of 34 collotypes after frottage, image: 10⅛ × 16⅝ in., sheet 12¾ × 19⅝ in. Museum of Modern Art, New York, Gift of James Thrall Soby, 29.1958.30

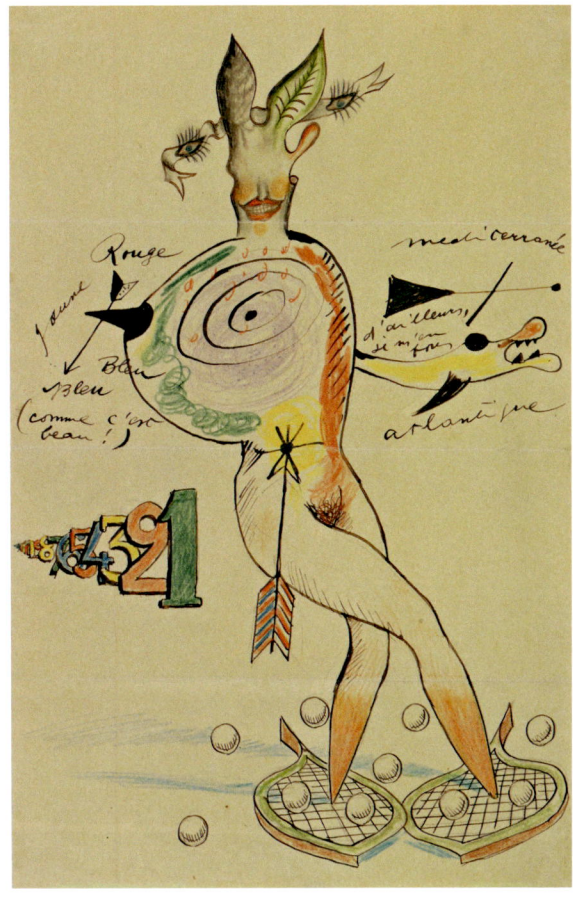

States, Surrealism debuted with the 1931 exhibition *Newer Super-Realism* at the Wadsworth Atheneum in Hartford, Connecticut, which included works by Ernst, de Chirico, Masson, and Joan Miró, as well as Dalí's *The Persistence of Memory* (1931, acquired by the Museum of Modern Art, New York, in 1934), a miniature landscape populated by melting and decaying timepieces. The following year, *Surrealism: Paintings, Drawings, and Photographs* opened at the Julien Levy Gallery in New York, featuring the work of Pablo Picasso, Ernst, Joseph Cornell, and Marcel Duchamp, as well as an encore showing of *The Persistence of Memory* and a screening of Dalí and Luis Buñuel's 1929 film *Un Chien Andalou*. Levy continued to establish Surrealism's presence in the United States, regularly showing the work of Ernst, René Magritte, and especially Dalí. In 1936, the Museum of Modern Art in New York further

bolstered the movement's North American presence when then-director Alfred Barr organized the blockbuster exhibition *Fantastic Art, Dada, Surrealism*, which positioned Surrealism and its antecedent, Dada, as intuitive and expressive alternatives to Cubism and the other geometric modes then favored in American abstraction. Between 1939 and 1941, many European Surrealists—including Breton, Ernst, Masson, Roberto Matta, Kurt Seligmann, and Tanguy—immigrated to the United States to escape the rise of totalitarianism in Europe, expanding Surrealism's presence on this side of the Atlantic. Led by Breton, they launched the landmark *First Papers of Surrealism* at the Whitelaw Reid Mansion in New York in 1942, an exhibition famously dominated by Duchamp's "mile of string," a web of twine that crisscrossed the gallery, obscuring the artworks on view.

Dalí was Surrealism's most notorious émigré in the United States. His reputation continued to grow when *The Persistence of Memory* and *Shades of Night Descending* (1931, plate 110) appeared at the Art Institute of Chicago in conjunction with the 1933 Chicago World's Fair; meanwhile, Levy regularly exhibited Dalí's work in New York and assiduously promoted his persona.[6] By the time Dalí actually visited the United States, in 1934, to attend one of his frequent solo exhibitions at the Julien Levy Gallery, he was already a media sensation.[7] In 1936, his visage appeared on the cover of *Time*, which proclaimed that "Surrealism would never have attracted its present attention in the U.S. were it not for a handsome thirty-two-year-old Catalan with a soft voice and a clipped cinema actor's mustache, Salvador Dalí."[8] His forays into popular culture and performance with the over-the-top "Dream of Venus" pavilion for the 1939 New York World's Fair and the orgiastic ballet *Bacchanale* that same year made him synonymous with Surrealism in the United States.[9] By this time, Dalí had taken up residence in New York, where he continued to regale the general public and art world alike with his controversial theatricality and the psychological shock value of his paintings—especially the fascinating double images in works such as *Bust of Voltaire* (1941, plate 111), products of his "paranoiac critical method," a deliberate state of disorientation that invited connections between unrelated forms and ideas.

Surrealism and American Art

Dalí's illusions, along with de Chirico's metaphysical scenes and Tanguy's incongruous spaces, modeled Surrealism for American artists active in the 1930s, many of whom were working in realistic pictorial modes that readily incorporated the uncanny. Indeed, it was not Breton's psychic automatism but a more illusionistic form of Surrealism that initially found its way into American art. Surrealism became established in the United States neither cohesively nor definitively but, instead, in the work of a diffuse assortment of artists who were open to embracing the illogical.[10] Painters such as O. Louis Guglielmi adapted Surrealist scenarios to Depression-era social realism, and in works such as the disquieting *Mental Geography* (fig. 10)—a portent of domestic invasion painted in protest against the Spanish Civil War—they repurposed the New Deal's preferred painterly mode into an instrument of dissent known as Social Surrealism.[11] Other artists took a Surrealist approach to a form of magic realism and—as in works such as Peter Blume's *The Rock* (ca. 1944–48, plate 115), a mysterious tableau of excavation, construction, and ultimately destruction—conjured the marvelous through shifts in scale, extreme illusionism, and puzzling adjacencies.[12]

Blume's *Light of the World* (1932, plate 116) offered Puget Sound artists and audiences an early and direct experience with Surrealism when it was exhibited at the Seattle Art Museum (SAM) in 1935. For the most part, Northwest artists knew of Surrealism through exhibition catalogues and art periodicals, media coverage (particularly around Dalí), and travel, but this exquisitely rendered yet unsettling painting gave them something to think about. In the center of the composition, a tower rises up in a public square reminiscent of the town of Sherman, Connecticut, where the artist lived. Composed of architectural fragments and the pivot mechanism used to erect Cleopatra's Needle in New York's Central Park, this strange contrivance is capped by a polychrome orb illuminated by two incandescent lightbulbs.[13] Four ordinary people look on in varying states of curiosity, shock, and horror. To the left of this obtuse tableau is a Gothic cathedral, and to the right is a brick structure in the North American vernacular, providing an incongruous setting for what seems to be an extraordinary event whose meaning is never disclosed. Rendered in painstaking yet unresolved detail, Blume's painting frustrated its Pacific Northwest audience. Callahan noted that, while *Light of the World* was "literally painted with minute care and precision [where] each countless separate detail tells its own little story," it was ultimately "a composite illustration of countless little stories, but the whole having no major meaning."[14] For him, Blume's—and Surrealism's—importance lay in technical skill, not poetic content:

> In looking at the painting one feels the balance of a well-organized composition, and realizes there is beautiful color and fine space feeling. It is in the realization of the last quality I think that the surrealists have their greatest claim to importance. But when one has enjoyed these sensations and the temporary intrigue aroused by the fact that the objects are unrelated, one's interest starts to wander, becoming lost in the little stories told in different parts of the painting.[15]

Nevertheless, with *Light of the World*, Surrealism had officially arrived in the Puget Sound, and Callahan, despite his bewilderment at the painting's disconnects and dead ends, took it upon himself to explain the broader movement to local audiences. His voice carried considerable weight. In addition to being

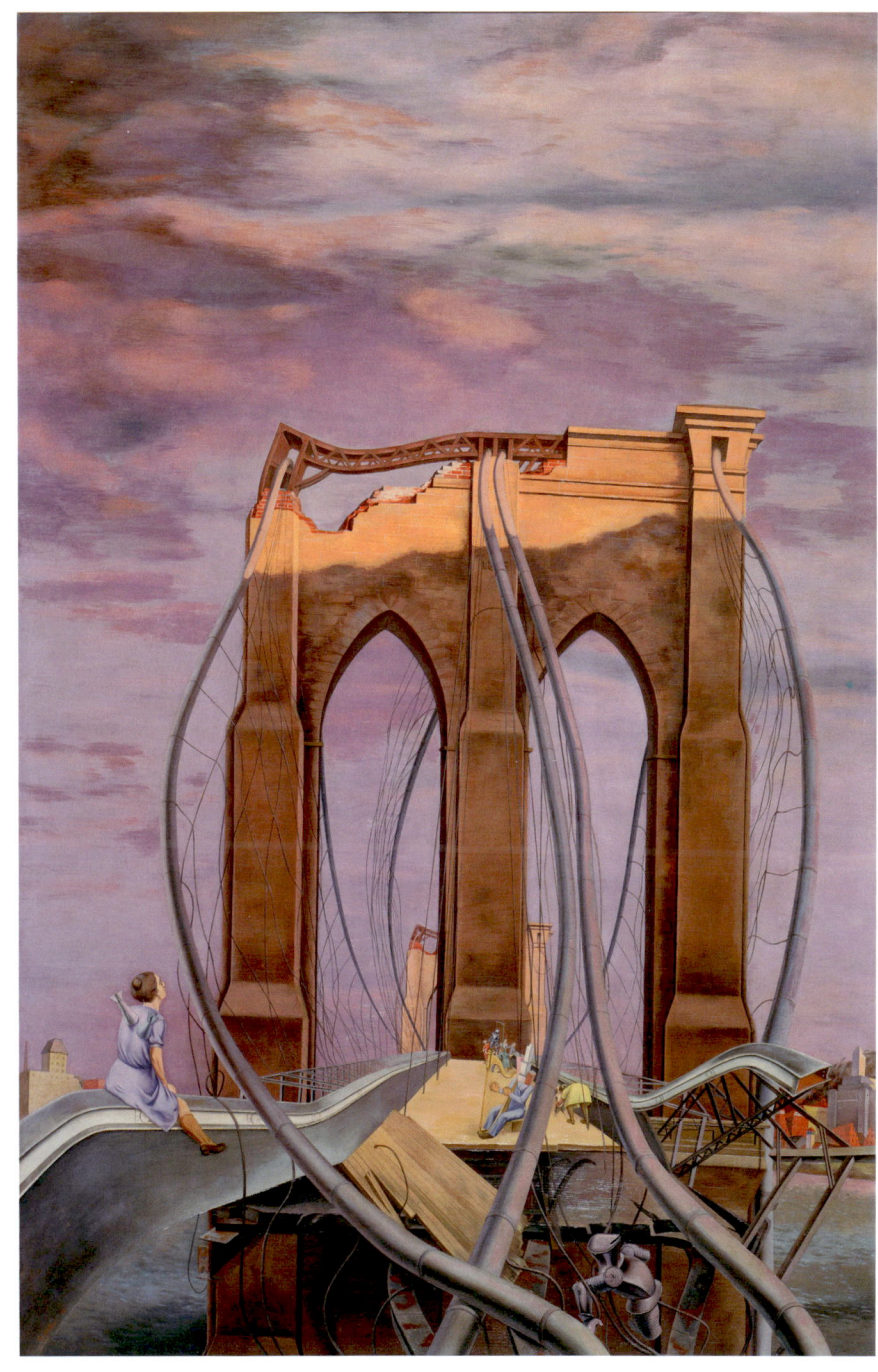

Fig. 10. O. Louis Guglielmi
(American, born in Egypt,
1906–1956), *Mental
Geography*, 1938, oil on
canvas, 24 × 35¾ in.
Private collection

one of the community's most visible Modernist artists, he curated exhibitions for SAM and covered art for the *Seattle Times*, and from this position of authority, he spread the word about artists, theories, movements, exhibitions, and various art-world events. Thus, when the exhibition *Paintings by Malcolm Roberts* went on view at SAM from December 9, 1936, to January 10, 1937, Callahan had mastered Surrealism sufficiently enough to articulate its key points:

> Seattle has had little opportunity of seeing surrealist paintings; no . . . local artist has attempted to enter this particular field of painting. I have heard definitions of surrealism by several surrealist painters and their attempt, as I understand it, is to make a conscious search of the subconscious. In doing this, they draw from their subconscious or dream impressions, recognizable objects of common usage which are placed in association with other objects unrelated in common usage, and together these are put in an atmosphere of unending space.[16]

The Surreal Northwest

While Callahan's commentaries explained the fundamentals of Surrealism for Seattle audiences, Roberts's groundbreaking solo show at SAM offered its most comprehensive local presentation to date. Remarkably, this exhibition focused not on an internationally renowned Surrealist but on a local artist with considerable grasp of the movement's visual and theoretical approaches. Roberts was born in Seattle and attended Broadway High School with fellow artists Morris Graves (a childhood friend) and George Tsutakawa, and he developed an early interest in art during a trip to Paris in 1929, at the age of sixteen.[17] After graduating from high school in 1931, he spent a year at the School of the Art Institute of Chicago and then returned to Seattle, in 1932, to practice and exhibit his artwork.

Roberts's meticulously rendered and highly theatrical paintings stage incongruous objects in vast and mysterious spaces redolent of the work of Dalí and Tanguy but also eerily evocative of the Pacific Northwest landscape. In *The Beach* (1935, plate 118), a shipping pallet, a fragment of driftwood resembling a female nude, and a railroad crossing sign meet on a rugged shoreline by moonlight, while in *View of Aurora Bridge* (ca. 1936, plate 119), two sailboats engage in a bizarrely intimate exchange against the nocturnal backdrop of the familiar Seattle landmark. Reviewing Roberts's exhibition at SAM, an unnamed critic for the *Seattle Post-Intelligencer* affirmed the enigma of the artist's works, assuring readers that "Roberts himself . . . doesn't know the meaning of many of his paintings."[18] For Roberts, however, Surrealism was not about ascribing significance to his painterly inconsistencies but about discovering visual equivalents for his subconscious ruminations. Insisting that his works "have no meaning . . . at all," he affirmed that "Surrealism is the artist taking material of the subconscious mind and explaining it and putting his discoveries on canvas by means of symbols."[19]

For the painter Louis Bunce, Surrealism was a bridge between social realism and expressionism. Although based in Portland, Oregon, he was on the radar of the Seattle art world thanks to his 1936 solo exhibition at SAM, *Paintings by Louis Demott Bunce*, as well as the long-standing support of Callahan, who regularly included Bunce in his writings on Northwest Modernism. Bunce had studied at the Art Students League of New York in 1927 with the painter Max Weber and was well versed in Modernism. An avid visitor to museums and galleries, he even hopped a freight train to attend the 1933 Chicago World's Fair, whose historically comprehensive visual arts section included works by Dalí, Ernst, Picasso, and other avant-garde painters.[20] During the Depression, after a decade spent creating Cézanne-inspired views of the landscape around Portland and the Columbia River, he turned to social realism and undertook mural commissions for the US Treasury Department and easel paintings for the Oregon Federal Art Project of the WPA. By this time, he had come under the influence of de Chirico's metaphysical cityscapes, whose lessons he applied to scenes of Portland, interspersing recognizable landmarks and industrial spaces with irreconcilable objects, structures, and figures.

In Bunce's *Structure #10* (1939, plate 121), an odd assortment of disparate items— impracticable scaffolding, a lone figure, a multicolored disk, a mysterious spilled substance, dark shadows, a portrait bust—adds absurd clutter to the city's overbuilt embankment and interrupts the sight line to the Lincoln steam plant in the distance, which disgorges toxic waste into a red sky. The subject of *Lumber Yard #514* (ca. 1940, plate 122) is the Oregon Lumber Company, whose logo is on the white signpost in the composition's middle ground. This mammoth timber conglomerate claimed vast tracts of land, much of it either illegally or through the Homestead Act of 1862, including a significant portion of the rainforest west of Portland. Here, Northwest social realism merges with American Social Surrealism as the lumber industry becomes the stuff of nightmares: A monstrous sawmill in a precipitous pictorial space feeds on a pile of timber, methodically chewing it up and spitting it out into planks as green, faceless figures look on helplessly. Bunce returned to New York in the early 1940s, and by then the city had become a center for Surrealism thanks to the presence there of European artists in exile and exhibitions of their work at the Julien Levy Gallery, the Museum of Modern Art, and other venues.[21] This direct experience with Surrealism gave rise to paintings such as *Dreamer* (1940, plate 123), whose anonymous somnolent subject suggests the artist's further assimilation of Surrealist ideas and opened the door to the intuitive approach that he brought to his abstractions a decade later.

Many of the environmental elements in Bunce's Social Surrealism—the overbuilt waterfront, the insatiable sawmill, water contamination, air pollution—align with his Seattle counterparts' rejoinders to urbanization, industrialization, and ecological devastation, and much of their work likewise shows the imprint of Surrealism. Morris Graves was no doubt thinking of Surrealism when he incorporated vessels, gloves, and other disconnected objects into his landscapes of the mid-1930s. In *Chalice Holding the Stimson Mill* (1936, plate 124), the eponymous cup rests, unbelievably and precariously, on an abandoned plowshare in an overcultivated field. The chalice cradles a miniature replica of a Stimson Lumber Company sawmill with smoke rising from its tiny smokestacks, like a censer used in some bizarre industrial sacrament. In the equally cryptic *Ancient Anthem* (1936, plate 125), a disembodied glove lies palm up in a mountainous setting, gesturing toward a forest of smokestacks; in the foreground, a cluster of battered coffins indicates the environmental fallout of logging primordial forests. These works reveal the ecocritical potential of Surrealism, for their emphasis on the irrational, the unexplained, and the organic visualized an understanding of the natural world that ran counter to the scientific empiricism responsible for industrialization.[22]

Graves's Surrealist paintings not only reinforced his ecocriticism but also signaled a shift in his practice toward a more deliberate exploration of the liberating potential of chance, the fantastic, and the irrational. In 1937, he attended a lecture at the Cornish School of Allied Arts in Seattle by the philosopher Nancy Wilson Ross on the relationship between Zen Buddhism and Dada, an important precursor to Surrealism that also embraced the unconscious and the illogical. Over the next few years, he staged a series of impromptu performances whose improvisational arrangements and unpermitted settings precipitated actions and reactions whose bizarre spontaneity were redolent of Dada and Surrealist interventions. In 1938, he arrived at a performance of the composer John Cage's *Quartet* carrying a sack of peanuts and wearing a lorgnette outfitted with googly eyes; during the third act, after spending the entire performance ostentatiously holding the lorgnette and audibly shelling and ingesting the peanuts, he bellowed, "Jesus in the Everywhere," causing pandemonium.[23] Cage was in residence in Seattle to teach at the Cornish School, and he and Graves, along with Roberts, shared a mutual interest in Dada, Surrealism, and Zen—as well as, briefly, a home in Seattle's Capitol Hill neighborhood. Perhaps their exchanges motivated Graves (often with Roberts as a willing participant) to continue to enliven everyday existence by shocking the Seattle public with the absurd and the unexpected.[24] It was in this spirit that Graves entered a luncheonette on a red carpet and, to the bewilderment of curious onlookers, ordered a lettuce sandwich; in a similar vein, he pushed a baby carriage full of rocks through the stately halls of the Olympic Hotel. These rebellious gestures—impromptu, astonishing, unpredictable, and ridiculous— generated unexpected reactions and unplanned inconsistencies that aligned with his Surrealist paintings. In turn, his paintings announced the holistic philosophy and much of the personal symbolism that formed the basis for his work from that point forward.

The Seattle painters Leo Kenney and Margaret Tomkins represent a second generation of Puget Sound artists who responded to Surrealism. For Kenney, Surrealism was an early and powerful influence. A prodigious art student and amateur art historian, he had his first exhibition, at the Little Gallery at Seattle's Frederick & Nelson department store, in 1944, when he was just nineteen; the following year, his painting *The Inception of Magic* (1945, plate 129) entered SAM's collection.[25] This ambitious composition, with its complex web of oscillating, transfiguring forms, reveals Kenney's familiarity with Surrealist automatism, and he centered Surrealism in his self-directed study of art history.[26] In addition to engaging with the broader Seattle Surrealist milieu, he saved his earnings from working overtime in his uncle's Pioneer Square

restaurant to purchase Dalí's wildly popular 1942 autobiography *The Secret Life of Salvador Dalí*. He also brought himself up to speed on the work of Matta, Ernst, and especially de Chirico; subscribed to the American Surrealist publication *View*; and was passingly aware of Freud's theory of psychoanalysis and its implications for Surrealism and psychic automatism. "Psychology was everything," Kenney said. "The Surrealists were all about that. Freud was just in the air when I was in my twenties."[27] He applied the lessons of Surrealism to his highly extemporaneous approach to painting, allowing forms to emerge, accumulate, and combine into unpremeditated compositions such as *Northern Image: The Muse III* (1948, plate 130) and *Third Offering* (1948, plate 132), both of which began with the figure but without a plan for its context, only the artist's intention to "invent a world to go around her, for her to inhabit . . . to [pull] her out into it like an obstetrician."[28]

Tomkins was born and educated in Los Angeles and moved to Seattle in 1939 to become "a citizen of the Northwest as a painter."[29] Although she exhibited her work regularly in SAM's Northwest Annuals and got to know many local artists, she held herself apart from the mainstream of Northwest Modernism, preferring to carve her own path as a Surrealist and, later, Abstract Expressionist. Frustrated by Seattle's lack of galleries and what she perceived to be SAM's neglect of local artists, she opened Artist Gallery in 1958 with her husband, the painter James FitzGerald, as well as Bunce, Manuel Izquierdo, William Ivey, and Alden Mason. The gallery provided a space for artists to show and sell their work independently, outside of institutional channels.

Tomkins was first exposed to Surrealism as an artist in Southern California, after seeing Picasso's *Guernica* at the Stendhal Art Galleries in Los Angeles in 1939, and subsequently encountered other works by exiled European artists on the West Coast, including Ernst, Miró, Tanguy, and Masson.[30] Surrealism's imprint is apparent in her work in the nightmarish spaces and transmogrifying organisms of *Metamorphosis* (1943, plate 135) and *Anamorphosis* (1944, plate 136). In *Metamorphosis*, terrifying creatures with swirling bodies and pointed wings dart and soar across a dull yellow sky, either bombarding or escaping the biomorphic rubble in the brown, wasted landscape around them. In *Anamorphosis*, chaos reigns, as the landscape—now inflected with shocking hues of magenta, violet, chartreuse, turquoise, and red—explodes and begins to reassemble into an even more frightening scenario. Both paintings visualize cosmic transitions and cycles of growth, energy, and decay outside the realm of physical reality. "I think it's fairly accurate [that these works were sympathetic to Surrealism]," she stated, elaborating on her intuitive process of tapping into the essence of the visible world to generate unforeseen forms and configurations:

> The metamorphosis [entails] . . . the changing possibility, mentally and physically, of objects you look at, depending upon how you view them, how your mind is, and how your thoughts are. And it was in that transfer of energies from, say, a material object into a more intuitive object. And the energies that would be inherent in the realistic form, having been developed through abstracting it and metamorphizing it into new shapes, created, re-created by the energy of the original thing in a whole new guise.[31]

In describing metamorphosis as the transformation of the mundane into the fantastic, Tomkins articulates a core notion of the Surrealist uncanny, and her work is but one manifestation of the movement's impact on Modernism in the Puget Sound during the 1930s and 1940s. After being accessible in the region only indirectly for the better part of a decade, Surrealism burst on the Seattle art scene in the mid-1930s with the veristic works of Blume and Roberts, and it took hold in the work of painters, among them Graves, Kenney, and Tomkins, who preferred to experiment more deliberately with automatism, intuition, and chance. For them, Surrealism was a powerful alternative to the literalness of social realism, for it offered a pathway to highly personal modes of expression, receptiveness to the marvelous, and a holistic approach to nature.

Notes

I would like to thank Abigail Susik for sharing her expertise on West Coast Surrealism and for her helpful feedback on an earlier version of this essay.

1. K. Callahan, "The Art Museum," 3 October 1936.

2. Wechsler, *Surrealism and American Art*, 32.

3. Breton, "Manifesto of Surrealism," in *Manifestoes of Surrealism*, 26.

4. Breton, "Second Manifesto of Surrealism," in *Manifestoes of Surrealism*, 142.

5. For Surrealism's international centers and reach, see D'Alessandro and Gale, *Surrealism Beyond Borders*.

6. Robert Lubar, "Salvador Dalí in America," 20.

7. Lubar, "Salvador Dalí in America," 20.

8. "Art: Marvelous and Fantastic," 60.

9. Lubar, "Salvador Dalí in America," 23.

10. For Surrealism in the United States, see Dervaux, *Surrealism USA*; Fort, *In Wonderland*; Michael Rosenfeld Gallery, *Exploring the Unknown*; and Wechsler, *Surrealism and American Art*.

11. For Social Surrealism, see Fort, "American Social Surrealism."

12. For magic realism in American Surrealism, see Wechsler, *Surrealism and American Art*, 35–38.

13. Cleopatra's Needle is a New Kingdom Egyptian obelisk given to the United States by the Khedivate of Egypt in the nineteenth century and erected in New York's Central Park in the 1870s, shortly after the construction of the Metropolitan Museum of Art.

14. K. Callahan, "Art Museum," 14 April 1935.

15. K. Callahan, "Art Museum," 14 April 1935.

16. K. Callahan, "Seattle Art Museum," 20 December 1936.

17. "Malcolm Roberts," artist file, Seattle Art Museum.

18. "It's Girl Friend—Painted via Subconscious Mind."

19. Malcolm Roberts, quoted in "It's Girl Friend."

20. Hull, *Louis Bunce*, 17.

21. Hull, *Louis Bunce*, 33.

22. For an ecocritical interpretation of Surrealism, see Noheden, "Toward a Total Animism," 53–61.

23. For descriptions of this event, see Herzogenrath, "John Cage," 8; and Cumming, *Sketchbook*, 114.

24. "Malcolm Roberts," artist file, Seattle Art Museum.

25. Farr, "Leo Kenney," 12.

26. Farr, "Leo Kenney," 13.

27. Leo Kenney, quoted in Farr, "Leo Kenney," 13.

28. Kenney, quoted in Farr, "Leo Kenney," 15.

29. Margaret Tomkins, quoted in Watkinson, *Margaret Tomkins*, 1.

30. For Margaret Tomkins, see Kendall, *Margaret Tomkins*; and Watkinson, *Margaret Tomkins*.

31. Tomkins and Guenther, "Oral History Interview," 6 June 1984.

PLATES

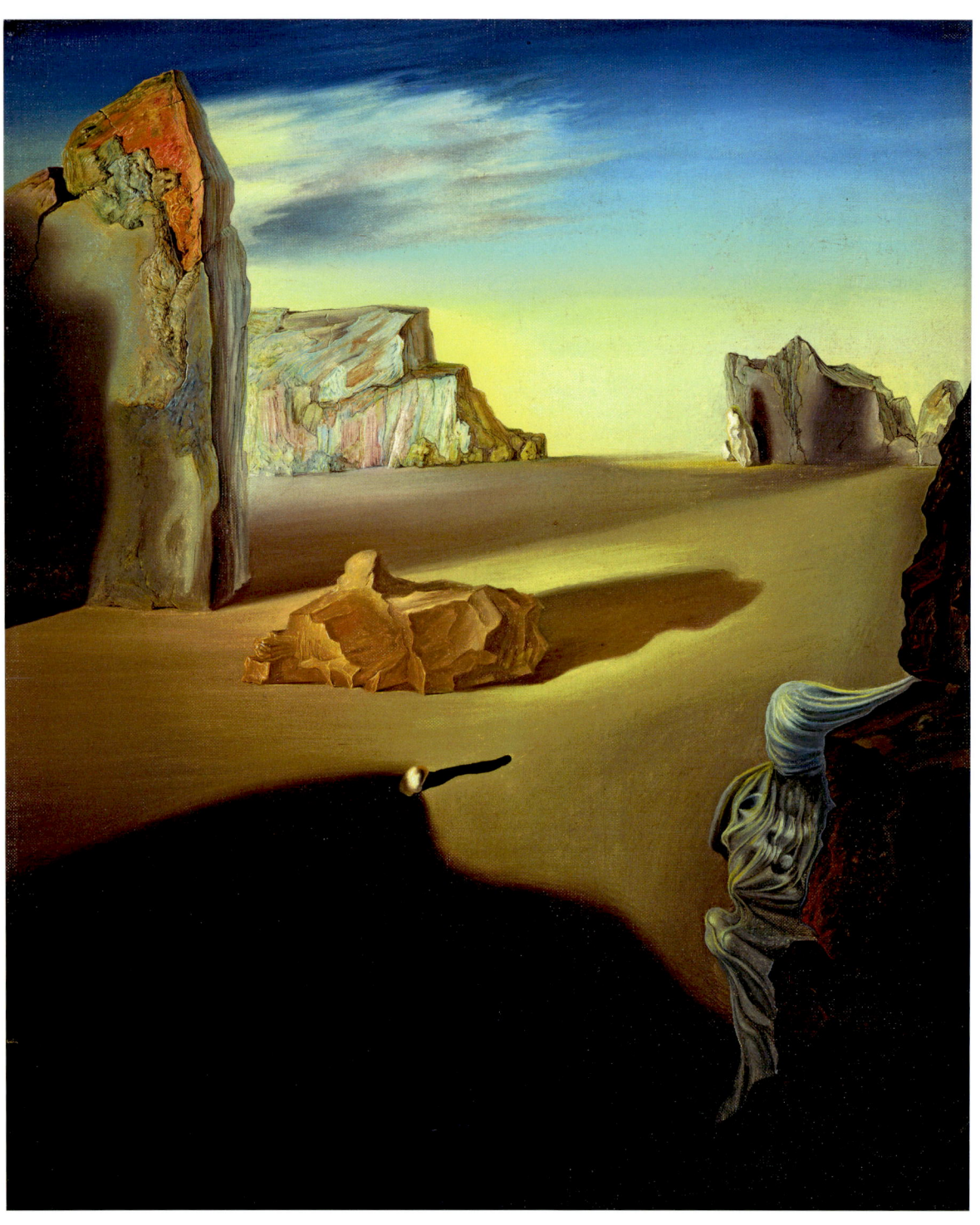

110 Salvador Dalí, *Shades of Night Descending*, 1931, oil on canvas

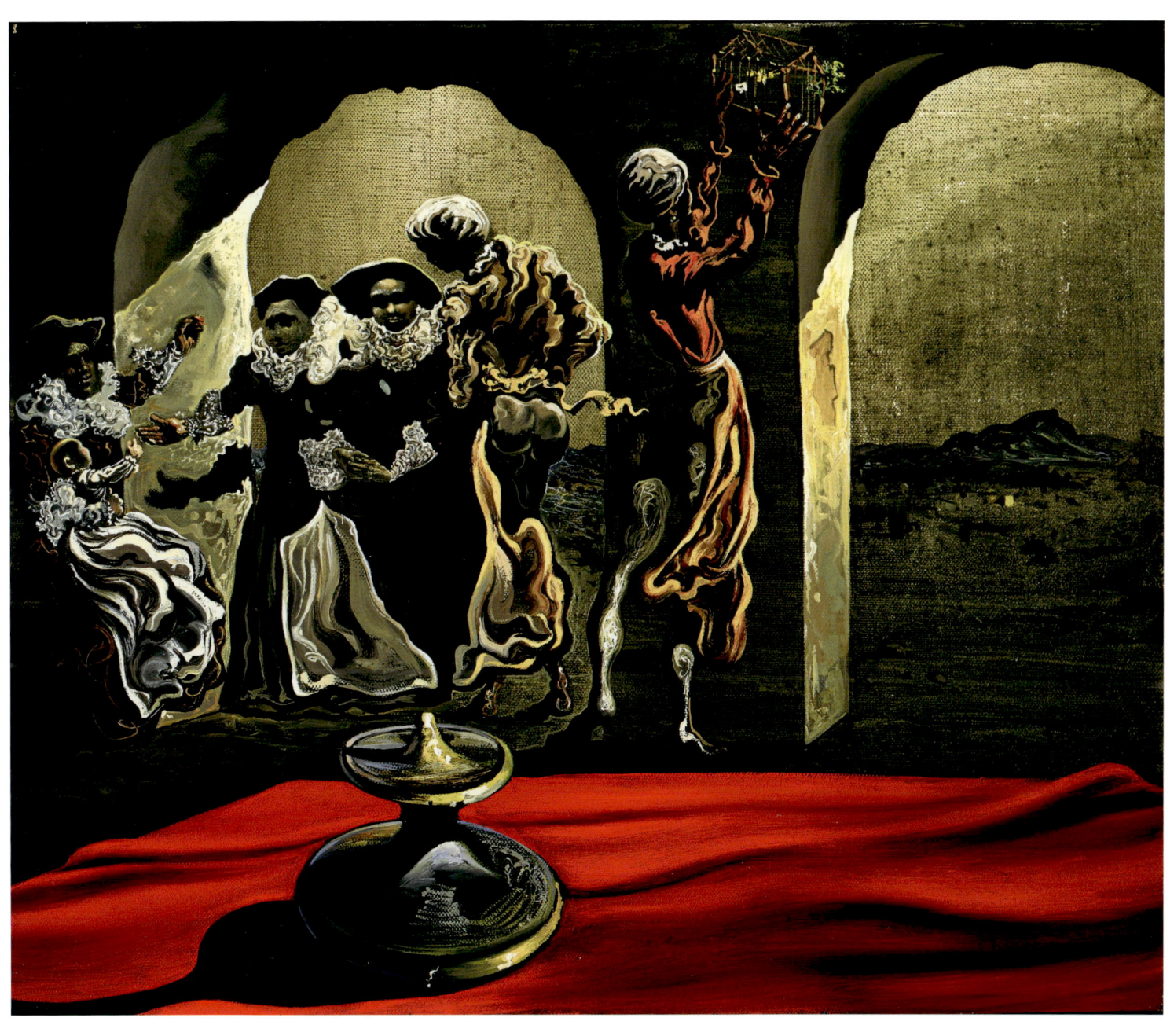

111 Salvador Dalí, *Bust of Voltaire*, 1941, oil on canvas

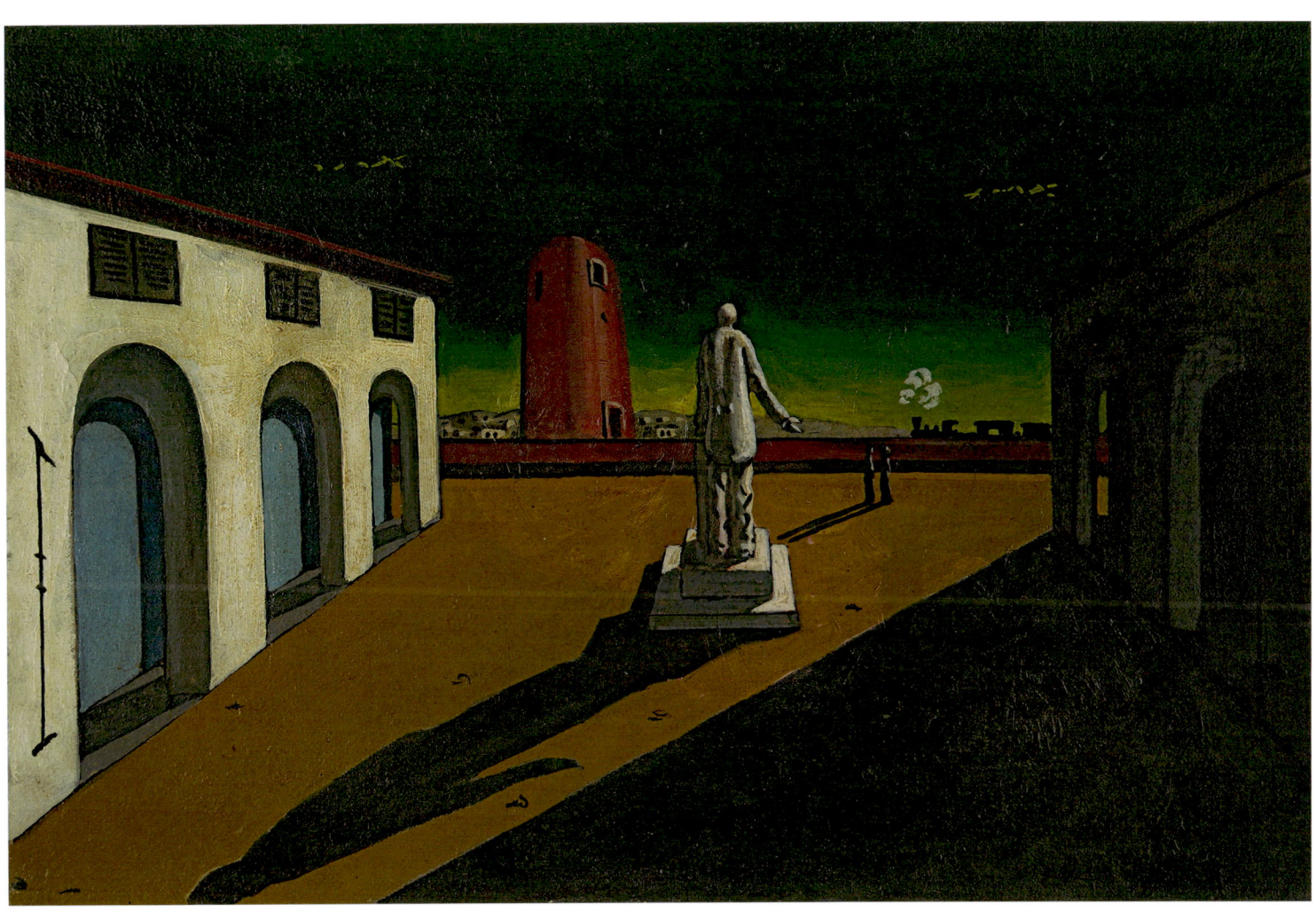

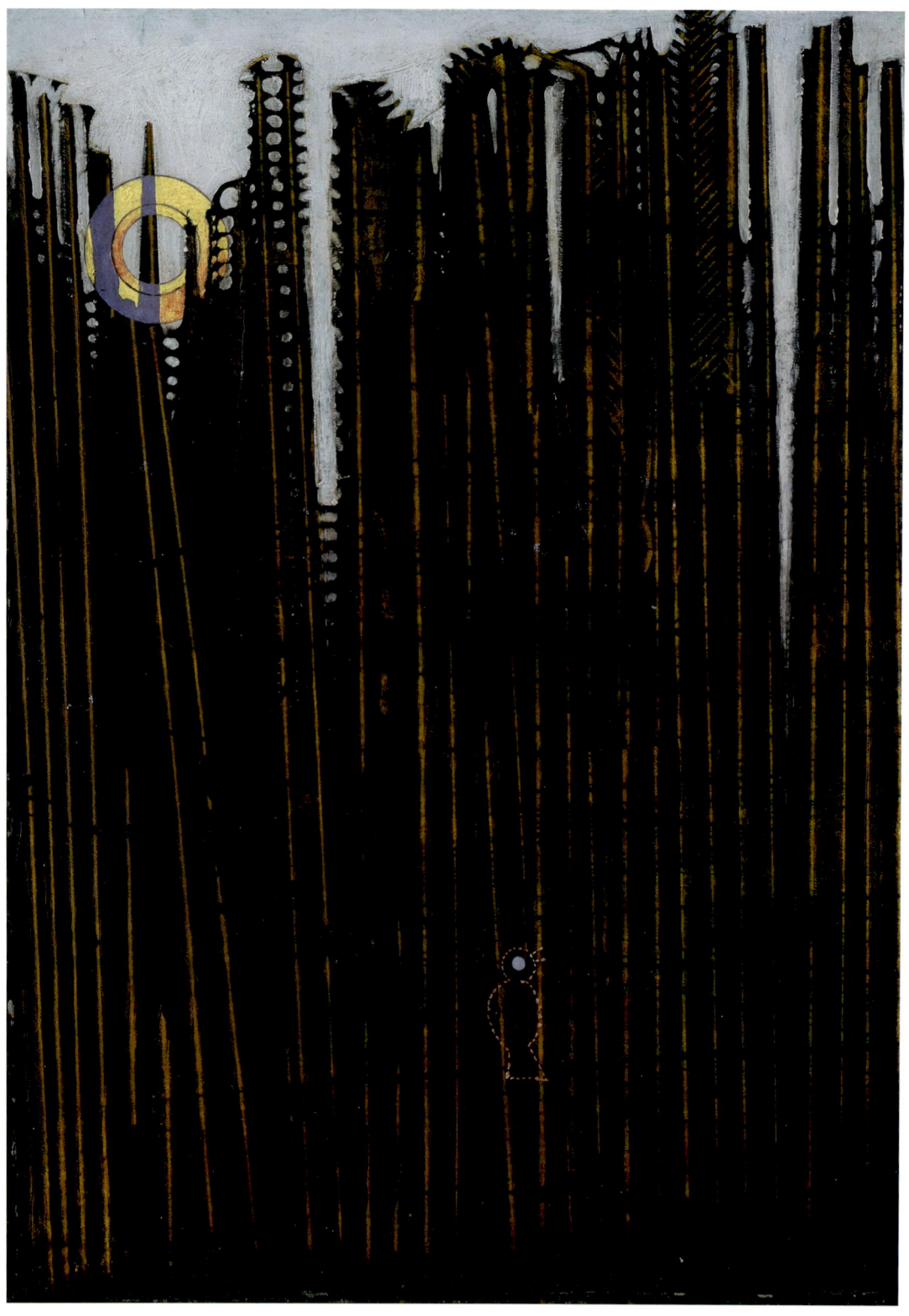

113 Max Ernst, *Forest* (*Forêt*), 1927, oil on paper mounted on canvas

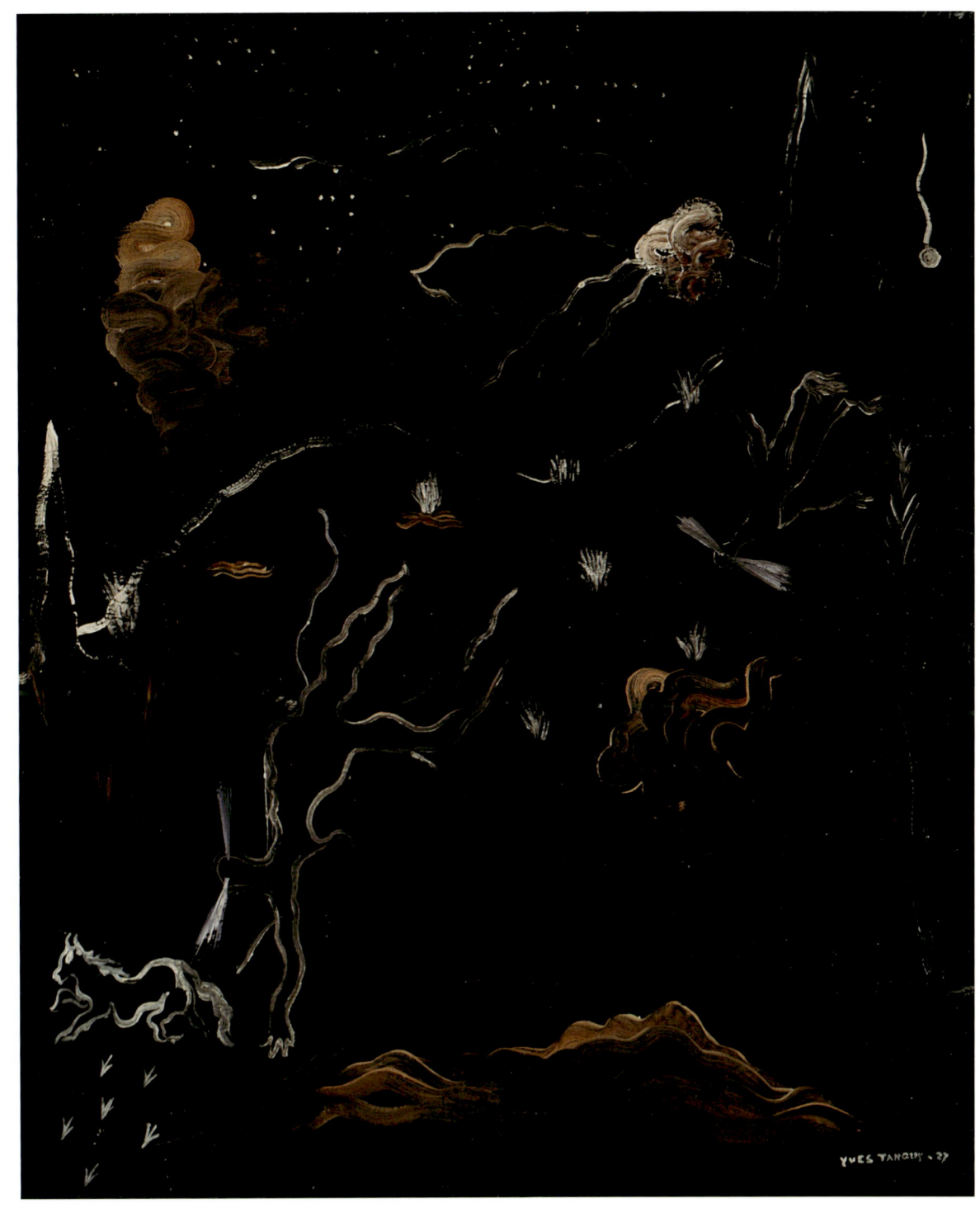

114 Yves Tanguy, *There! (The Evening Before)* (*Et voilà! [La veille au soir]*), 1927, oil on canvas

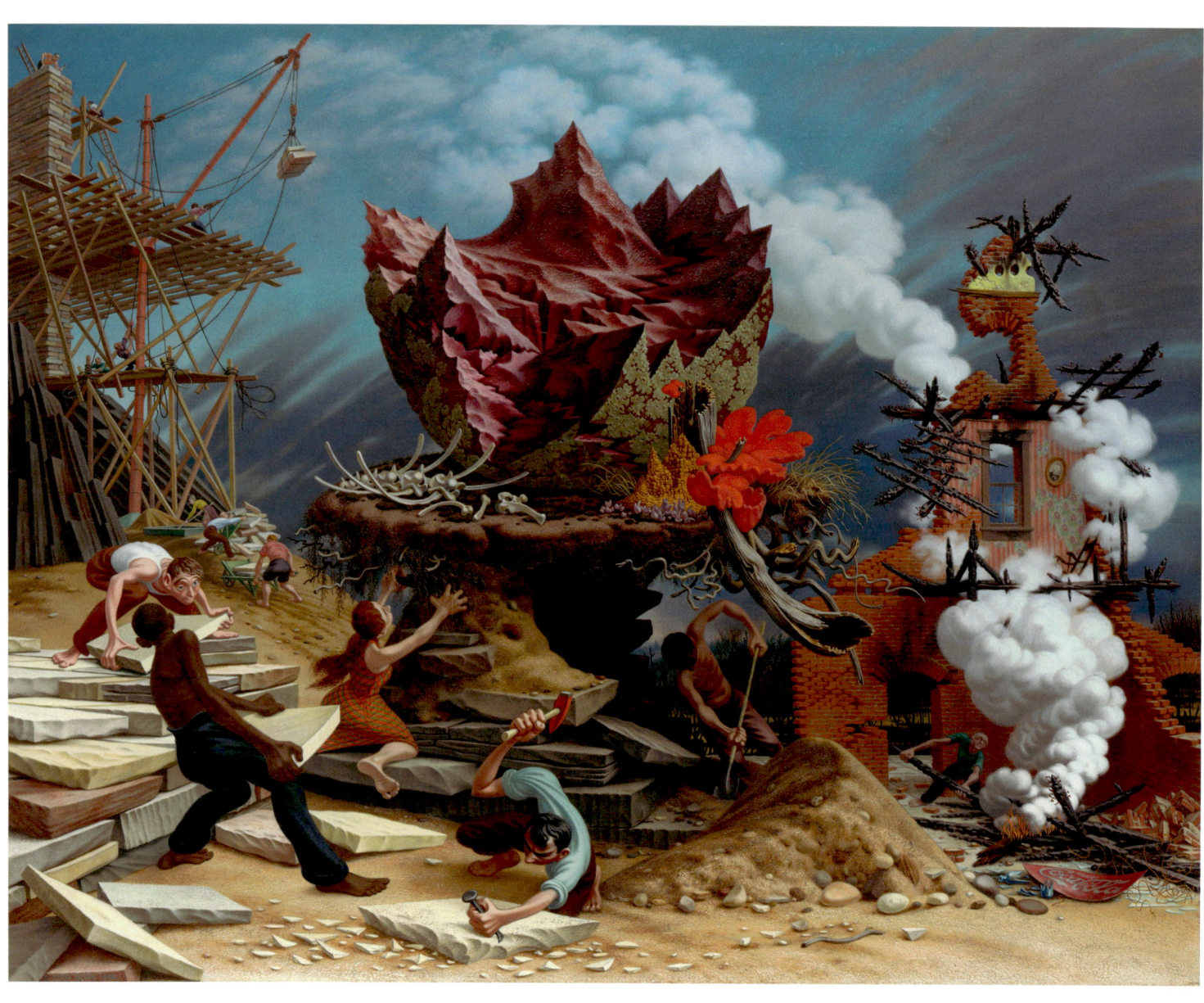

115   Peter Blume, *The Rock*, ca. 1944–48, oil on canvas

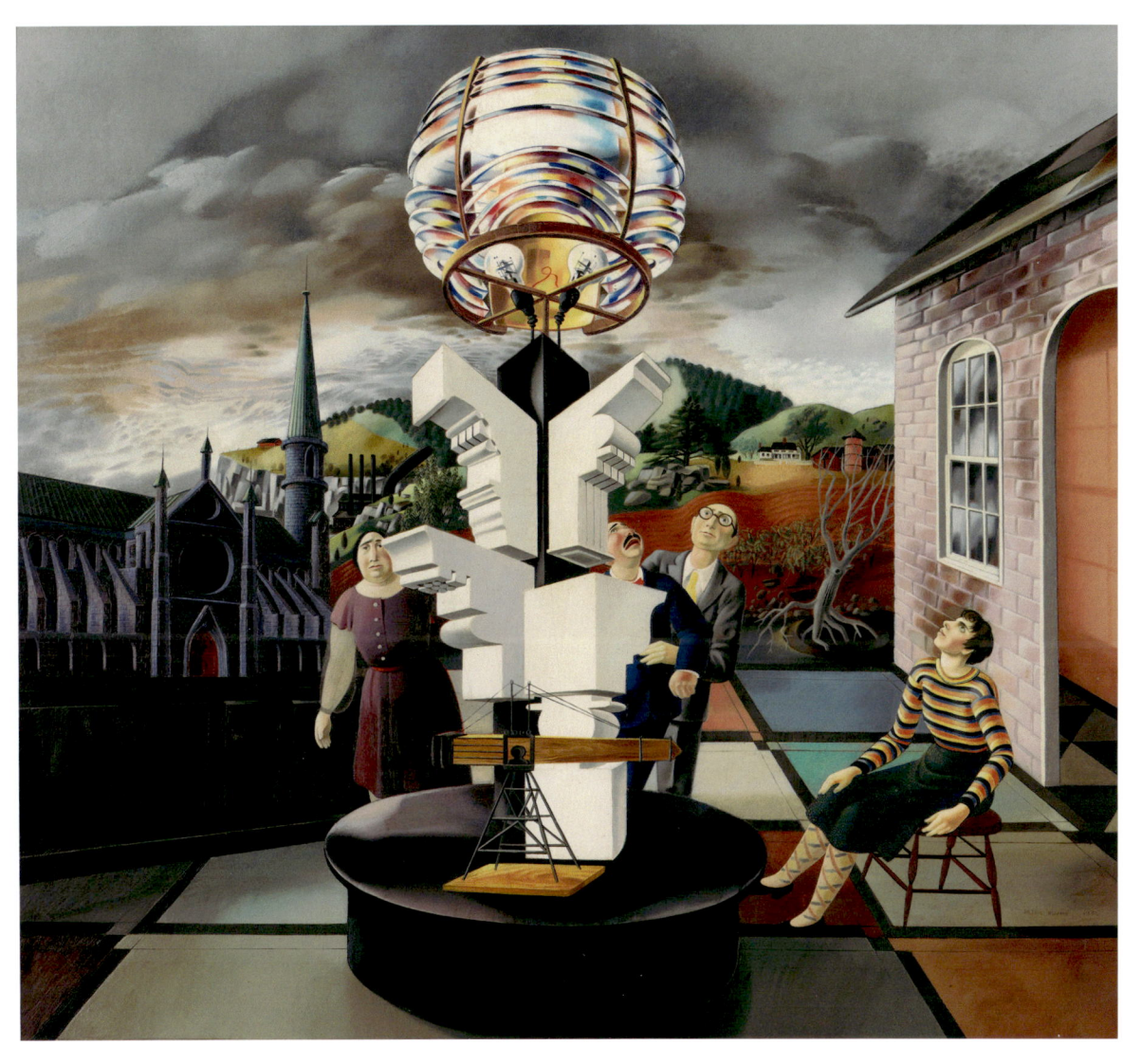

116   Peter Blume, *Light of the World*, 1932, oil on composition board   141

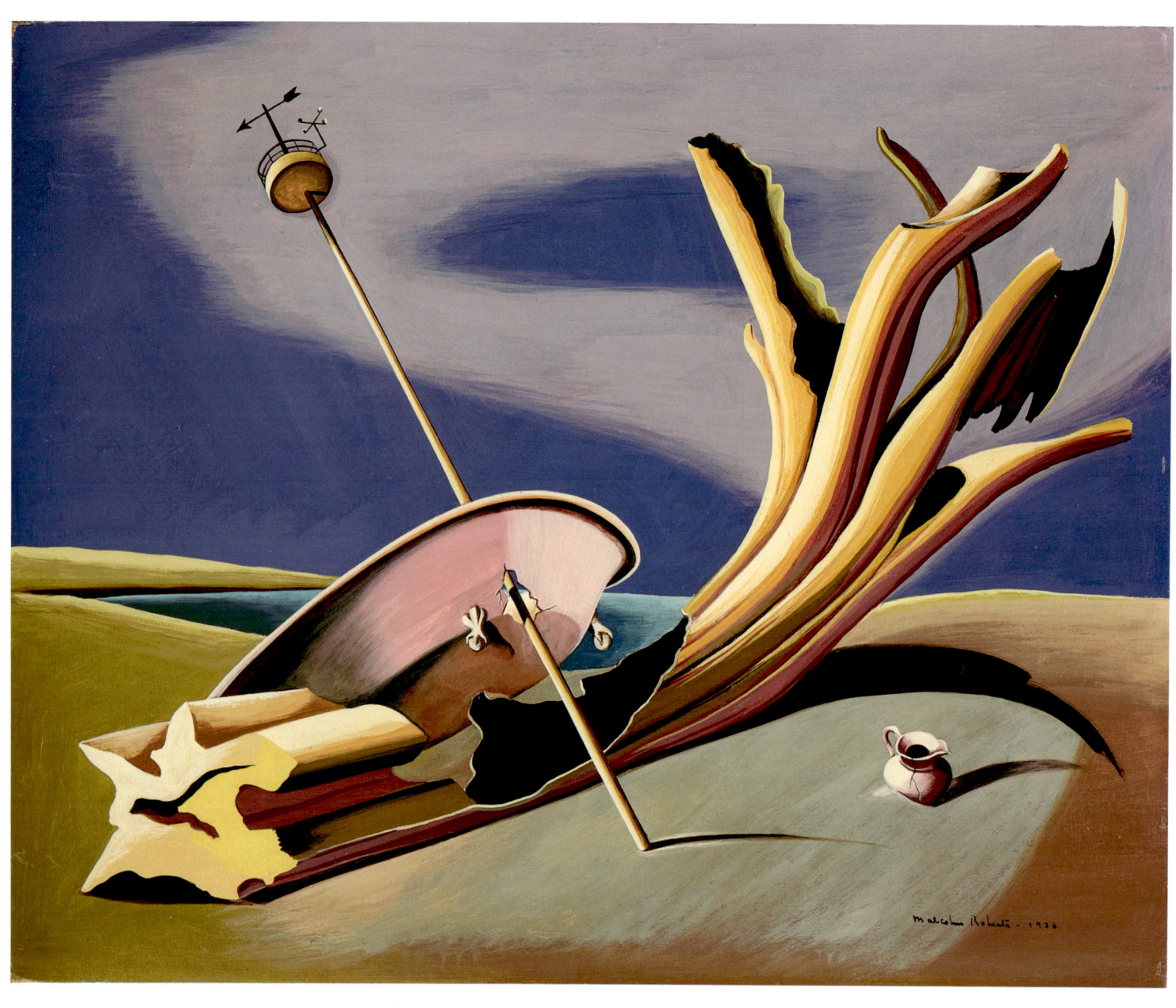

117 Malcolm M. Roberts, *Drift No. 2*, 1936, tempera on board

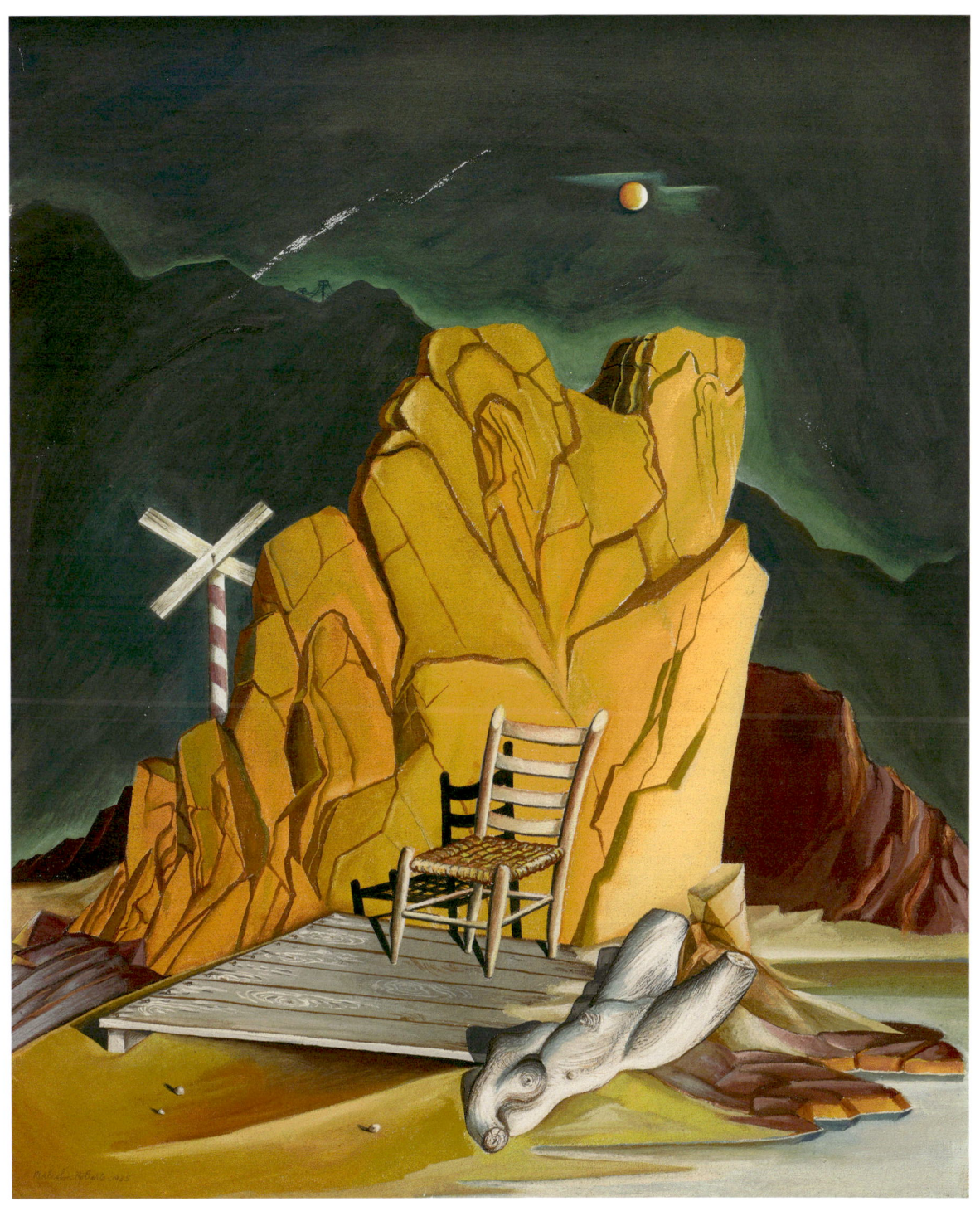

118 Malcolm M. Roberts, *The Beach*, 1935, tempera on canvas

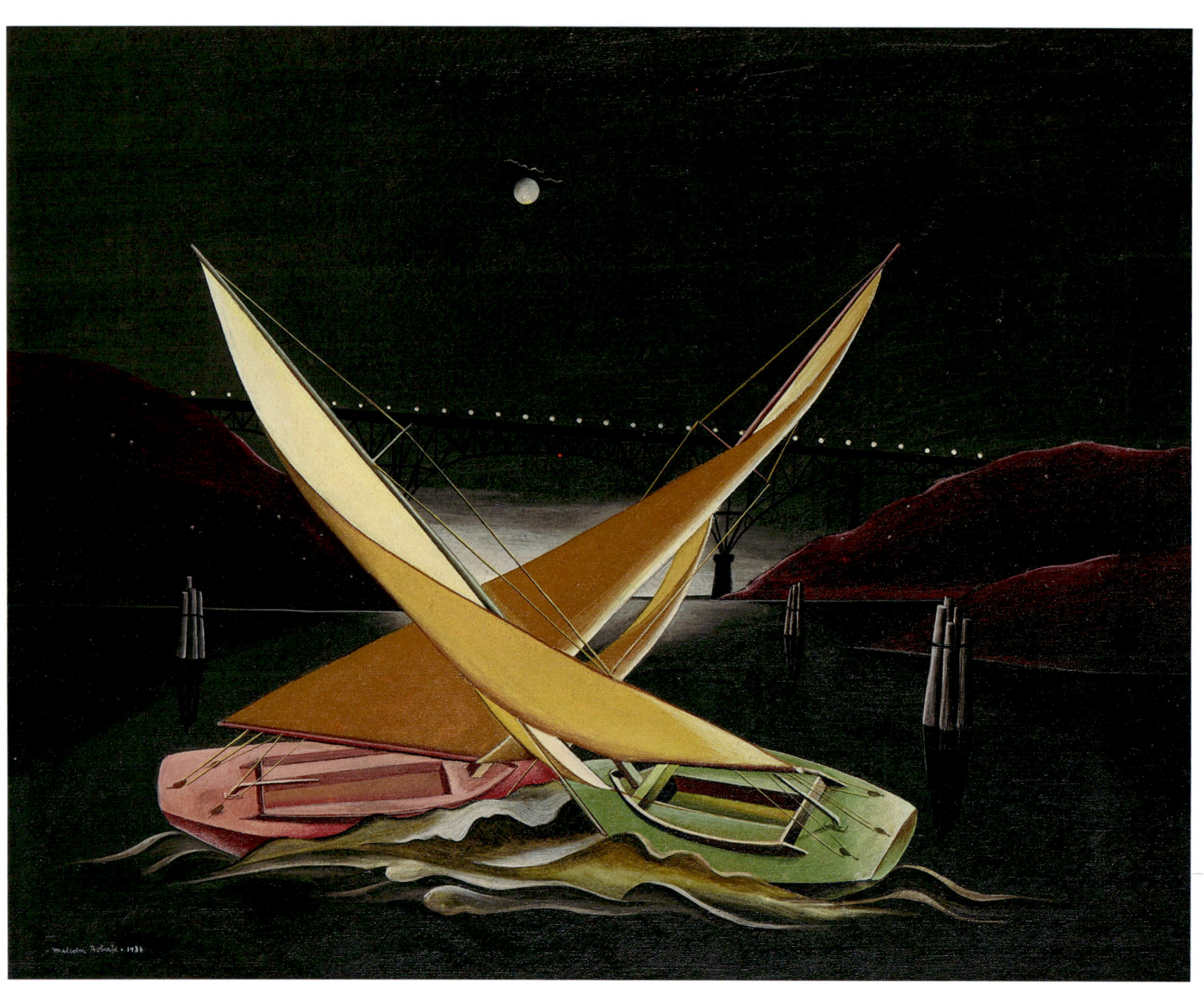

119 Malcolm M. Roberts, *View of Aurora Bridge*, ca. 1936, tempera on canvas and linen

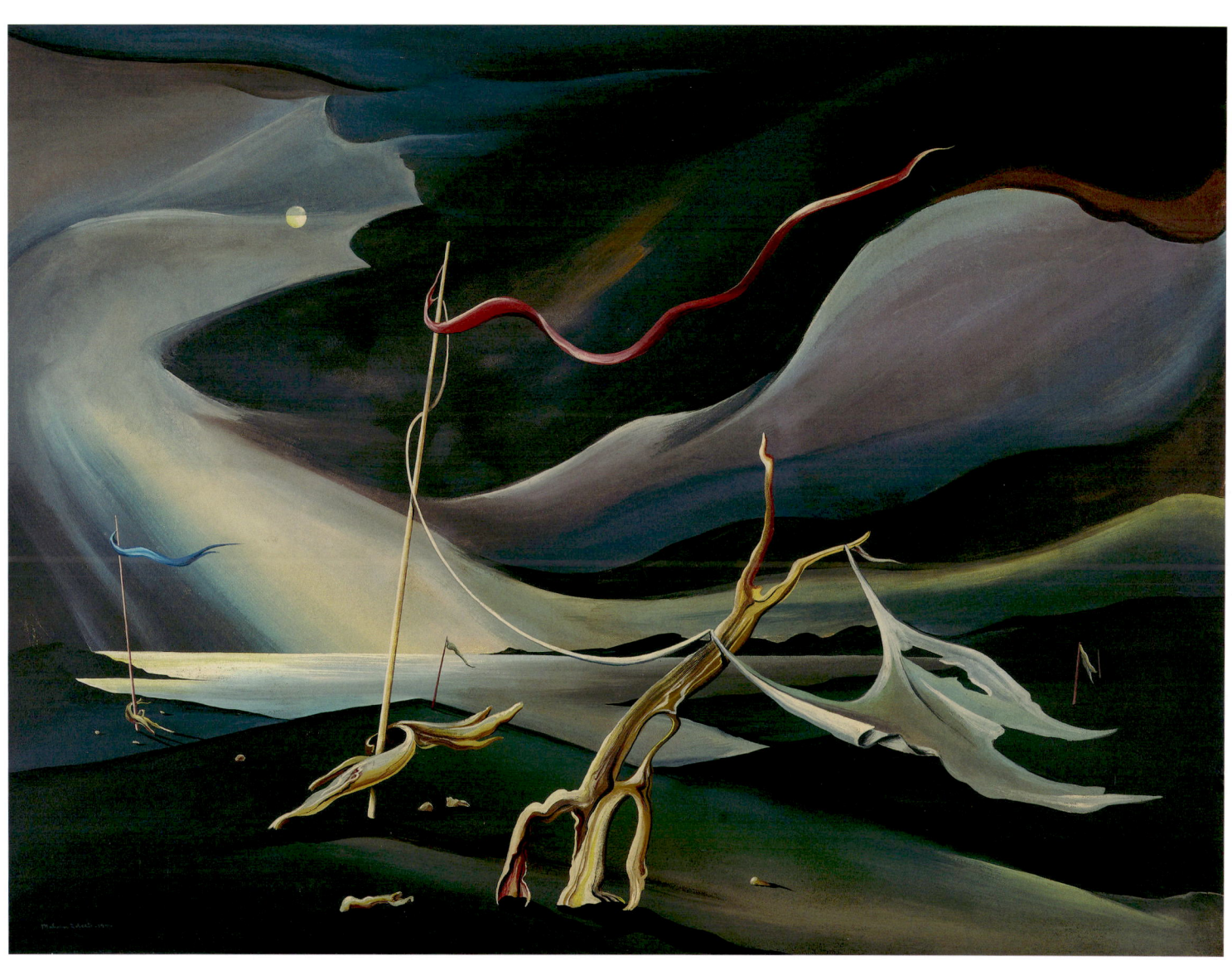

120 Malcolm M. Roberts, *Lunar Landscape*, 1941, tempera on cardboard

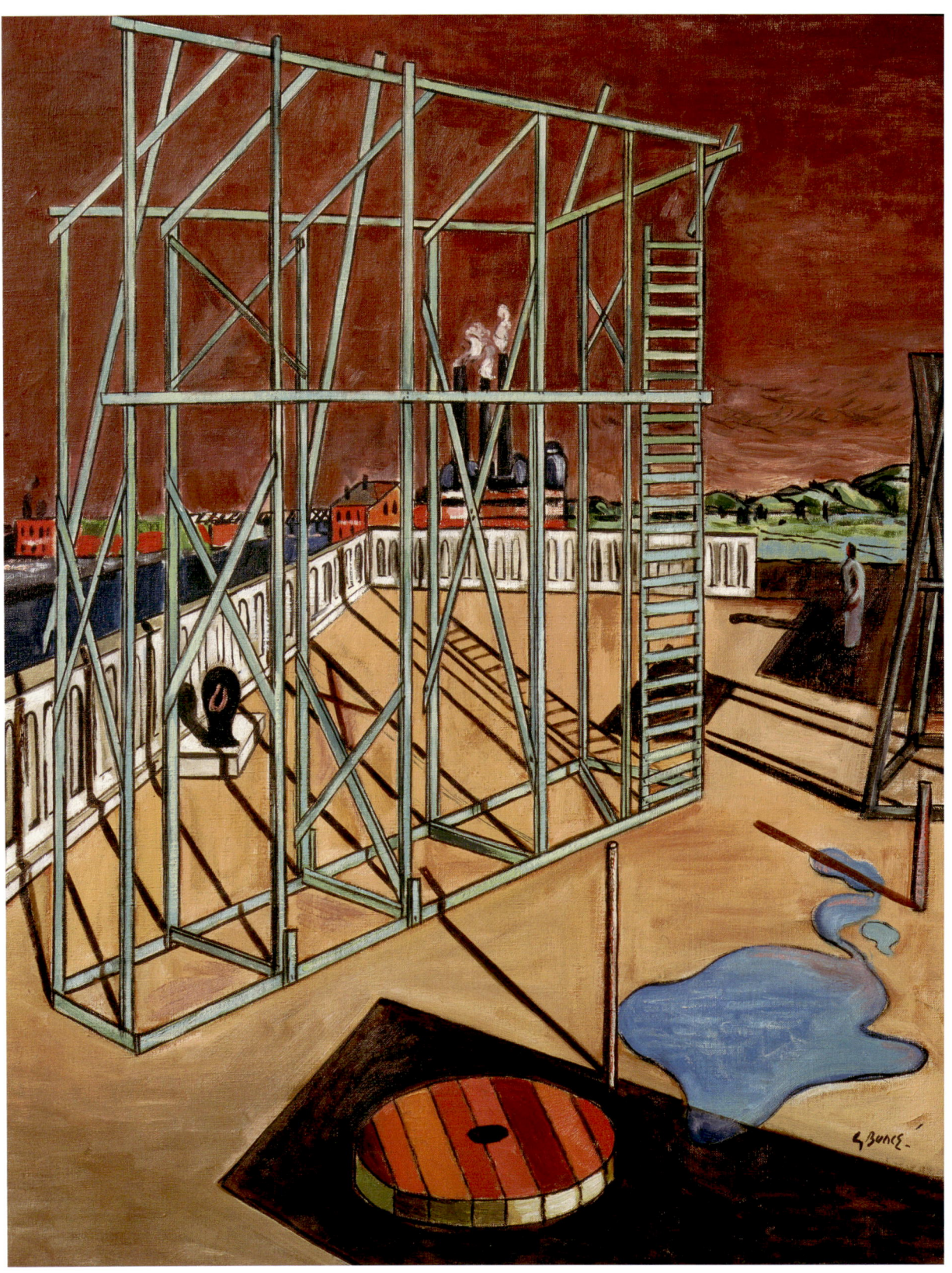

121 Louis Bunce, *Structure #10*, 1939, oil on canvas

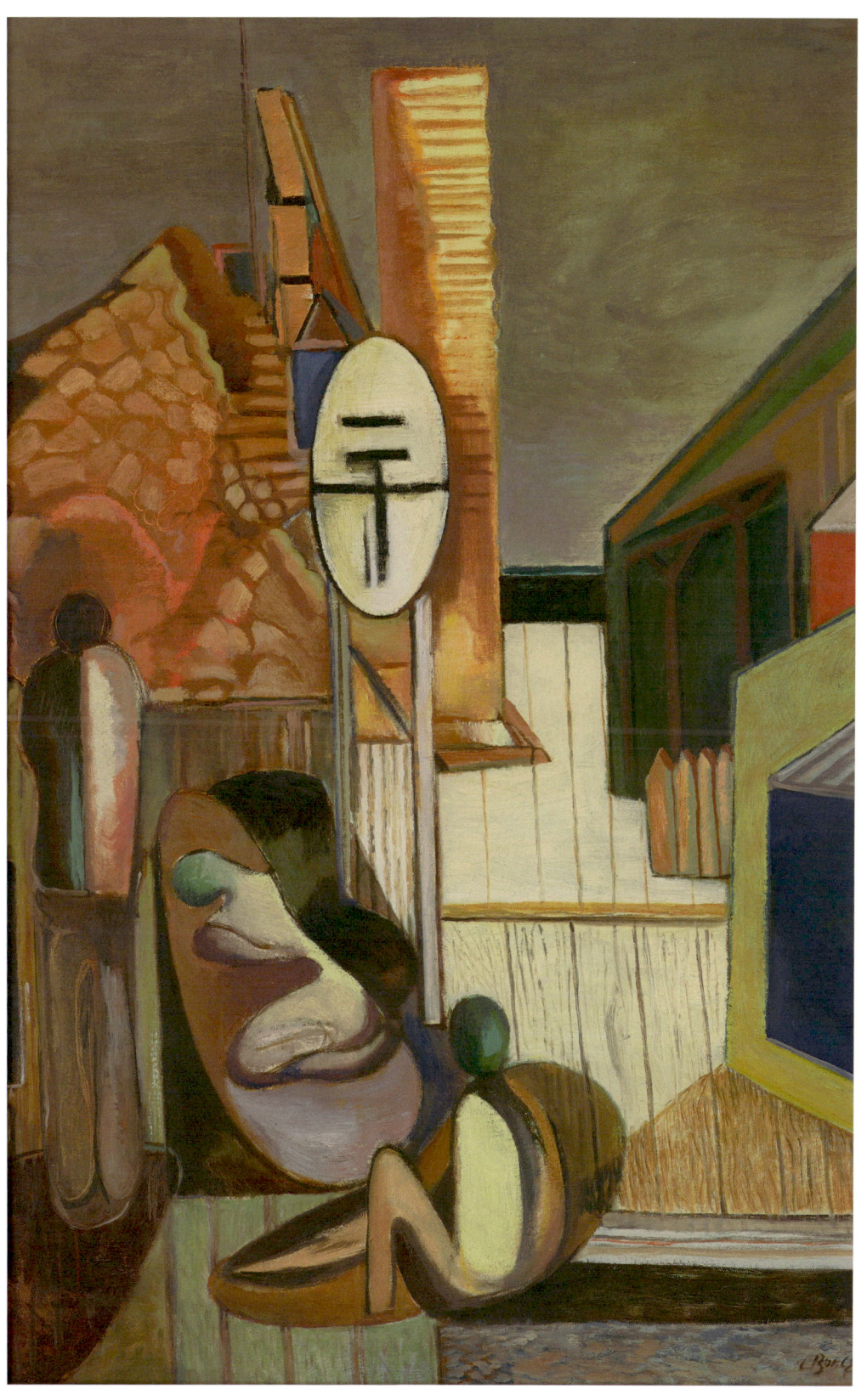

122 Louis Bunce, *Lumber Yard #514*, ca. 1940, oil on canvas

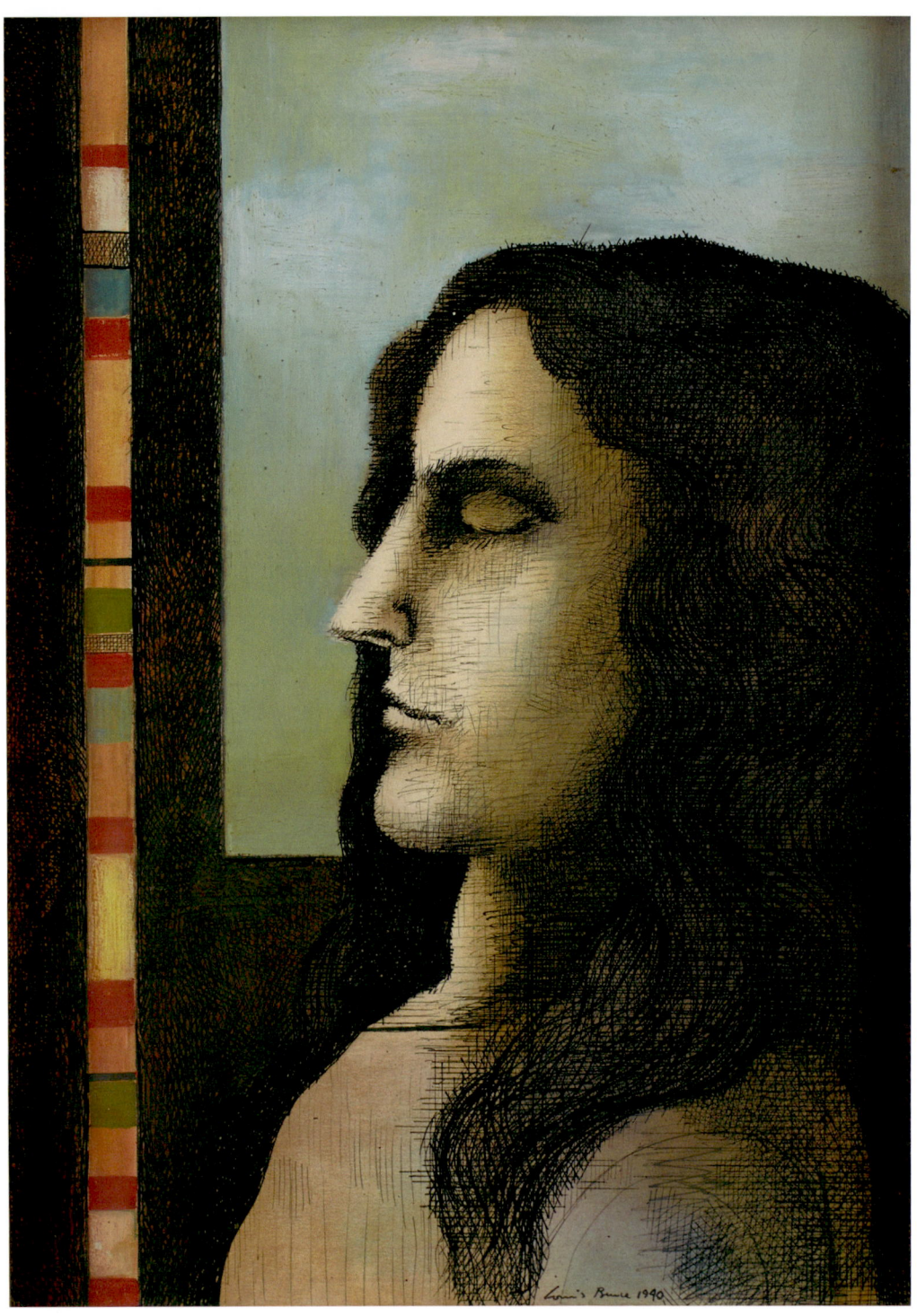

123 Louis Bunce, *Dreamer*, 1940, oil and ink on paperboard

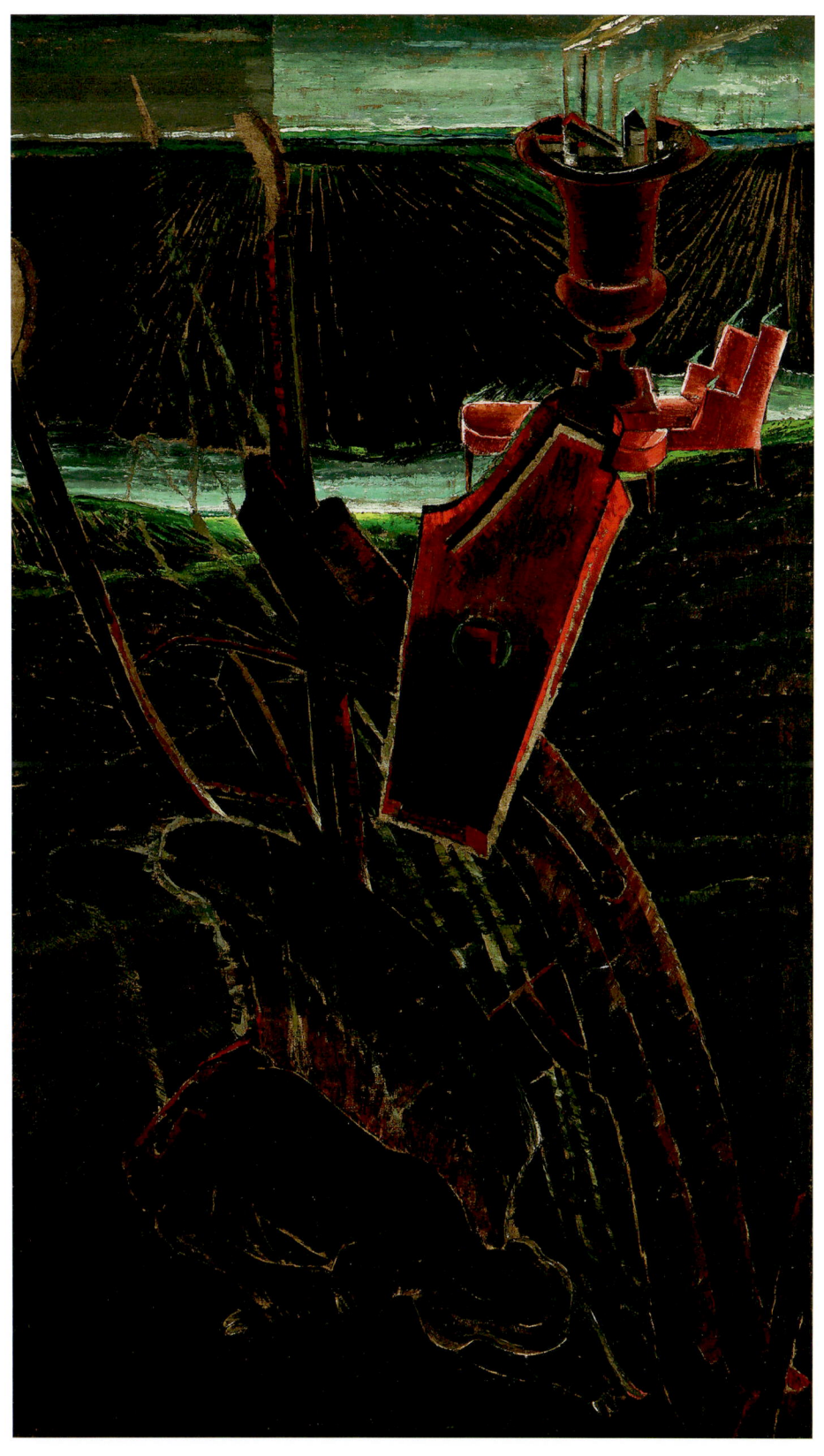

124 Morris Graves, *Chalice Holding the Stimson Mill*, 1936, oil on canvas

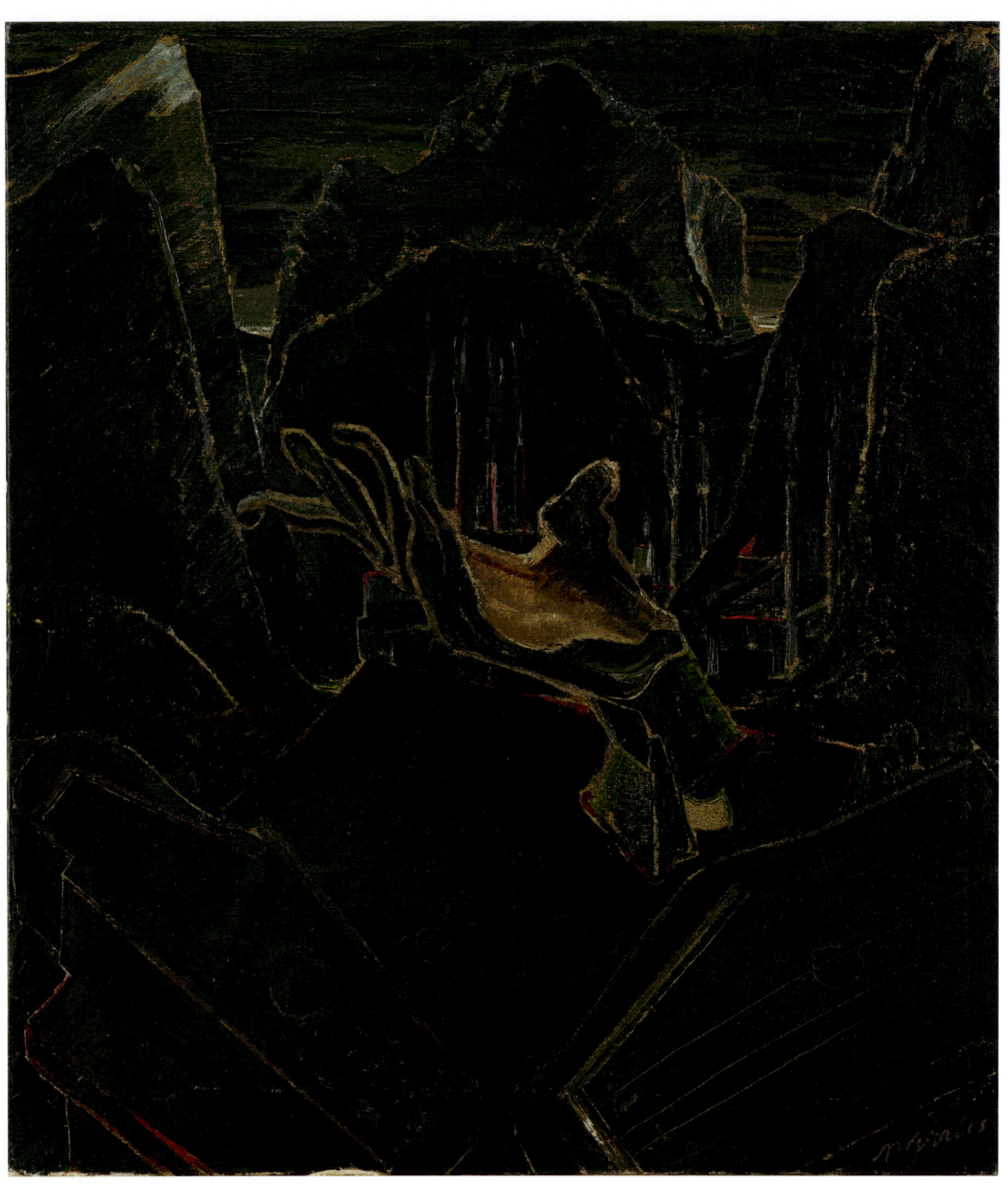

125 Morris Graves, *Ancient Anthem*, 1936, oil on burlap

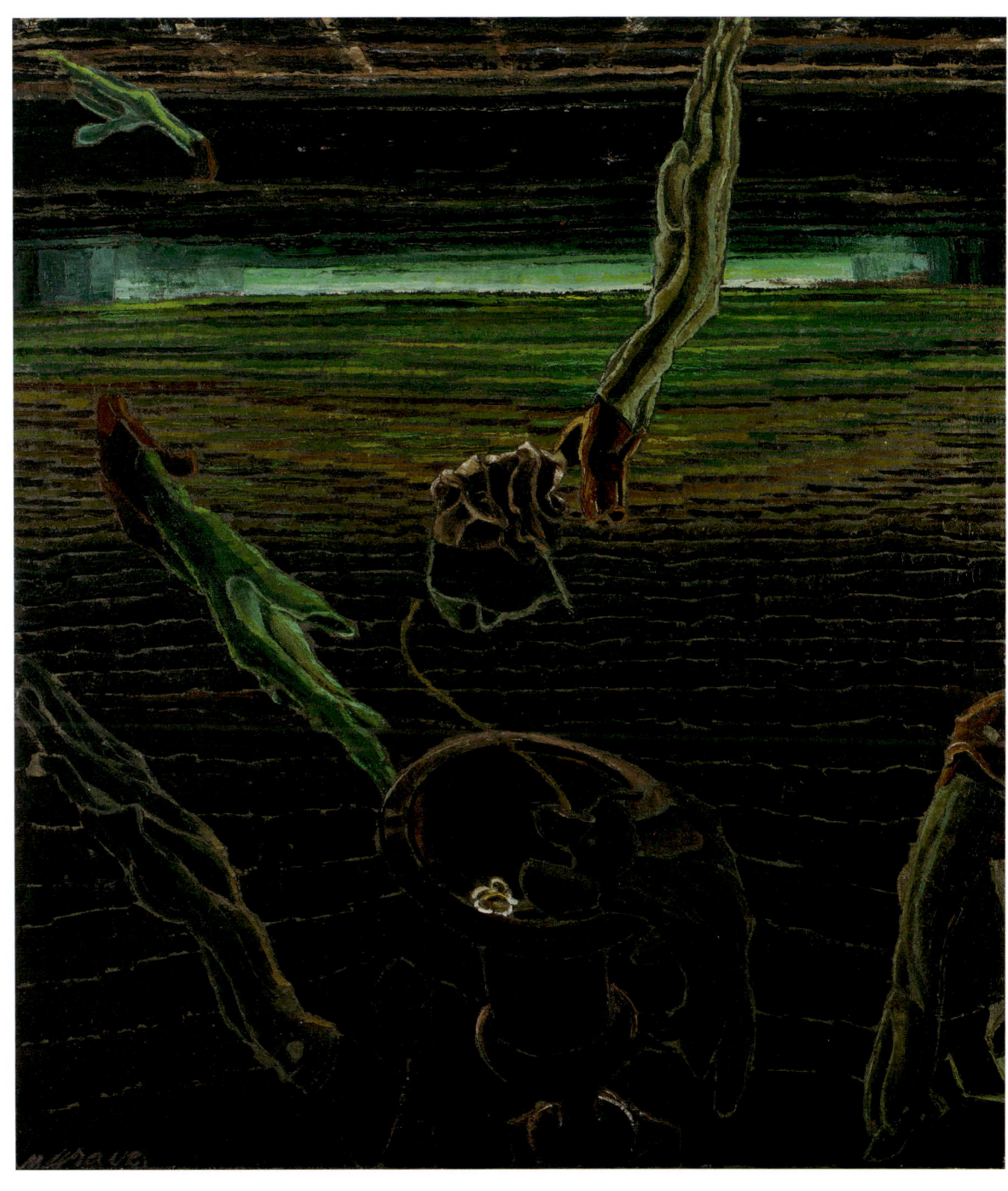

126 Morris Graves, *Burial of the New Law*, 1936, oil on canvas

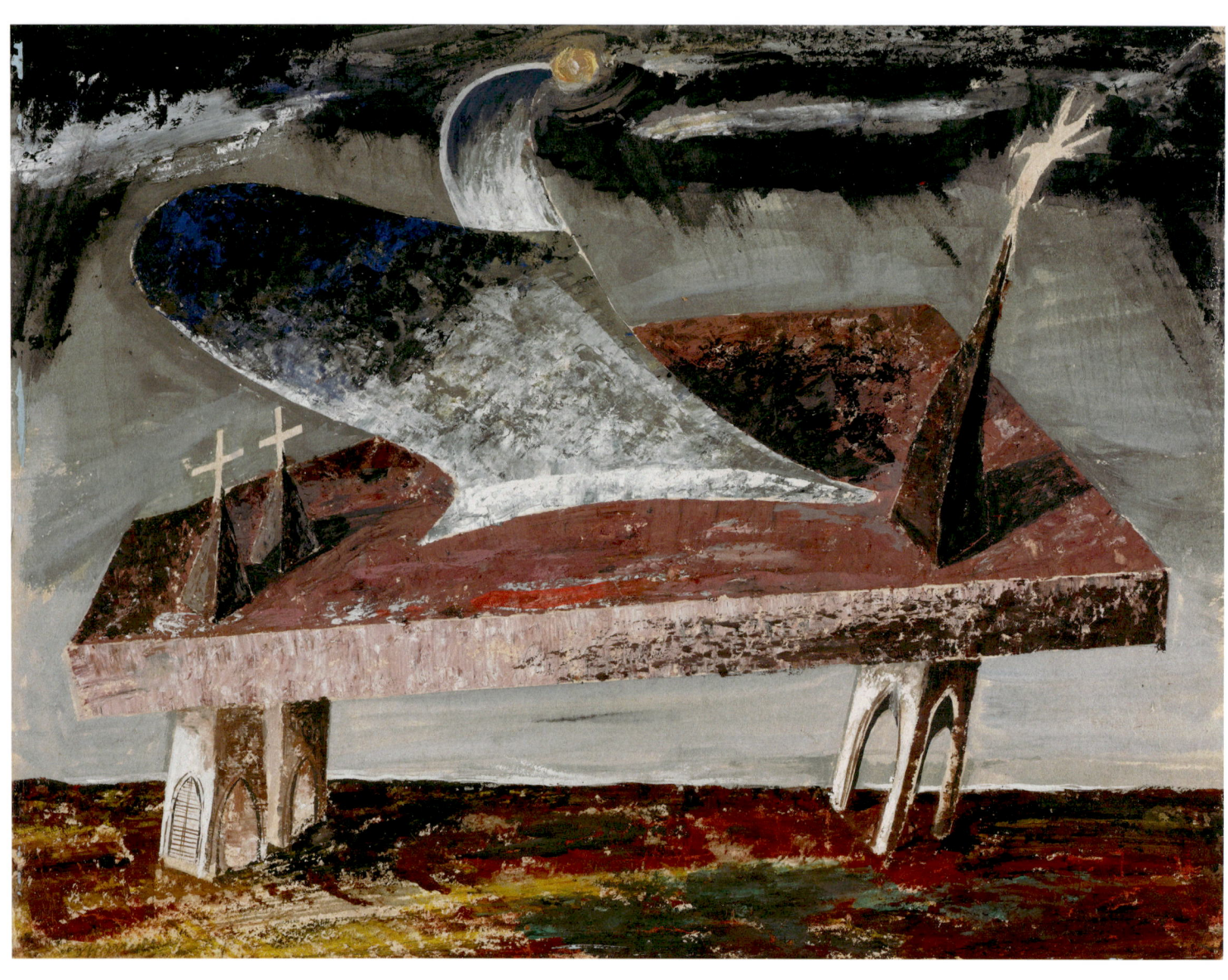

127 Morris Graves, *Untitled (Altar)*, 1937, watercolor, tempera, and oil pastel or encaustic on paper mounted on composite board

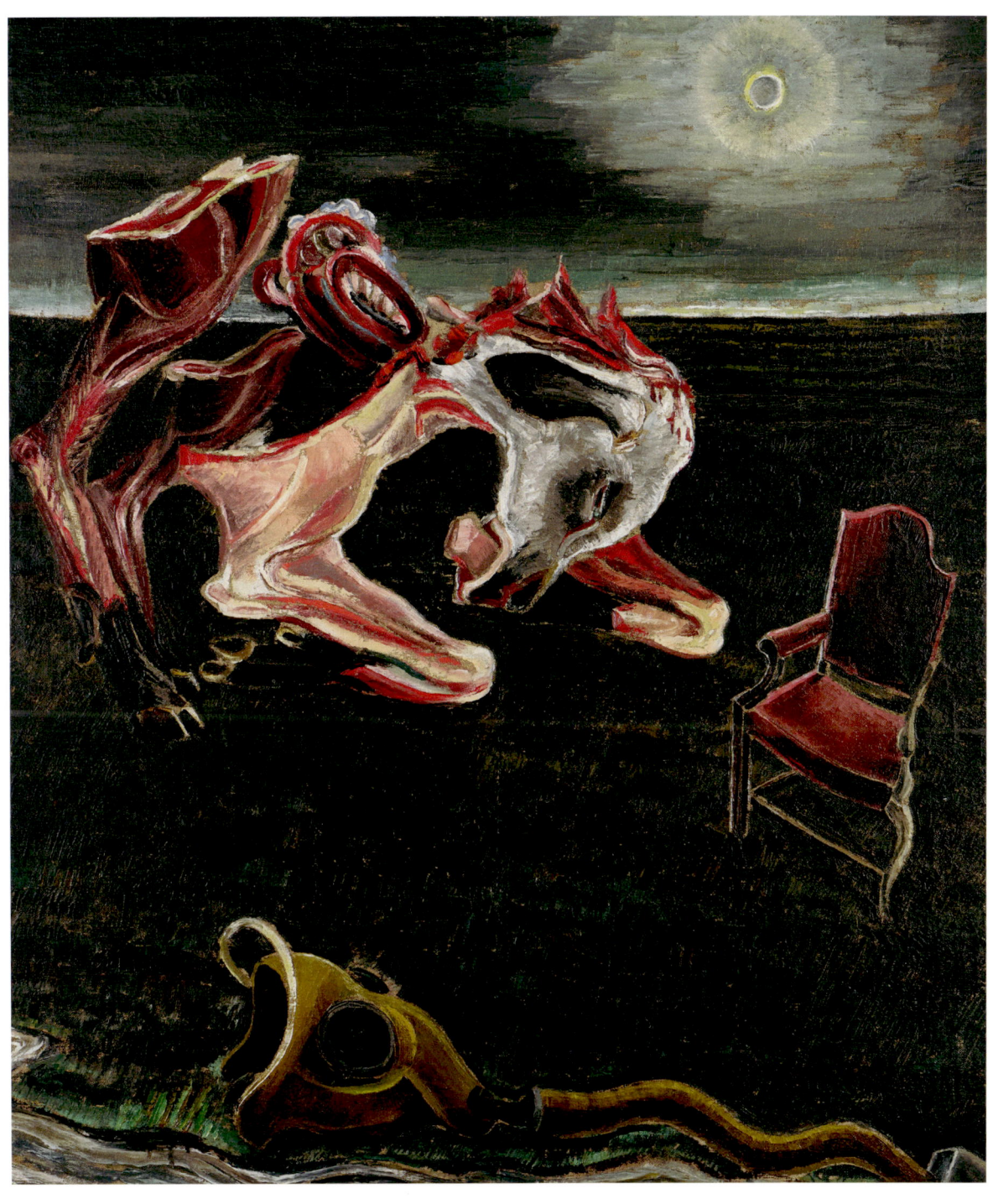

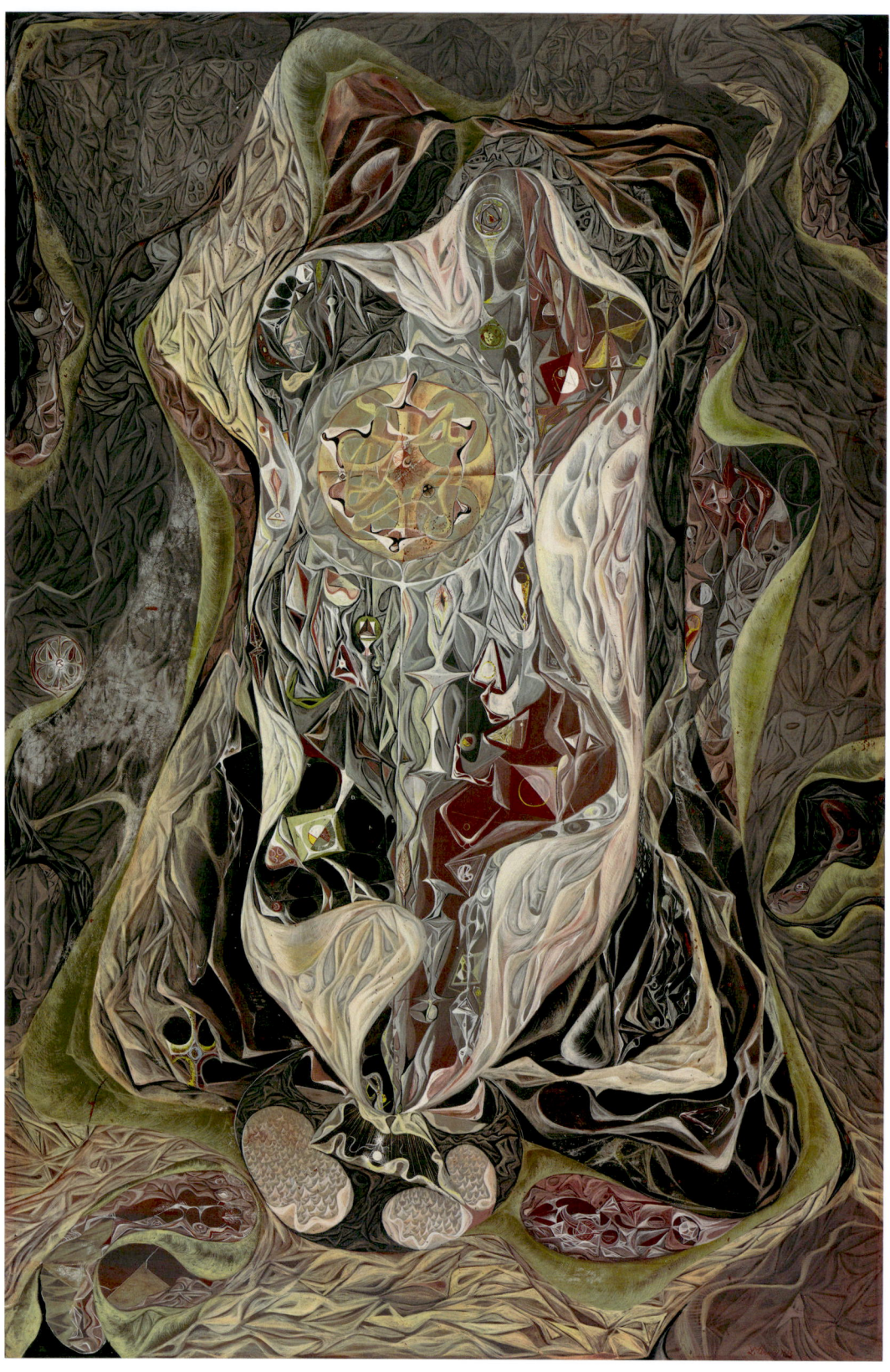

129 Leo Kenney, *The Inception of Magic*, 1945, tempera on composite board

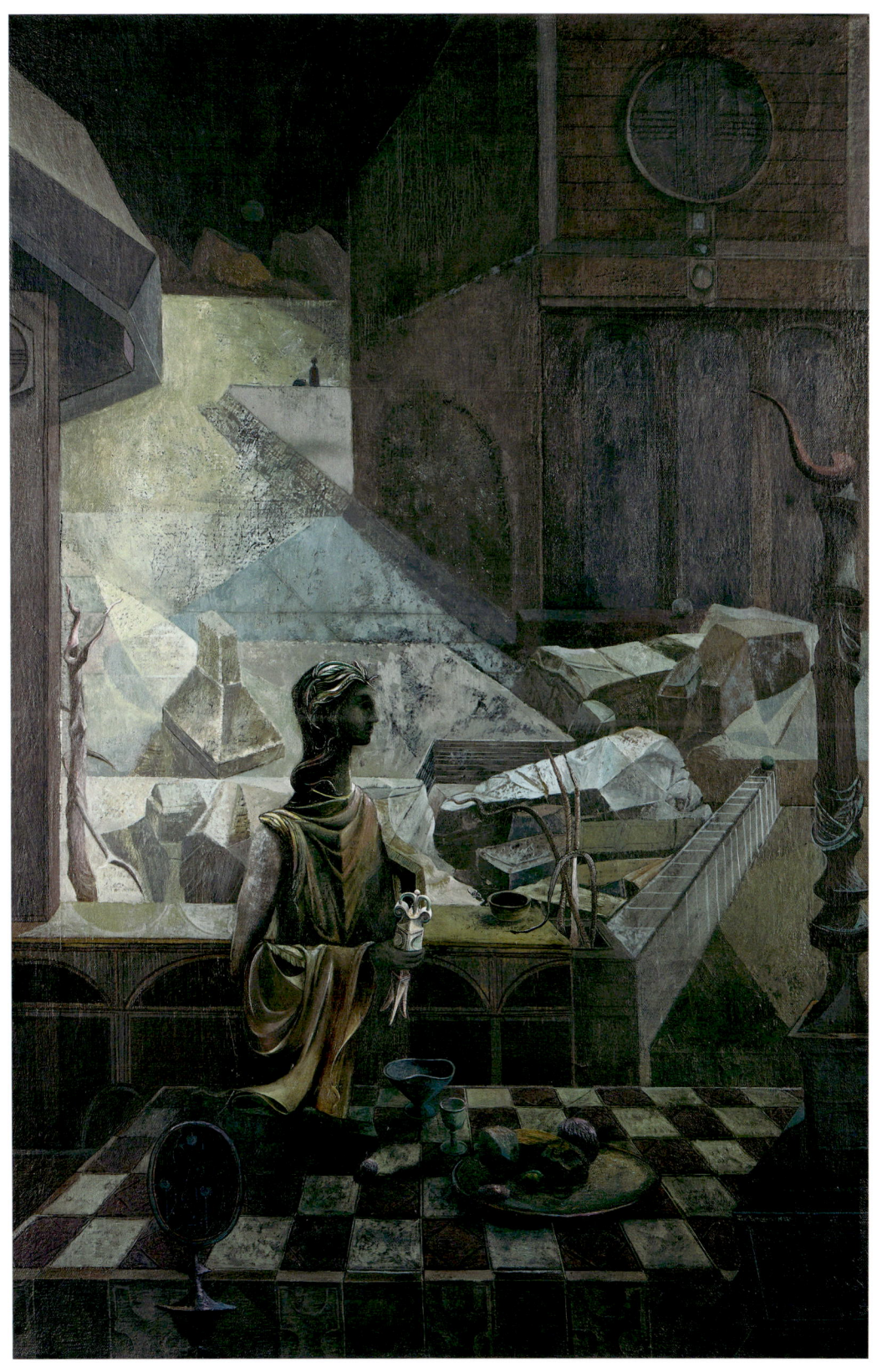

130 Leo Kenney, *Northern Image: The Muse III*, 1948, oil on canvas

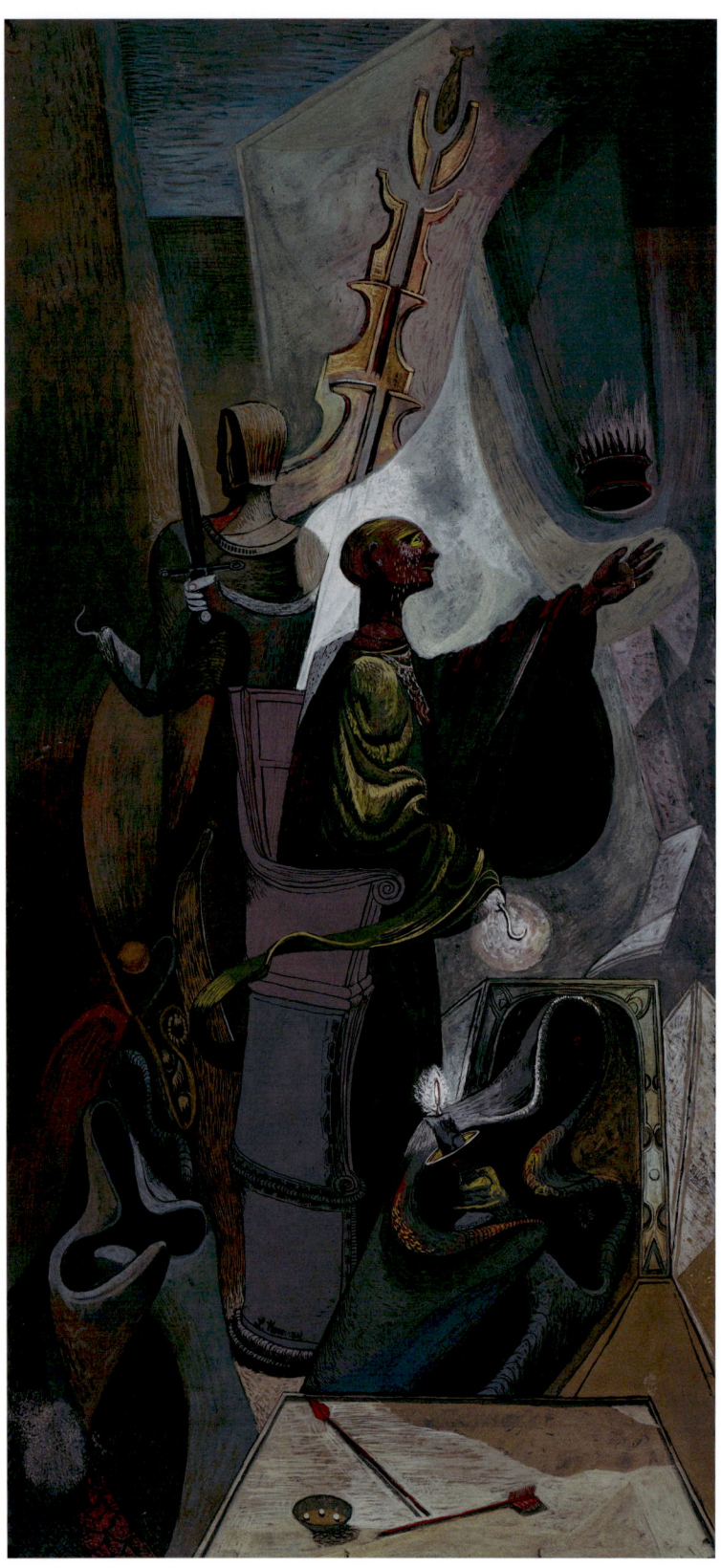

131 Leo Kenney, *Lamentation*, 1947, watercolor on black paper

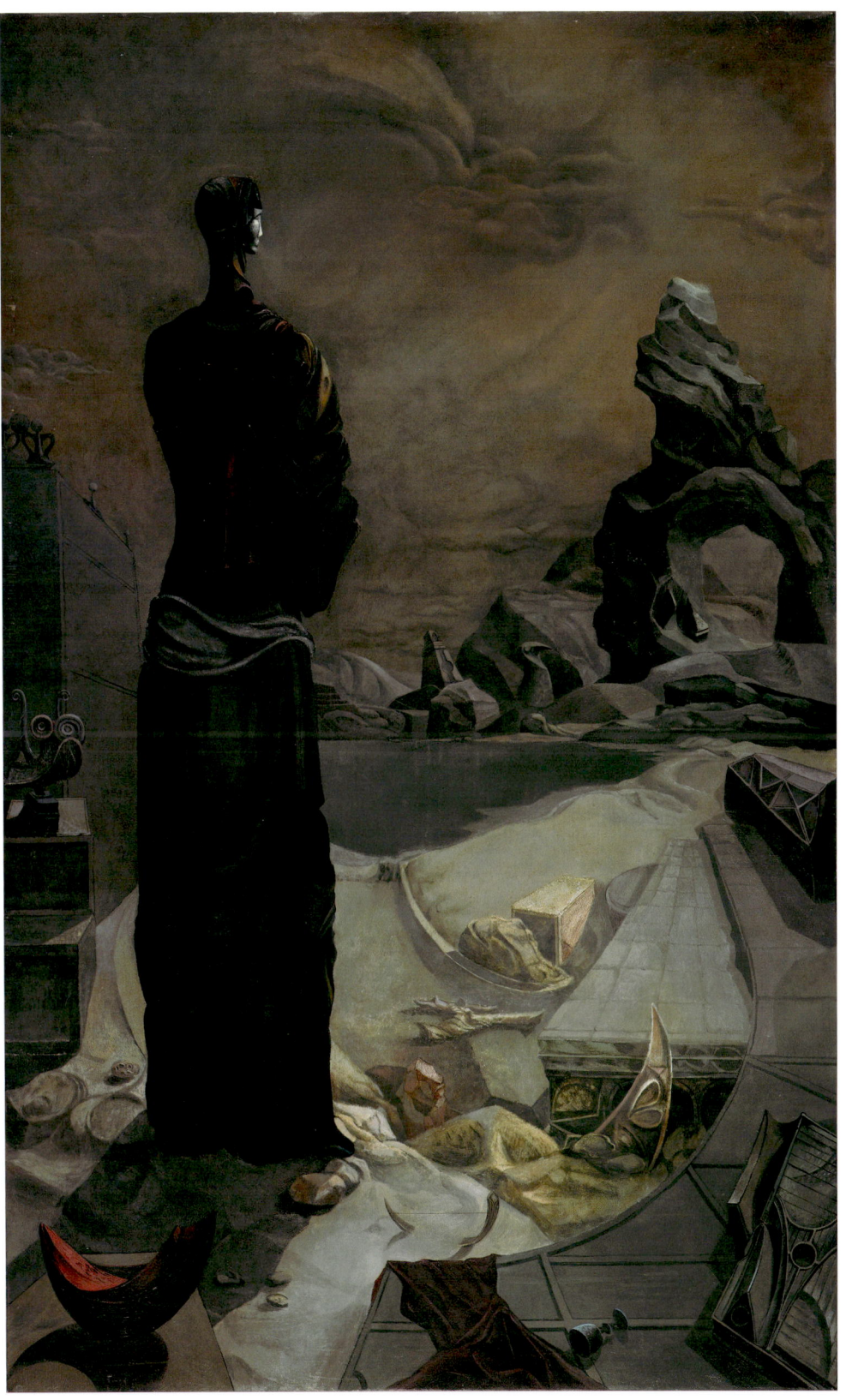

132 Leo Kenney, *Third Offering*, 1948, oil on canvas

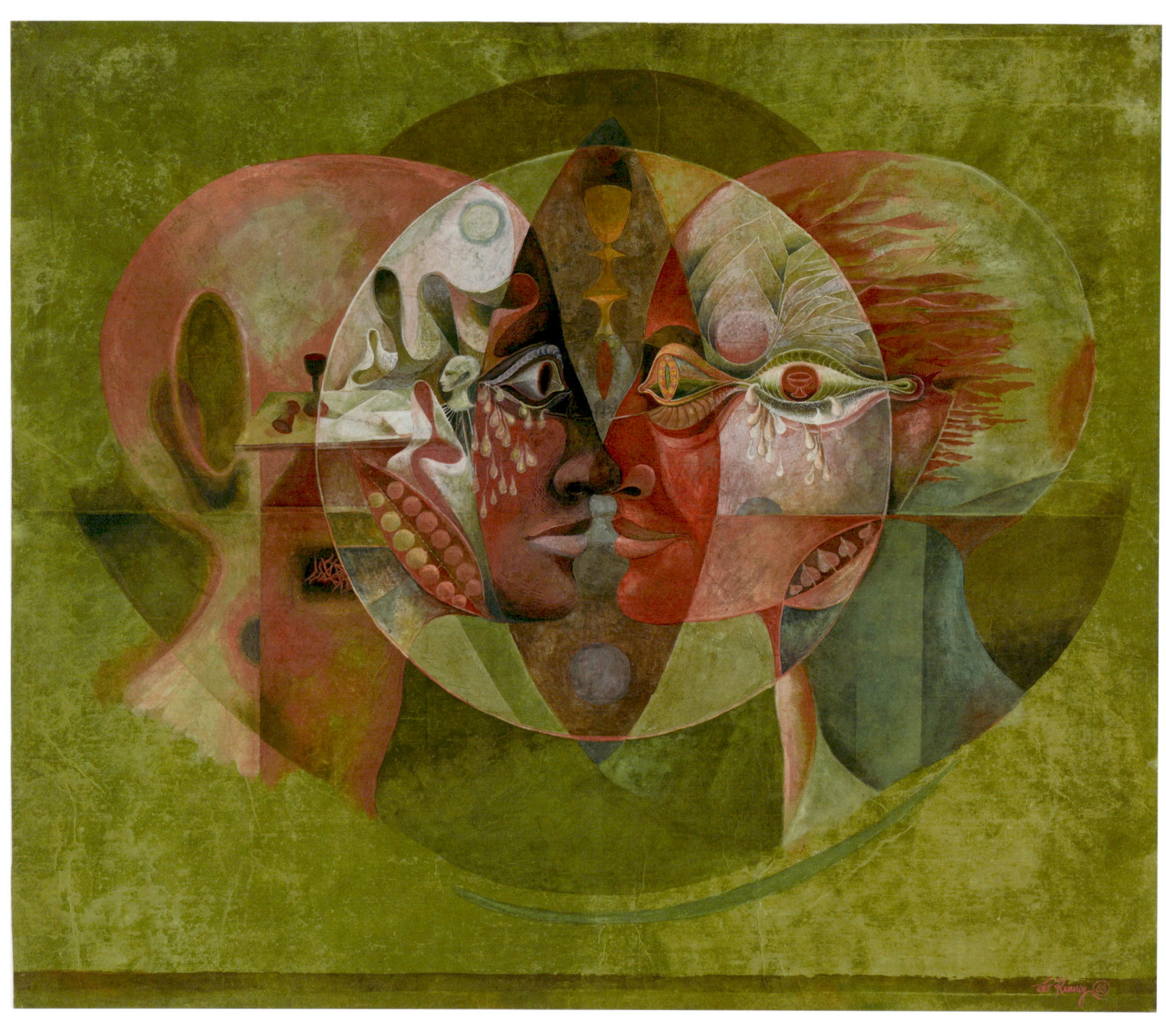

133 Leo Kenney, *Voyage for Two*, 1953, gouache on Chinese paper

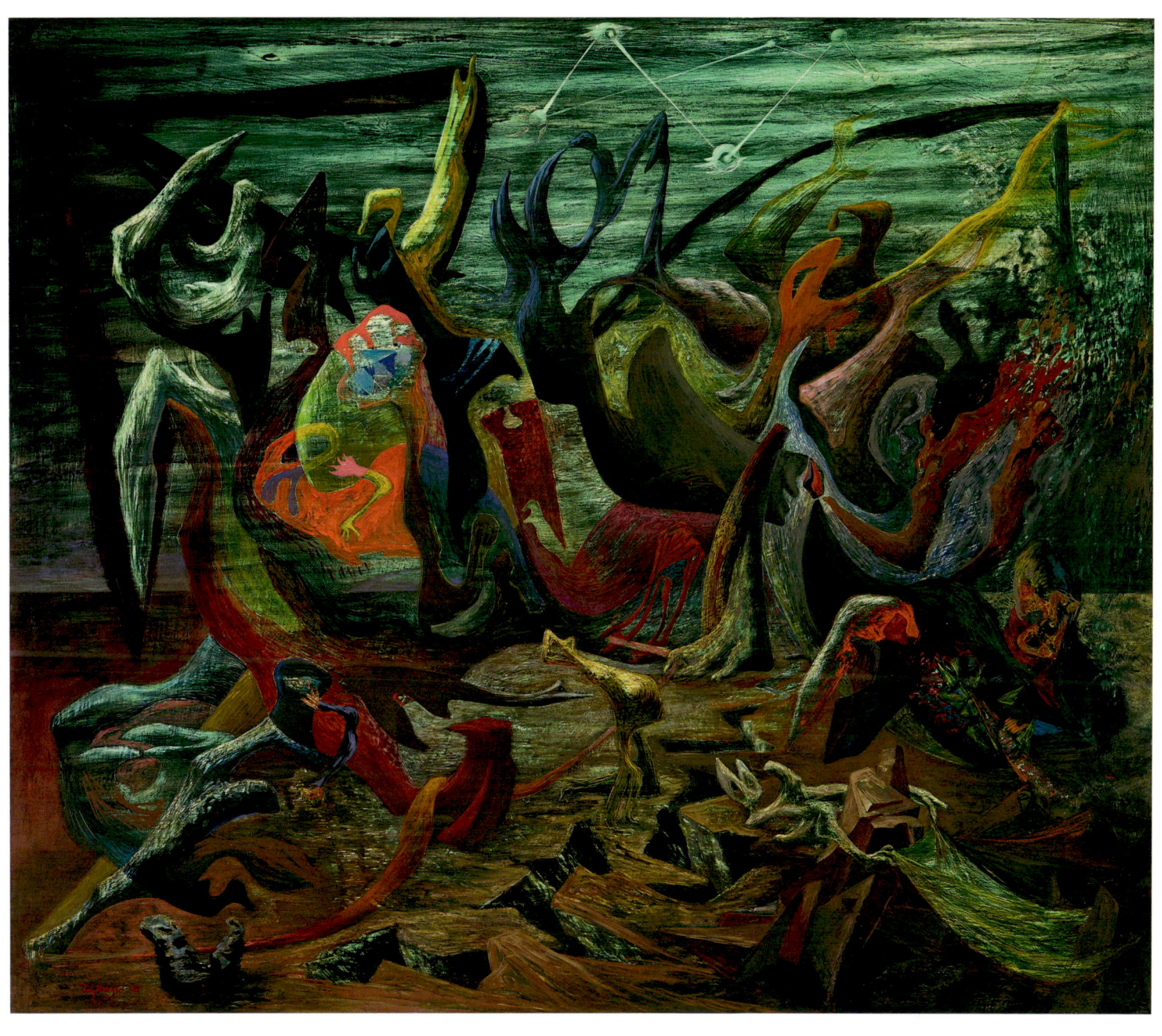

134 James H. FitzGerald, *Resurgent Sea*, 1945, oil and tempera on board

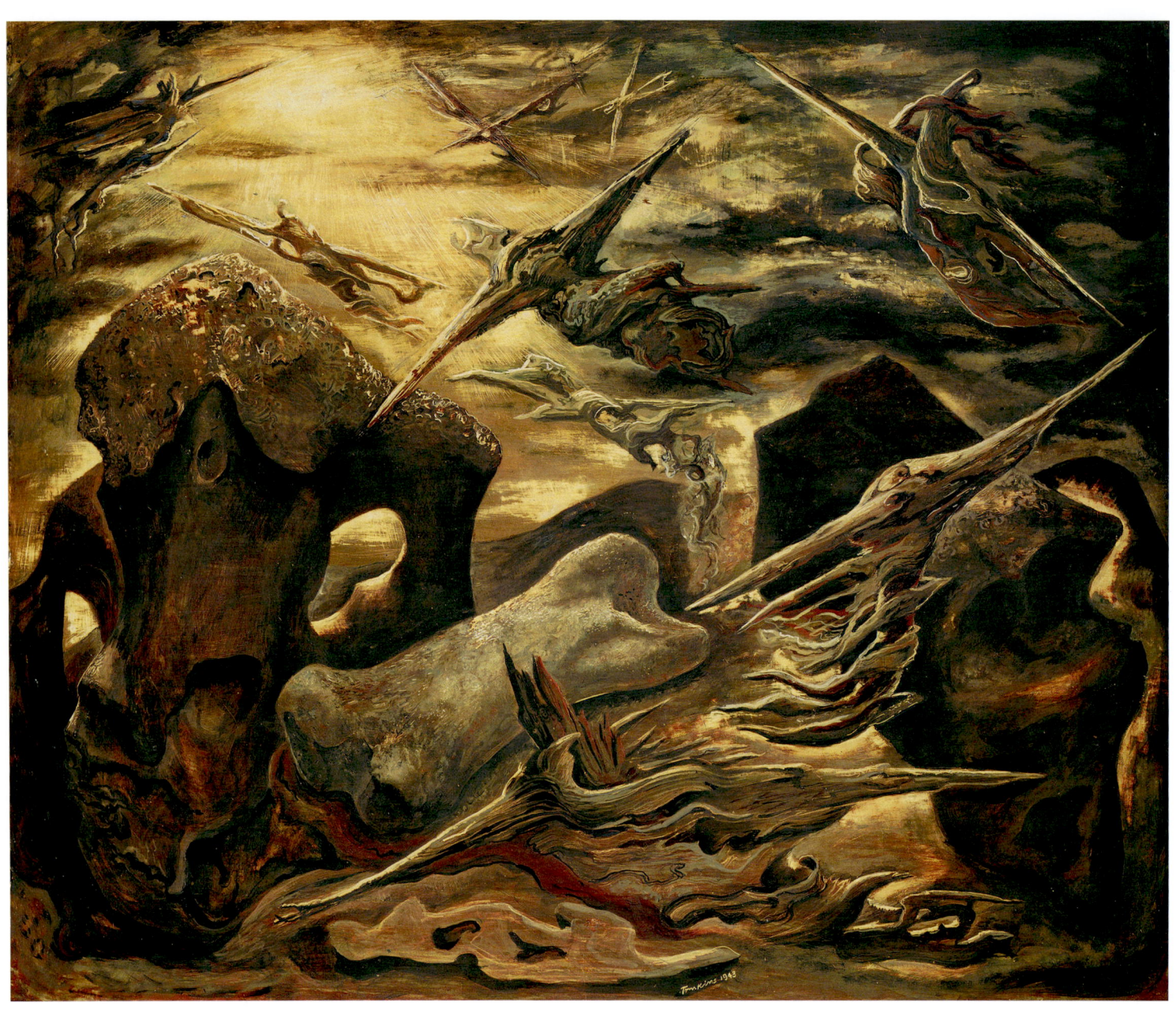

135 Margaret Tomkins, *Metamorphosis*, 1943, tempera on Masonite

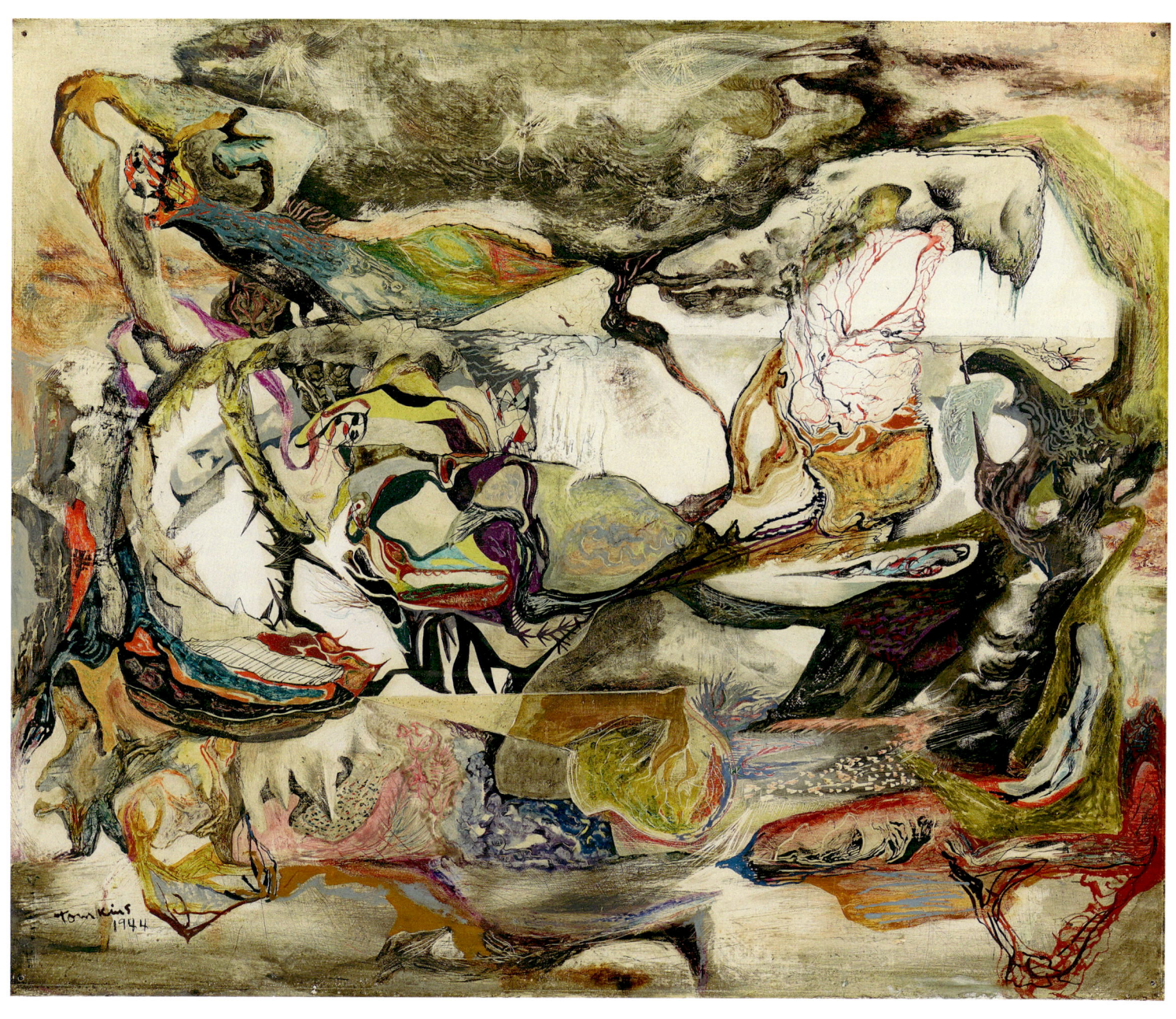

136 Margaret Tomkins, *Anamorphosis*, 1944, ink and tempera on board

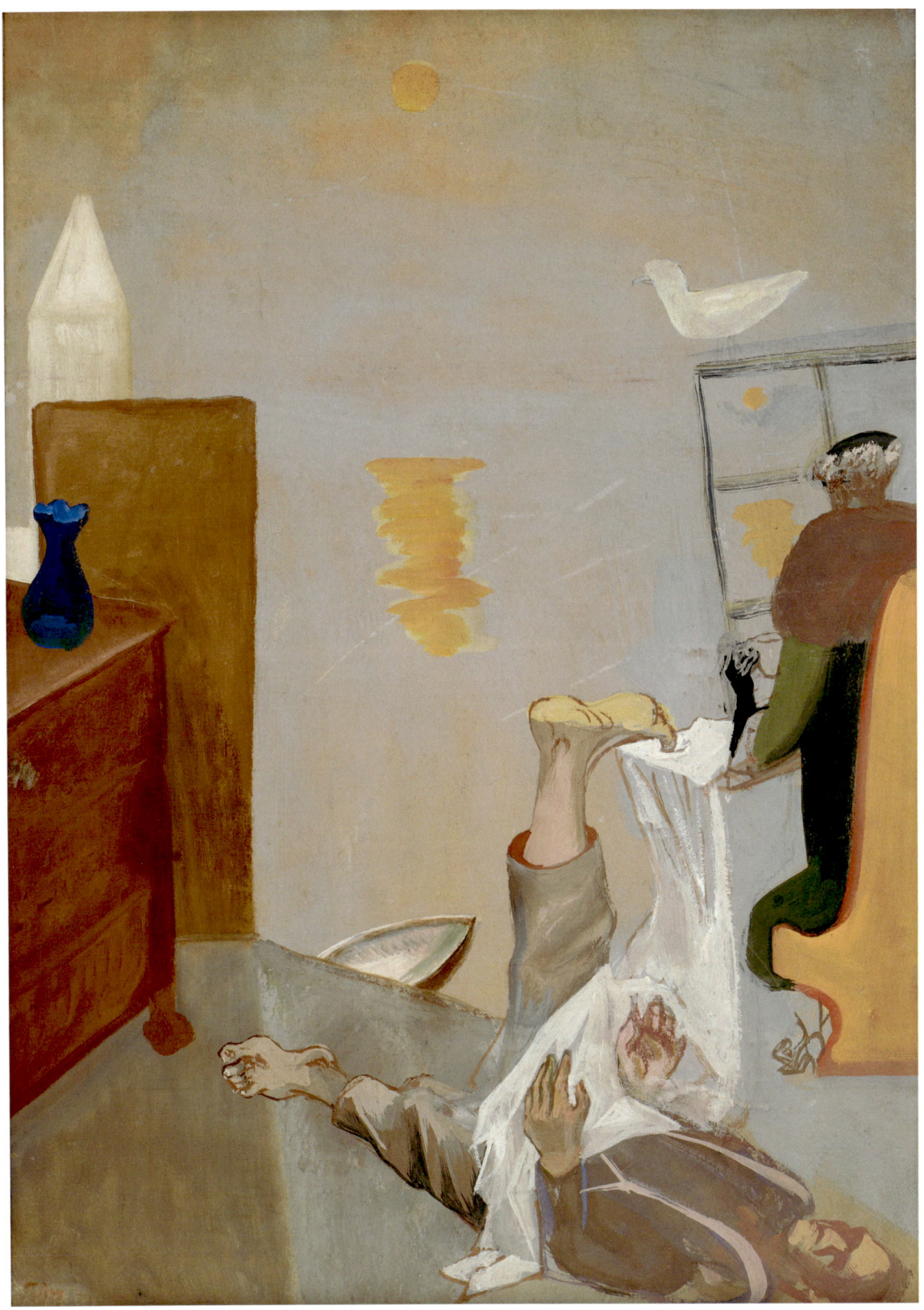

137 Mark Tobey, *Market Fantasy*, ca. 1940, tempera on paperboard

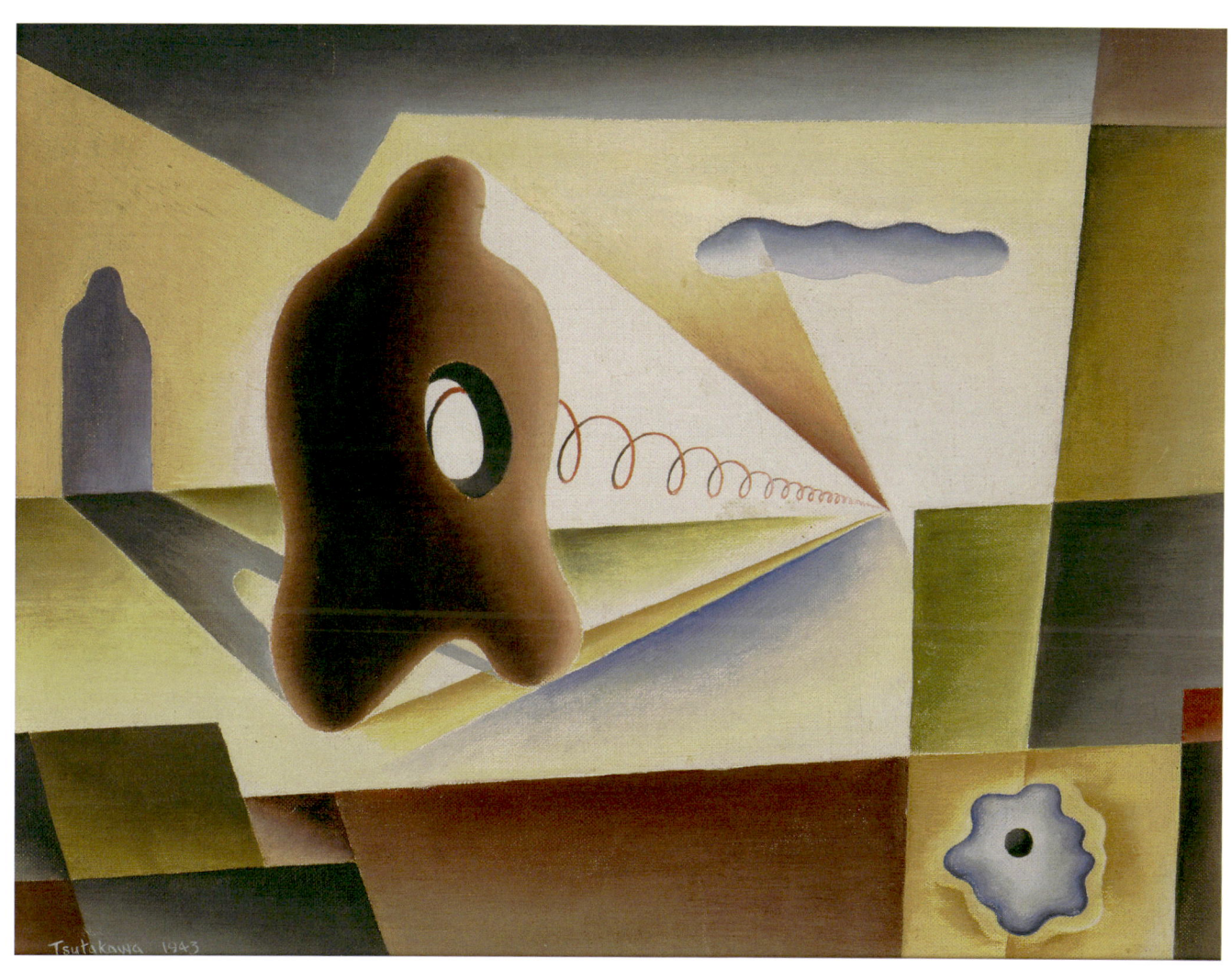

138 George Tsutakawa, *Self-Portrait*, ca. 1941, oil on canvas

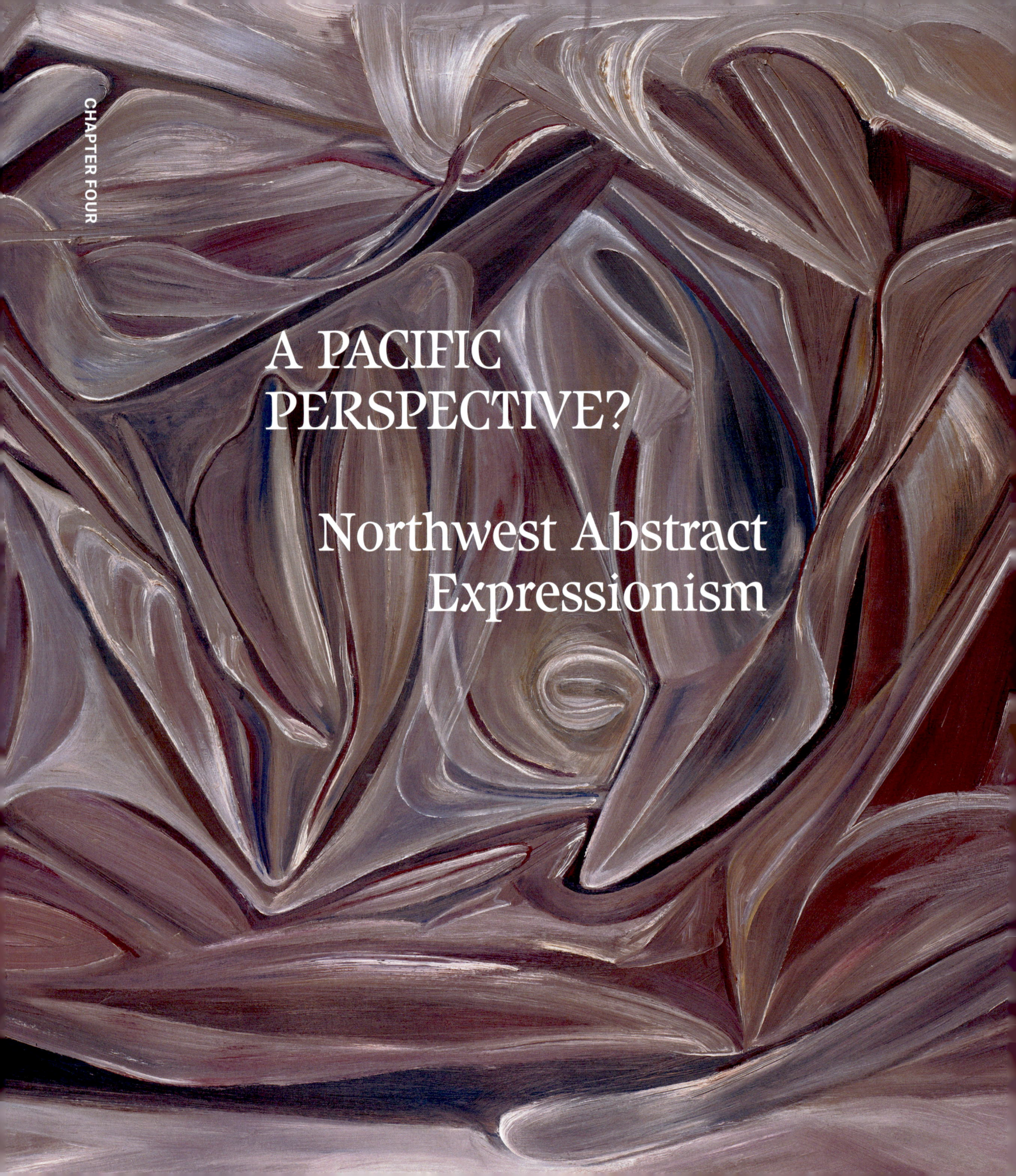

CHAPTER FOUR

A PACIFIC PERSPECTIVE?

Northwest Abstract Expressionism

In 1933, Mark Tobey unveiled a painting that announced a new direction for Modernism in the Pacific Northwest. The diminutive pastel, titled *Cirque d'hiver* (1933, plate 141), was nearly monochromatic, completely non-objective, and dominated by an intricate web of kinetic black lines meant as visual equivalents for movement. He elaborated his linear networks in subsequent abstract paintings such as *White Night* (1942, plate 142), switching black pigment for white and applying it spontaneously and calligraphically in the spirit of Surrealist automatism and the electrified energy of the urban environment. His "white writing," as his gestural technique has come to be known, both reflects his knowledge of Chinese calligraphy and aligns his work with Abstract Expressionism, an affinity he shared with many Northwest Modernists, including Kenneth Callahan, Morris Graves, Paul Horiuchi, and George Tsutakawa.

Beginning in the 1940s, these artists, following the lead of Tobey's groundbreaking paintings, were developing a regional form of abstraction allegedly inspired by the artistic and philosophical traditions of the Pacific Rim, most notably those of East Asia and Northwest Coast Native communities.[1] The paradigm of a Northwest version of Abstract Expressionism oriented more to the Pacific than to Europe, however, merits closer examination. On the one hand, this paradigm unfolded in a place—Seattle—where ties to Asia and the Pacific Northwest hinterland, as well as their expression in visual culture, had

long been established. On the other hand, it relied heavily on the priorities and assumptions of midcentury art criticism, which at times offered overly simplistic accounts of artistic influence and also often failed to consider how Asian, Asian American, and Native artists in the Puget Sound region negotiated modernity on their own terms.

In 1896, the steamship *Miike Maru* of the Japanese shipping company Nippon Yusen Kaisha pulled into the Seattle waterfront, announcing regular trade and passenger service between Japan and North America. That same year, gold was struck in Yukon Territory, and Seattle became the headquarters for gear and transportation targeted to prospectors hoping to cash in on the Klondike Gold Rush. Thirteen years later, in 1909, with its commercial and political networks in Alaska and Asia well established, Seattle entered the world stage as an industrial, technological, and resource-rich powerhouse, proudly presenting the Alaska-Yukon-Pacific Exposition (AYPE) to celebrate the development and economic growth of the Pacific Northwest.[2] Held on undeveloped land on what is now the University of Washington campus, the AYPE was one in a long line of world's fairs organized since the mid-nineteenth century to flaunt the latest in industry, culture, and technology. (Recent studies have exposed the subtexts of colonial expansion, unfair racial stereotypes, and harmful resource extraction in the early universal expositions held in Europe and North America.)

In celebrating the Pacific Northwest's natural and cultural assets, the fair positioned the Puget Sound at the center of a global network that encompassed the entire Northwest Coast and extended into the Pacific, and its architecture and advertising reinforced this triad of Seattle, the greater Pacific Northwest, and Asia. The AYPE emblem (fig. 11), for example, designed by Adelaide Hanscom Leeson, shows a cluster of three women rendered in the Arts and Crafts style: One, seated among fir trees, holds a miniature train to symbolize trade over land; a second, shaded by a bonsai tree, bears a tiny ship to symbolize trade by sea; and the third, illuminated by the northern lights, offers an armful of gold nuggets to symbolize the promise of resources for this commerce. Moreover, the fair's South Gate (fig. 12)—a structure loosely based on a Japanese torii and composed of mock totem poles whose crest figures had light bulbs for eyes—was a

crass conflation of Asian and Northwest Native architectural forms and symbols. Meanwhile, the AYPE's advertising was dominated by the Seattle Totem Pole, a plundered Tlingit monument that had been reinstalled in Pioneer Square.[3] Northwest Abstract Expressionism must be understood within the context of this climate of miscellany, misrepresentation, and misappropriation. This essay examines some of its points of intersection with Asian and Northwest Coast Native art, culture, and thought; the critical fortunes of these art forms in the Western popular and scholarly imaginations; and the ways in which Asian American and Native artists also engaged with modernity.

Asian Influences and Orientalism

That Northwest Abstract Expressionists, particularly those active in the Puget Sound region, were interested in Asian art is widely acknowledged and rarely questioned. After all, Asian art and culture were all around them: in Seattle's substantial diasporic communities; in the region's many artists of East Asian descent; and in the Seattle Art Museum's collection, which was dominated not by masterworks of the Western tradition but by the world-class examples of Asian art collected and donated by the museum's founder, Richard Fuller. Callahan remarked that the "source for seeing first-class painting was the Oriental paintings [at SAM]," which offered him and his fellow artists an abundance of instructional exemplars and, for some of them, a point of departure for further experimentation.[4]

Tobey's study of Chinese calligraphy, for example, began in Seattle in the 1920s with visits to the museum and study with Teng Kuei, a Chinese artist-in-residence at the University of Washington. In 1934, Tobey traveled to China to visit Teng and practice sumi-e before going on to Japan to study haiku and calligraphy at a Zen monastery outside Kyoto.[5] He demonstrated his knowledge of sumi-e in paintings such as *Space Ritual No. 1* and *Space Ritual No. 18* (both 1957, plates 143, 144), in which

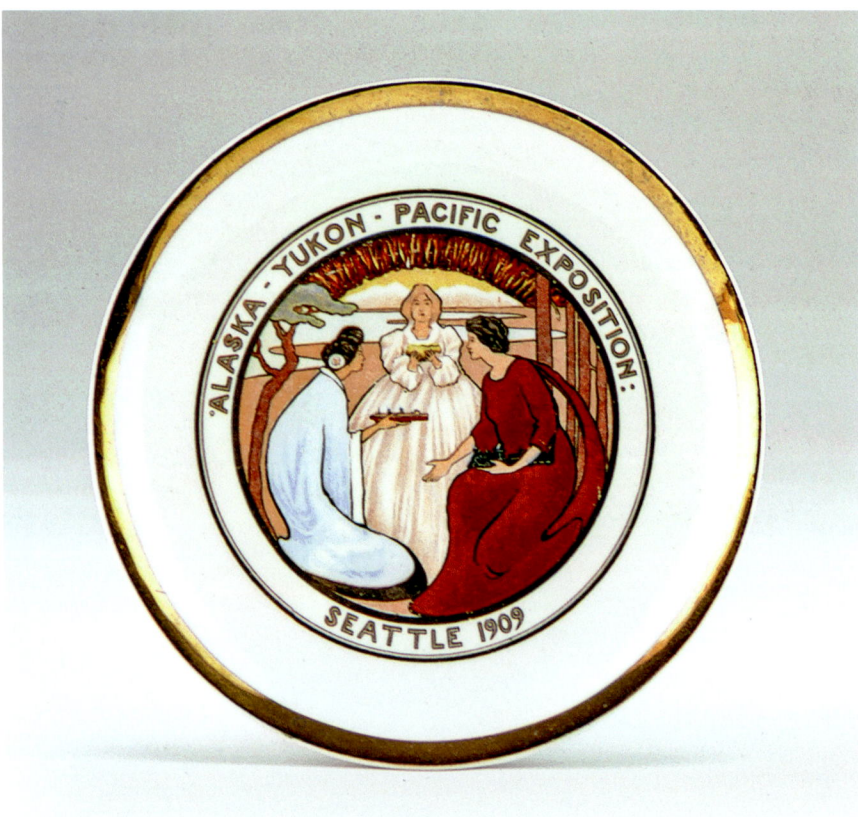

Fig. 11. Plate with Alaska-Yukon-Pacific Exposition emblem designed by Adelaide Hanscom Leeson (American, 1875–1931), 1909, ceramic, paint; height: ¾ in., diameter: 6½ in. Museum of History and Industry, Seattle, 1954.678.2

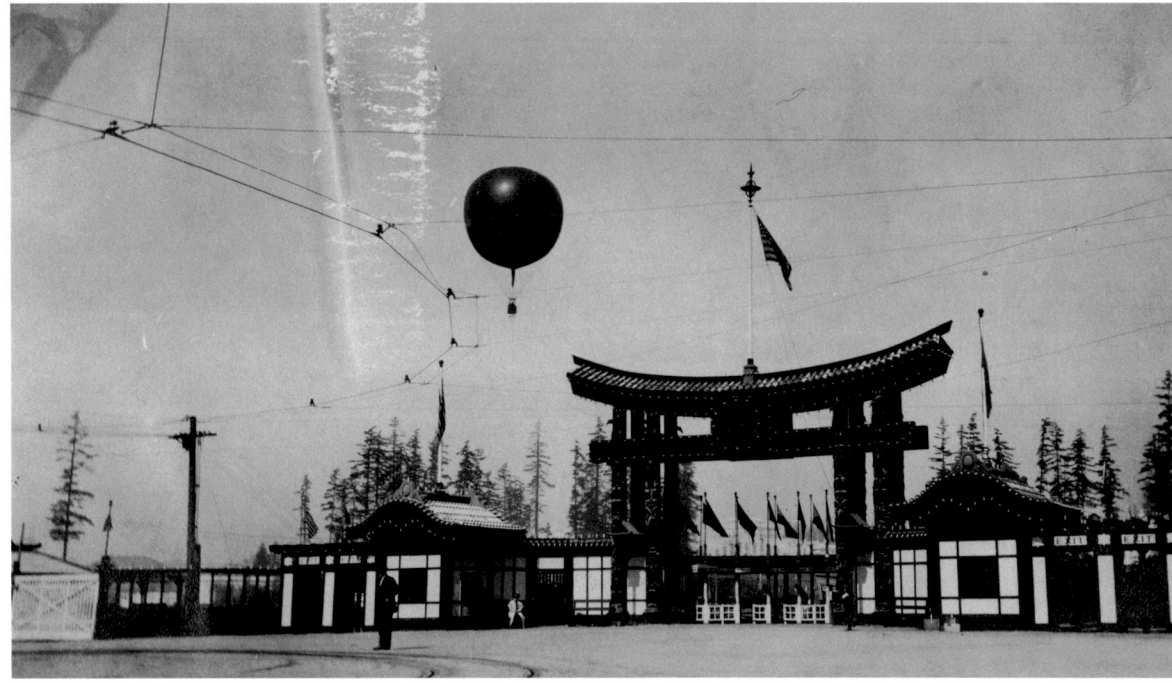

Fig. 12. South Gate, Alaska-Yukon-Pacific Exposition, 1909. University of Washington Special Collections

calligraphic ink strokes merge with the gesturalism of Abstract Expressionism. As he wrote in a 1957 letter to the dealer Marian Willard, these works synthesize Western painting technique and Eastern self-awareness: "Standing as I am here between East and West cultures, I sometimes get dizzy as I find I can't always make a synthesis and that I admire both paths which should and will, I suppose, merge."[6] By this time, he was practicing calligraphy alongside the Seattle artists Paul Horiuchi and George Tsutakawa, as well as the Zen master Tamotsu Takizaki, who owned the local antiques store Far West. From Takizaki, Tobey learned to "let nature take over in [his] work" and get out of his own way enough "not [to] look for fine draughtsmanship nor fine color—perhaps no color—but directness of spirit [as] a new point of view as the arts of the East and of the West draw closer together."[7]

For Tobey, an alignment of Eastern and Western art would lead to greater aesthetic awareness and spiritual knowledge. For Horiuchi and Tsutakawa, it offered a way of reclaiming their Japanese ancestry as American Modernists. Chikamasa Horiuchi—who called

himself Paul after the Post-Impressionist painter Paul Cézanne—studied calligraphy and painting as a child in his hometown of Oishi, Japan.[8] At the age of sixteen, he immigrated to Seattle and the temporary custody of his cousin Shigetoshi Horiuchi, a dealer and collector of Japanese antiquities, before traveling to Wyoming to join his family and begin a career with the Union Pacific Railroad (a career that was cut short with World War II and the subsequent brutal discrimination against Japanese Americans). In Wyoming, he enjoyed moderate success as a Sunday painter specializing in conventional, Impressionist landscapes, but after the war and his permanent return to Seattle, he found his voice as a full-time artist. In his backroom studio at his antique shop, Tozai, which also served as his gallery and a gathering space for fellow artists, he created works that earned him material and critical success. Encouraged by Tobey, Horiuchi tapped into his early exposure to Japanese aesthetics to break through to his signature style: collages made of hand-dyed rice paper that he tore and arranged in balanced abstraction, such as *Monolithic Impasse* (1964, plate 151).

Tsutakawa was born in Seattle and educated in Fukuyama, Japan, where he was sent at the age of seven to live with his highly cultivated maternal grandparents. Under their tutelage—especially that of his grandfather—he learned Kabuki and Noh drama, ikebana, tea ceremony, and calligraphy before returning to Seattle at the age of sixteen. During World War II, he was drafted into the US Army; upon his discharge, after pursuing his MFA at the University of Washington on the GI Bill, he embarked on a career as an artist specializing in calligraphic watercolors, ink paintings, and sculpture.[9] Throughout his adult life, Tsutakawa visited Japan regularly, and in 1956, following one such sojourn (and at Tobey's suggestion), he began to apply his long-standing interest in Asian culture and aesthetics to his work. He often said that it was the non-Asian artists, especially Tobey, who rekindled his interest in Asian art.[10] This influence is evident in Tsutakawa's *Obos* (plates 155, 156), a series of sculptures composed of freestanding abstract forms that, stacked with balance and perfect proportion, echo the ritual piles of stones he encountered in Japan and the Himalayas. The *Obos* announce the direction Tsutakawa's work would take thereafter, most notably in his fountain designs, which embody the harmony between nature and its inhabitants that he discerned from Asian philosophy. Reflecting on the impact of Asian thought in this work, he wrote:

> For me, 1960 or thereabouts was a time to take another look at the philosophy and art of the Orient—particularly Japanese art—that I had become familiar with in my youth. Through my travels and my studies of traditional Japanese arts I was able to reaffirm my conviction in the Oriental view of nature which sees man as one part of nature, a part that must live in harmony with the rest of nature.[11]

The influence of Asian art and thought on the work of Tobey, Horiuchi, and Tsutakawa, however, while rich with suggestion, is easily overstated and aligns less with their direct experience (save for Horiuchi's and Tsutakawa's early educations) than with their overall views that Asian philosophy and aesthetics signal harmony in nature. Their reception of Asian philosophy, like that of many American artists in the mid-twentieth century, bears the mark of a Westernized, romanticized version of Zen Buddhism that focused on agency, individual wholeness, and the unpredictability of change and had its roots in Orientalist constructs of Asia from a Western perspective. Indeed, Orientalism provided the prevailing context for the influence of Asian art and thought on Northwest Abstract Expressionism, whether it was Tobey's spiritualized approach to calligraphy, Horiuchi's embrace of Asian materials, or Tsutakawa's views on nature's balance.

Zen entered postwar American culture with the 1948 publication of the German philosopher Eugen Herrigel's *Zen in the Art of Archery*, which offered a road map for applying basic Zen principles to secular pursuits, and Richard Wilhelm's 1950 English translation of the *I Ching*, which, with a foreword by Carl Jung, described a world in constant flux and governed by chance. But even before this, Zen flowed into Pacific Northwest artistic circles through the conduit of the avant-garde Cornish School of Allied Arts, where, during the 1930s, the composer John Cage taught his indeterminate and holistic approach to music and, in 1937, the philosopher Nancy Wilson Ross delivered lectures on the relationship between Zen and Dadaism.

For American artists, Zen, as filtered through Western epistemologies, was a sustaining mode for artistic philosophies predicated on chance, spontaneity, and unity, which were themselves founded on Jungian notions of mythological commonalities, comparative religion, and the collective unconscious.[12] In Seattle, this aesthetic Orientalism was amplified by the city's deliberate self-positioning as a gateway to Asia, which led to uncritical assumptions that Puget Sound Modernists were influenced by Asian art and thought, regardless of its Westernization and irrespective of degree.

Native American Influences and Artists

Many Northwest Modernists were drawn to the art and cultural practices of the Native communities of the Pacific Northwest. Guy Anderson, Graves, and Tobey, for example, were frequent visitors to the Washington State Museum (now the Burke Museum of Natural History and Culture) in Seattle and its vast collections of totems and other carvings; they also collected Northwest Coast Native masks, baskets, and other objects and, along with the painter Helmi Juvonen, were drawn to the ceremonial practices of local tribes.[13] In 1938, the pioneering anthropologist Erna Gunther, who was well connected with tribal communities in the Puget Sound region, brought a group of artists, including Anderson, Graves, the painter William Cumming, and the dancer Eleanor

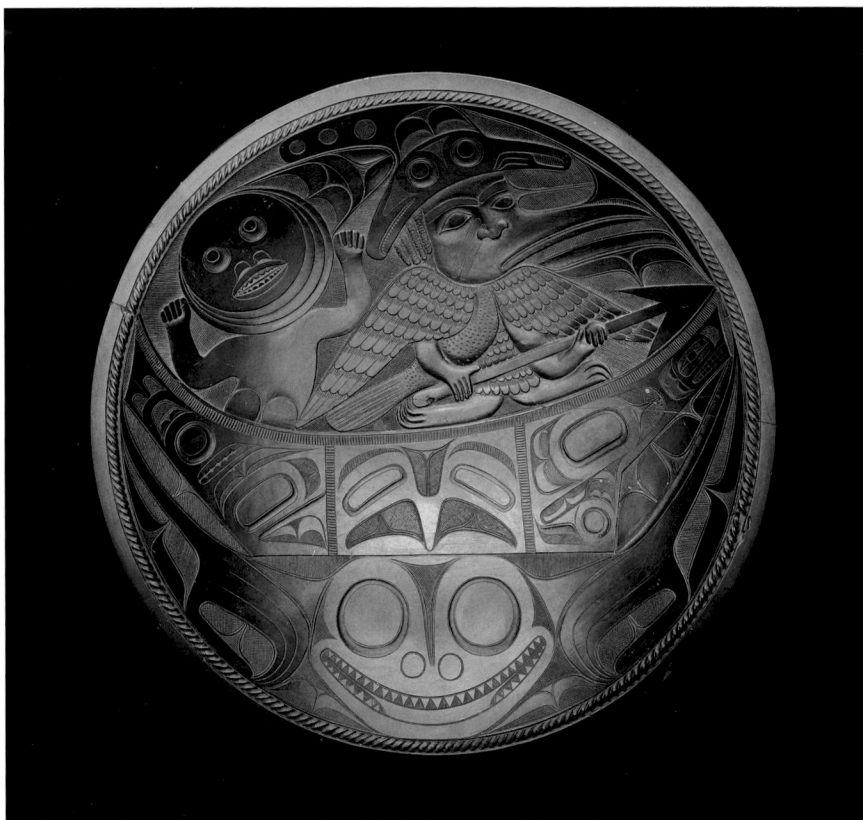

Fig. 13. Charles Edenshaw (First Nations, Haida, 1839–1920), *Platter*, ca. 1885, argillite, height: 2¼ in., circumference: 13 in. Seattle Art Museum, Gift of John H. Hauberg, 91.1.127

King, to the dances at the Snohomish long-house near La Conner, Washington. Typically closed to all but tribal members, these rituals were deliberately unintelligible to outsiders; therefore, while the non-Native contingent of Northwest artists gained access thanks to Gunther, they were forced to rely on their Western sensibilities in their attempts to interpret what they had witnessed. This left considerable room for romantic projection and, at times, outright misunderstanding. According to the highly cynical Cumming, the group spent "a dispirited evening watching Indians of the Northwest coastal areas dance for their conquerors," where "the dancers were listless. The fires smoldered dull. We were invaders and intruders, bringing to the ceremonies only our curiosity and our patronizing minds."[14] Anderson's comments suggest that he found the performance impenetrable and himself able to do little more than watch the practitioners "going into a trance," where they made "very strange noises" and "[danced] around the bonfires and in the smoke."[15] To him, "the dances were always the same; they weren't very inventive. . . . They just kind of jumped from one foot to the other . . . [and] always made this sound when they were jumping. . . . The ones in trance seemed to do the same thing; they weren't dancing as a kind of dance; it was a thing of therapy, I think."[16]

Anderson's indifferent misreading of the ritual aspects of Snohomish ceremony carried over into his appropriation of Northwest Coast Native formal strategies in his paintings. For him, these visual languages symbolized universal human experience and natural wholeness, a sweeping understanding that he shared with many of his fellow artists.[17] While paintings such as *Dream of the Language Wheel* (1962, plate 157) superficially resemble the graphic forcefulness of formline—a style of bold, swooping and tapering linear designs used in unique expressions among various Northwest Coast Indigenous cultures (fig. 13)—they are ultimately pure abstractions that lack formline's iconographic specificity and symbolic weight.

Similarly, Tobey incorporated elements of the Native masks he collected into paintings such as *Esquimaux Idiom* (1946, plate 160), whose central figures, with their extreme frontality and outstretched arms, are loosely based on Yup'ik River wind maker masks, and whose supporting cast of fish and other creatures echoes the vertical orientation of totem poles.[18]

Tobey's and Anderson's highly generalized conceptions of Northwest Coast Native art find their counterpart in the broader, pan-Indian context of Seattle and its environs. Indeed, a vast assortment of Northwest Coast Native art was everywhere in Seattle at midcentury—in the wide-ranging collections at the Washington State Museum; in the totem poles that stood in the city's parks and public spaces; in the baskets, beadwork, and carvings marketed by local Native vendors; and in the retail outlets (most famously Ye Olde Curiosity Shop) that offered everything from inexpensive curios and kitschy trinkets to genuine artifacts and the craftwork of legitimate carvers, serving a clientele that encompassed tourists bound for Alaska and serious collectors alike.[19] This kaleidoscope of Native things—whether from the Puget Sound, the Pacific Northwest hinterland, or even farther afield—effectively conflated multitudes of cultures, communities, and histories into a single "Indian" entity for the general public's indiscriminate consumption, with little consideration for the Puget Sound's actual living Native populations and their diverse cultural practices.[20]

This pluralism is reflected in approaches to and interpretations of Native American art within Modernism more broadly, whose advance coincided with the recognition of Native cultural production as art—alongside primitivizing assumptions that Native people were close to nature, untouched by modernity, and, importantly, frozen in time.[21] Driving this was the notion of the Vanishing Indian, a hypothetical pure aboriginal who had been effectively contaminated and ultimately eradicated through contact with non-Natives, leaving behind nothing but ancient cultural production

that was seen as evidence of unadulterated, unmediated creativity. East Coast avant-garde artists—including Marsden Hartley, John Sloan, Mabel Dodge Luhan, and Walter Pach—flocked to Southwestern outposts such as Taos, New Mexico, believing modern Pueblo communities there to be deeply connected to the ancient inhabitants of their traditional homelands. These Modernists felt that contemporary Pueblo pottery and other artifacts were therefore authentically and essentially Native.[22]

The Surrealists Max Ernst, André Breton, Kurt Seligmann, and Wolfgang Paalen, moreover, built vast and complex collections of art and artifacts from throughout the Pacific Northwest, which they viewed as timeless examples of fundamental expression imbued with mystery and uncorrupted by logic.[23] In exile in the United States during World War II, these artists frequented New York's American Museum of Natural History and its collections of Northwest Coast native art. They also purchased Yup'ik, Kwakwaka'wakw, and other Northwest Coast Native objects from Julius Carlebach's New York gallery, which was well stocked with Canadian and Alaskan ceremonial artifacts, as well as masks acquired from George Gustav Heye's Museum of the American Indian in Manhattan, itself a clearinghouse for North American Native art.[24] They consumed and acquired this art with little awareness of its provenance or ritual purpose; in the spirit of Modernist primitivism, they were interested only in what they saw as its alignment with Surrealism.

The Modernist aestheticization of Native American art reached its high point in 1941 with the blockbuster exhibition *Indian Art of the United States* at the Museum of Modern Art, New York. Organized by the Indian Arts and Crafts Board, established in 1935 under the US Department of the Interior, this exhibition was curated by the museum's then-director, René d'Harnoncourt, in collaboration with the Denver Art Museum Curator of Indian Art Frederic Huntington Douglas and the architect Henry Klumb, who designed the installation.[25] With more than a thousand ancient, historical, and contemporary examples representing communities throughout North America, the exhibition celebrated the nation's Indigenous arts as an integral part of its cultural heritage, essentially decontextualizing these objects from traditional practice and modern-day purpose and recontextualizing them as American art.[26] A thirty-foot totem pole carved by the contemporary Haida artist John Wallace stood at the museum's Fifty-Third Street entrance as both a generic symbol of "Indianness" (by 1941, totem poles, along with other disparate emblems such as war bonnets, tomahawks, and teepees, had come to represent all things Native) and as an announcement of the rich array of Northwest Coast Native art housed within, including an entire room dedicated to totem poles.[27] Critics analyzed the exhibition's contents through the lens of primitivism and in Surrealist terms as evidence of what they perceived as Indigenous artists' deep connection to the preternatural energy and marvelous entities present in the subconscious. George Vaillant, for example, writing in the *Art Bulletin*, remarked that "the supernatural forces, with whom the Indian has always been in such intimate and uncomfortable contact, seemed dramatically concentrated here, overawing even the case-hardened New Yorker," while Jeannette Lowe, writing in *Art News*, described "the carved raven, killer-whale and devil fish [which] may strike the eye, more accustomed to such fauna in the world of Surrealism, as symbols of the unconscious mind."[28] Their fetishization of Native American arts as mystical and mythical offers a broader Modernist context for non-Native Northwest artists' interest in and appropriation of Native Northwest Coast art.

Modernist readings of Native American art not only extracted it from its communities of origin and their cultural practices but also failed to recognize modernity within Native communities. Native artists active throughout the Pacific Northwest in the mid-twentieth century were, like their non-Native counterparts, responding to the commercial, physical, and material realities of their time. Far from being suppressed as a result of contact with non-Natives and assimilation into mainstream American culture, Indigenous artists were alive, well, and active in the Pacific Northwest and were creating work both for their communities and for sale to outsiders. During the nineteenth and early twentieth centuries, this happened under the radar, as in the beadwork practices of Tlingit women, but this all changed during the Depression with the Indian Reorganization Act (IRA) of 1934, also known as the Indian New Deal.[29] Established by the Bureau of Indian Affairs Director John Collier, the IRA relaxed federal policies impacting Native people, supported Native cultural practices, and ushered Native epistemologies into the American mainstream as a form of spiritual healing.[30] Their blatant primitivism and gatekeeping notwithstanding, IRA programs reversed course on official policies aimed at curbing Native cultural production, and they paved the way for new programs designed to provide space and opportunities for Native artists. In Alaska, Haida and Tlingit men were enrolled in the Civilian Conservation Corps (CCC) and tasked with removing totem poles from ancestral villages, restoring them, and relocating them to parks in Southeast Alaska.[31] Within these parks, carvers reclaimed their sculptural skills, raised awareness for their craft, and in doing so asserted their sovereignty.[32] The Ute artist Julius Twohy likewise benefited from New Deal programs. One of several Native artists employed by the Works Progress Administration's Federal Arts Project, he was commissioned to paint the *Legend of the Thunderbird* mural for the dining room of Cushman Indian Hospital in Puyallup (fig. 14), as well as a series of prints that merged pan-Indian forms with Modernist style (plates 161–66).[33]

In the Puget Sound, the craft of carving brought Coast Salish artists into the orbit of Northwest Modernism. The history of this practice in the region is complicated and linked to

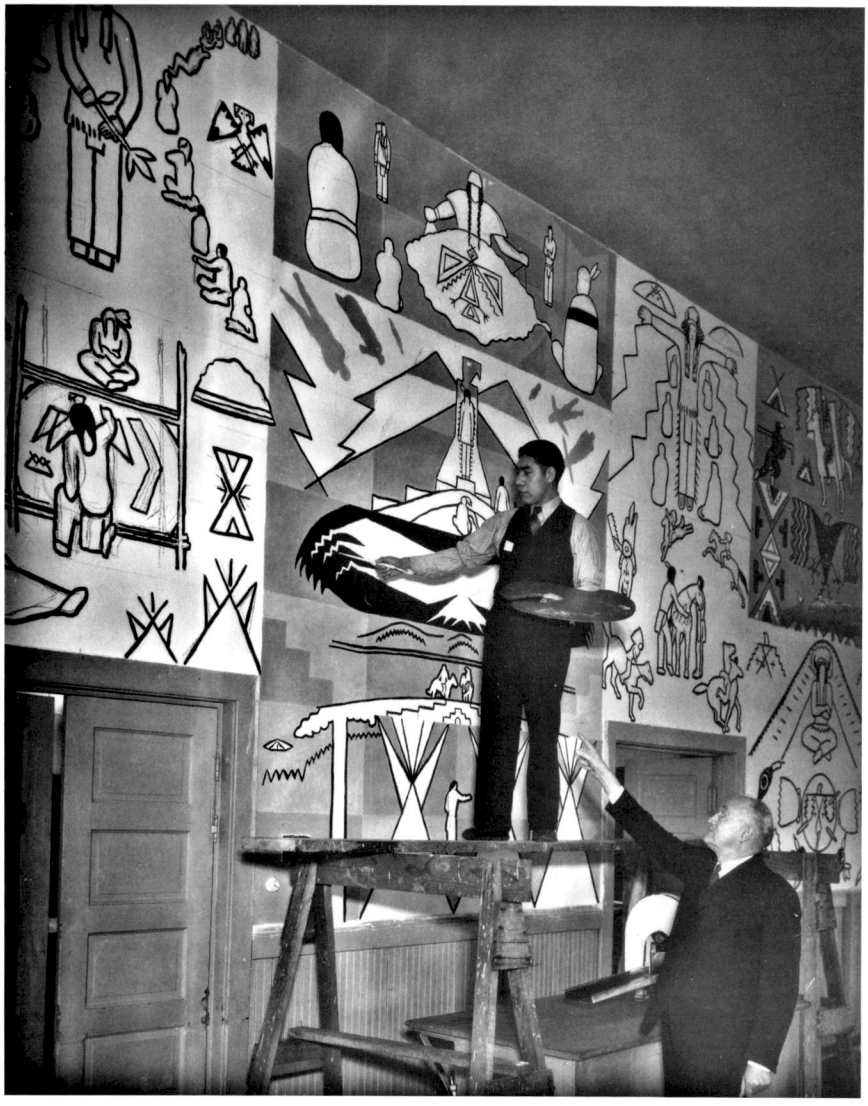

Fig. 14. Julius Twohy working on *Legend of the Thunderbird*, in the dining room of Cushman Indian Hospital, Puyallup, Washington, January 1937. Northwest Room at the Tacoma Public Library, Richards Studio T145-1

the broader critical fortune of a specific form: the totem pole. Totem poles are thought to have originated on Haida Gwaii, an archipelago off the coast of British Columbia, as heraldic vehicles for identifying ancestors and sequencing clan lineages, and they spread and were amplified throughout Alaska and Northern British Columbia with colonial contact and the consolidation of Native communities into larger villages.[34] By the early twentieth century, the totem pole had entered American popular culture as an all-purpose symbol for Northwest Coast Native Americans and, indeed, Native Americans in general, and examples, both

ersatz and genuine, proliferated throughout Seattle—in Pioneer Square, in city parks, along the waterfront, and in curio shops—where they were appropriated as civic mascots, despite their origins far from the Puget Sound. Local carvers, such as the Tulalip artist William Shelton, were enlisted to meet the demand for more and more poles, and, because Coast Salish belief systems did not accommodate visual symbols associated with ancestry, the purpose of the pole form expanded. Shelton, who was dedicated to introducing local non-Native audiences to Puget Sound Native communities and to preserving the oral histories of these communities, developed the story pole, a type of pole that both aligned with Coast Salish belief systems and fulfilled his mission of education and cultural preservation (fig. 15). Narrative rather than heraldic, his story poles were pictorial chronicles of the history, cultural values, and spiritual power of his community.[35] His legacy was passed down to carvers such as Joseph Hillaire (Lummi), who, through his own work and performances, likewise acted as a liaison between Native and non-Native populations (fig. 16).[36]

Shelton's, Hillaire's, and other Coast Salish artists' deliberate interactions with non-Native audiences, though often hybrid and shaped by disparate Native cultures, served as a creative presence operating in parallel to the appropriation of Northwest Coast Native aesthetics within the region's iteration of Abstract Expressionism. Mid-twentieth-century visual culture in the Pacific Northwest also included Native Modernists like Twohy, who both responded to and helped shape the contemporary art world, alongside their Asian and Asian American peers. A nuanced understanding of the role Asian and Northwest Coast Native art played in the work of Northwest Abstract Expressionists must acknowledge the creativity and fortunes—not only in the Pacific Northwest but also in North America more generally—of these communities, as well as the cultural blind spots of the Modernist artists indebted to them. This recognition further

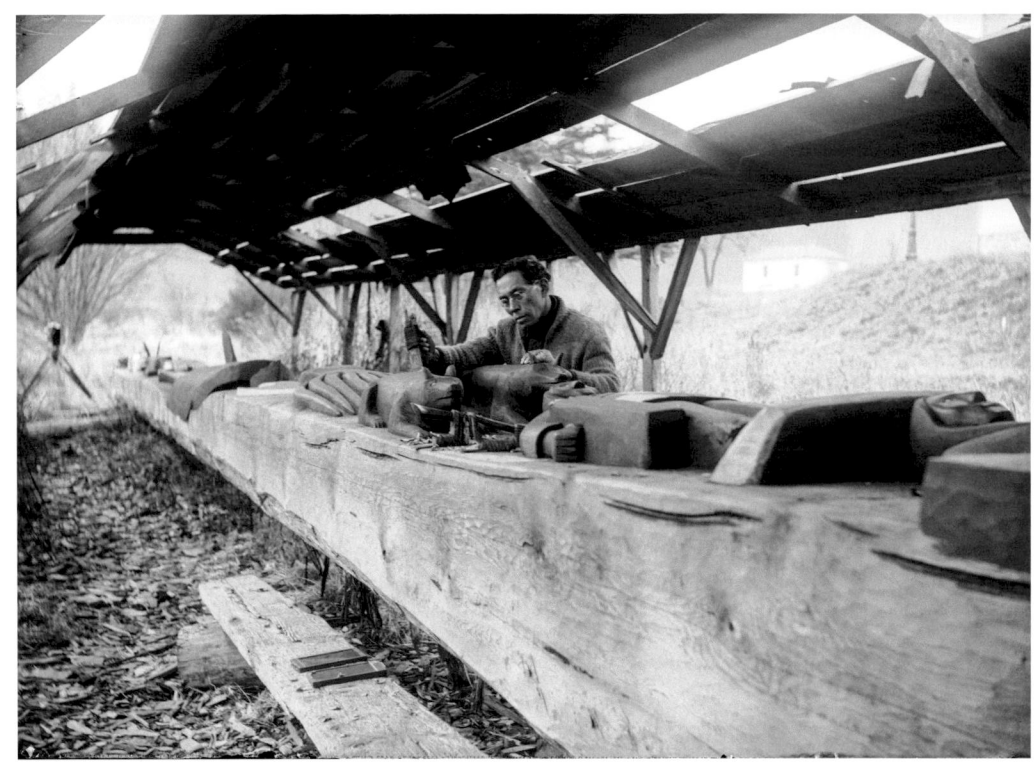

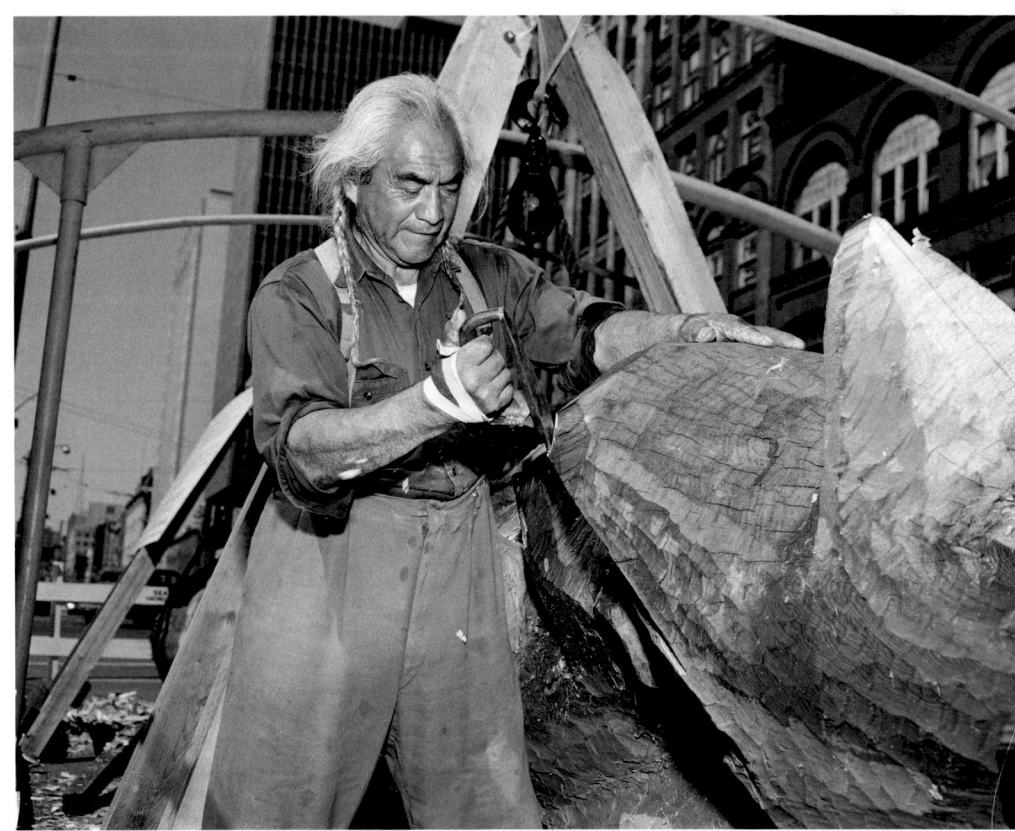

Fig. 15. William Shelton carving a totem pole, ca. 1925. Museum of History and Industry, Seattle, 1983.10.10923.2

Fig. 16. Joseph Hillaire in Pioneer Square, Seattle, carving totem pole for Kobe, Japan, 1961. Museum of History and Industry, Seattle, 1986.5.28648.2

expands the idea of Northwest Modernism beyond the tropes established by *Life*'s "Mystic Painters of the Northwest" in 1953, focusing on the influence of Asian aesthetics and inspiration by Indigenous forms, to embrace the rich and varied artistic world these artists inhabited —a world shaped by urbanization, industrialization, environmental disruption, reflective introspection, and cultural resilience in the Puget Sound.

Notes

I would like to thank Colin Browne, Katherine Bunn-Marcuse, and Christopher Greene for sharing their thoughts and expertise on intersections between Native and non-Native Modernism during research for this essay.

1. For Pacific Northwest Abstract Expressionism, see Papanikolas, "Abstract Expressionism"; and Junker, *Modernism in the Pacific Northwest*.

2. For the AYPE, see Stein, *Alaska-Yukon-Pacific Exposition*.

3. For the Seattle Totem Pole, see Jonaitis and Glass, *Totem Pole*, 142–50.

4. K. Callahan and Kendall, "Oral History Interview."

5. For Tobey's relationship with Teng, see Danzker and Lawrimore, *Mark Tobey /*
Teng Baiye. Teng Kuei was known in China by his pen name, Teng Baiye.

6. Mark Tobey to Marian Willard, August 1957, quoted in Musée des arts décoratifs, *Mark Tobey*, n.p.

7. Tobey to Willard, August 1957.

8. For Horiuchi's life and work, see Johns, *Paul Horiuchi*; for the development of his abstraction, see Papanikolas, "Abstract Expressionism."

9. For Tsutakawa's life and work, see Kingsbury, *George Tsutakawa*.

10. Kingsbury, *George Tsutakawa*, 75

11. Quoted in Papanikolas, "Abstract Expressionism," 26.

12. For Zen's reception in the Pacific Northwest, see
Kingsbury, "Four Artists in the Northwest Tradition," 16.

13. For the spirit dance performances, see Conkleton, "Pantheon of Dreams," 72

14. Cumming, *Sketchbook*, 99.

15. Anderson and Kingsbury, "Oral History Interview."

16. Anderson and Kingsbury, "Oral History Interview."

17. Junker, *Modernism in the Pacific Northwest*, 42.

18. Junker, wall label for *Esquimaux Idiom*, Seattle Art Museum records.

19. For the history of Ye Olde Curiosity Shop, see Duncan, *1,001 Curious Things*.

20. For the fortunes of totem poles in Seattle, see Thrush, *Native Seattle*, 116; for the fortunes of the term "Indian" to describe Puget Sound Native communities, see Harmon, *Indians in the Making*.

21. For the Modernist interest in Native American art, see Rushing, *Native American Art*.

22. Rushing, *Native American Art*.

23. For Surrealist collections of Northwest Coast Native art, see Browne, "Scavengers of Paradise."

24. Browne, "Scavengers of Paradise." Heye's collection
would become the core of the Smithsonian Institution's National Museum of the American Indian George Gustav Heye Center in New York City.

25. Rushing, *Native American Art*, 104ff.

26. Rushing, *Native American Art*.

27. Jonaitis and Glass, *Totem Pole*, 138.

28. Both quoted in Jonaitis and Glass, *Totem Pole*, 38 and 140.

29. For the history of Tlingit beadwork, see Smetzer, *Painful Beauty*.

30. For the IRA, see Rushing, *Native American Art*, 103–4.

31. For the history of the CCC's totem parks, see Moore, *Proud Raven, Panting Wolf*.

32. Moore, *Proud Raven, Panting Wolf*.

33. Ng, "Work of Julius 'Land Elk' Twohy."

34. For the history and fortunes of the totem pole, see Jonaitis and Glass, *Totem Pole*.

35. Christodoulides, "Carved Legacy."

36. For Hillaire's work, see Brotherton, "Joseph Raymond Hillaire."

PLATES

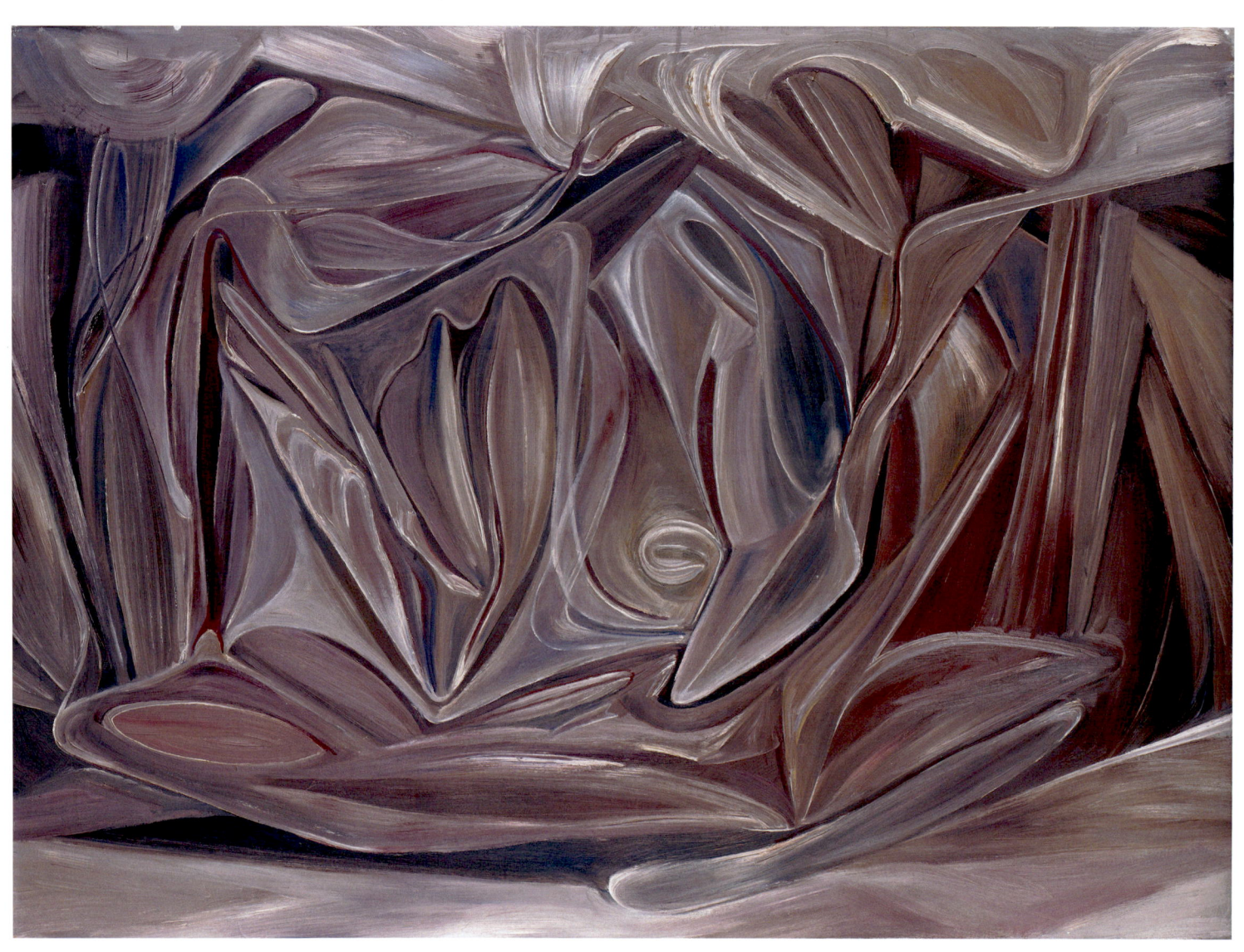

139 Mark Tobey, *Modal Tide*, 1940, oil on canvas

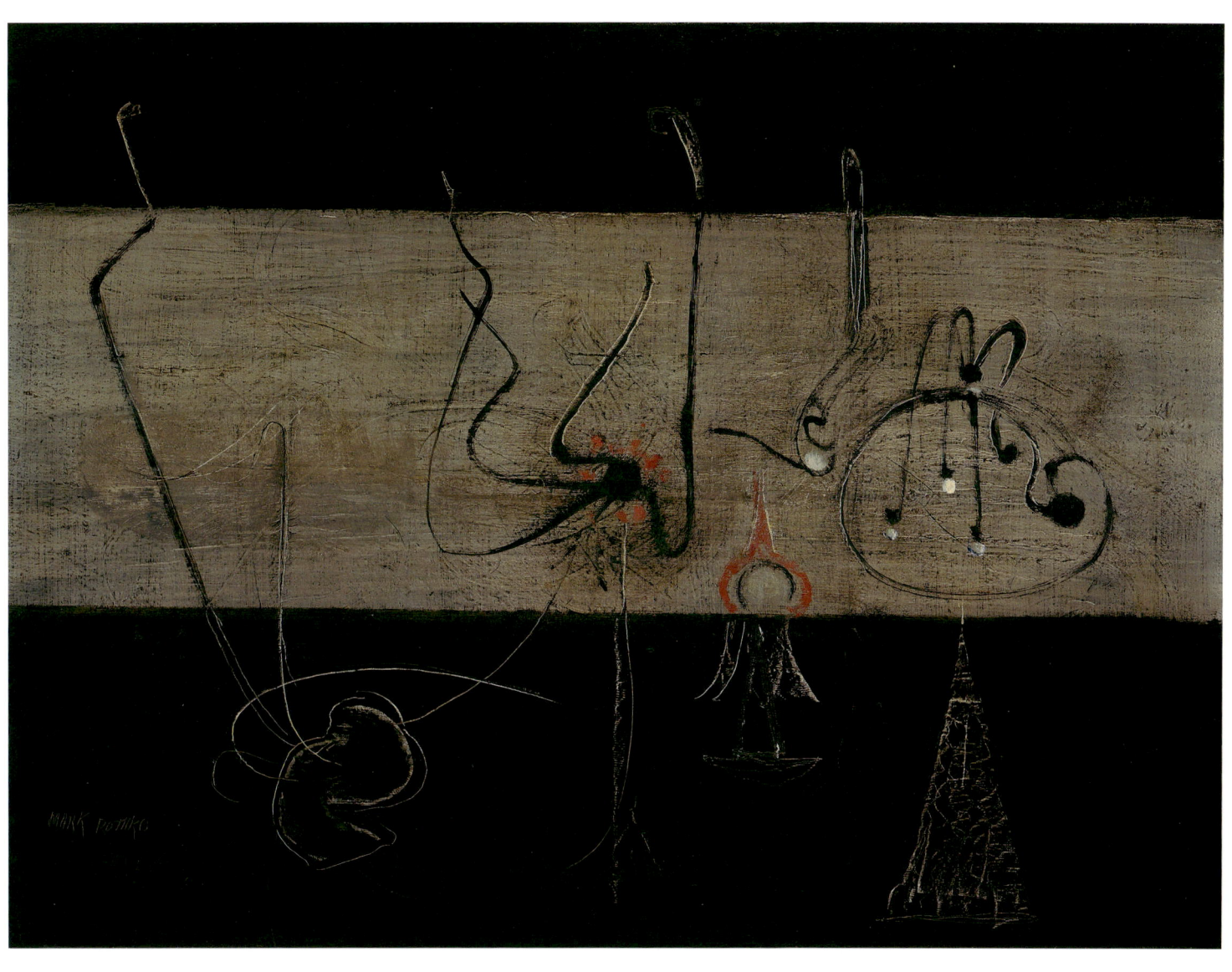

140 Mark Rothko, *Untitled*, ca. 1945, oil on canvas

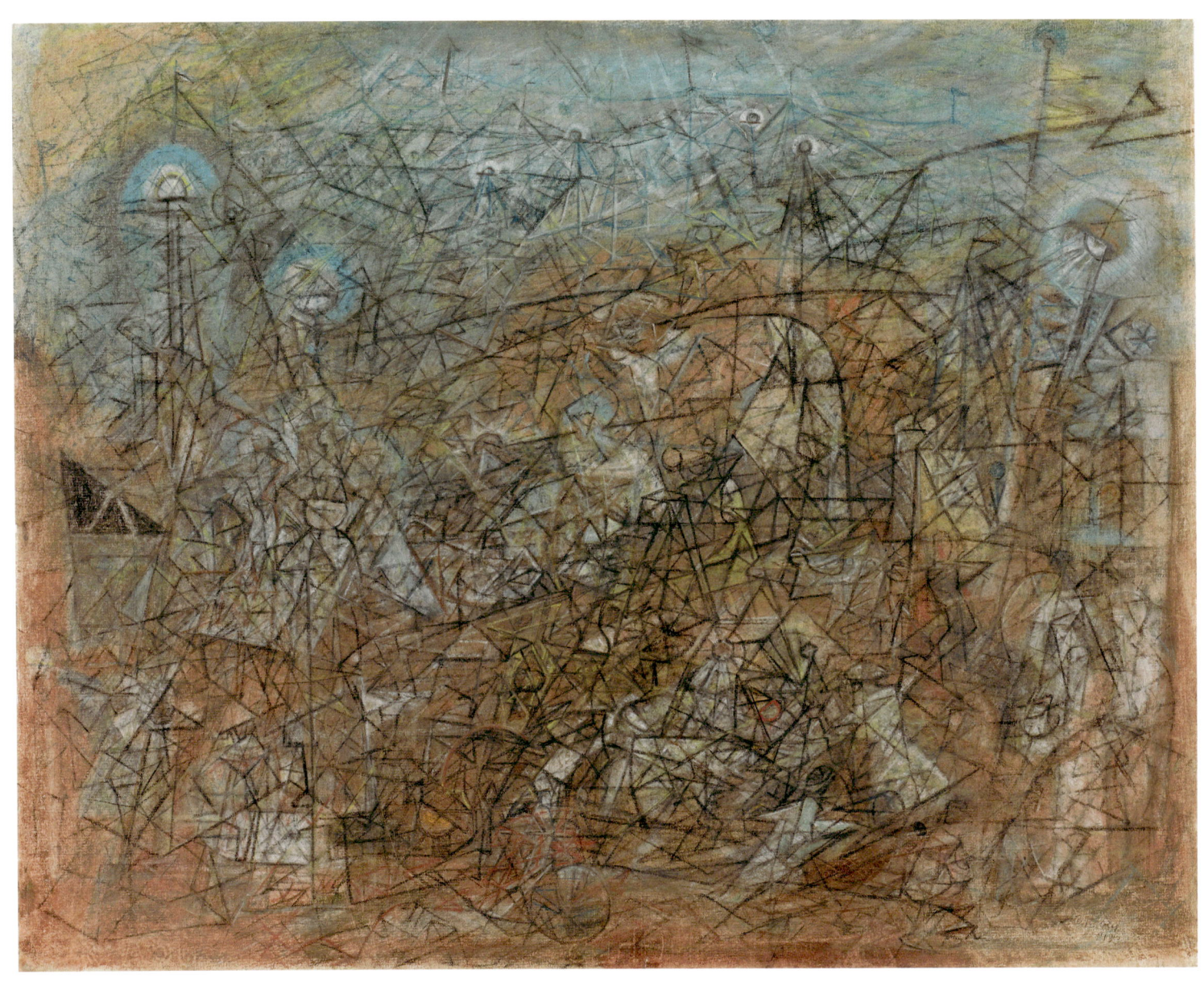

141 Mark Tobey, *Cirque d'hiver*, 1933, pastel on paper

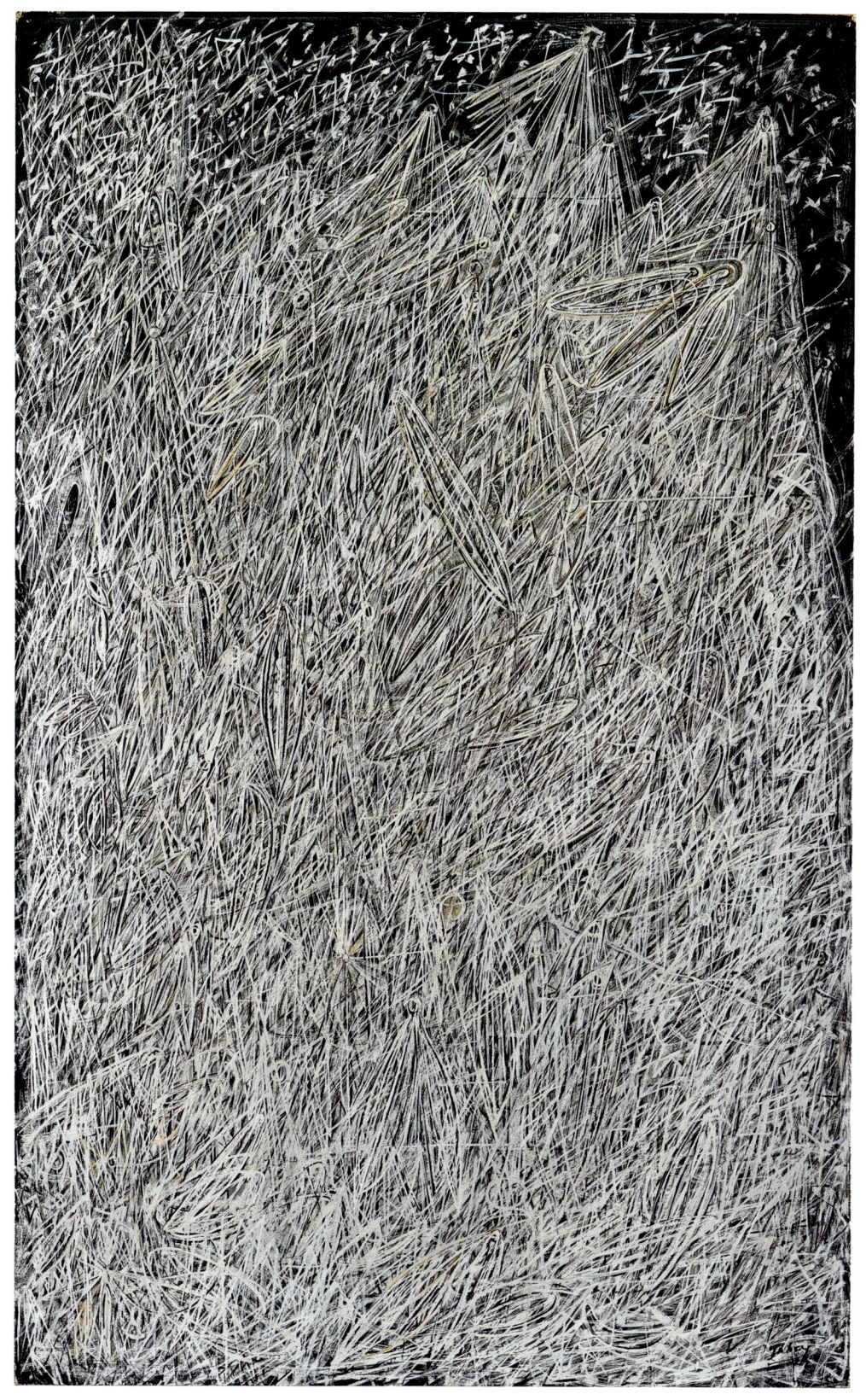

142 Mark Tobey, *White Night*, 1942, tempera on paperboard mounted on composition board

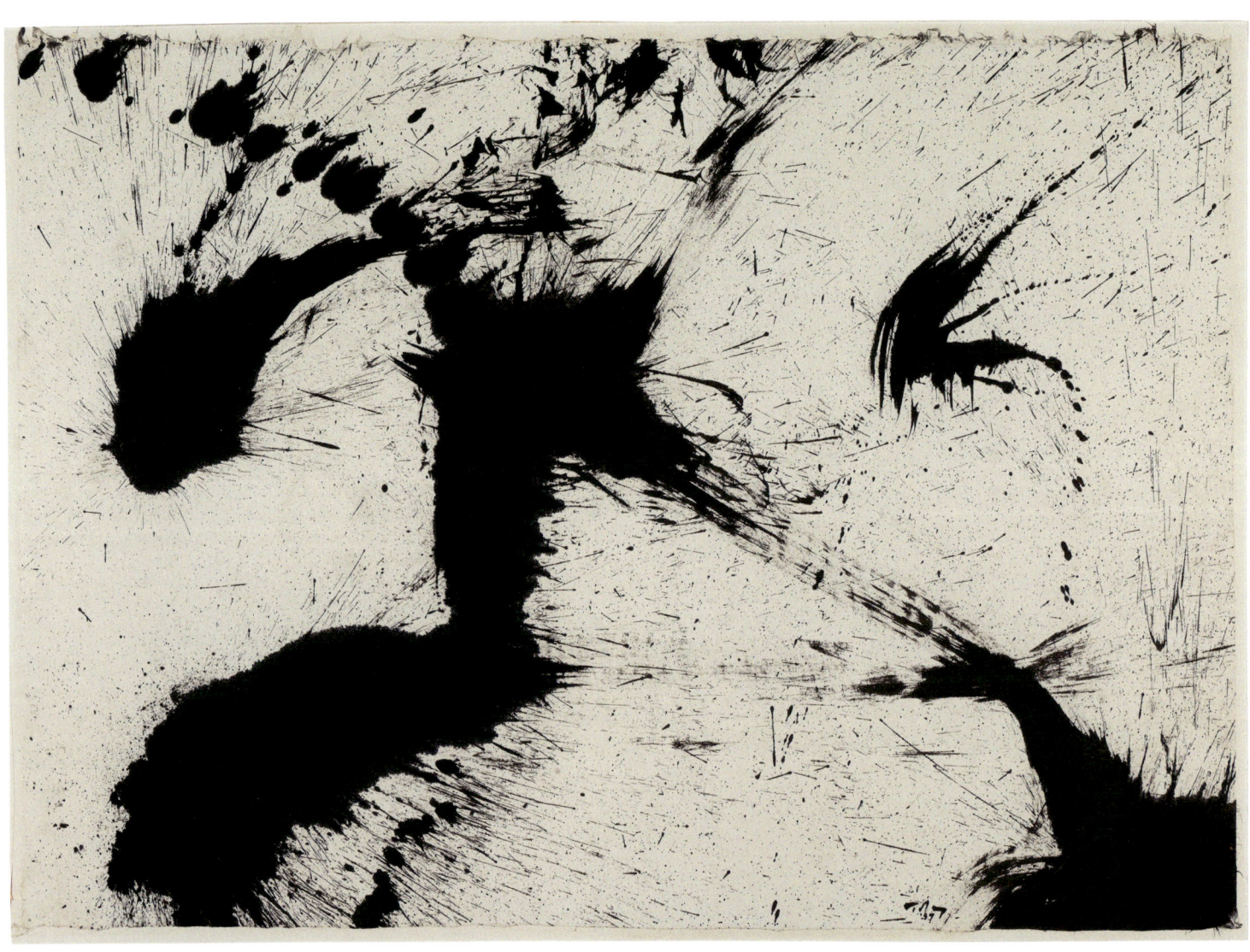

143 Mark Tobey, *Space Ritual No. 1*, 1957, sumi ink on paper

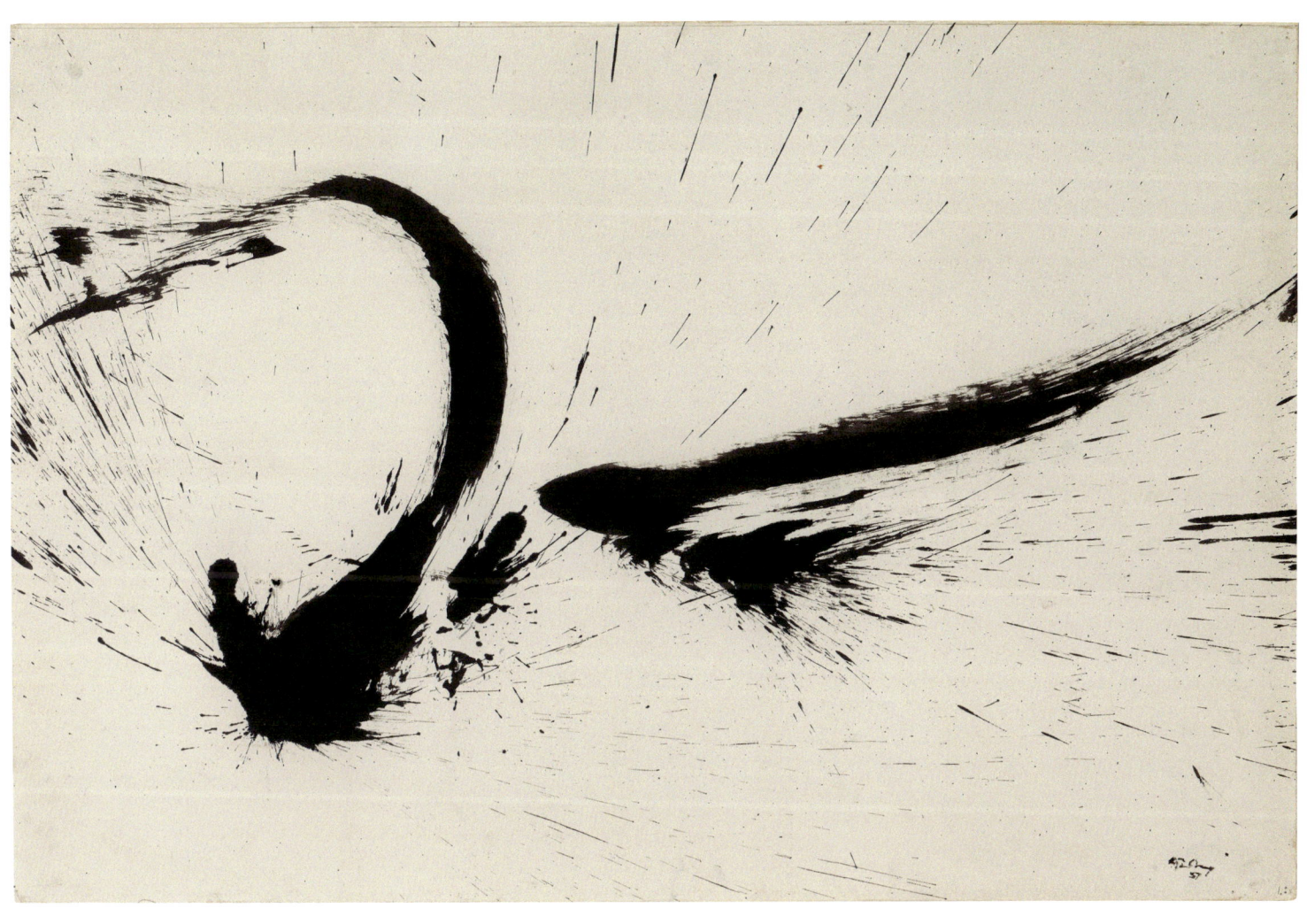

144 Mark Tobey, *Space Ritual No. 18*, 1957, sumi ink on wove paper mounted on board

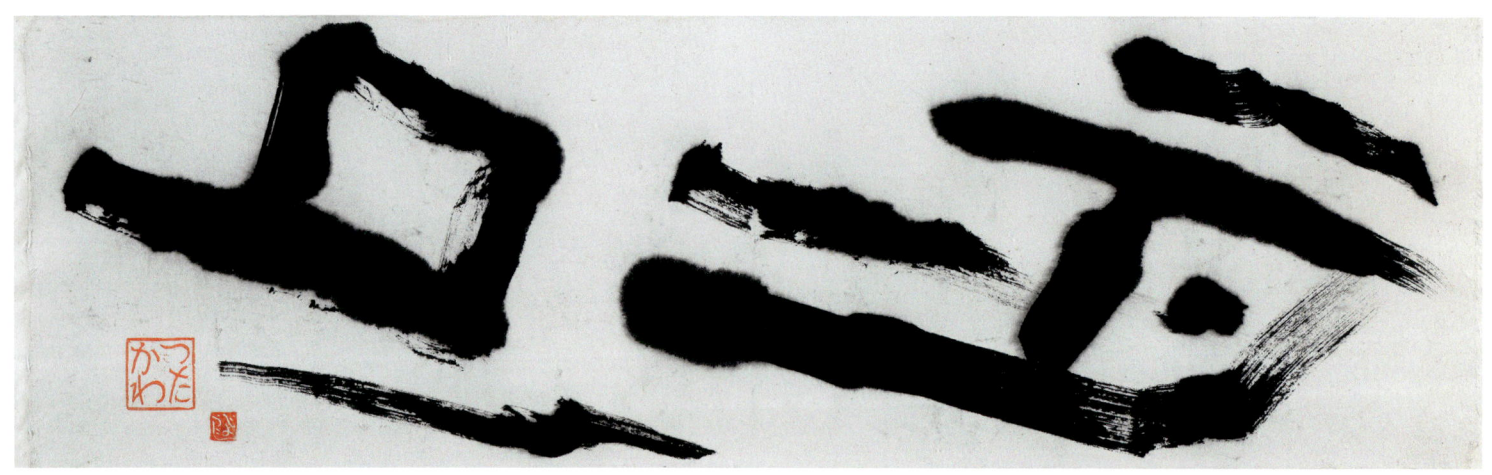

145 George Tsutakawa, *Gust*, 1980, ink on medium-weight Japanese paper, mounted on lightweight Japanese paper 182

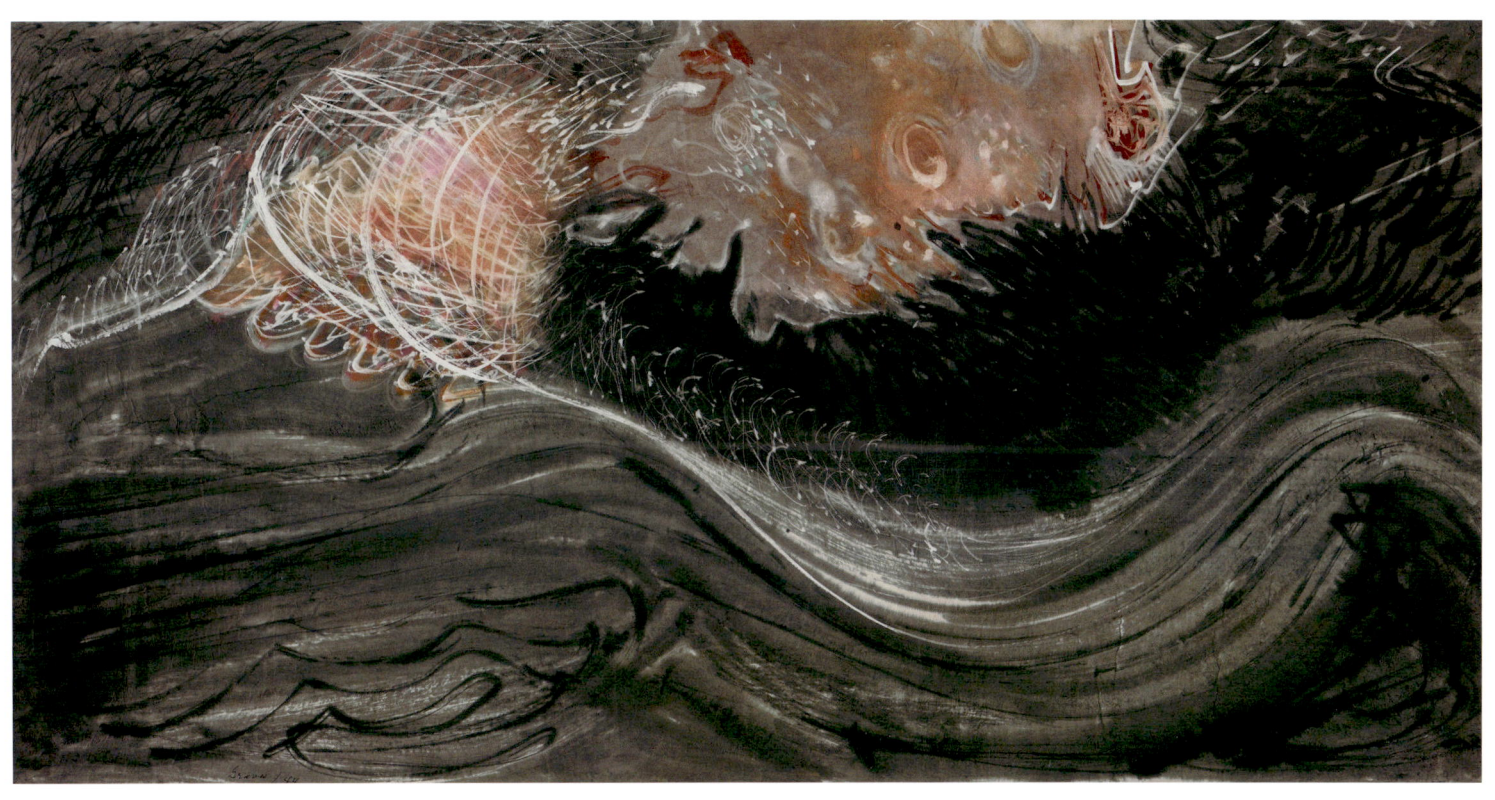

146 Morris Graves, *The Genesis of Life Lay Deep and Anticipant Under the Sky*, 1944, ink and watercolor

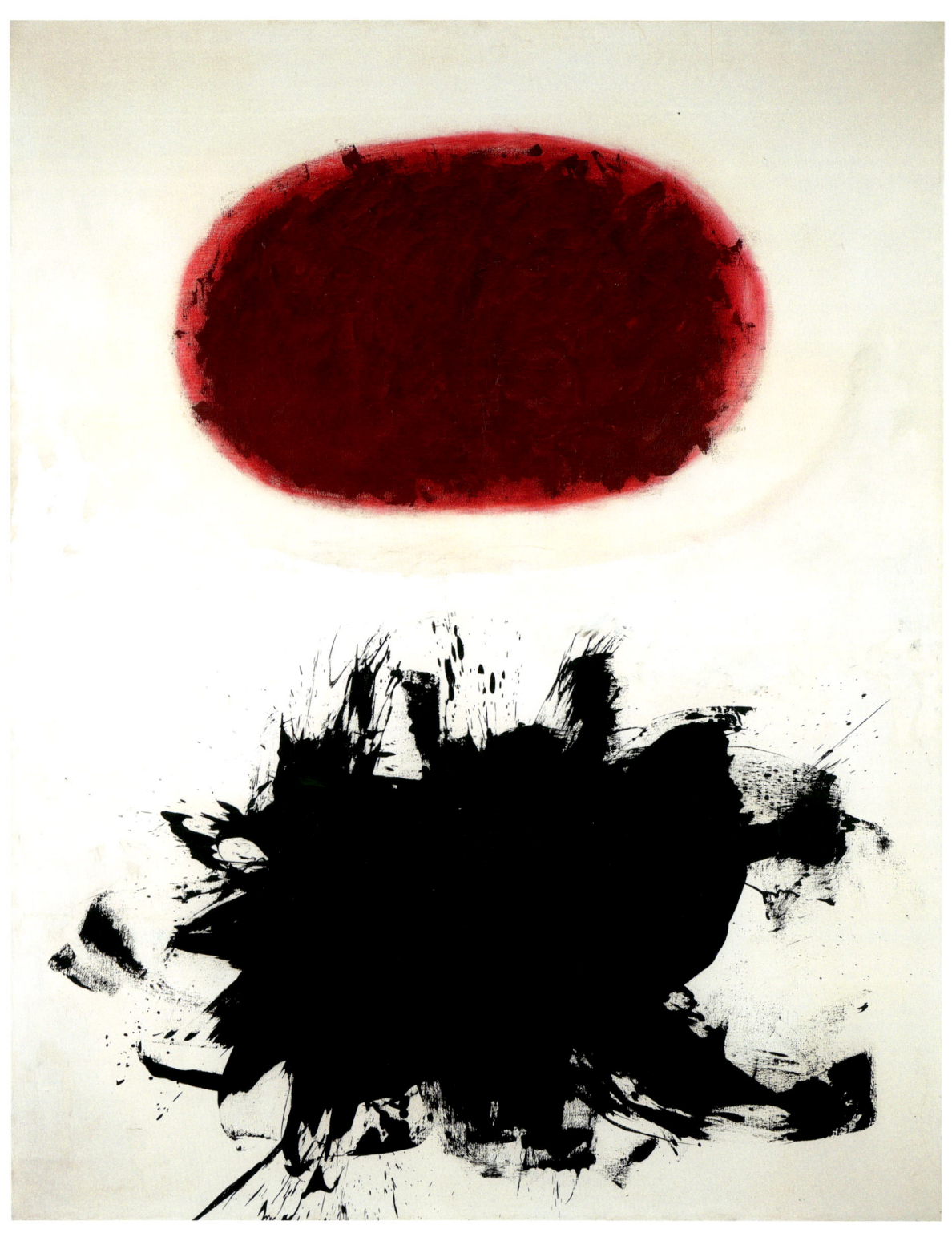

147 Adolph Gottlieb, *Crimson Spinning #2*, 1959, oil on canvas

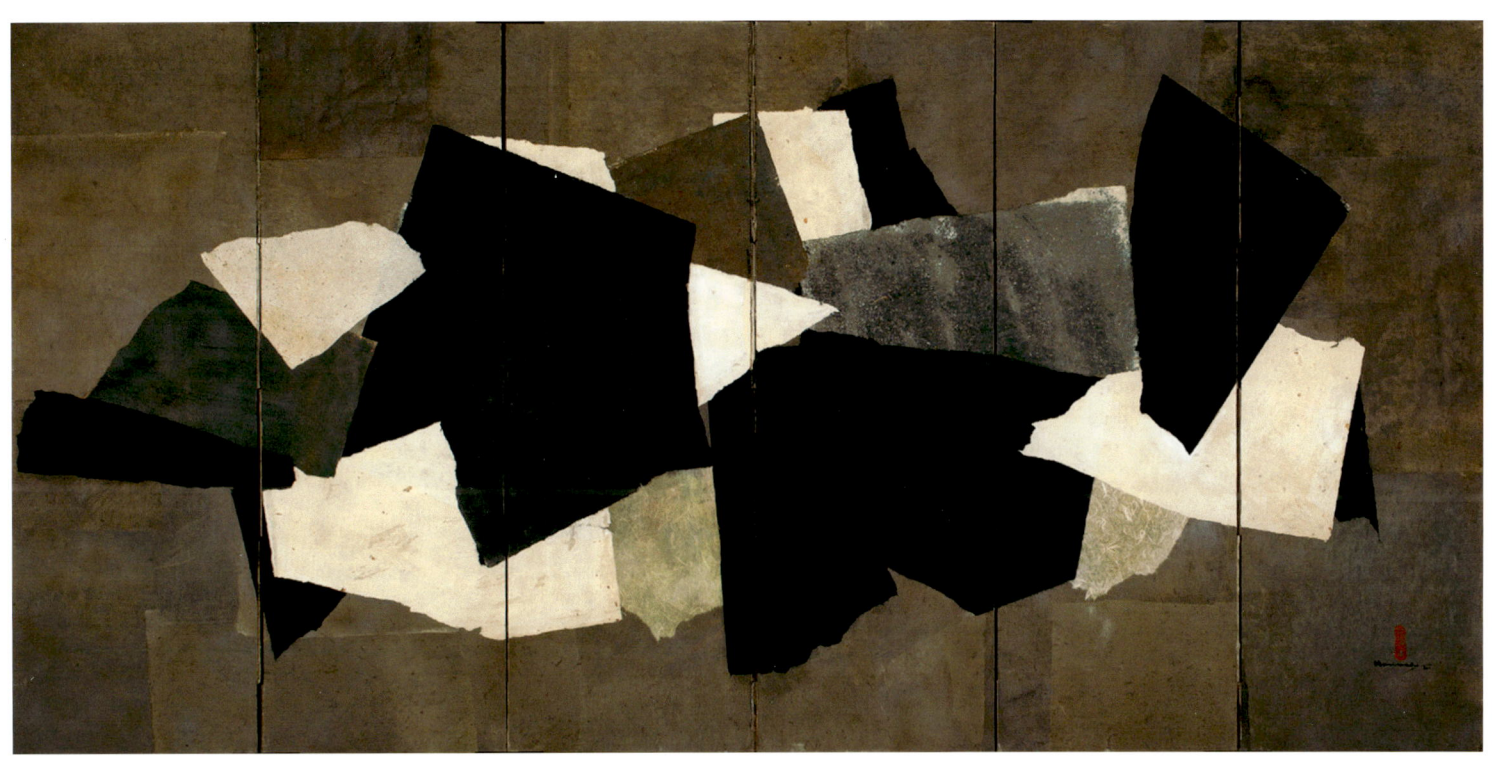

148 Paul Horiuchi, *Untitled*, 1961, paper collage with gouache on six-panel screen

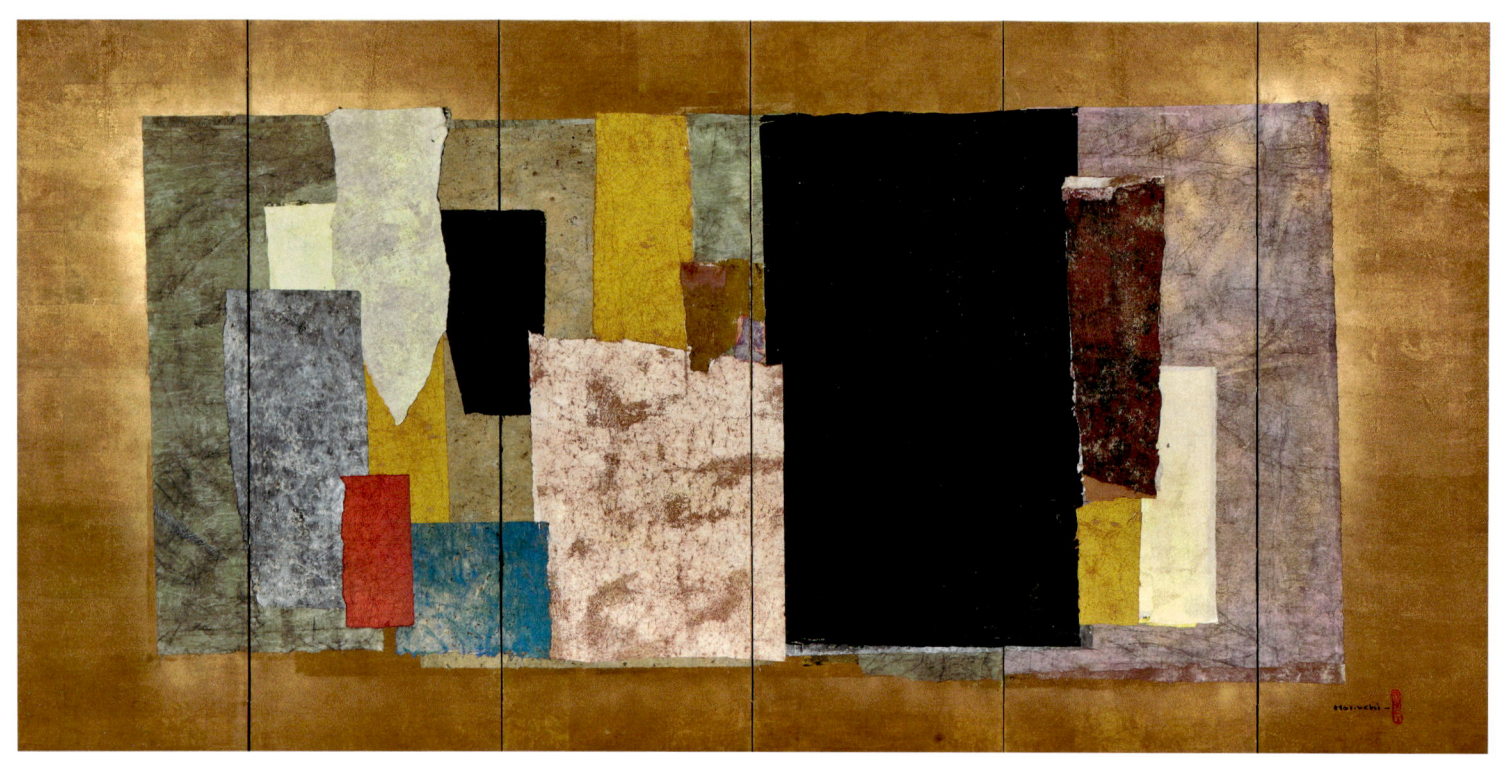

149 Paul Horiuchi, *Colors and Patterns from Heian Period*, 1969, casein and paint on paper mounted on board 186

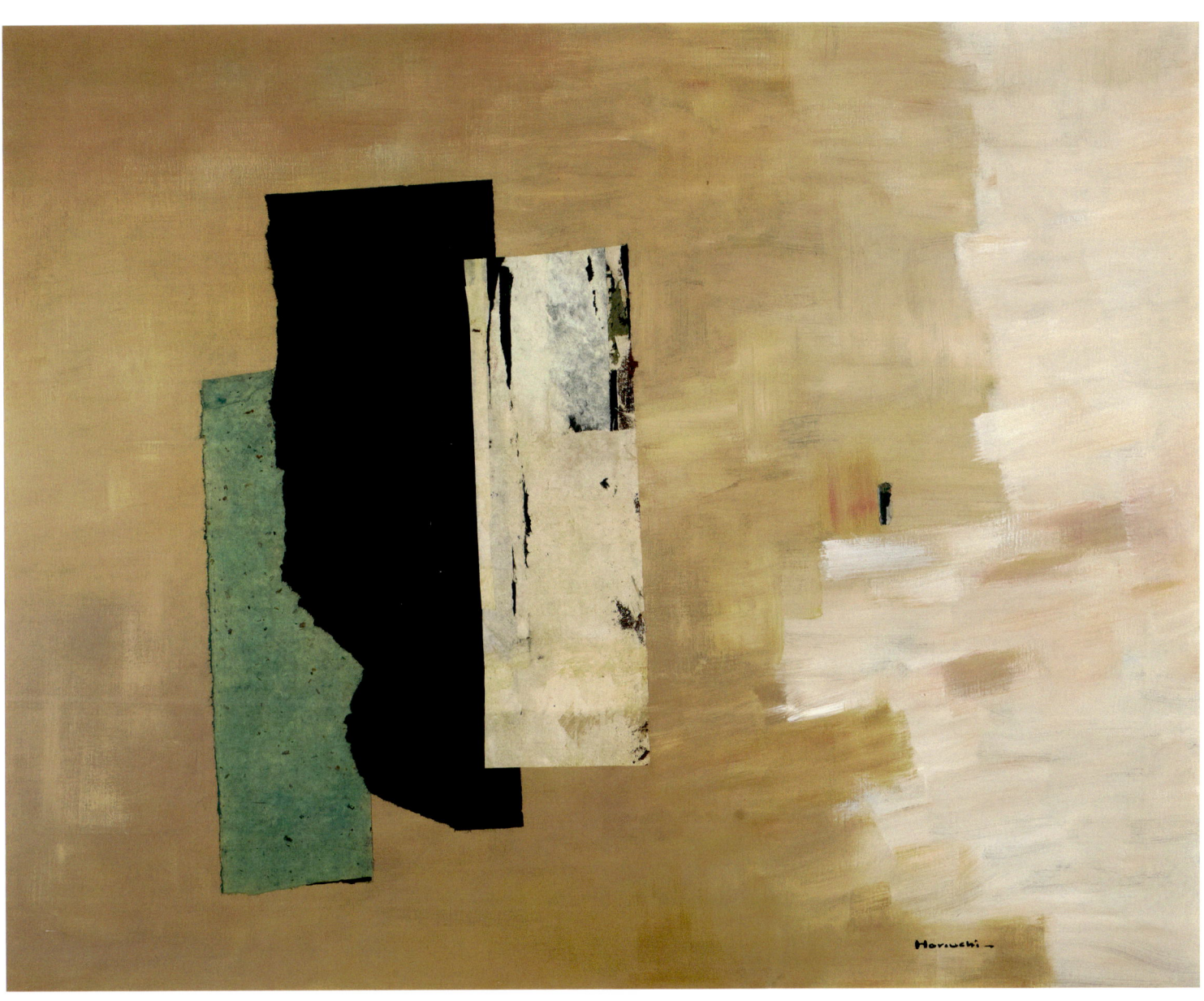

150 Paul Horiuchi, *Definition*, 1976, casein on paper mounted on canvas

151 Paul Horiuchi, *Monolithic Impasse*, 1964, casein on mulberry paper mounted on canvas

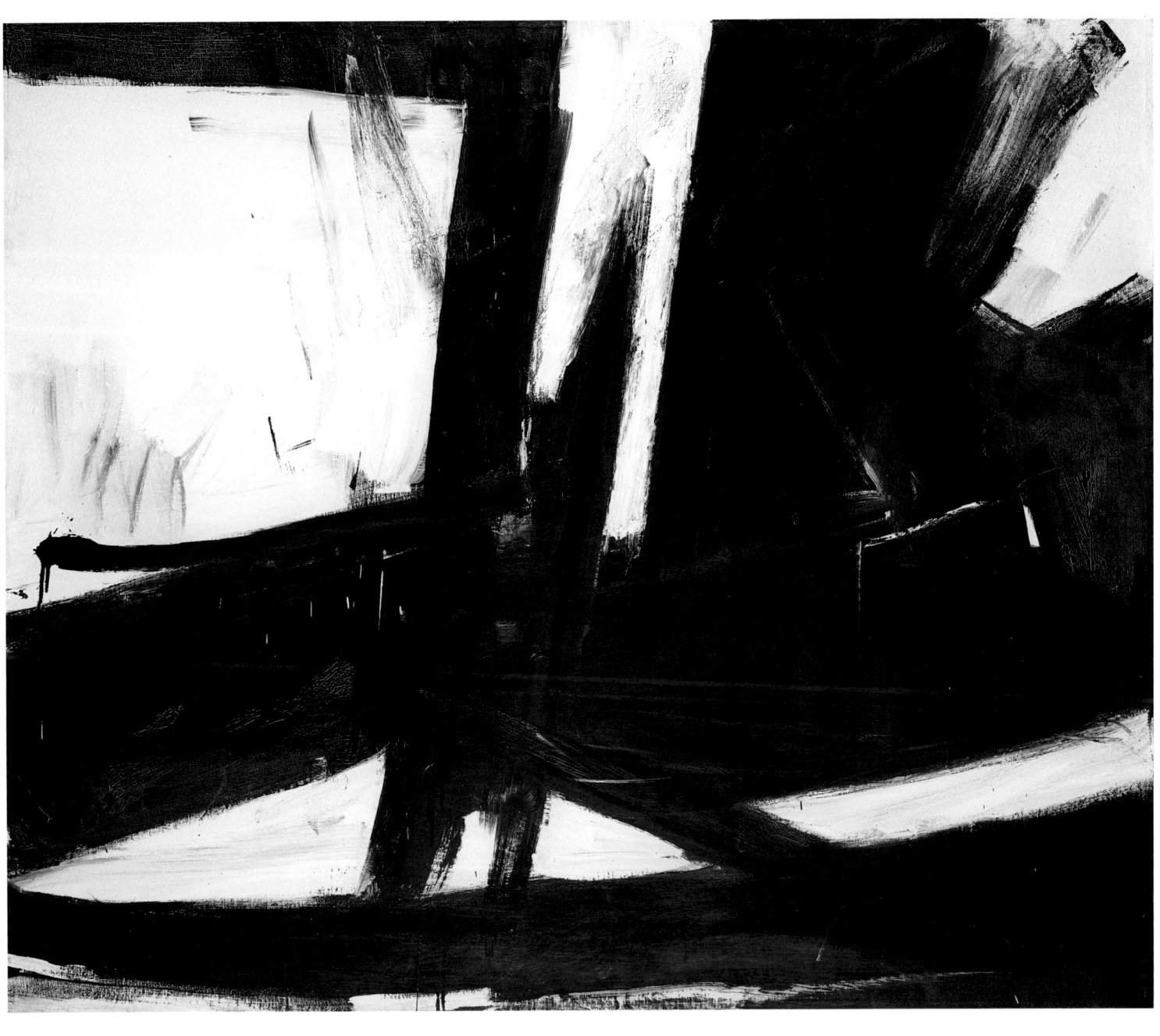

152 Franz Kline, *Cross Section*, 1956, oil on canvas

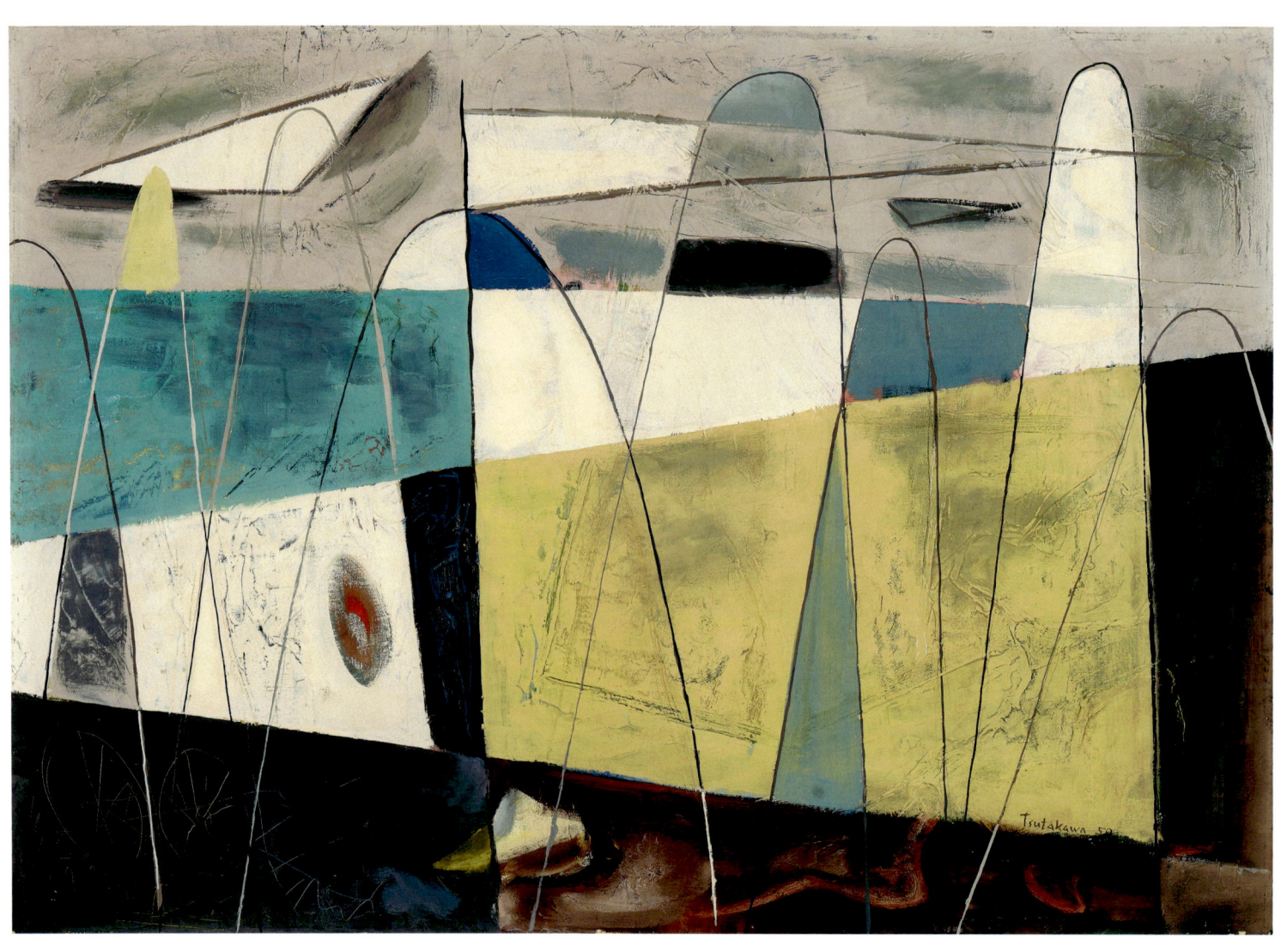

153 George Tsutakawa, *The Ascent*, 1950, oil on canvas board

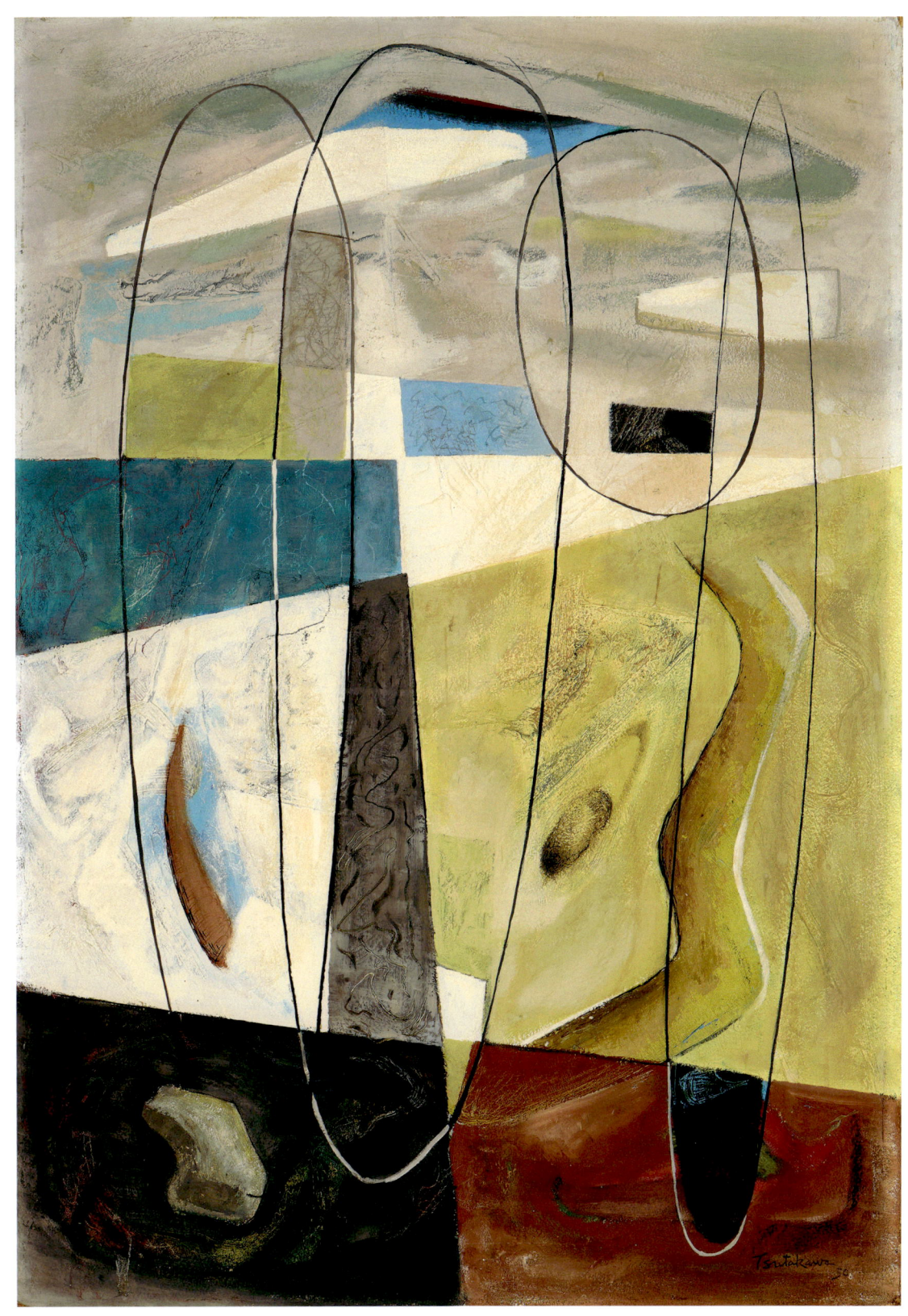

154 George Tsutakawa, *The Descent*, 1950, oil on board

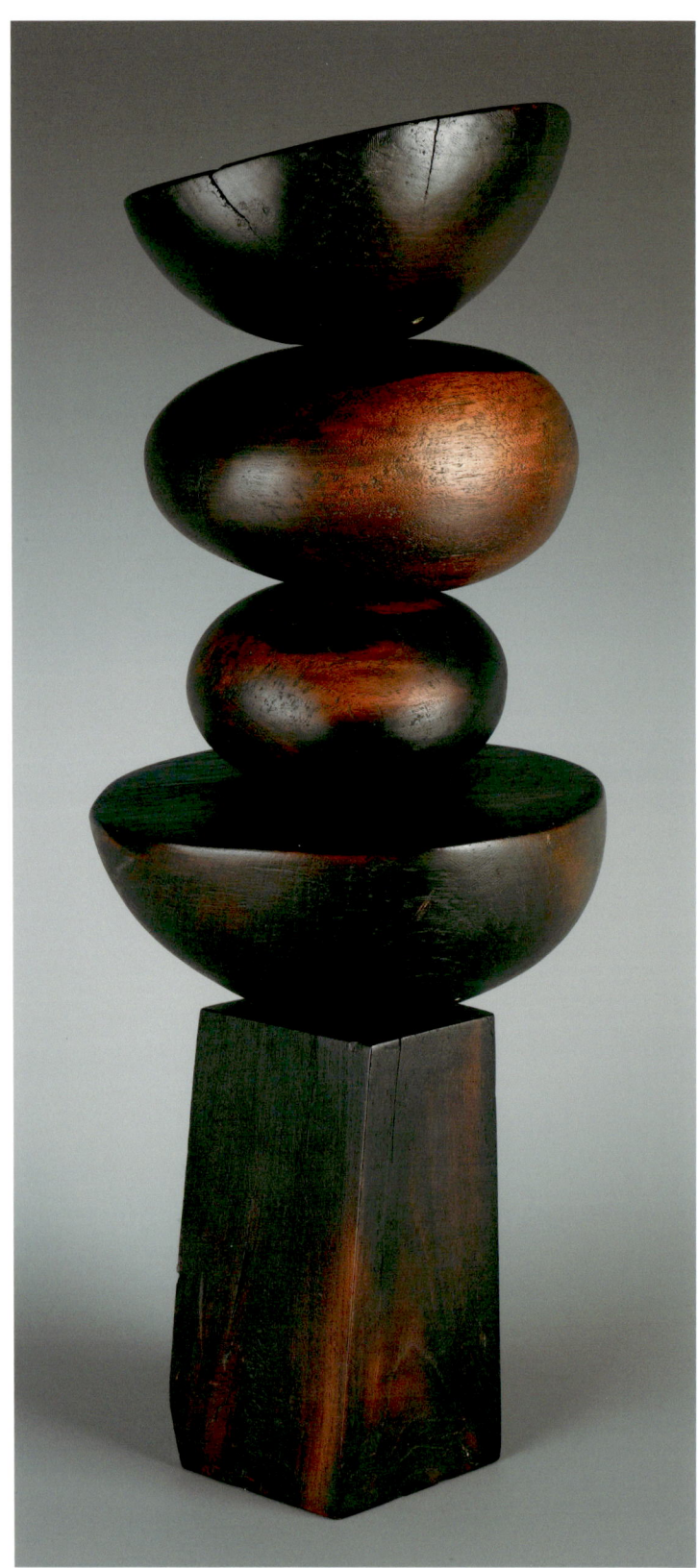

155 George Tsutakawa, *Obos I*, 1956, teak

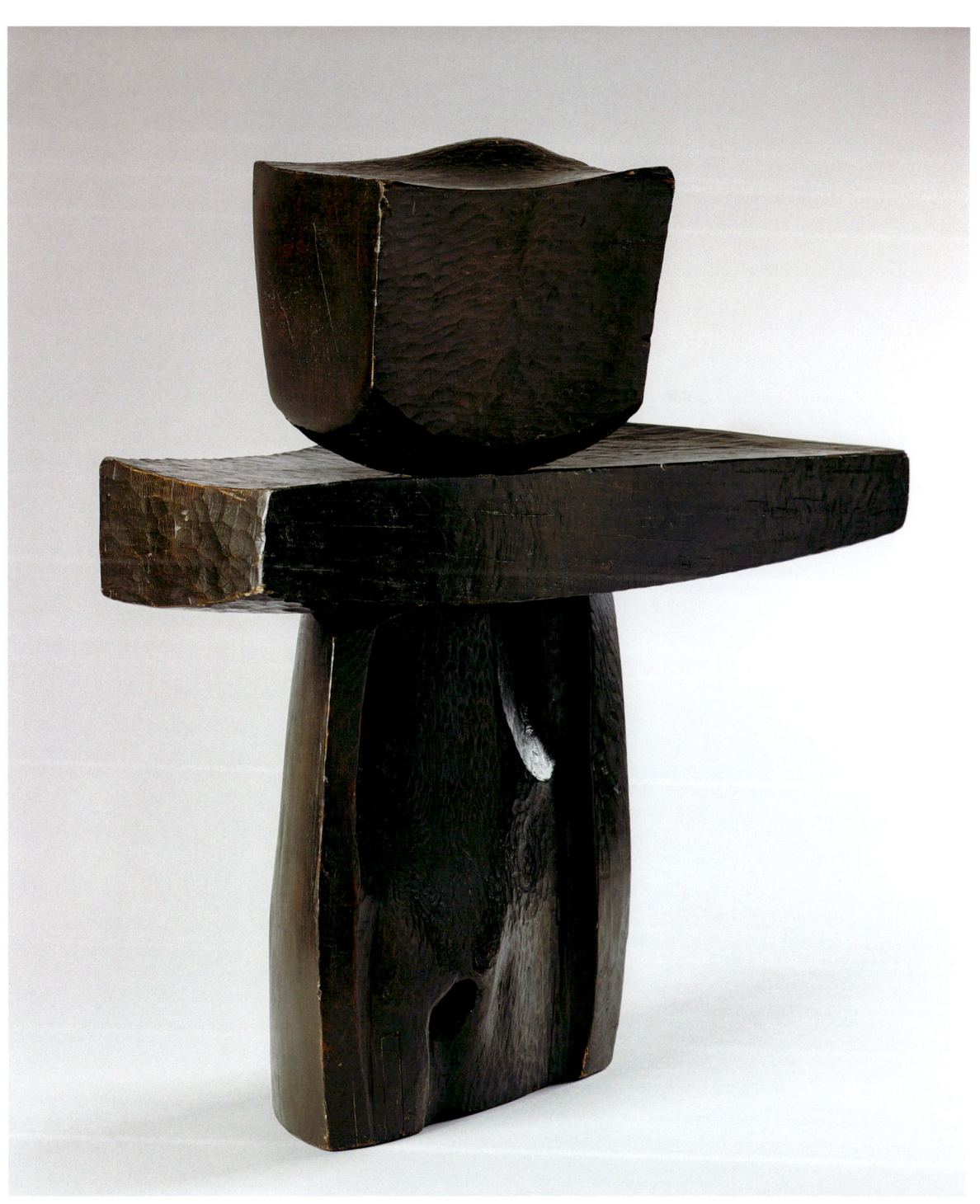

156   George Tsutakawa, *Obos 15*, 1961, cedar

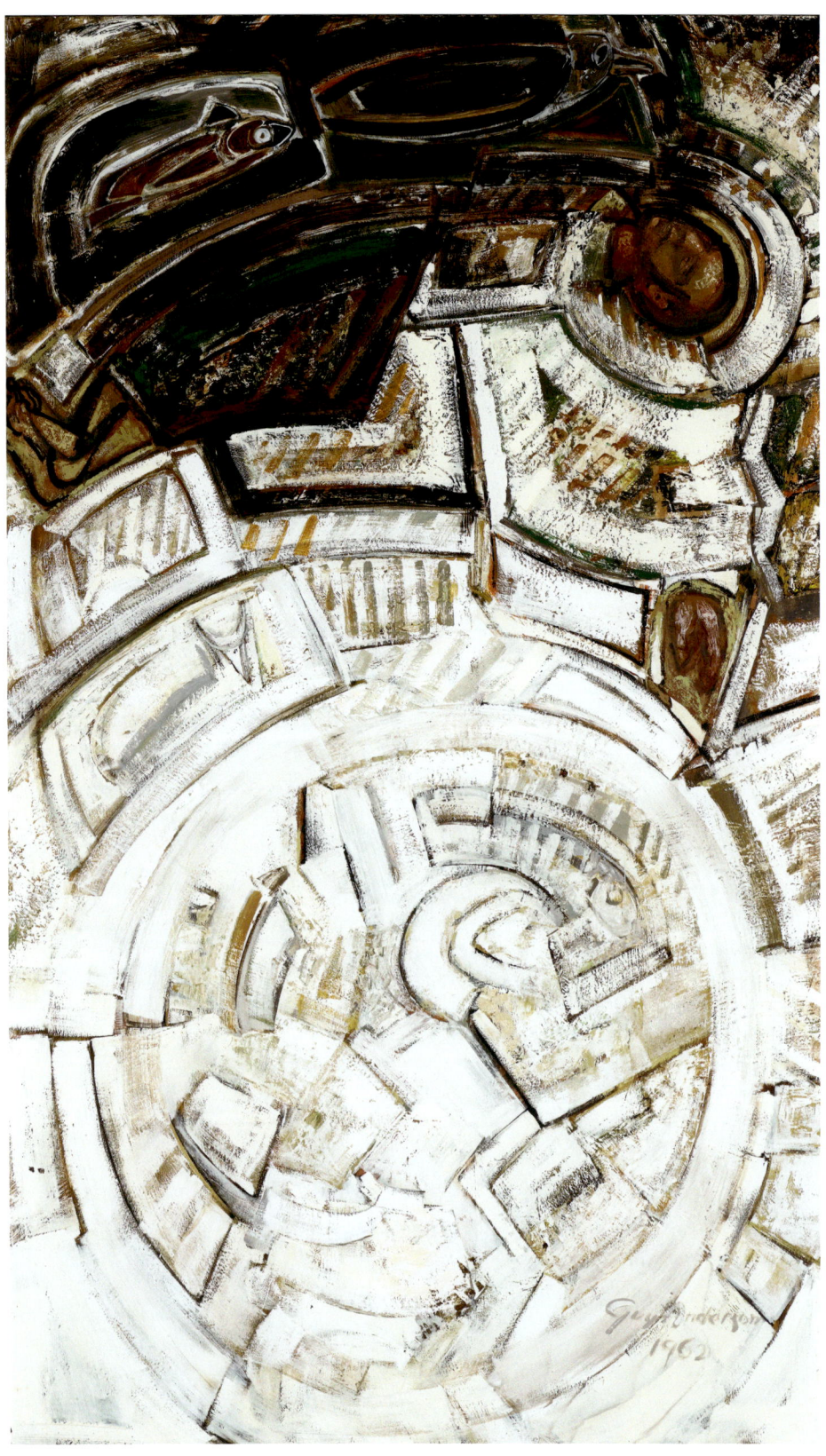

157 Guy Anderson, *Dream of the Language Wheel*, 1962, oil on canvas

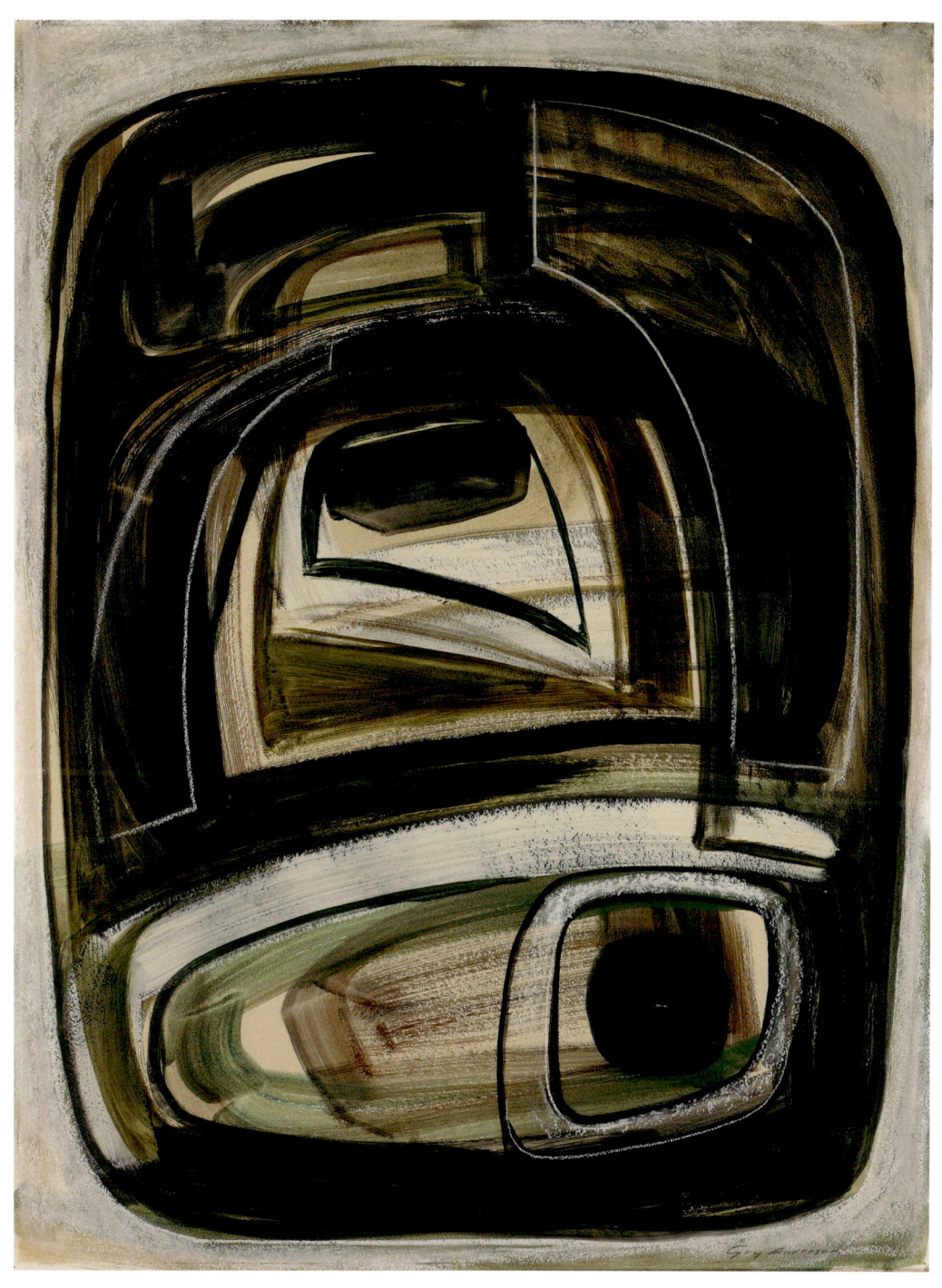

158 Guy Anderson, *Primitive Forms II*, 1962, oil on composition board

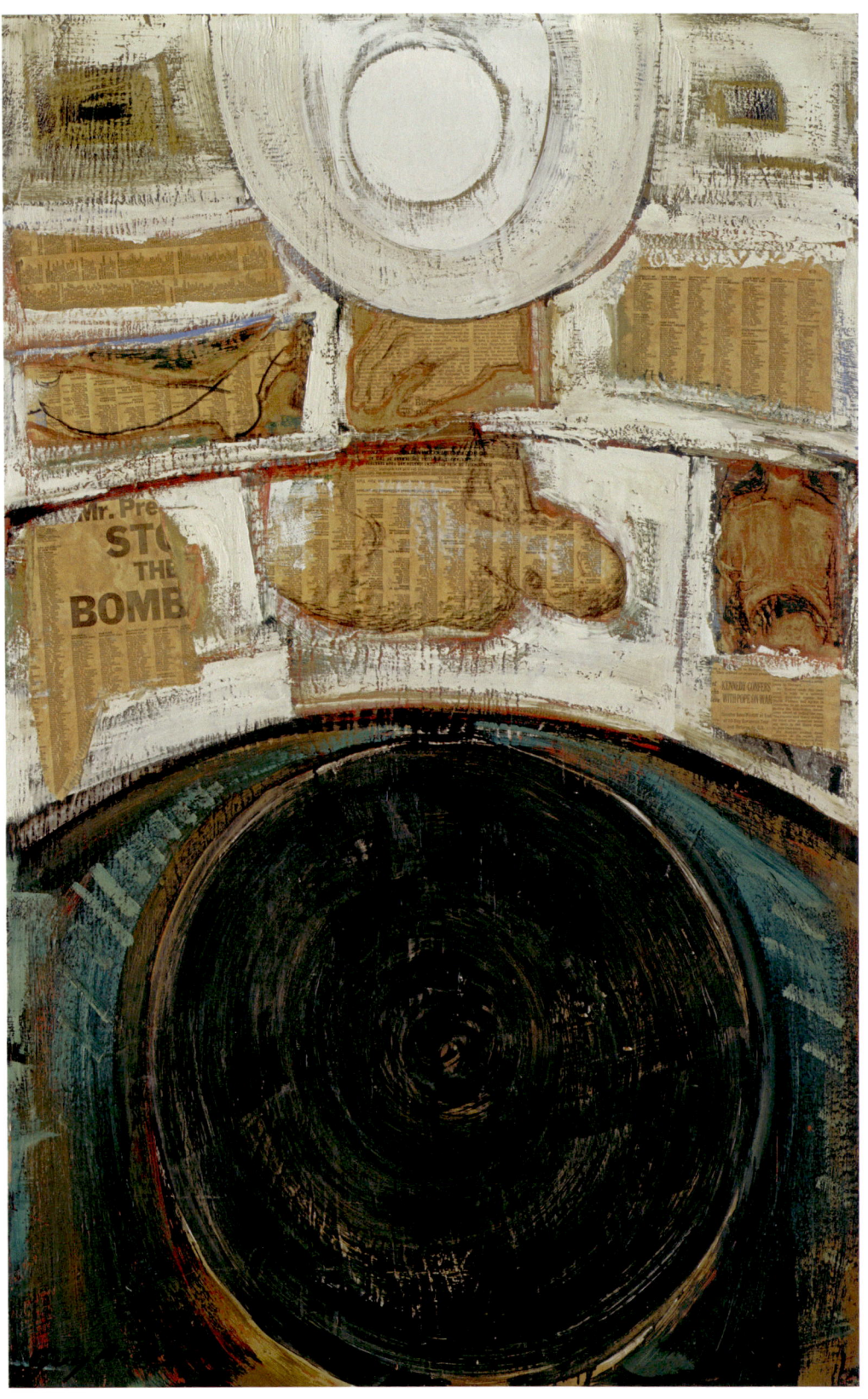

159 Guy Anderson, *Spring*, 1967, oil on newspaper mounted on plywood

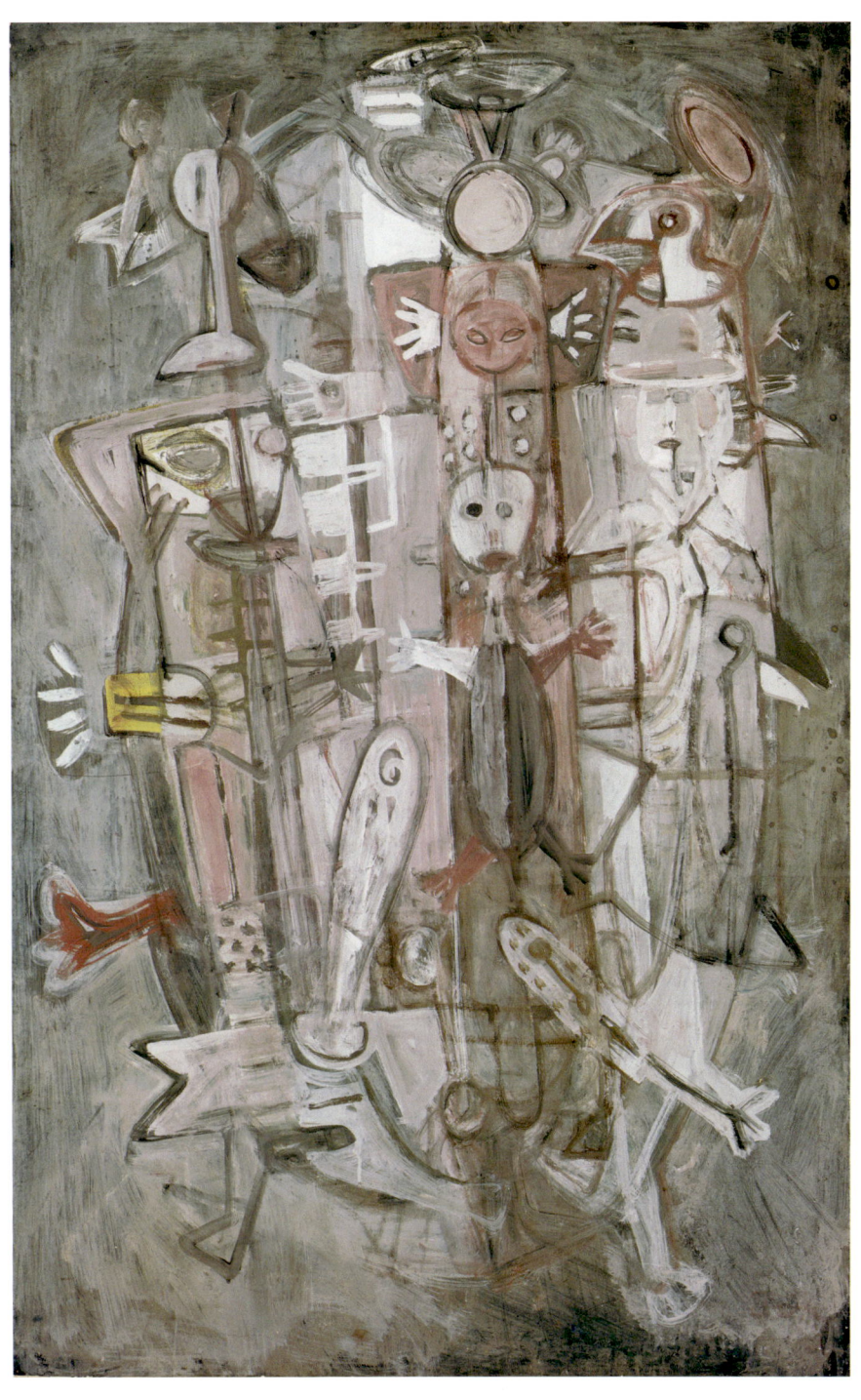

160 Mark Tobey, *Esquimaux Idiom*, 1946, tempera with graphite on composition board   197

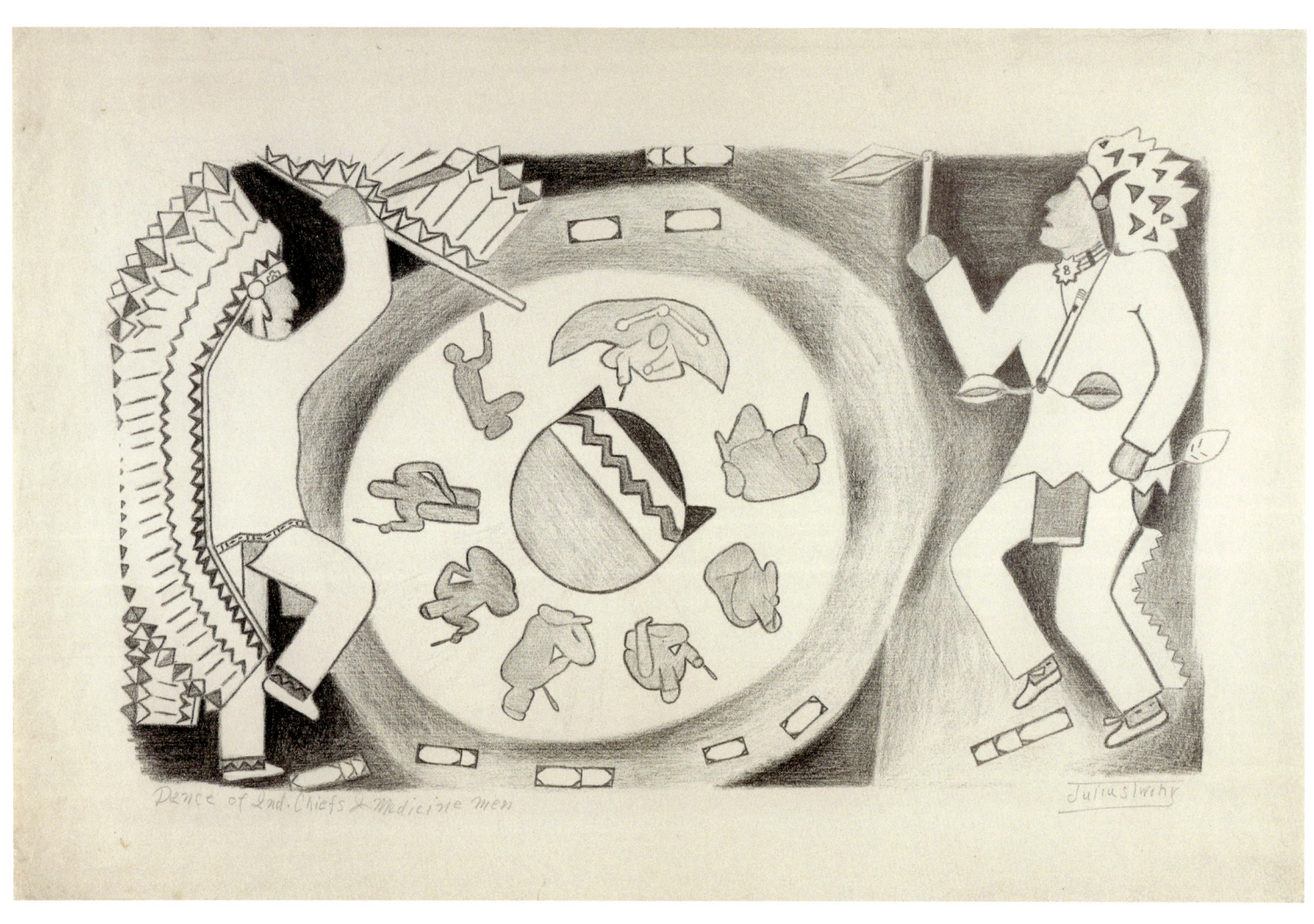

161 Julius Twohy, *Dance of Indian Chiefs and Medicine Men*, ca. 1936–37, lithograph on wove paper

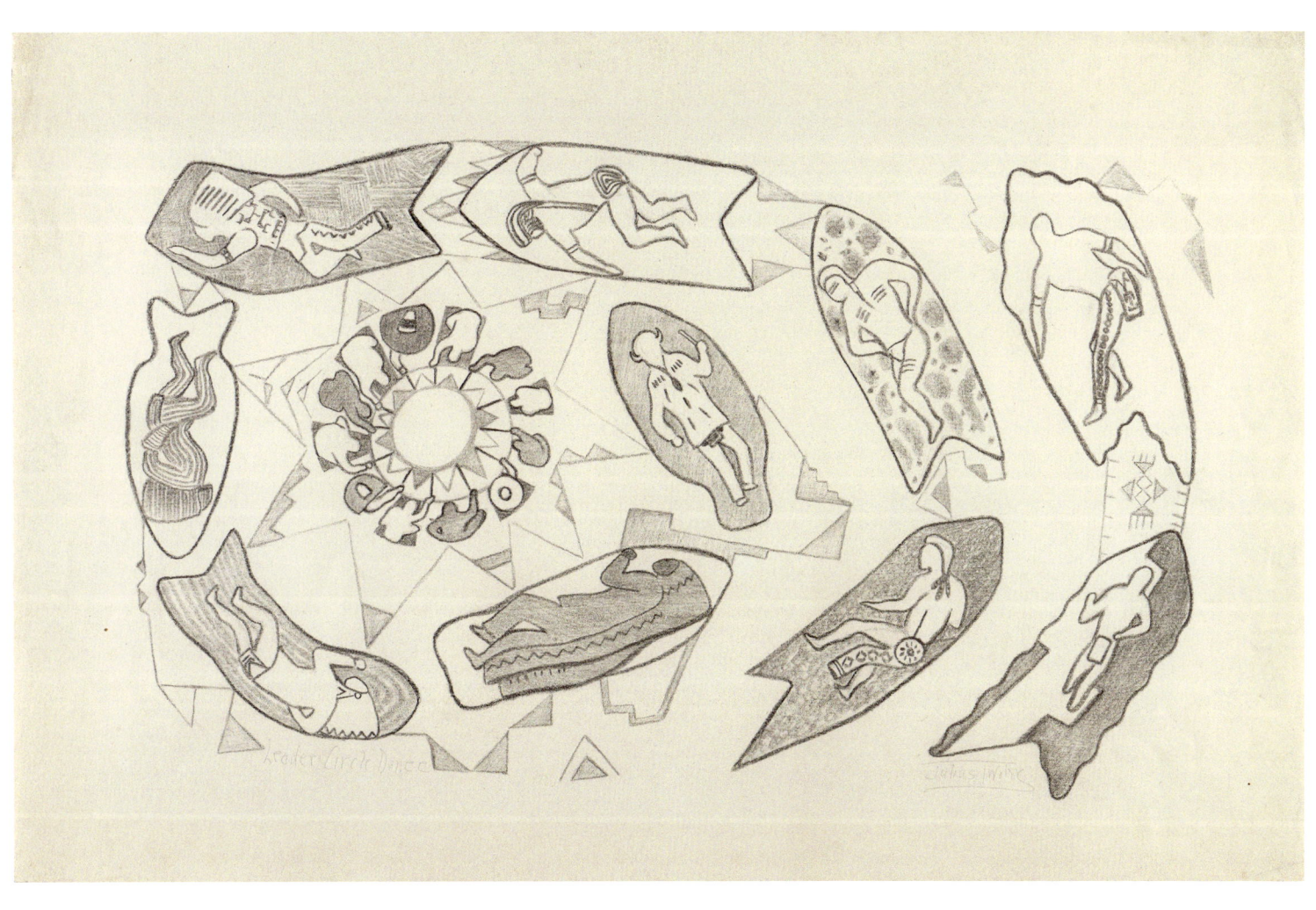

162 Julius Twohy, *Leader, Circle Dance*, ca. 1936–37, lithograph on wove paper

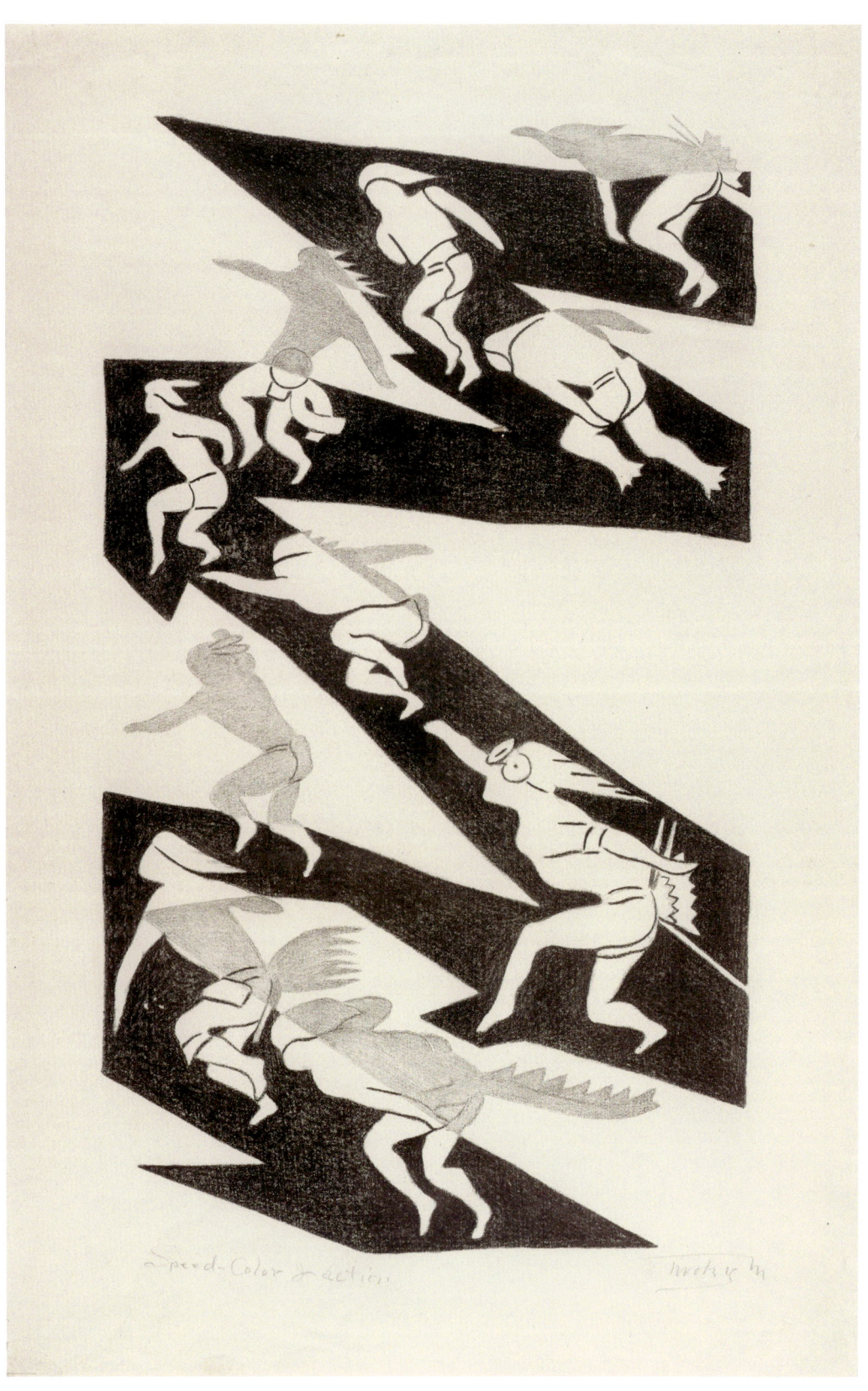

163 Julius Twohy, *Speed, Color, and Action*, ca. 1938–39, lithograph on wove paper

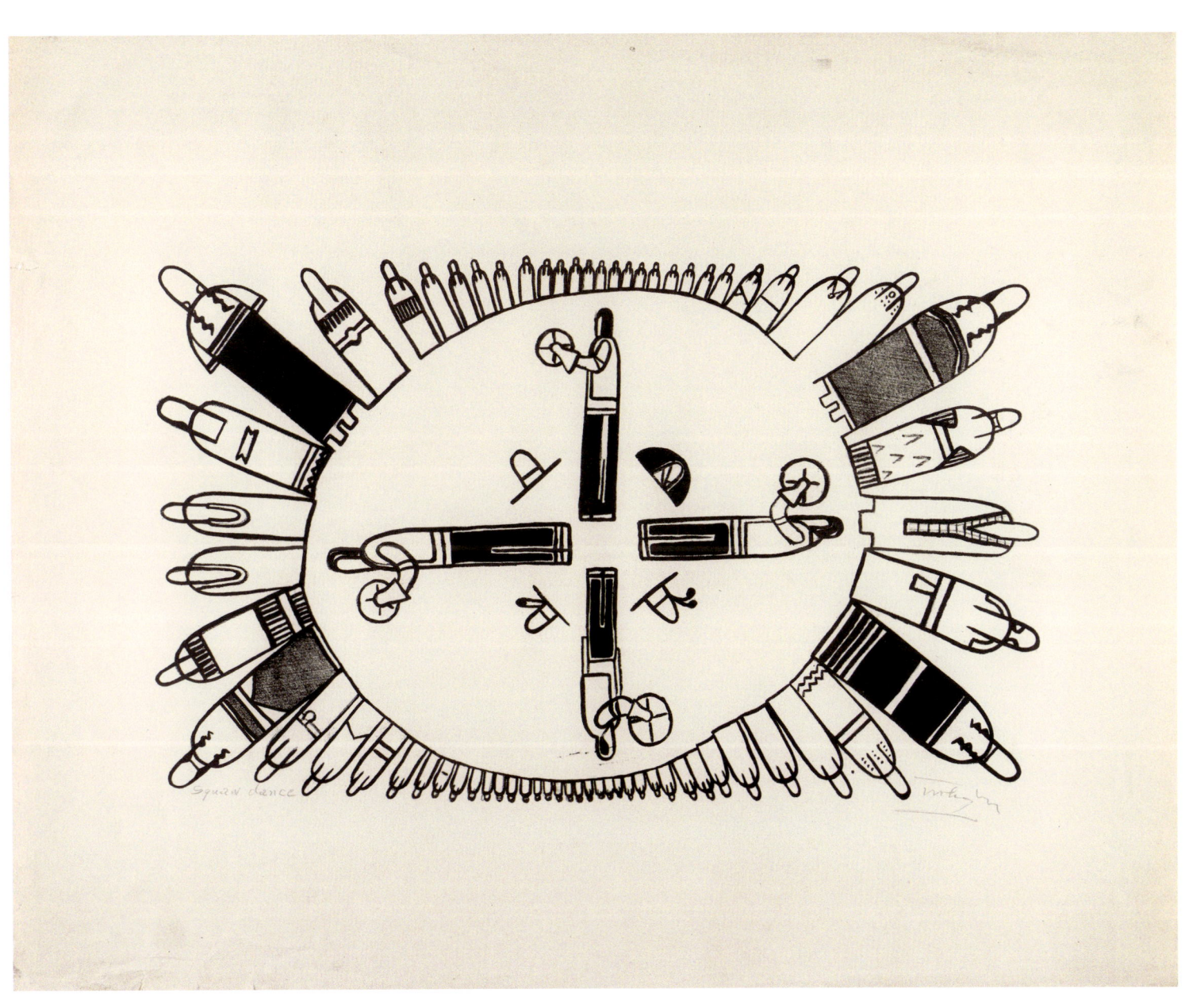

164 Julius Twohy, *Squaw Dance*, 1939, lithograph on wove paper

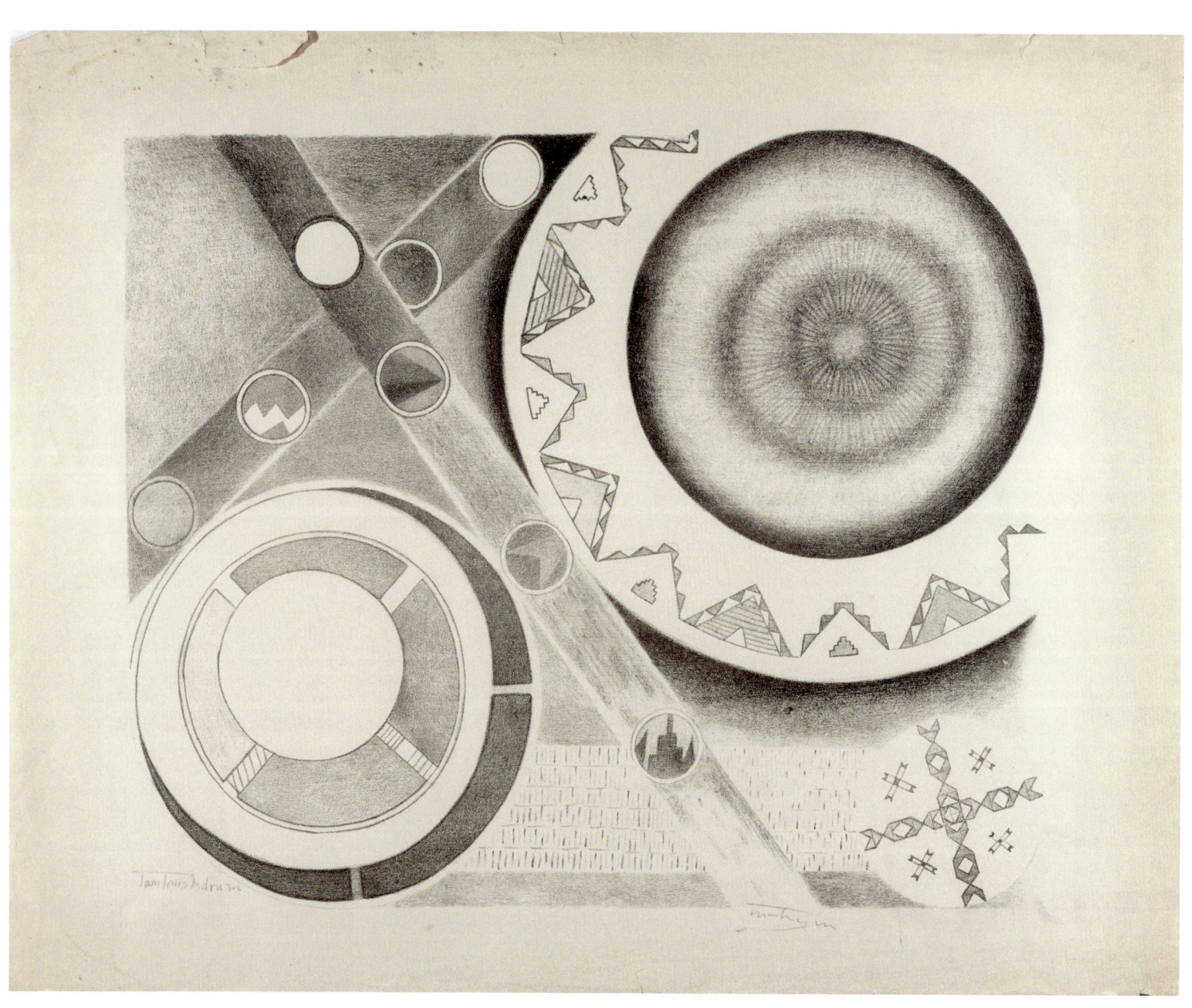

165 Julius Twohy, *Tom Toms and Drum*, 1939, lithograph on wove paper

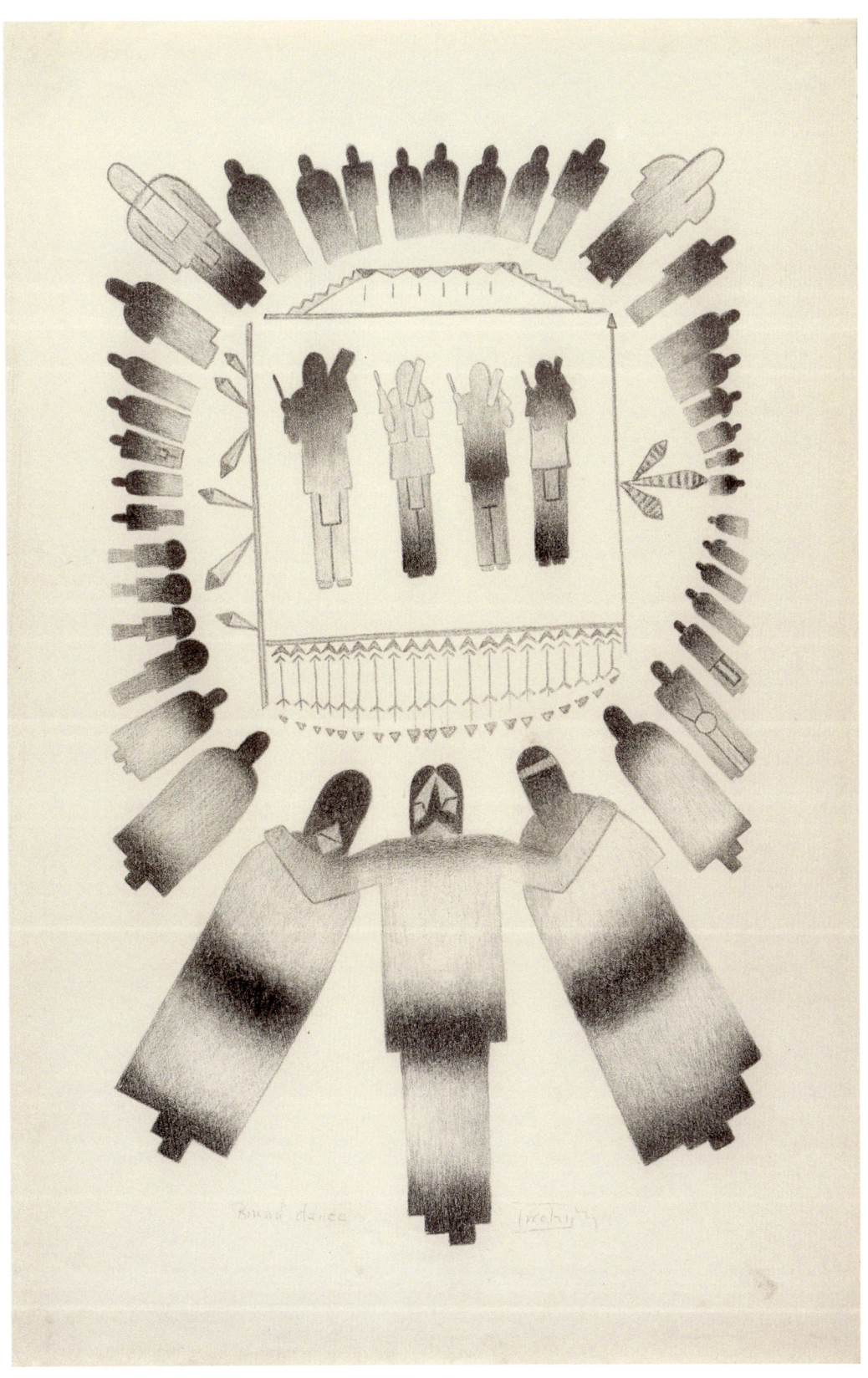

166 Julius Twohy, *Round Dance*, ca. 1938–39, lithograph on wove paper

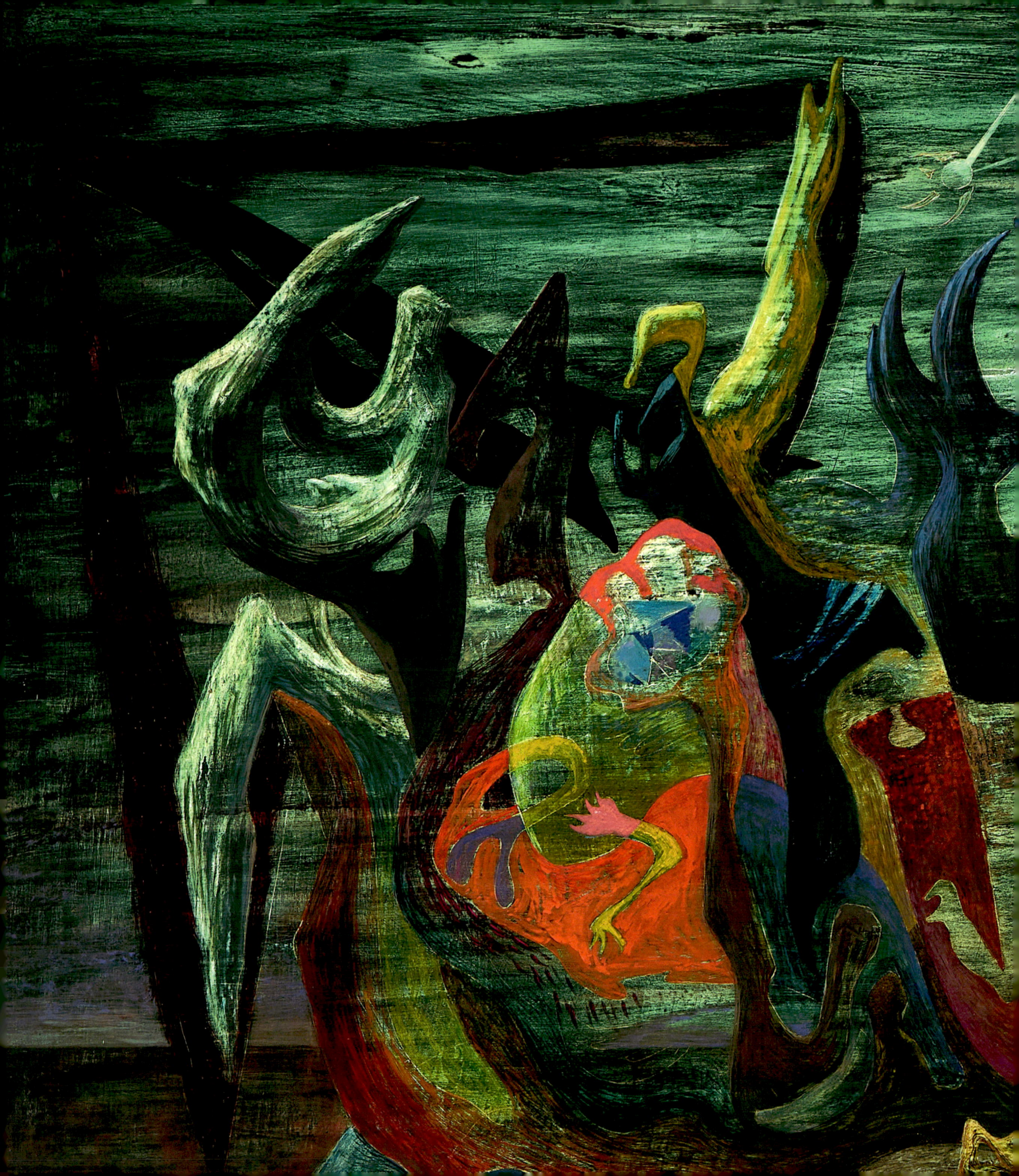

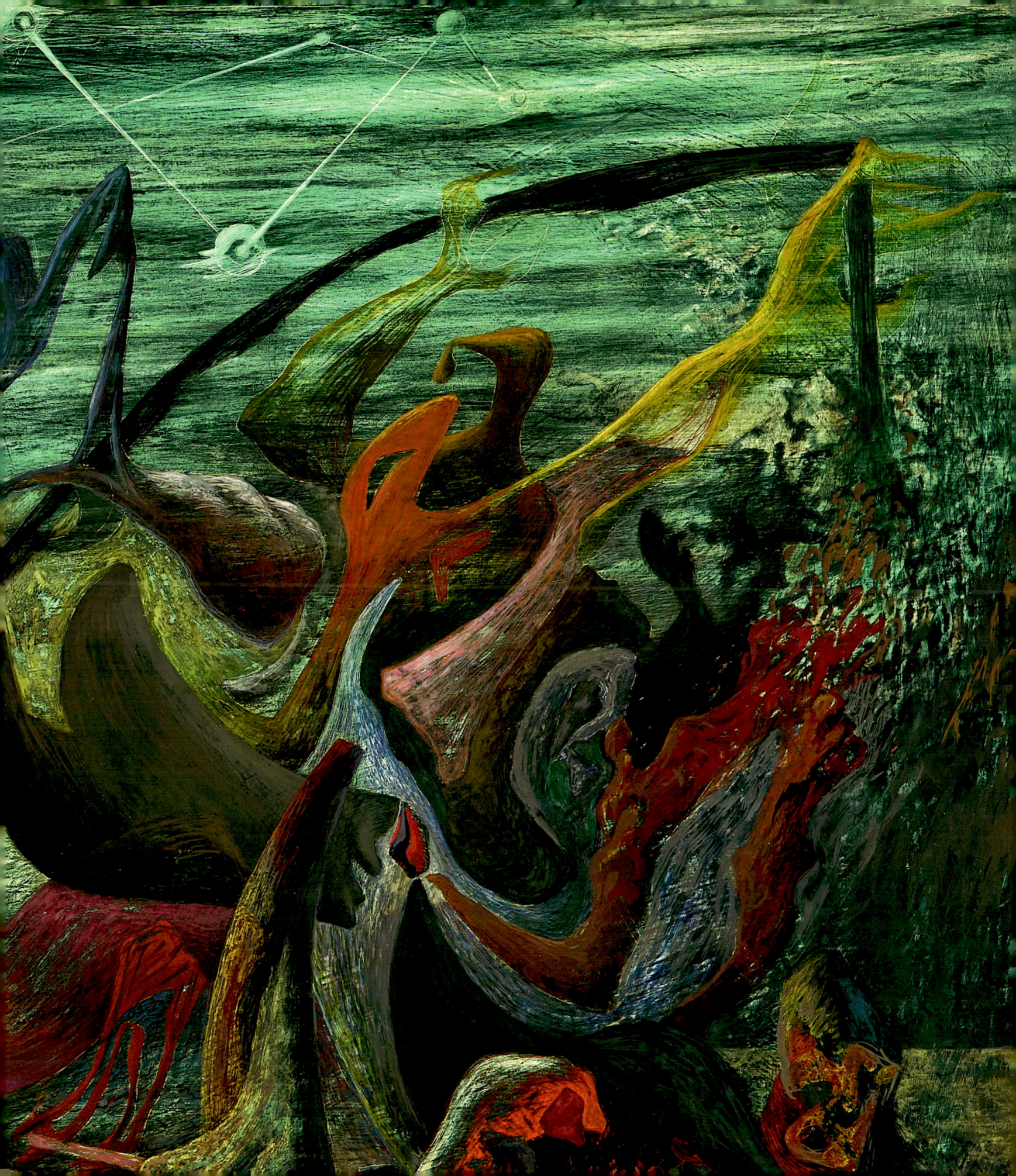

LIST OF PLATES

Guy Anderson

(American, 1906–1998)

Dream of the Language Wheel, 1962

Oil on canvas
81 × 48 in.
Seattle Art Museum, Gift of the Marshall and Helen Hatch Collection, in honor of the 75th Anniversary of the Seattle Art Museum, 2012.15.3
Plate 157

Primitive Forms II, 1962

Oil on composition board
39½ × 29⅝ in.
Seattle Art Museum, Eugene Fuller Memorial Collection, 63.88
Plate 158

Spring, 1967

Oil on newspaper mounted on plywood
46½ × 30 in.
Seattle Art Museum, Purchased with funds from the Pacific Northwest Arts Council and with funds from the National Endowment for the Arts, 77.69
Plate 159

Peter Blume

(American, born in Belarus, 1906–1992)

Light of the World, 1932

Oil on composition board
16⅝ × 18⅞ in.
Whitney Museum of American Art, New York, Purchase, 33.5
Plate 116

The Rock, ca. 1944–48

Oil on canvas
57⅝ × 74⅜ in.
Art Institute of Chicago, Gift of Edgar Kaufmann Jr., 1956.338
Plate 115

Louis Bunce

(American, 1907–1983)

Structure #10, 1939

Oil on canvas
40¾ × 36¼ in.
Portland Art Museum, Courtesy of the Fine Arts Collection, US General Services Administration, New Deal Art Project, L42.5
Plate 121

Dreamer, 1940

Oil and ink on paperboard
12⅜ × 8⅞ in.
Portland Art Museum, Museum purchase: Caroline Ladd Pratt Fund, 77.35
Plate 123

Lumber Yard #514, ca. 1940

Oil on canvas
34⅞ × 23 in.
Portland Art Museum, Courtesy of the Fine Arts Collection, US General Services Administration, New Deal Art Project, L42.13
Plate 122

Kenneth Callahan

(American, 1905–1986)

Feller, 1934

Oil on board
31⅛ × 22 in.
Seattle Art Museum, Eugene Fuller Memorial Collection, 40.51
Plate 71

Northwest Landscape, 1934

Oil on board
34 × 47 in.
Seattle Art Museum, Eugene Fuller Memorial Collection, 34.137
Plate 82

Mail Boxes, 1935

Oil on canvas
32¾ × 26¾ in.
Seattle Art Museum, Eugene Fuller Memorial Collection, 35.91
Plate 86

Logging Rail Road Construction, 1937

Oil on canvas
34½ × 44½ in.
Seattle Art Museum, Eugene Fuller Memorial Collection, 37.47
Plate 89

Mountain Landscape, ca. 1938

Oil on board
19¾ × 29 in.
Seattle Art Museum, Gift of the Marshall and Helen Hatch Collection, in honor of the 75th Anniversary of the Seattle Art Museum, 2012.15.4
Plate 83

The Storm, 1938

Oil on wood
17 × 12 in.
Seattle Art Museum, Eugene Fuller Memorial Collection, 38.28
Plate 74

The Accident, 1939

Tempera on canvas
40 × 34 in.
Seattle Art Museum, Eugene Fuller Memorial Collection, 42.41
Plate 73

Evening Mist in Mountains, ca. 1940

Tempera on board
23½ × 35¾ in.
Seattle Art Museum, Eugene Fuller Memorial Collection, 48.48
Plate 80

First Seed into Last Harvest, 1943

Tempera on canvas
14½ × 18¼ in.
Seattle Art Museum,
Eugene Fuller Memorial
Collection, 46.65
Plate 106

Weyerhaeuser Company Mill B Mural Panel (Loggers with Chokers), 1944

Oil on canvas
48 × 105½ in.
Tacoma Art Museum,
Washington, Gift of the
Weyerhaeuser Company,
2003.39.1
Plate 70

Weyerhaeuser Company Mill B Mural Panel (Weyerhaeuser Mill), 1944

Oil on canvas
47¾ × 95¾ in.
Tacoma Art Museum,
Washington, Gift of the
Weyerhaeuser Company,
2003.29.2
Plate 90

The Mountain, 1945–46

Tempera on board
34⅞ × 22¼ in.
Seattle Art Museum,
Eugene Fuller Memorial
Collection, 47.60
Plate 104

Rocks and People, ca. 1945–46

Tempera on wood panel
22⅜ × 26⅛ in.
Seattle Art Museum,
Eugene Fuller Memorial
Collection, 46.58
Plate 105

The Seventh Day (The Seed Was in Itself), 1952–53

Tempera on paperboard
34 × 46¾ in.
Seattle Art Museum,
Northwest Annual
Purchase Fund, 53.123
Plate 107

Fay Chong

(American, born in China, 1912–1973)

Lake Union Mooring, ca. 1942

Watercolor
14⅜ × 19⅝ in.
Seattle Art Museum,
Eugene Fuller Memorial
Collection, 42.23
Plate 5

Yesler Housing Project, ca. 1942

Watercolor
13 × 19 in.
Seattle Art Museum,
Eugene Fuller Memorial
Collection, 42.24
Plate 34

William Cumming

(American, 1917–2010)

Abandoned Factory, 1939

Tempera on board
9⅞ × 13 in.
Seattle Art Museum,
Eugene Fuller Memorial
Collection, 41.46
Plate 78

Skidroad Group, ca. 1940

Tempera on board
14⅞ × 19⅝ in.
Seattle Art Museum,
Eugene Fuller Memorial
Collection, 41.45
Plate 79

Worker Lifting a Rock, 1940

Tempera on board
23¾ × 33½ in.
Seattle Art Museum,
Seattle Art Museum
Purchase Prize in
Watercolor, 40.71
Plate 75

Worker Resting, 1941

Tempera on board
15 × 19¾ in.
Seattle Art Museum,
Eugene Fuller Memorial
Collection, 41.44
Plate 76

Planting the Flare, ca. 1945

Gouache on board
21¼ × 14½ in.
Seattle Art Museum,
Eugene Fuller Memorial
Collection, 47.156
Plate 77

Salvador Dalí

(Spanish, 1904–1989)

Shades of Night Descending, 1931

Oil on canvas
30⅜ × 26 in.
The Dalí Museum,
St. Petersburg, Florida,
Gift of A. Reynolds &
Eleanor Morse, 2007.22
Plate 110

Bust of Voltaire, 1941

Oil on canvas
18¼ × 21¾ in.
The Dalí Museum,
St. Petersburg, Florida,
Gift of A. Reynolds &
Eleanor Morse, 2007.9
Plate 111

Giorgio de Chirico

(Italian, 1888–1978)

The Piazza, 1914

Oil on canvas
13¼ × 20 in.

Seattle Art Museum, Gift
of Mrs. John C. Atwood Jr.,
55.210
Plate 112

Arthur Dove

(American, 1880–1946)

Power Plant I, 1938

Oil on canvas
25 × 35 in.
Seattle Art Museum,
Partial and promised gift
of Mr. and Mrs. Howard S.
Wright, in honor of the
museum's 50th year, 84.64
Plate 33

Jacob Elshin

(American, born in Russia, 1892–1976)

Mill, 1934

Oil on canvas
29 × 38 in.
Seattle Art Museum, Public
Works of Art Project,
Washington State, 34.138
Plate 3

Max Ernst

(German, 1891–1976)

Forest (Forêt), 1927

Oil on paper mounted
on canvas
27⅛ × 19⅝ in.
The Menil Collection,
Houston, X 484
Plate 113

James H. FitzGerald

(American, 1910–1973)

Resurgent Sea, 1945

Oil and tempera on board
41 × 48 in.
Seattle Art Museum,
Eugene Fuller Memorial
Collection, 45.91
Plate 134

Takuichi Fujii

(American, born in Japan, 1891–1964)

Rock Island Dam, 1935

Oil on canvas
28½ × 34 in.
Wing Luke Museum, Seattle, Gift of Sean M. and Teddi L. Callihan
Plate 30

Adolph Gottlieb

(American, 1903–1974)

Crimson Spinning #2, 1959

Oil on canvas
90 × 72 in.
Seattle Art Museum, Gift of the Friday Foundation in honor of Richard E. Lang and Jane Lang Davis, 2020.14.9
Plate 147

Morris Graves

(American, 1910–2001)

Moor Swan, 1933

Oil on canvas
36 × 34¾ in.
Seattle Art Museum, Gift of West Seattle Art Club, Katherine B. Baker Memorial Purchase Prize, 19th Annual Exhibition of Northwest Artists, Seattle Art Museum, 1933, 33.219
Plate 93

Summer Still Life, ca. 1935

Oil on burlap
44 × 39 in.
Seattle Art Museum, Purchased in memory of Solomon Katz with funds from the Estate of Mark Tobey and contributions by friends of Solomon Katz, 89.187
Plate 91

Logged Mountains, ca. 1935–43

Oil on canvas
27⅛ × 36⅛ in.
Smithsonian American Art Museum, Washington, DC, Transfer from the General Services Administration, 1971.447.33
Plate 81
*Not in exhibition

Ancient Anthem, 1936

Oil on burlap
44 × 39 in.
Seattle Art Museum, Eugene Fuller Memorial Collection, 36.32
Plate 125

Burial of the New Law, 1936

Oil on canvas
43 × 38 in.
Seattle Art Museum, Eugene Fuller Memorial Collection, 36.33
Plate 126

Chalice Holding the Stimson Mill, 1936

Oil on canvas
67 × 39½ in.
Tacoma Art Museum, Washington, Gift of Robert Ohashi, Arnold Ohashi, and Ross Ohashi, 2007.14
Plate 124

Departure via Cedron, 1936

Oil on canvas
41 × 35½ in.
Seattle Art Museum, Gift of the Marshall and Helen Hatch Collection, in honor of the 75th anniversary of the Seattle Art Museum, 2009.52.11
Plate 128

Untitled (Altar), 1937

Watercolor, tempera, and oil pastel or encaustic on paper mounted on composite board
12 × 16 in.

Seattle Art Museum, Gift of the Marshall and Helen Hatch Collection, in honor of the 75th anniversary of the Seattle Art Museum, 2009.52.12
Plate 127

Still Life with Onions, ca. 1937

Oil on canvas
29 × 34⅛ in.
Seattle Art Museum, Gift of the Marshall and Helen Hatch Collection, in honor of the 75th anniversary of the Seattle Art Museum, 2009.52.102
Plate 92

Crow, Surf and Moon, 1943

Ink and watercolor on Japanese paper, later mounted on rag board
25½ × 30¾ in.
Seattle Art Museum, Gift of the Marshall and Helen Hatch Collection, in honor of the 75th anniversary of the Seattle Art Museum, 2005.170
Plate 94

Bird Sensing the Essential Insanities, 1944

Tempera on paper mounted on composition board
26¾ × 53¼ in.
Seattle Art Museum, Eugene Fuller Memorial Collection, 56.47
Plate 108

The Genesis of Life Lay Deep and Anticipant Under the Sky, 1944

Ink and watercolor
26¾ × 52½ in.
Seattle Art Museum, Gift of the Marshall and Helen Hatch Collection, in honor of the 75th anniversary of the Seattle Art Museum, 2009.52.16
Plate 146

Night Sky No. 2, 1944

Ink and watercolor on toned Japanese paper
52¼ × 26⅞ in.
Seattle Art Museum, Gift of the Marshall and Helen Hatch Collection, in honor of the 75th anniversary of the Seattle Art Museum, 2005.171
Plate 95

Each Time You Carry Me This Way, 1953

Ink and charcoal on paper mounted on heavyweight paper and fiber board
25 × 43¼ in.
Seattle Art Museum, Gift of the Marshall and Helen Hatch Collection, in honor of the 75th anniversary of the Seattle Art Museum, 2007.115
Plate 109

Spring with Machine Age Noise No. 3, 1957

Ink and watercolor on paper
26¼ × 54¾ in.
Seattle Art Museum, Gift of the Marshall and Helen Hatch Collection, in honor of the 75th anniversary of the Seattle Art Museum, 2005.172
Plate 96

Marsden Hartley

(American, 1877–1943)

Log Jam, Penobscot Bay, 1940–41

Oil on board
30 × 40⅞ in.
Detroit Institute of Arts, Gift of Robert H. Tannahill, 44.5
Plate 101
*Not in exhibition

Z. Vanessa Helder

(American, 1904–1968)

Coulee Dam Construction: Skip Way and Grout Shed, 1939
Watercolor
18¼ × 14⅞ in.
Seattle Art Museum, Eugene Fuller Memorial Collection, 39.54
Plate 29

B Street—Residence District, 1939–41
Watercolor
15½ × 20½ in.
Northwest Museum of Arts and Culture, Spokane, Washington, Museum purchase, 1954, 2085.22
Plate 7

Cement Silos, 1939–41
Watercolor
14¾ × 22¼ in.
Northwest Museum of Arts and Culture, Spokane, Washington, Museum purchase, 1954, 2585.1
Plate 8

Cliff Drive, 1939–41
Watercolor
15⅛ × 20½ in.
Northwest Museum of Arts and Culture, Spokane, Washington, Museum purchase, 1954, 2085.12
Plate 9

Construction Crew, 1939–41
Watercolor
14⅞ × 20½ in.
Northwest Museum of Arts and Culture, Spokane, Washington, Museum purchase, 1954, 2585.2
Plate 10

Conveyor Belt, 1939–41
Watercolor
18¼ × 22½ in.
Northwest Museum of Arts and Culture, Spokane, Washington, Museum purchase, 1954, 2085.22
Plate 12

Coulee Dam, Looking West, 1939–41
Watercolor
18 × 21 in.
Northwest Museum of Arts and Culture, Spokane, Washington, Museum purchase, 1954, 2585.3
Plate 11

East Grout Shed, 1939–41
Watercolor
15½ × 21 in.
Northwest Museum of Arts and Culture, Spokane, Washington, Museum purchase, 1954, 2585.7
Plate 14

Grand Coulee, 1939–41
Watercolor
18¼ × 22¼ in.
Northwest Museum of Arts and Culture, Spokane, Washington, Museum purchase, 1954, 2085.22
Plate 13

Grand Coulee Heights, 1939–41
Watercolor
15 × 19½ in.
Northwest Museum of Arts and Culture, Spokane, Washington, Museum purchase, 1954, 2085.11
Plate 16

Hilltop House, 1939–41
Watercolor
18⅛ × 22½ in.
Northwest Museum of Arts and Culture, Spokane, Washington, Museum purchase, 1954, 2085.5
Plate 15

Hooverville, Coulee Dam, 1939–41
Watercolor
14½ × 19¼ in.
Northwest Museum of Arts and Culture, Spokane, Washington, Museum purchase, 1954, 2585.10
Plate 17

Jackhammer Crew, 1939–41
Watercolor
15½ × 20½ in.
Northwest Museum of Arts and Culture, Spokane, Washington, Museum purchase, 1954, 2585.14
Plate 18

Kettle Falls, 1939–41
Watercolor
17⅝ × 22⅛ in.
Northwest Museum of Arts and Culture, Spokane, Washington, Museum purchase, 1954, 2085.6
Plate 19

Methodist Church in Coulee Heights, 1939–41
Watercolor
14 × 20½ in.
Northwest Museum of Arts and Culture, Spokane, Washington, Museum purchase, 1954, 2085.18
Plate 20

Neighbors, 1939–41
Watercolor
26¼ × 29⅞ in.
Northwest Museum of Arts and Culture, Spokane, Washington, Museum purchase, 1954, 2585.17
Plate 22

Pool Below Kettle Falls, 1939–41
Watercolor
18¼ × 22½ in.
Northwest Museum of Arts and Culture, Spokane, Washington, Museum purchase, 1954, 2085.8
Plate 21

Rainy Afternoon, 1939–41
Watercolor
14 × 19½ in.
Northwest Museum of Arts and Culture, Spokane, Washington, Museum purchase, 1954, 2085.11
Plate 24

Rocks and Concrete, 1939–41
Watercolor
22¼ × 16¼ in.
Northwest Museum of Arts and Culture, Spokane, Washington, Museum purchase, 1954, 2015.16
Plate 23

Sand and Gravel Works, 1939–41
Watercolor
20½ × 26¼ in.
Northwest Museum of Arts and Culture, Spokane, Washington, Museum purchase, 1954, 2585.19
Plate 25

Stiff-Legged Crane, 1939–41
Watercolor
14¾ × 20 in.
Northwest Museum of Arts and Culture, Spokane, Washington, Museum purchase, 1954, 2585.4
Plate 26

Sunday Morning in Grand Coulee, 1939–41
Watercolor
18⅛ × 22¼ in.
Northwest Museum of Arts and Culture, Spokane, Washington, Museum purchase, 1954, 2585.9
Plate 27

Tanks and Track,
1939–41

Watercolor
18⅜ × 22⅝ in.
Northwest Museum of
Arts and Culture, Spokane,
Washington, Museum pur-
chase, 1954, 2585.15
Plate 28

Alexandre Hogue

(American, 1898–1994)

Erosion No. 2—
Mother Earth Laid
Bare, 1936

Oil on canvas
40 × 55 in.
Philbrook Museum of Art,
Tulsa, Museum purchase,
1946.4
Plate 102

Crucified Land, 1939

Oil on canvas
47 × 65 in.
Gilcrease Museum,
Tulsa, Gift of the Thomas
Gilcrease Foundation,
1955, 01.2000
Plate 103

Paul Horiuchi

(American, born in Japan,
1906–1999)

Untitled, 1961

Paper collage with gouache
on six-panel screen
52¾ × 108 in.
Collection of Fay Hauberg
Page and Nathaniel
Blodgett Page
Plate 148

Monolithic Impasse,
1964

Casein on mulberry paper
mounted on canvas
77½ × 78½ in.
Seattle Art Museum, Gift
of the Seattle Art Museum
Guild, 79.6
Plate 151

Colors and Patterns
from Heian Period,
1969

Casein and paint on paper
mounted on board
54 × 105 in.
Seattle Art Museum, Gift
in memory of Elisabeth A.
Smithson by her son,
Richard B. Smithson, 71.52
Plate 149

Definition, 1976

Casein on paper mounted
on canvas
60 × 72 in.
Seattle Art Museum, Gift
of Gordon Woodside, 76.67
Plate 150

Yvonne Twining Humber

(American, 1907–2004)

Suburban Street,
1940

Oil on canvas
20 × 29 in.
Seattle Art Museum,
Margaret E. Fuller Pur-
chase Prize, 31st Annual
Exhibition of Northwest
Artists, 45.84
Plate 36

Spoiled Carnival,
1946

Oil on canvas
22 × 38 in.
Seattle Art Museum,
Eugene Fuller Memorial
Collection, 47.154
Plate 39

Leo Kenney

(American, 1925–2001)

The Inception of
Magic, 1945

Tempera on composite
board
36⅛ × 24⅛ in.
Seattle Art Museum,
Eugene Fuller Memorial
Collection, 45.52
Plate 129

Lamentation, 1947

Watercolor on black paper
18½ × 9 in.
Seattle Art Museum, Gift
of the Estate of Robert M.
Shields, 2013.4.4
Plate 131

Northern Image:
The Muse III, 1948

Oil on canvas
29⅝ × 19½ in.
Seattle Art Museum,
Eugene Fuller Memorial
Collection, 49.129
Plate 130

Third Offering, 1948

Oil on canvas
41¼ × 25½ in.
Seattle Art Museum,
Lowman and Hanford Pur-
chase Prize, 48.199
Plate 132

Voyage for Two, 1953

Gouache on Chinese paper
19¾ × 23½ in.
Seattle Art Museum, Gift
of the artist, 66.87
Plate 133

Franz Kline

(American, 1910–1962)

Cross Section, 1956

Oil on canvas
53½ × 63 in.
Seattle Art Museum, Gift
of the Virginia and Bagley
Wright Collection, in honor
of the 75th Anniversary of
the Seattle Art Museum,
2020.15.17
Plate 152

Reginald Marsh

(American, born in France,
1898–1954)

Tuesday Night at the
Savoy Ballroom, 1930

Tempera on composition
board
44 × 56 in.
Rose Art Museum, Brandeis
University, Waltham,

Massachusetts, Gift of the
Honorable William Benton,
New York, 1962.36
Plate 51

Archibald John Motley Jr.

(American, 1891–1981)

Nightlife, 1943

Oil on canvas
36 × 47¾ in.
Art Institute of Chicago,
Purchased with funds
provided by Jamee J.
and Marshall Field, Jack
and Sandra Guthman,
Ben W. Heineman, Ruth
Horwich, Lewis and Susan
Manilow, Beatrice C.
Mayer, Charles A. Meyer,
John D. Nichols, and
Mr. and Mrs. Edward
Byron Smith, Jr.; James W.
Alsdorf Memorial Fund;
Goodman Endowment
Fund, 1992.89
Plate 52

William L. Nellor

(American, 1923–2020)

Merry Pranks, 1949

Tempera on paperboard
14⅜ × 19½ in.
Seattle Art Museum,
Lowman and Hanford
Co. purchase prize in any
medium, 49.209
Plate 6

Kenjiro Nomura

(American, born in Japan,
1896–1956)

Street, ca. 1932

Oil on canvas
23¾ × 28¾ in.
Seattle Art Museum,
Gift of West Seattle Art
Club, Katherine B. Baker
Memorial Purchase Award,
33.225
Plate 35

Red Barns, 1933

Oil on canvas
28 × 36 in.
Seattle Art Museum,
Eugene Fuller Memorial
Collection, 33.224
Plate 84

Ernest Ralph Norling

(American, 1892–1974)

The Timber Bucker,
ca. 1934

Oil on canvas
34⅛ × 40 in.
Smithsonian American
Art Museum, Washington,
DC, Transfer from the US
Department of the Inte-
rior, National Park Service,
1965.18.35
Plate 69

Georgia O'Keeffe

(American, 1887–1986)

A Celebration, 1924

Oil on canvas
34⅞ × 18 in.
Seattle Art Museum, Gift
of the Georgia O'Keeffe
Foundation, 94.89
Plate 87

*Dead Tree Bear Lake
Taos*, 1929

Oil on canvas
32 × 17 in.
Art Bridges Foundation,
Bentonville, Arkansas
Plate 88

Malcolm M. Roberts

(American, 1913–1990)

The Beach, 1935

Tempera on canvas
24⅛ × 20⅛ in.
Seattle Art Museum,
Eugene Fuller Memorial
Collection, 36.79
Plate 118

Drift No. 2, 1936

Tempera on board
20⅝ × 25½ in.

Seattle Art Museum,
Eugene Fuller Memorial
Collection, 37.103
Plate 117

*View of Aurora
Bridge*, ca. 1936

Tempera on canvas and
linen
17¾ × 22½ in.
Seattle Art Museum,
Eugene Fuller Memorial
Collection, 37.104
Plate 119

Lunar Landscape,
1941

Tempera on cardboard
29⅜ × 39½ in.
Seattle Art Museum,
Eugene Fuller Memorial
Collection, 41.205
Plate 120

Mark Rothko

(American, born in Russia
[now Latvia], 1903–1970)

Untitled, ca. 1945

Oil on canvas
22½ × 30⅜ in.
Seattle Art Museum, Gift
of the Friday Foundation
in honor of Richard E.
Lang and Jane Lang Davis,
2020.14.3
Plate 140

Charles Sheeler

(American, 1883–1965)

Classic Landscape,
1931

Oil on canvas
25 × 32¼ in.
National Gallery of Art,
Washington, DC, Collec-
tion of Barney A. Ebsworth,
2000.39.2
Plate 31
*Not in exhibition

*Composition Around
White*, 1957

Tempera on plexiglass
7½ × 8¼ in.

Collection of Bill and Holly
Marklyn
Plate 32

Albert Smith Sr.

(American, 1916–2008)

*Louis Armstrong
Onstage at the Civic
Auditorium, Seattle,
July 17, 1944*, 1944

Digital scan of a black-and-
white acetate negative
2¼ × 2¼ in.
Museum of History and
Industry (MOHAI), Seattle,
Al Smith Collection,
2014.49.002-027-0214
Plate 41

*Jazz Trio on Stage at
the Basin Street Club,
Seattle, March 24,
1945*, 1945

Digital scan of a black-and-
white acetate negative
2¼ × 2¼ in.
Museum of History and
Industry (MOHAI), Seattle,
Al Smith Collection,
2014.49.002-035-0162
Plate 40

*Count Basie at
the Piano, Seattle,
November 27, 1946*,
1946

Digital scan of a black-and-
white acetate negative
5 × 4 in.
Museum of History and
Industry (MOHAI), Seattle,
Al Smith Collection,
2014.49.002-016-0049
Plate 42

*Lionel Hampton and
His Orchestra Playing
at Civic Auditorium,
Seattle, August 7,
1946*, 1946

Digital scan of a black-and-
white acetate negative
5 × 4 in.

Museum of History and
Industry (MOHAI), Seattle,
Al Smith Collection,
2014.49.002-013-0197
Plate 43

*Cab Calloway Singing
on Stage at the Civic
Auditorium, Seattle,
circa 1947*, ca. 1947

Digital scan of a black-and-
white acetate negative
5 × 4 in.
Museum of History and
Industry (MOHAI), Seattle,
Al Smith Collection,
2014.49.002-019-0060
Plate 44

*Ernestine Anderson
Singing at the Black
& Tan, Seattle,
circa 1947*, ca. 1947

Digital scan of a black-and-
white acetate negative
3¼ × 2¼ in.
Museum of History and
Industry (MOHAI), Seattle,
Al Smith Collection,
2014.49.002-023-0074
Plate 45

*Group Around Table
at the Black & Tan,
Seattle, circa 1947*,
ca. 1947

Digital scan of a black-and-
white acetate negative
4 × 5 in.
Museum of History and
Industry (MOHAI), Seattle,
Al Smith Collection,
2014.49.010-051-0102
Plate 46

*Hazel Scott at the
Piano at the Civic
Auditorium, Seattle,
October 11, 1947*, 1947

Digital scan of a black-and-
white acetate negative
5 × 4 in.
Museum of History and
Industry (MOHAI), Seattle,
Al Smith Collection,
2014.49.002-014-0043
Plate 47

Jitterbug Dancers at Cab Calloway Performance, Seattle, circa 1947, ca. 1947

Digital scan of a black-and-white acetate negative
5 × 4 in.
Museum of History and Industry (MOHAI), Seattle, Al Smith Collection, 2014.49.002-019-0062
Plate 48

Singer and Jazz Band at the Black & Tan, Seattle, circa 1947, ca. 1947

Digital scan of a black-and-white acetate negative
2½ × 2½ in.
Museum of History and Industry (MOHAI), Seattle, Al Smith Collection, 2014.49.002-036-0175
Plate 50

Dizzy Gillespie and His Orchestra Performing at the Senator Ballroom, Seattle, February 19, 1949, 1949

Digital scan of a black-and-white acetate negative
5 × 4 in.
Museum of History and Industry (MOHAI), Seattle, Al Smith Collection, 2014.49.002-011-0034
Plate 49

Yves Tanguy

(French, 1900–1955)

There! (The Evening Before) (Et voilà! [La veille au soir]), 1927

Oil on canvas
25¾ × 21⅜ in.
The Menil Collection, Houston, 1985-023 DJ
Plate 114

Mark Tobey

(American, 1890–1976)

Dancing Miners, ca. 1922–27

Oil on canvas
67 × 39¼ in.
Seattle Art Museum, Eugene Fuller Memorial Collection, 42.19
Plate 72

Cirque d'hiver, 1933

Pastel on paper
17¼ × 22 in.
Seattle Art Museum, Gift of Windsor and Josephine Utley, 96.80
Plate 141

12 Market Scenes, Being Sketches of Seattle Public Market Between 1939 and 1941, 1939–41

Ink and watercolor on paper
Each: 7½ × 5¾ in.
Seattle Art Museum, Bequest of Frank S. Bayley III, 2023.11.49–60
Plates 53–64

Market Fantasy, ca. 1940

Tempera on paperboard
22 × 16 in.
Seattle Art Museum, Gift of William S. and Janice K. Street in honor of the museum's 50th year, 83.165
Plate 137

Modal Tide, 1940

Oil on canvas
34½ × 47⅜ in.
Seattle Art Museum, Gift of the West Seattle Art Club, Katherine B. Baker Memorial Purchase Prize, 26th Annual Exhibition of Northwest Artists, 40.58
Plate 139

Rummage, 1941

Watercolor on paperboard
38⅜ × 25⅞ in.
Seattle Art Museum, Eugene Fuller Memorial Collection, 42.28
Plate 66

Time Off, 1941

Oil on board
19⅝ × 15½ in.
Seattle Art Museum, Eugene Fuller Memorial Collection, 42.21
Plate 68

E Pluribus Unum, 1942

Watercolor on paper mounted on paperboard
19¾ × 27¼ in.
Seattle Art Museum, Gift of Mrs. Thomas D. Stimson, 43.33
Plate 65

White Night, 1942

Tempera on paperboard mounted on composition board
22¼ × 14 in.
Seattle Art Museum, Gift of Mrs. Berthe Poncy Jacobson, 62.78
Plate 142

Working Man, 1942

Gouache on board
43½ × 27½ in.
Seattle Art Museum, Eugene Fuller Memorial Collection, 42.33
Plate 67

Esquimaux Idiom, 1946

Tempera with graphite on composition board
43½ × 27½ in.
Seattle Art Museum, Gift of Gladys and Sam Rubinstein, 69.79
Plate 160

Space Ritual No. 1, 1957

Sumi ink on paper
29¼ × 37½ in.
Seattle Art Museum, Eugene Fuller Memorial Collection, 60.85
Plate 143

Space Ritual No. 18, 1957

Sumi ink on wove paper mounted on board
23¼ × 34¾ in.
Seattle Art Museum, Gift of the Estate of Mark Tobey, 87.20
Plate 144

Kamekichi Tokita

(American, born in Japan, 1897–1948)

Alley, ca. 1929

Oil on canvas
20½ × 16½ in.
Seattle Art Museum, Gift of the artist, 33.229
Plate 37

House, ca. 1930

Oil on canvas
17⅜ × 21¾ in.
Seattle Art Museum, Gift of the artist, 33.228
Plate 38

Bridge, 1931

Oil on canvas
23¼ × 19 in.
Seattle Art Museum, Gift of the artist, 33.230
Plate 4

Billboard, 1932

Oil on canvas
19 × 23 in.
Seattle Art Museum, Gift of the artist, 35.214
Plate 2

Drugstore, 1933

Oil on canvas
16⅝ × 20½ in.
Seattle Art Museum, Gift of the artist, 33.227
Plate 1

Margaret Tomkins

(American, 1916–2002)

Metamorphosis, 1943

Tempera on Masonite
25 × 30 in.
Seattle Art Museum,
Eugene Fuller Memorial
Collection, 43.24
Plate 135

Anamorphosis, 1944

Ink and tempera on board
17⅜ × 21¾ in.
Seattle Art Museum,
Eugene Fuller Memorial
Collection, 45.93
Plate 136

George Tsutakawa

(American, 1910–1997)

Self-Portrait, ca. 1941

Oil on canvas
11¼ × 15¼
Tsutakawa Art Legacy LLC
Plate 138

The Ascent, 1950

Oil on canvas board
21 × 30 in.
Seattle Art Museum, Gift
of Mr. and Mrs. Dwight E.
Robinson, 54.153
Plate 153

The Descent, 1950

Oil on board
29⅜ × 20¼ in.
Seattle Art Museum, Gift
of Sidney and Anne Gerber,
65.174
Plate 154

Obos I, 1956

Teak
23¼ × 9¾ × 8⅞ in.
Seattle Art Museum, Gift
of Seattle Art Museum
Guild, 79.7
Plate 155

Obos 15, 1961

Cedar
30 × 26 × 18 in.
Seattle Art Museum,
General Acquisition Fund,
Northwest Art Fund,

American Art Acquisition
Fund, 2022.37
Plate 156

Gust, 1980

Ink on medium-weight
Japanese paper, mounted
on lightweight Japanese
paper
11½ × 36⅜ in.
Seattle Art Museum, Gift
of the Estate of Robert M.
Shields, 2013.4.1
Plate 145

Julius Twohy

(Native American, Ute,
1902–1986)

*Dance of Indian
Chiefs and Medicine
Men*, ca. 1936–37

Lithograph on wove paper
Image: 10 × 16⅝ in., sheet:
12½ × 19 in.
Henry Art Gallery,
University of Washington,
Seattle, FA 69.83
Plate 161

Leader, Circle Dance,
ca. 1936–37

Lithograph on wove paper
Image: 9½ × 16 in., sheet:
12¼ × 19 in.
Henry Art Gallery,
University of Washington,
Seattle, FA. 69.86
Plate 162

Round Dance,
ca. 1938–39

Lithograph on wove paper
Image: 15¼ × 11 in.; sheet:
19 × 12½ in.
Henry Art Gallery,
University of Washington,
Seattle, 69.84
Plate 166

*Speed, Color, and
Action*, ca. 1938–39

Lithograph on wove paper
Image: 16⅝ × 9½ in., sheet:
19⅛ × 12½ in.

Henry Art Gallery,
University of Washington,
Seattle, FA 69.82
Plate 163

Squaw Dance, 1939

Lithograph on wove paper
Image: 10 × 16 in., sheet:
16⅞ × 21 in.
Henry Art Gallery,
University of Washington,
Seattle, FA 69.85
Plate 164

Tom Toms and Drum,
1939

Lithograph on wove paper
Image: 15 × 18 in., sheet:
17½ × 21⅝ in.
Henry Art Gallery,
University of Washington,
Seattle, FA 69.87
Plate 165

Celilo Falls, 1945

Tempera on paper
8¾ × 11¾ in.
Seattle Art Museum, Gift
of the Marshall and Helen
Hatch Collection, in honor
of the 75th Anniversary of
the Seattle Art Museum,
2009.52.87
Plate 85

**James
Washington Jr.**

(American, 1909–2000)

*Young Bird of the
Swamp*, 1959

Granite on wood mount
Stone sculpture: 6½ ×
5¾ × 7¼ in.; wood mount:
4½ × 4½ × 3 in.
Seattle Art Museum,
Eugene Fuller Memorial
Collection, 59.165
Plate 97

Bird, 1961

Stone
1¼ × 2 × 1½ in.
Seattle Art Museum, Mark
Tobey Estate, 2000.104
Plate 98

The Woodchuck,
1962

Granite on wood mount
Stone sculpture: 5½ ×
6½ × 9 in.; wood mount:
1¾ × 6½ × 8⅜ in.
Seattle Art Museum, Gift
of Edward B. Thomas,
62.149
Plate 99

*Wounded Eagle
No. 10*, 1963

Granite on wood mount
Stone sculpture: 8 × 10⅝ ×
13¼ in.; wood mount: 1¾ ×
6½ × 8⅜ in.
Seattle Art Museum,
Eugene Fuller Memorial
Collection, 68.159
Plate 100

REFERENCES

Anderson, Guy, interviewed by Martha Kingsbury. "Oral History Interview with Guy Anderson, 1983 February 1–8." Transcript, Archives of American Art, Smithsonian Institution, Washington, DC. https://www.aaa.si.edu/collections/interviews/oral-history-interview-guy-anderson-12009.

"Art: Marvelous and Fantastic." *Time*, 14 December 1936, 60–62.

Asaka, Megan. *Seattle from the Margins: Exclusion, Erasure, and the Making of a Pacific Coast City.* University of Washington Press, 2022.

Barter, Judith A., ed. *America After the Fall: Painting in the 1930s.* Art Institute of Chicago, 2016. Distributed by Yale University Press, 2016.

Blecha, Peter. "Al Smith." HistoryLink. Posted 6 August 2015. https://www.historylink.org/file/11095.

Breton, André. *Manifestoes of Surrealism.* Translated by Richard Seaver and Helen R. Lane. First paperback edition. University of Michigan Press, 1972.

Brotherton, Barbara. "Joseph Raymond Hillaire: Lummi Artist-Diplomat." In *A Totem Pole History: The Work of Lummi Carver Joe Hillaire*. Edited by Pauline Hillaire and Gregory Fields. University of Nebraska Press, 2012.

Browne, Colin. "Scavengers of Paradise." In *The Color of My Dreams: The Surrealist Revolution in Art*. Edited by Dawn Ades. Vancouver Art Gallery, 2011.

Bullock, Margaret E., et al. *New Deal Art in the Northwest: The WPA and Beyond.* Tacoma Art Museum, 2020. Distributed by University of Washington Press.

Burns, Jennifer. *Weyerhaeuser Murals.* Everett Public Library, 2002.

Calhoun, Anne. *A Seattle Heritage, the Fine Arts Society.* Lowman & Hanford, 1942.

Callahan, Kenneth. "The Art Museum." *Seattle Sunday Times.* 14 April 1935.

Callahan, Kenneth. "The Art Museum." *Seattle Times.* 3 October 1936.

Callahan, Kenneth. "Seattle Art Museum." *Seattle Times.* 16 February 1936.

Callahan, Kenneth. "The Seattle Art Museum." *Seattle Times.* 20 December 1936.

Callahan, Kenneth, interviewed by Sue Ann Kendall. "Oral History Interview with Kenneth Callahan, 1982 October 27–December 19." Transcript, Archives of American Art, Smithsonian Institution, Washington, DC. https://www.aaa.si.edu/collections/interviews/oral-history-interview-kenneth-callahan-12975.

Callahan, Margaret Bundy. *Margaret Callahan: Mother of Northwest Art.* Edited by Brian Tobey Callahan. Trafford, 2009.

Chiang, Connie Y., with Michael Reese. "Seeing the Forest for the Trees: Placing Washington's Forests in Historical Context." Center for the Study of the Pacific Northwest, University of Washington Department of History. Not dated. https://www.washington.edu/uwired/outreach/cspn/Website/Classroom%20Materials/Curriculum%20Packets/Evergreen%20State/Evergreen%20Main.html.

Christodoulides, Christy. "The Carved Legacy of Snohomish Cultural Leader William Shelton." Burke Museum blog. 13 December 2012. https://www.burkemuseum.org/news/carved-legacy-snohomish-cultural-leader-william-shelton.

Conkleton, Sheryl. "Pantheon of Dreams." In *Northwest Mythologies: The Interactions of Mark Tobey, Morris Graves, Kenneth Callahan, and Guy Anderson*. Edited by Sheryl Conkleton and Laura Landau. Tacoma Art Museum, in association with University of Washington Press, 2003.

Conkleton, Sheryl, et al. *What It Meant to Be Modern: Seattle at Mid-Century.* Henry Art Gallery, University of Washington, 2000.

Cornish, Nellie C. *Miss Aunt Nellie: The Autobiography of Nellie C. Cornish.* Edited by Ellen Van Volkenburg Browne and Edward Nordhoff Beck. University of Washington Press, 1964.

Cumming, William. *Sketchbook.* University of Washington Press, 1984.

D'Alessandro, Stephanie, and Matthew Gale. *Surrealism Beyond Borders.* Metropolitan Museum of Art, New York, 2021. Distributed by Yale University Press.

Danzker, Jo-Anne Birnie, and Scott Lawrimore, eds. *Mark Tobey / Teng Baiye: Seattle/Shanghai.* Frye Art Museum, 2014.

De Barros, Paul. *Jackson Street After Hours: The Roots of Jazz in Seattle*. Sasquatch, 1993.

Dervaux, Isabelle, et al. *Surrealism USA*. National Academy Museum, in association with Hatje Cantz, 2005.

Duncan, Kate C. *1,001 Curious Things: Ye Olde Curiosity Shop and Native American Art*. University of Washington Press, 2000.

Faltys-Burr, Kaegan. "Jazz on Jackson Street: The Birth of a Multiracial Musical Community in Seattle." Great Depression in Washington State. Posted 2010. https://depts .washington.edu/depress /jazz_jackson_street _seattle.html.

Farr, Shelia. "Leo Kenney; The Seed and Beyond." In *Celebrating the Mysteries: Leo Kenney, a Retrospective*. Edited by Barbara Straker James and Sheila Farr. Museum of Northwest Art, in association with University of Washington Press, 2000.

Fort, Ilene. "American Social Surrealism." *Archives of American Art Journal* 22, no. 3 (1982): 8–20.

Fort, Ilene, ed. *In Wonderland: The Surrealist Adventures of Women Artists in Mexico and the United States*. Los Angeles County Museum of Art, in association with Museo de Arte Moderno, Mexico City, and Delmonico Books / Prestel, 2012.

Graves, Morris. *Morris Graves: Selected Letters, 1910–2001*. Edited by Vicki Halper and Lawrence M. Fong. University of Washington Press, 2013.

Gregory, James. "Seattle Labor History Highlights." Seattle Civil Rights and

Labor History Project. 2017. https://depts.washington .edu/civilr/labor_history .htm.

Griffey, Randall R. "Ambivalent Prodigal." In *Marsden Hartley's Maine*. By Donna M. Cassidy, Elizabeth Finch, Randall R. Griffey et al. Metropolitan Museum of Art, New York, 2017. Distributed by Yale University Press.

Harmon, Alexandra. *Indians in the Making: Ethnic Relations and Indian Identities Around Puget Sound*. University of California Press, 1998.

Haskell, Barbara, ed. *Vida Americana: Mexican Muralists Remake American Art, 1925–1945*. Whitney Museum of American Art, in association with Yale University Press, 2020.

Herzogenrath, Wulf. "John Cage: An Artist Who Accepts Life." In *John Cage, Mark Tobey, Morris Graves: Sounds of the Inner Eye*. Edited by Wulf Herzogenrath and Andreas Kreul. English edition. Museum of Glass: International Center for Contemporary Art, in association with Kunsthalle Bremen and University of Washington Press, 2002.

Hull, Roger. *Louis Bunce: Dialogue with Modernism*. Hallie Ford Museum of Art, 2017. Distributed by University of Washington Press.

"It's Girl Friend—Painted via Subconscious Mind." *Seattle Post-Intelligencer*. 24 December 1936.

Johns, Barbara. *Kenjiro Nomura, American Modernist: An Issei Artist's Journey*. Cascadia Art Museum, 2021. Distributed by University of Washington Press.

Johns, Barbara. "Knowing Your Place: Issei Artists in Seattle: Kenjiro Nomura, Kamekichi Tokita, and Takuichi Fujii." PhD diss., University of Washington, 2014.

Johns, Barbara. *Paul Horiuchi: East and West*. University of Washington Press, in association with Museum of Northwest Art, 2008.

Johns, Barbara. *Signs of Home: The Paintings and Wartime Diary of Kamekichi Tokita*. University of Washington Press, 2011.

Jonaitis, Aldona, and Aaron Glass. *The Totem Pole: An Intercultural History*. University of Washington Press, in association with Douglas & McIntyre, 2010.

Junker, Patricia. *Modernism in the Pacific Northwest: The Mythic and the Mystical*. Seattle Art Museum, in association with University of Washington Press, 2014.

Karasoulas, Margarita. "Marsden Hartley's Maine." *Panorama: Journal of the Association of Historians of American Art*. Fall 2017. https://journalpanorama .org/article/marsden -hartleys-maine/.

Kass, Ray. *Morris Graves: Vision of the Inner Eye*. George Braziller, in association with the Phillips Collection, 1983.

Kendall, Sue Ann. *Margaret Tomkins, 1975–1981*. Bellevue Art Museum, 1982.

Kingsbury, Martha. "Four Artists in the Northwest Tradition." In *Northwest Traditions*. Edited by Sarah Clark and Charles Cowles. Seattle Art Museum, 1978.

Kingsbury, Martha. *George Tsutakawa*. Bellevue Art

Museum, in association with University of Washington Press, 1990.

Klingle, Matthew W. *Emerald City: An Environmental History of Seattle*. Yale University Press, 2007.

Klingle, Matthew W. "Reclaiming Nature: Flattening Hills and Digging Waterways in Seattle." In *Building Nature: Topics in the Environmental History of Seattle and Spokane, a Curriculum Project for Washington Schools*. Not dated. Center for the Study of the Pacific Northwest, University of Washington Department of History. https://www .washington.edu/uwired /outreach/cspn/Website /Classroom%20Materials /Curriculum%20Packets /Building%20Nature /IV.html.

Lawson, Jacqueline E. A. *Seattle on the Spot: The Photographs of Al Smith*. Museum of History and Industry, 2017. Distributed by University of Washington Press.

Leighten, Patricia, and Mark Antliff. "Kandinsky and Radical Ecology: States of Mind, States of Abstraction." In *Vasily Kandinsky: Around the Circle*. Edited by Tracey Bashkoff and Megan Fontanella. Guggenheim Museum, 2021.

Long, Priscilla. "Fisher Flouring Mills Officially Opens on Harbor Island in Elliott Bay on June 1, 1911." HistoryLink. Posted 28 August 2002. https:// www.historylink.org/file /3927.

Lubar, Robert. "Salvador Dalí in America." In *Surrealism USA*. By Isabelle Dervaux et al. National Academy

Museum, in association with Hatje Cantz, 2005.

Martin, David. *Austere Beauty: The Art of Z. Vanessa Helder*. Tacoma Art Museum, 2013. Distributed by University of Washington Press.

Martin, David F., and Nicholette Bromberg. *Shadows of a Fleeting World: Pictorial Photography and the Seattle Camera Club*. University of Washington Press, in association with University of Washington Libraries, 2011.

Merchant, Carolyn. "Anarchist Social Ecology." In *Radical Ecology: The Search for a Livable World*. Routledge, 2005.

Michael Rosenfeld Gallery. *Exploring the Unknown: Surrealism in American Art*. Michael Rosenfield Gallery, 1995.

Miller, Angela. *The Empire of the Eye: Landscape Representation and American Cultural Politics, 1825–1875*. Cornell University Press, 1993.

Moore, Emily L. *Proud Raven, Panting Wolf: Carving Alaska's New Deal Totem Parks*. University of Washington Press, 2018.

Morgan, Murray. *Skid Road: An Informal Portrait of Seattle*. University of Washington Press, 2018.

Musée des arts décoratifs. *Mark Tobey*. Musée des Arts Décoratifs, Palais du Louvre, 1961.

"The Mystic Painters of the Northwest: They Translate Reality into Symbolic and Distinctive Art." *Life*, 28 September 1953, 84–89.

Ng, Nick. "Work of Julius 'Land Elk' Twohy Highlighted in Cascadia's Native American Modern Exbibit." *MyEdmondsNews*,

July 30, 2023. https://www.cascadiaartmuseum.org/work-of-julius-land-elk-twohy-highlighted-in-cascadias-native-american-modern-exhibit/.

Noheden, Kristoffer. "Toward a Total Animism: Surrealism and Nature." In *The Routledge Companion to Surrealism*. Edited by Kirsten Strom. Routledge, 2023.

Orton, Thomas. "Kenneth Callahan." In *Kenneth Callahan*. Edited by Patricia Grieve Watkinson and Thomas Orton. Museum of Northwest Art, in association with University of Washington Press, 2000.

Papanikolas, Theresa. "Abstract Expressionism: Looking East from the Far West." In *Abstract Expressionism: Looking East from the Far West*. By Theresa Papanikolas and Stephen Salel. Honolulu Museum of Art, 2017.

Park, Marlene, and Gerard E. Markowitz. *Democratic Vistas: Post Offices and Public Art in the New Deal*. Temple University Press, 1984.

Reclus, Élisée. *The History of a Mountain*. Harper and Brothers, 1881.

Reed, Norman. "Flour Milling in Washington: A Brief History." History-Link. Posted 11 July 2010. https://www.historylink.org/file/9474.

Rubin, Ida E. *The Drawings of Morris Graves*. New York Graphic Society, 1974.

Rudnick, Allison, et al. *Art for the Millions: American Culture and Politics in the 1930s*. Metropolitan Museum of Art, New York, 2023. Distributed by Yale University Press.

Rushing, W. Jackson. *Native American Art and the New York Avant-Garde:*

A History of Cultural Primitivism. University of Texas Press, 1995.

Saab, A. John. *For the Millions: American Art and Culture Between the Wars*. University of Pennsylvania Press, 2004.

Smetzer, Megan. *Painful Beauty: Tlingit Women, Beadwork, and the Art of Resilience*. University of Washington Press, 2021.

Some Works of the Group of Twelve, Seattle, Washington. Dogwood Press, 1937.

Stein, Alan J., and Paula Becker. *Alaska-Yukon-Pacific Exposition: Washington's First World's Fair, a Timeline History*. History Ink / HistoryLink, in association with University of Washington Press, 2009.

Takami, David. "Japanese Farming." HistoryLink. Posted 29 October 1998. https://www.historylink.org/file/298.

Taylor, Joshua, et al. *Art of the Pacific Northwest: From the 1930s to the Present*. Smithsonian Institution Press, 1974.

Taylor, Quintard. *The Forging of a Black Community: Seattle's Central District from 1870 Through the Civil Rights Era*. University of Washington Press, 1994.

Thrush, Coll. *Native Seattle: Histories from the Crossing-Over Place*. Foreword by William Cronon. Second edition. University of Washington Press, 2017.

Tobey, Mark. *Mark Tobey: The World of a Market*. University of Washington Press, 1964.

Tomkins, Margaret, interviewed by Bruce Guenther. "Oral History Interview

with Margaret Tomkins, 1984 June 6." Transcript, Archives of American Art, Smithsonian Institution, Washington, DC. https://www.aaa.si.edu/collections/interviews/oral-history-interview-margaret-tomkins-12308.

Truettner, William H. "Ideology and Image." In *The West as America: Reinterpreting Images of the Frontier*. Edited by William H. Truettner. Smithsonian Institution Press, 1991.

Tsutakawa, Mayumi. "A Canvas Diary: Painters Before the War. In *Turning Shadows into Light: Art and Culture of the Northwest's Early Asian/Pacific Community*. Edited by Mayumi Tsutakawa and Alan Chong Lau. Young Pine Press, 1982.

Wagner, Ann Prentice. *1934: A New Deal for Artists*. Smithsonian American Art Museum, in association with D. Giles Limited, 2009.

Watkinson, Patricia Grieve. *Margaret Tomkins*. Washington State University Press, 1977.

Wechsler, Jeffrey. *Surrealism and American Art, 1931–1947*. Rutgers University Art Gallery, 1977.

White, Mark. "Alexandre Hogue's Passion: Ecology and Agribusiness in the Crucified Land." In *A Keener Perception: Eco-critical Studies in Art History*. Edited by Alan C. Braddock and Christoph Irmscher. University of Alabama Press, 2009.

Wilma, David. "Harbor Island, at the Time the World's Largest Artificial Island, Is Completed in 1909." HistoryLink. Posted 6 November 2011. https://www.historylink.org/File/3631.

LENDERS TO
THE EXHIBITION

Art Bridges Foundation, Bentonville, Arkansas

Art Institute of Chicago

The Dalí Museum, St. Petersburg, Florida

Gilcrease Museum, Tulsa

Henry Art Gallery, University of Washington, Seattle

Bill and Holly Marklyn

The Menil Collection, Houston

Museum of History and Industry (MOHAI), Seattle

Northwest Museum of Arts and Culture, Spokane, Washington

Fay Hauberg Page and Nathaniel Blodgett Page

Philbrook Museum of Art, Tulsa

Portland Art Museum, Oregon

Private collection

Rose Art Museum, Brandeis University, Waltham, Massachusetts

Smithsonian American Art Museum, Washington, DC

Tacoma Art Museum, Washington

Tsutakawa Art Legacy LLC

Whitney Museum of American Art, New York

Wing Luke Museum, Seattle

INDEX

IMAGE CREDITS

Published on the occasion of the exhibition *Beyond Mysticism: The Modern Northwest* organized by Theresa Papanikolas, Ann M. Barwick Curator of American Art, Seattle Art Museum, and on view at Seattle Art Museum, March 5– August 2, 2026.

Generous support for this publication was provided by:

Presenting Sponsors

CULTURE

ARTSFUND

Major Sponsors
Bette and David Sprague Exhibition Endowment
Wyeth Foundation for American Art

Supporting Sponsors
Eric Peterson and Barbara Pomeroy
The Twining Humber Fund

Library of Congress Control Number: 2025939471
ISBN: 978-0-295-75484-0

Published by Seattle Art Museum
1300 First Avenue
Seattle, WA 98101
seattleartmuseum.org

University of Washington Press
4333 Brooklyn Avenue NE
Seattle, WA 98105
uwapress.uw.edu

Produced by Marquand Books, Seattle
marquandbooks.com

Designed by Thomas Eykemans
Copyedited by Kristin Swan
Proofread by Janice Lee
Indexed by Dave Luljak
Typeset in Atlas Grotesk and Isbell by Maggie Lee
Color management by I/O Color, Seattle
Printed and bound in in China by Artron Art Group

Front cover: Detail of Malcolm M. Roberts, *Drift No. 2*, 1936 (plate 117)
Back cover: Detail of Kenneth Callahan, *Evening Mist in Mountains*, ca. 1940 (plate 80)
Frontispiece: Detail of Julius Twohy, *Celilo Falls*, 1945 (plate 85)
Page 14: Detail of Kamekichi Tokita, *Bridge*, 1931 (plate 4)
Page 80: Detail of Detail of Kenneth Callahan, *Mail Boxes*, 1935 (plate 86)
Page 122: Detail of Margaret Tomkins, *Metamorphosis*, 1943 (plate 135)
Page 164: Detail of Mark Tobey, *Modal Tide*, 1940 (plate 139)
Pages 204–5: Detail of James H. FitzGerald, *Resurgent Sea*, 1945 (plate 134)